VISUAL
CONSULTING
DESIGNING & LEADING CHANGE
ACTION
STAKEHOLDER RELATIONSHIPS
GOALS
VISION
HINDER
SUPPORTS
BOLD STEPS
DAVID SIBBET &
GISELA WENDLING PhD

The following are registered trademarks of The Grove Consultants International—Group Graphics®, Graphic Guides®, Digital Graphic Guides®, and The Drexler/Sibbet Team Performance Model®. Trademarks in use include Storymaps™, Visual Planning Systems™, Strategic Visioning Model™, Liminal Pathways Framework™ and the Seven Challenges of Change™.

Published by John Wiley & Sons, Inc., Hoboken, New Jersey.
Published simultaneously in Canada.

For general information on our other products and services or for technical support, please contact our Customer Care Department within the United States at (800) 762-2974, outside the United States at (317) 572-3993 or fax (317) 572-4002.

Wiley publishes in a variety of print and electronic formats and by print-on-demand. Some material included with standard print versions of this book may not be included in e-books or in print-on-demand. If this book refers to media such as a CD or DVD that is not included in the version you purchased, you may download this material at http://booksupport.wiley.com. For more information about Wiley products, visit www.wiley.com.

Library of Congress Cataloging-in-Publication Data is available

ISBN 978-1-119-37534-0 (pbk)
ISBN 978-1-119-37536-4 (ebk)
ISBN 978-1-119-37533-3 (ebk)

Printed in the United States of America

V10003955 082418

This book is dedicated to all the visual facilitators, consultants, and activists working to make their organizations and communities more collaborative, creative, and compassionate places to work and live, and to Hannah, Thom, Val, Jerda, Phil, and all their children as they face the new challenges ahead.

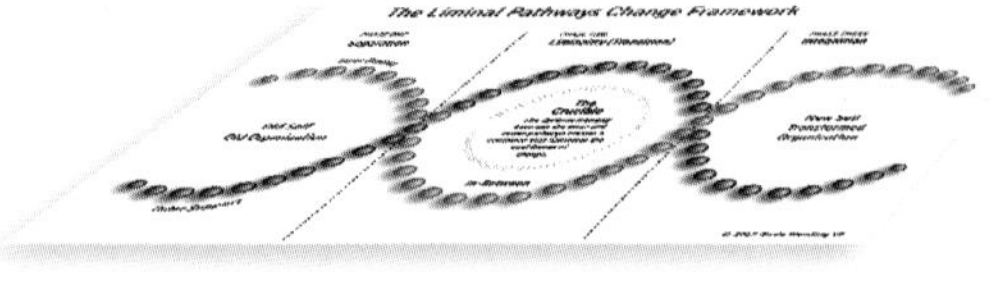
The Liminal Pathways Change Framework

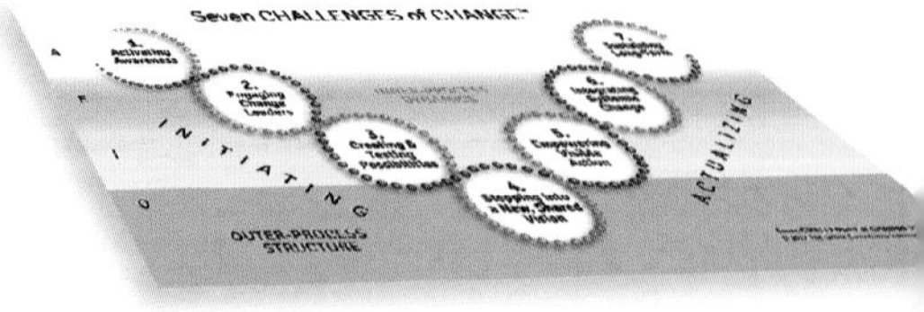
Seven CHALLENGES of CHANGE
INITIATING
ACTUALIZING
OUTER-PROCESS
STRUCTURE

Contents

Part I.
Imagining Visual Consulting
Jumping into the Flow

Part II.
Visualizing Change
Helping Clients Look Ahead

Part III.
Visual Consulting Practices
Responding to the Challenges of Change

Part IV. Expanding Your Resources
Continuing the Journey

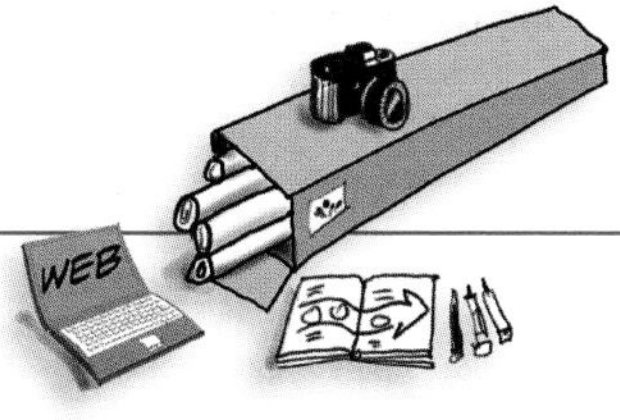

The Wiley Visual Facilitation Series

Figure 1.1

Visual Meetings: How Graphics, Sticky Notes & Idea Mapping Can Transform Group Productivity, was a best seller in 2009. It's been translated in more than a dozen languages and stimulated many to begin consulting practices using these methods.

Visual Teams: Graphic Tools for Commitment, Innovation, & High Performance followed in 2010 and explained how teams using visual facilitation function over time. It also explains the underlying Theory of Process that informs this and other process models designed by David Sibbet.

Visual Leaders: New Methods for Visioning, Management & Organization Change came out in 2013 in full color. It guides leaders on how to think about developing personal visual literacy and guide their organizations to become visually adept.

Introduction

This book is the fourth in a series sponsored by Wiley & Sons to comprehensively explore the rapidly expanding field of visual practice for facilitation, group leadership and consulting. (See Figure I.1). *Visual Consulting: Designing & Leading Change* (Figure I.2) builds on prior books, but assumes a more general level of understanding of the purpose and power of visualization than when the series began. Since *Visual Meetings* was published an entire body of literature has emerged with an ever-widening delta of practitioners, and attendant confusions about how these methods really work in practice.

A deeper purpose for writing *Visual Consulting* emerges from our experience of current events on local and global levels moving very quickly in complex and polarizing ways. We believe there is a need for practitioners who can be constructively involved in responding to these challenges and help guide change using the tools that visualization and dialogic practice provides. Both of us authors are fully engaged in long-term projects working on organizational and community change, often combined with supporting practitioner development. We feel called to share what we are learning more now than ever. We are eager to reach consultants in general who are becoming aware of the power of visualization, but also to visual practitioners who are awakening to the possibility of using their skills to help design and facilitation change in a more expanded way.

As with the other books, what we are sharing is based on experience enlivened by relevant theory. We know practitioners need concepts and light scaffolding to guide their developmental work, and specific, useful practices that can be applied. And we also know that reading stories of how these approaches work in actual practice can bring the theories, skills, and approaches to life.

Figure I.2

Visual Consulting: Designing & Leading Change explores the integration of visual facilitation, dialogic practice, and change work, as practiced by co-authors David Sibbet and Gisela Wendling, Ph.D. It introduces a new Seven Challenges of Change model.

Blending Three Fields

We are integrating three fields of practice in our conception of visual consulting: **Visual facilitation—Dialogic practice—Change work** (Figure 1.3). Each of these fields has disciplines, associations, literature, practices, and special language. What makes it possible

Figure I.3

to integrate them is they share a need for process awareness and process thinking.

Visual facilitation is my (David Sibbet,) lifelong passion with decades of organization and community consulting across multiple sectors. I, Gisela Wendling, have spent my professional life researching and supporting change work with a continuous focus on integrating the principles and practices of dialogue in my work. We are excited to introduce readers to several new visual frameworks that have been especially powerful with our own work in this regard. One is the *Consulting Framework for Respectful Engagement* that will help consultants of any type understand their roles and the type of relationship they hope to establish with clients.

A second, the *Liminal Pathways Change Framework*, has grown out of my, Gisela's, research at Fielding Graduate University. It re-conceptualizes the basic archetype of change embedded in traditional rites of passages as a human systems change framework, offering insights not only into the phases and milestones of change but also inner process and outer process dynamics that accompanies it. This framework has been consistently eye-opening and useful to people who are participating in our workshops.

The third model is a *Seven Challenges of Change framework* that integrates The Grove Consultants International traditional organization change model (described in Visual Leaders) with the Liminal Pathways work.

Being Aware of the Inner & Outer Dimensions of Change

These frameworks and process models are outgrowths of our joint leadership of many change projects and our work of teaching process consultants about these methods. Over the course of our professional practice we have became increasingly convinced that one's own inner awareness and how this applies to the use of oneself as an instrument for change is as important as the supportive outer structures consultants create, including the hands-on practices and tools they use with clients.(Figure I.4) Of course this dual focus on the inner and outer dimensions applies not only to consultants and their development but also reflects the dual focus that is needed to effectively support change in client systems. As we began sharing these ideas, we found more and more colleagues coming to similar conclusions or feeling confirmed by what they have sensed or known all along but had not seen simultaneously well-integrated before. Throughout the chapters we come back to this dual focus and share specific approaches and practices to working with each of the seven challenges of change.

Figure 1.4

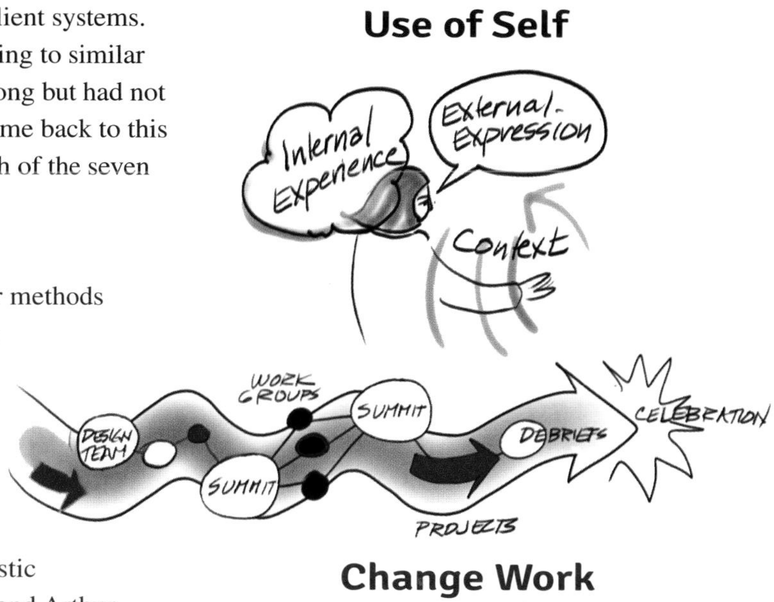

Anchored in Student-Centered Learning

We bring 70 years of collective, field-tested knowledge to our writing. Our methods have been refined through actual practice in the field, informed by reading and extensive exchange with colleagues. Underlying this we share rich, formative experiences in student-centered learning.

I, Gisela, as a student in the humanistic-oriented psychology department at Sonoma State University was part of a several-years-long extraordinary learning community modeled after the principles of student-centered learning. This community was guided by true elders in the field of humanistic psychology—William McCreary, who had been a student of Carl Rogers, and Arthur Warmoth, a student of Abraham Maslow. In this approach it is the learner and not the content, the instructor, or the institution that is at the center of the learning process. It taught me what it means to be an empowered learner, to locate my self-authority, to pursue my callings, and embrace community as a deep resource for personal and collective learning and development.

My passion for supporting transformative learning processes grew while I was in the masters program in Organization Development, also at SSU, learning the trade by participating in immersive action research projects—a program which I later directed. Being part of the scholar/practitioner doctoral program at the Fielding Graduate University further deepened my appreciation for self-direction and peer learning. My approach to

Figure 1.5

THE GLEN
GLOBAL LEARNING
& EXCHANGE NETWORK

Colleagues from the Global Learning & Exchange Network worked extensively with David and Gisela in refining the core ideas in this book. The GLEN's purpose is to evolve methodologies of collaboration and change to better face the problems of our times. This network is supported by The Grove Consultants International. For more information about both check:

https://glen.grove.com

www.grove.com

working with organizations and fellow learners is deeply rooted in these experiences.

I, David, worked for many years with the Coro Center for Civic Leadership before starting my consulting firm, The Grove Consultants International, in 1977. Coro pioneered experience-based leadership development in its nine-month Fellowship in Public Affairs, now offered in six cities across the country. Many of The Grove's visual and other methods were seeded in that experience of helping Fellows learn from their own experiences.

This shared orientation to designing and facilitating empowering person- and client-centered approaches, along with her global perspectives and focus on human systems change led to Gisela joining The Grove as its VP of Global Learning. She and David launched a Designing & Leading Change Intensive at The Grove in 2014 to explore the integration of their fields of work. Response to this work resulted in them co-creating a Global Learning & Exchange Network (or The GLEN) with the help of a half-dozen colleagues and Grove consultants. Its purpose is to evolve methodologies of collaboration within and across organization, communities, and cultures to better face the problems of our times. Through eight on-line inquiries, or what we call Exchanges at The GLEN, we shared our emerging Seven Challenges of Change framework and tested it's depictions of the inner and outer challenges against the extensive experience of our colleagues.

Structure of the Book

In general, this book is oriented to the less experienced consultants in the beginning chapters, making the case for visualization, dialogue, and change working together and providing frameworks and explicit, practical examples of how to get started. As the book progresses we address the more subtle aspects of change, continuing with specific methods and tools.

The book is, itself, highly visual and designed to be scanned as well as read. We invite you to move between sections to find the parts that resonate with your current interests. But if you want to follow our main case (the UC Merced Vision & Change Alignment process) from beginning to end it is best to read the chapters sequentially.

Part I: Imagining Visual Consulting, *Jumping into the Flow*, is written to orient you to this way of working.

Chapter 1: The Potential of Visual Consulting begins with a story of the California Roundtable on Water & Food Supply, and how Gisela, as a consultant who does not work on the wall graphically, extensively used visualization as a way to both support dialogue and catalyze new, holistic thinking to address some of the tough water issues California is facing. She eventually involved David as a visual facilitator, so this story embodies many of the themes of this book.

Chapter 2: What Kind of Consultant Are You? introduces the Consulting Framework for Respectful Engagement, an extension of Ed Schein's traditional definition of process consulting. This overview provides you with a sense of where you are entering this field.

Chapter 3: Capabilities You'll Need, orients you to capabilities we believe are needed to practice visual facilitation, dialogic practice, change work, and use of self. These are framed in the context of the four flows of process, a powerful set of distinctions from Arthur M. Young's Theory of Process that underlies this and all The Grove's other work. These capabilities deal with both inner practices and outer structures.

Part II: Visualizing Change, *Helping Clients Look Ahead*, heads directly into the challenge of finding clients, scoping your projects, and contracting for success, and at an overview level thinking about change not only in terms of stages of process, but also the weave between inner and outer considerations.

Chapter 4: Finding & Contracting Clients, begins with the story of a Visioning & Change Alignment project at the University of California at Merced. This year-long consulting engagement threads through subsequent chapters provides many examples of best practices for designing and leading change. This chapter is a must for anyone beginning the consulting journey.

SideStory 1.1

SideStory Format

Throughout this book there are side stories that are formatted like this one, with a simple headline and a box of text.

These feature visual consultants, key concepts you can use in sketch talks, and explanations of graphics that illustrate various formats you can use.

Side stories and all graphic figures have a number in the upper right, so when this book is translated to electronic versions the text can link to the appropriate visuals. It will also work as a cross reference between chapters as you read. The sidestory and figure numbers are the chapter number followed by the number of the specific sidestory or figure in that chapter., i.e. SideStory 2.3 is in Chapter 2 as the third sidestory. The numbers are an additional way to know what chapter you are reading.

SideStory 1.2

Practices & Activities You Can Do Look Like This

Throughout the book there are specific activities you can do to assess yourself, learn a new practice, or use as a checklist to remember key elements in a process.

All activities have either checkboxes or numbered steps.

- [ ] Checkboxes look like this.

1. Numbered steps look like this.

Chapter 5: Basic Patterns of Change introduces the *Liminal Pathways Framework*, a way of looking at how traditional peoples have supported change for tens of thousands of years. This work is an outgrowth of Gisela's field study of indigenous rites and ceremonies in Peru, Africa, and Australia and her doctoral research. This framework applies to change in general and transformational change in particular.

Chapter 6: Seven Challenges of Change provides an overview of the framework that will guide Part III on visual consulting practices. It explains the integration of the basic pattern of change illustrated in the Liminal Pathways framework with The Grove's organizational change model (described in Visual Leaders). This framework evolved during the writing of this book as colleagues and others reflected on the themes that were most important for practitioners.

Part III: Visual Consulting Practices, *Responding to the Challenges of Change*, moves through the Seven Challenges of Change Framework one at a time, and elucidates core principles for working with inner process dynamics and outer process structures, as well as best practices for each.

Chapter 7: Activating Awareness Shares how to be aware of the surprise, shock, hopefulness, and preparedness. We describe outer structures for doing scoping, initial client meetings, mapping drivers of change, interviewing stakeholders, using conceptual models to hold a systemic perspective, assessing readiness, and contracting for change.

Chapter 8: Engaging Leaders of Change moves into the formation of design teams, visual stakeholder analysis, roadmapping, role clarification, and working with resistance. We speak to the fears, and feelings of uncertainty connected with this early stage. It continues the UC Merced case with explicit examples of charting, dialogic practices and overall design for a change process.

Chapter 9: Creating & Sharing Opportunities explores how to design and hold a strong container for design thinking, visual facilitation, visioning, scenario planning, creating large storymaps, and dialogue practices to support this challenge. Exploring assumptions, resistance, caring, and creativity are inner aspects. The UC Merced story continues, showing elements in practice that create strong containers for the work.

Chapter 10: Stepping into a new Shared Vision brings the UC Merced story to culmination as the University agrees on its vision and priorities moving forward. We describe how to stay connected to purpose, hold complexity, and cross the threshold in decision crucibles, and large-scale visioning processes.

Chapter 11: Empowering Visible Action looks at the importance of taking enough time to involve new leaders, support emergence, and learn from experience. It explores communicating early wins, keeping a clear rhythm, supporting work groups, building capacity, and facilitating learning opportunities. A case from Cal Poly Pomona's College of Business Administration shows how visioning work materialized in visible results for the college.

Chapter 12: Integrating Systemic Change uses the iceberg model to look into the systemic issues and mental models that need to shift to support change. How do you persist courageously, clearing old habits and nurturing new patterns of working systemwide? How can consultants amplify successes, clear blocks, design new processes, and evolve new rituals for creating and sustaining culture change.

Chapter 13: Sustaining Long Term moves into the challenge of evolving culture change over a period of time—both appreciating the gifts of change and living with impermanence. How do you evolve the culture, celebrate completions, invest in renewal, and maintain and refine?

Part IV: Expanding Your Resources, *Continuing the Journey*, contains a last chapter, the appendix, bibliography, and index.

Chapter 14: Toward Mastery wraps up with our hopes for where these concepts, principles, and practices will be used, and how you as a visual consultant can begin the longer road of personal practice and development in this field. It includes sidestories of consultants who are working at this level.

Appendix and Bibliography. The back of the book has a short overview of the Theory of Process, which underlies Grove models, as well as links and a bibliography of the references that have inspired us in writing this book.

SideStory 1.3

Assumptions About Visual Book Design

This book, like the preceding ones, is rich with use of visual imagery that dances with the writing to bring across these new ideas. We actually "wrote" the book in Adobe's InDesign software, writing and drawing our way through the ideas, making sure the page text explains and bounces off the imagery. This will of course be reformatted in e-book form, but we have added figure numbers of all images so the links can continue.

Cognitive scientists agree that our embedded mental models and metaphors drive perception and behavior in fundamental ways. Active visualization of this material is a direct way to both uncover and upgrade your systemic thinking. If you actively sketchnote while reading you can get some of this value.

Visualizing as a process is already integral to design thinking, prototyping, strategy formation, implementation, change management, and planning in general, but it is not appreciated enough as a core thinking tool for leadership and social change. Nor is it sufficiently appreciated how powerful the person-hood of the practitioner is to getting results. We move to story telling to bring in this dimension, and exercises you can do on your own.

Visual Consultants as Vanguards of Integrated Thinking and Practice

In a time of specialization and polarization, we are writing into the space of integration and collaboration. We have been hugely inspired by the response of our clients to this blending of dialogue, visualization, and change (Sidestory 1.3). Take any away and you do not have the potential we are describing.

- ❑ As you will discover, this is not a book about the traditional use of visuals as static pictures that explain things, but of **using visualization as an active language, central to the social construction** of what we consider valid and real, and understandable in the world.
- ❑ This is not a book about dialogue separated from the work of the world, but about the **important integration of inner and outer ways of knowing** and relating while working IN the world.
- ❑ This is not a book about change management—the smoothing of organizational transitions, project and process optimization, and the many operational capabilities needed to run any organization. It is **about stepping up to support change that transforms and touches the deeper currents of culture and the paradigms that we use to make sense of the world**.

We hope you consultants and others who read this book can become adept at BOTH the use of visualization to guide consulting processes in a structured way, and the use of your own visual imagination to become adept at enhancing dialogic explorations, guiding consulting processes in a structured way AND using your own visualization to become aware of your and your clients' inner dynamics. For visual facilitators stepping into consulting, we hope you can come to see the path forward as a wonderful expansion of your receptive, improvisational capabilities, and learn to listen to parts that can't be visualized explicitly, but can be honored by how you show up and the quality of your being while holding the processes of change.

Acknowledgements

There are many people who have contributed to our collective development and the themes in this book. Alan Briskin, co-author of *The Power of Collective Wisdom* and GLEN colleague, had an initial perception that the bringing together of visual facilitation and dialogic practice was a new edge for our field. Subsequently he and a group of colleagues met over two years to evolve the GLEN and the core ideas of this book. They included Aftab Omer, president of Meridian University; Amy Lenzo of Clear Light Communications; Rob Eskridge, president of Growth Management Center; Bill Bancroft of Conbrio Consulting; Laurie Durnell, copresident of The Grove, and Rachel Smith, former Grove director of Digital Facilitation. This book was then greatly improved by these and additional GLEN members in Visual Consulting Exchanges held to test our thinking. Thanks to Bassam Alkarashi of ES Consulting; Bob Horn of MacroVu; John Schinnerer of the Sociocratic Consulting Group; Joy Keller-Weidman with the Udal Foundation; Karen Wilhelm-Buckley of Communicorp Consulting; Marco Ceretti of Otherwise; Mary Gelinas of Gelinas James, Inc.; and Phil Bakelaar professor of OD at Montclair University,

We owe special thanks to the visual consultants we feature—to Diana Arsenian and her work with Appreciative Inquiry; to Holger Balderhaar and his internal consulting in Hamburg; to Bassam Alkarashi of ES Consulting, bringing visual facilitation to transformational change in Saudia Arabia; to Bill Bancroft of ConBrio and his applications in strategic visioning and leadership development; to Maaike Doyer of Business Models Inc. for modeling adept use of graphic wall templates; to Rob Eskridge of Growth Management Center and his work evolving templates for strategic planning; to Mary Gelinas (*Talk Matters*) for her work in leadership and brain sciences applied to collaboration; to Meryem LeSaget and her work in deep visioning and sustainable organizations in France; to Dan Roam (*Back of the Napkin; Blah, Blah, Blah;* and other books); to Holger Scholz, founder of kommunikationslotsen in Germany, and co-founder of bikablo; and to Kevin Souza and his applications of visual consulting as director of Educational Services at the University of California San Francisco Medical Center.

We have collaboratively learned this field with some special clients. Thanks to Ann Hayden,

We owe special thanks to Michael Reese, f. vice chancellor of Business & Administration at the University of California at Merced, Chancellor Dorothy Leland, and Erik Rolland, f. acting dean of the UC Merced School of Engineering, for the wonderful case study that brings many of these tools and practices to life.

We also are indebted to the cohort of process leaders in our Leading Change Program at the Metropolitan Council of the Twin Cities in Minnesota, whose eagerness to learn about change inspired many parts of this book.

senior director of the California Habitat Exchange at the Environmental Defense Fund; Barbara Waugh, f. HR director of HP Labs; Bryce Pearsall and Griff Davenport of DLR Group; Erik Rolland, dean of the College of Business Administration at Cal Poly Pomona; John Schiavo, f. CEO of Otis Spunkmeyer; Joseph McIntyre, f. executive director at Ag Innovations; Leisa Thompson, general manager of Environmental Services Division of the Metropolitan Council in Minnesota; and Rick Reed f. program manager of the Garfield Foundation, funders of RE-AMP.

We could not have written this book without the full support of our team at The Grove Consultants International. This includes Laurie Durnell, Tiffany Forner. Danielle Hansen, Megan Hinchliffe, Cody Keene, Malgosia Kostecka, Eddie Palmer, Robert Pardini, and Jan Thomas.

The many people who have influenced David and the growth of the visual facilitation field are well noted in earlier books in this series. For Gisela, special thanks to William McCreary and Art Warmoth, formerly at Sonoma State for their inspiration with student centered learning; to Fielding Graduate School's Fred Stier on reflexive research, Matt Hamabatta for love of qualitative data, and Charlie Seashore, on use of self; to Saul Eisen as early mentor in the field of OD; to Edie and Charlie Seashore, mentors at NTL; to Tony Petrella for moral support and consulting at the "C" level; to Kathy Danemiller for large-scale change; to Barry Oshry for helping "see" systems through his Power Labs; to Don Americo Yabar and Juan Nunes del Prado, meztiso paqos from Peru; to Bradford Keeny and his work with the Kalihari Bushmen, and Frank Ansel, an Aboriginal n'ankari, and Aunti Nellie Patterson, a traditional elder from the central deserts of Australia for direct experiences in indigenous ceremony.

In learning about the deep process of being a life-long consultant, Gisela has been part of Chakra, a peer circle of women committed to supporting each other through life's transitions—meeting three to four weekends a year since 1997. It includes Ann Dosher, Andrea Dyer-Miller, Kristen Cobble, Linda Boose Sweeney, Peggy Sebera, Ronita Johnson, Sarita Chawla, Stephany Ryan, Teresa Ruelas. David engaged in similar learning with the Pathfinders, a consultant developmental circle formed by Bill and Marilyn Veltrop in 2001. The initial cohort continues today as Pathwalkers, following a decade and a half of monthly, full-day meetings covering every theme imaginable. This group includes Amy Lenzo, Babara Waugh, Brian Dowd, Diego Navarro, Firehawk Hulin, Gary Merrill, Pele Rouge, Peter Gaarn, Susan Christy, and Vivian Wright.

Part I.

Imagining Visual Consulting

Jumping into the Flow

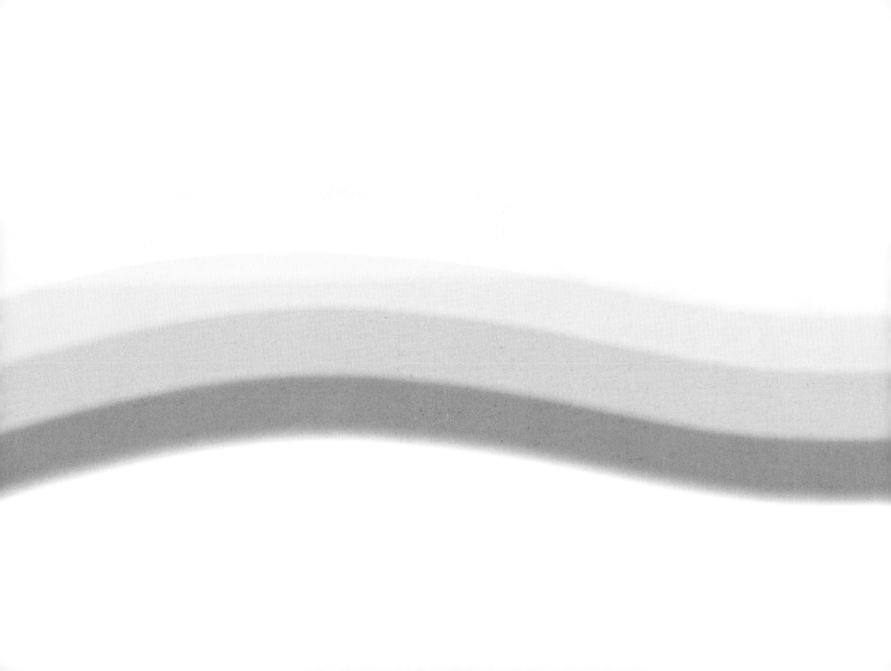

1. The Potential of Visual Consulting

Integrating Methods to Get Results

You are about to begin a learning journey into an intersection of three fields that are giving rise to a new way of working we are calling "visual consulting." One is the field of visualization, and visual facilitation in particular. A second is dialogic practice, as used in consulting. And a third is change consulting, specifically designing and leading change in organizations and communities. What they have in common is an orientation to process thinking and process leadership. Applied in the interests of clients seeking innovation, culture change, alignment on new visions, process transformation, and sustainable results, they come together as "visual consulting."

Like anyone learning something new, you'll need to orient to what it will mean for you. What is your interest in visualization? What's your interest in consulting? And what does this have to do with designing and leading change? Stay with these questions as we begin with a real client story that illustrates the power of visualization in a consulting engagement (Figure 1.1). It contains a number of practices you can add to your tool set right away. Starting with a story will help make the later chapters come alive.

Figure 1.1

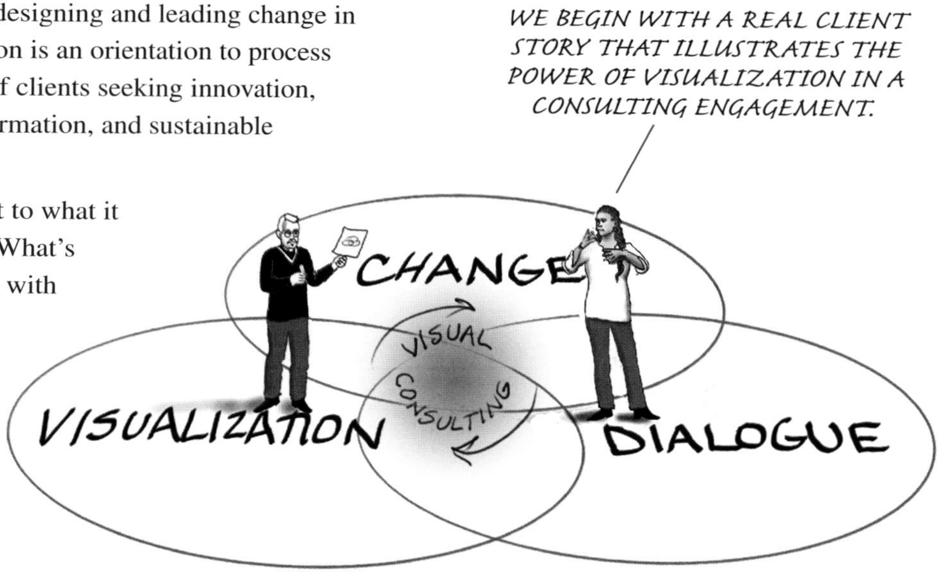

California Drought Calls for Change

In 2013 I, Gisela, joined Ag Innovation Network as director of Water Programs and took on the role of facilitating the California Roundtable on Water & Food Supply (CRWFS). It had 25 members. They were beginning their third year of dialogue identifying top water issues in the state and writing white papers to respond. The program was funded by the California Water Foundation and others. I would be acting as a process consultant/

facilitator, with the support and help of Ag Innovations staff. The participants were leaders in big agriculture, small agriculture, science, environment, state and local government, lawyers, regulators, and general water managers from all around the state. They were already a trusting group appreciating the off-the-record safety of the Roundtable, and our commitment to publish only what they consensually agreed upon. Being a diverse group this was the challenge. What was the most pressing issue to focus on this year?

I knew asking the right questions is the key to good dialogue. I asked, "Given what we are looking at, what key question should the Roundtable take on for this year?"... My question surfaced a deeper question that led to a new focus "What would it take to create connections, re-connections, or effective alignments to address these systemic issues?"

My Way in to Water Management

I began by using a tried-and-true group process, being experienced in large system change and a wide variety of organizational development practices and skills with extensive experience in process design and facilitation of dialogue. In spite of some early training in draftsmanship, drawing on the wall is not my forte. This story is about how the visualization I used helped the Roundtable come to significant consensus on a critical issue in our state—water management. It is also a story of how I reached out to David, who is very skilled in visual representation and facilitation, and together we took the work further, and began a professional journey that has convinced us of the power of more deeply blending these fields we are in. We'll share more stories about our findings as we go along.

Inviting a Conversation on Issues

The Roundtable had already developed an explicit group charter. Building on that, as well as individual interviews with all members, I facilitated a series of half-day meetings. In these full-group sessions we sat around tables set in a big "U" shape that suggested everyone was equal. I would create agendas on a flip chart. Confidentiality was key. My first task was to invite a conversation about what key California water issues they had on their mind. "What key question should the Roundtable take on for this year?" was on their mind. Historically this group was best at re-framing issues. An earlier report had argued for moving from "water conservation" to "stewardship." A second year they pushed to move from "water storage" to "retention." To get the group going this time I asked everyone to go around and have each person speak to what they considered to be the top issues and crises. They began to realize how many ways the water system was broken and disconnected.

In a second meeting they broke into small groups and identified the disconnections on sticky notes. We then clustered them on a big wall and identified 18 clusters. The huge wall of disconnections vividly visualized the complexity and extent of the systemic dysfunction. We typed up the clusters into a meeting report that was then fed back to all participants.

Asking the right questions is the key to good dialogue. I asked a lot. My questions and their resulting dialogue then surfaced even deeper questions and eventually a new focus. "What would it take to create connections, re-connections, or effective alignments to address the wide range of systemic issues?" they asked. "What kind of thinking would be needed to generate truly new solutions?" Their inquiry led them to a new learning edge. Thinking about disconnection led to ideas about reconnection and eventually the exploration of a connectivity model. The wall was a doorway for them to look at things systemically. I think that the visualization of issues plus the dialogue worked together to catalyze this new focus.

Initial Draft Visualizations

In following sessions we dug deeper into on a system-level depiction of their insights about disconnection, drawing an initial diagram in PowerPoint of what I had heard them say about connectivity. This simple image (Figure 1.2) provided enough visual language for the group to engage more deeply at a systemic level, and is a great example of how visuals work in facilitation. My illustration showed the human systems acting upon the physical

Figure 1.2

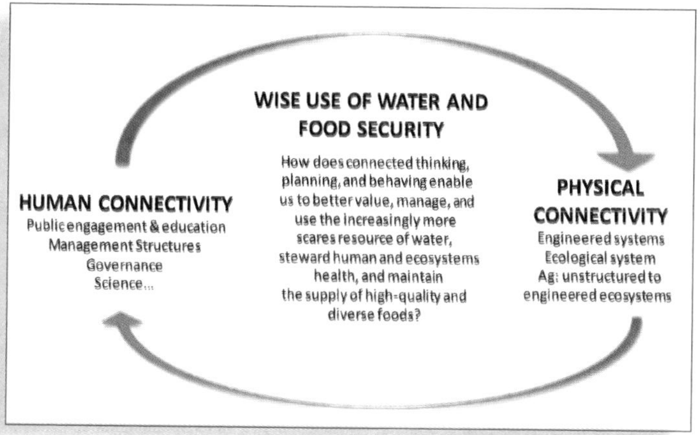

A Flawed View of the Water System

This PowerPoint slide shows my initial depiction of what I heard them talking about as the common view of connectivity, but it was flawed, and that was its value. It reflected and reinforced one of the most fundamental disconnects—the pervasively shared and often unexamined belief about the relationship between human systems and the larger ecosystem—that they are two separate systems, with distinct features and operational dynamics that act upon one another.

Figure 1.3

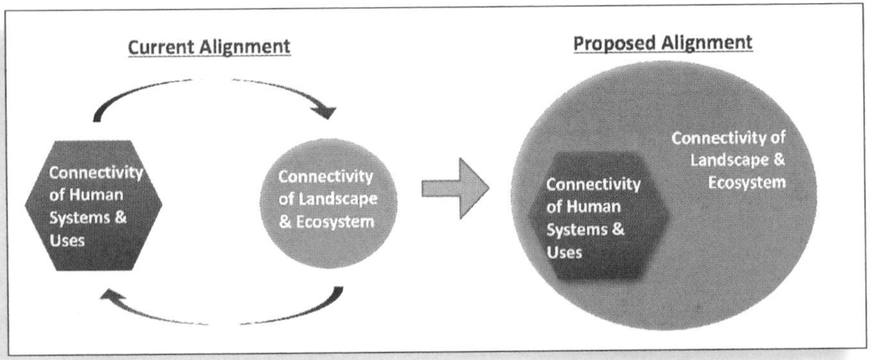

Connectivity Illustrated

This is my second illustration of the connectivity idea, using nesting as a way to show the human system embedded as part of the ecosystem.

system, in which I included the natural ecosystem. Because they are both physical. I used a very simple action diagram format. BUT it was flawed. The Roundtable participants pushed right back. They saw that it reflected one of the most fundamental disconnects—the pervasively shared and often unexamined belief about the relationship between human systems and the larger ecosystem—that they are two separate systems, with distinct features and operational dynamics.

This two-systems point of view leads us to think that we use our human-created engineering, management, and economic systems to act upon the ecosystem to shape it in order to serve our human systems' needs, and that this ecosystem in turn impacts the infrastructure we build—i.e. dams and tunnels to bring water to urban areas and agricultural lands, and manage through the ecosystem's seasonal weather, precipitation, and hydrological cycles, including drought and other global warming impacts. I had reinforced this misconception by showing two separate entities and the interaction arrows (left side of Figure 1.3).

Surfacing that this common belief may be wrong or insufficient, made it even more important that we clarify what is actually part of the human systems and the ecosystems and what the relationship between these two really looks like. I had follow-on conversations with members, and specifically a biologist who encouraged me that the right way to align these would be to put the human system as a subsystem of the ecosystem. This generated a more promising image of connectivity (Figure 1.3).

Note that the incorrect first draft is what precipitated this insight! Accepting this dynamic, of having your first drafts be challenged and considered "wrong," is a first step in learning to be a visual consultant. But it needs to be paired with dialogic practice that challenges and surfaces deeply held assumptions.

How Dialogue and Generative Images Deepen Insight

Studies of the importance of dialogic practice in organizational change are emphasizing that meaningful change is always accompanied by a change in people's conversation. Diagnosis by itself is inadequate. But with inquiry, learning, and hearing all perspectives, a new, coherent narrative can emerge, and this is what shapes the change. Because systemic, transformative change is always an evolving and emergent process, sustained dialogue about possibilities is needed on an ongoing basis. Generative images and metaphors that result in new insights and action often emerge during the dialogue, but we have discovered that they can also be introduced purposefully.

During the Roundtable's ensuing dialogue on how to depict the system, the imagery evolved further. A water management specialist at the California Water Institute, said that if we look at water as a system we have to look at different uses over time that have led to the current water infrastructure. He provided a simple diagram (Figure 1.4) illustrating three types of water users who compete on water projects—the agricultural interests, the urban interests, and the environmental interests.

I worked it into a Venn diagram with three overlapping circles (Figure 1.5), checked and refined it with the specialist, and shared it with Roundtable members. It showed single-use benefits and the overlap as dual benefits and the center as the "sweet spot" for connectivity projects. This visual was the seed of a depiction of "connected benefits" that serviced not just individual users but the whole.

Figure 1.4

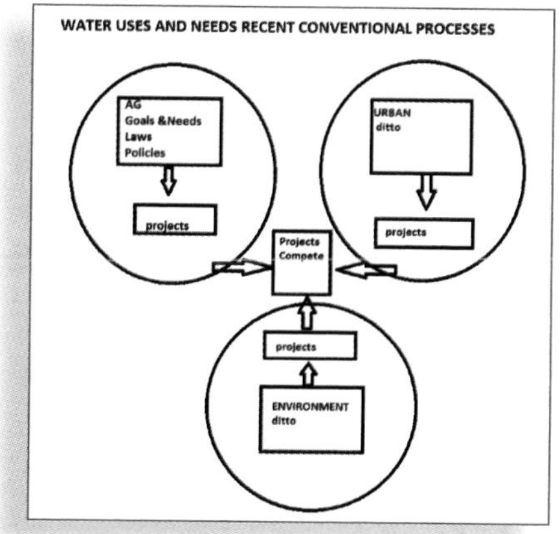

Water Users

This diagram was shared to illustrate three user categories.

Figure 1.5

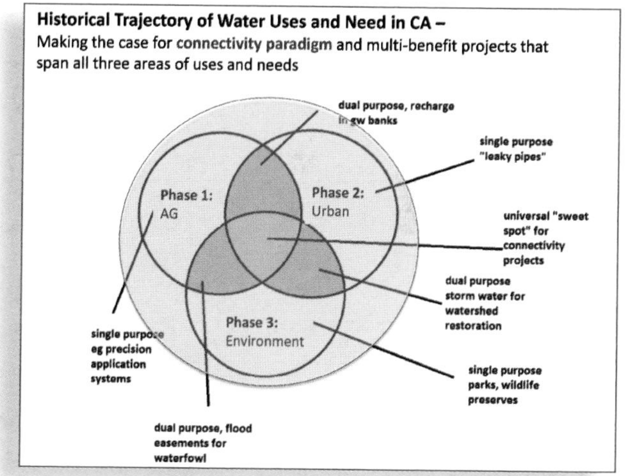

The Roundtable Sweet Spot

Blended with the earlier connectivity diagram, this integrated view illustrated the CRWFS sweet spot.

Figure 1.6

First Sketches

These simple sketches of an abstract graphic invite imagination. The more complex ones showing detail raised issues.

Figure 1.7

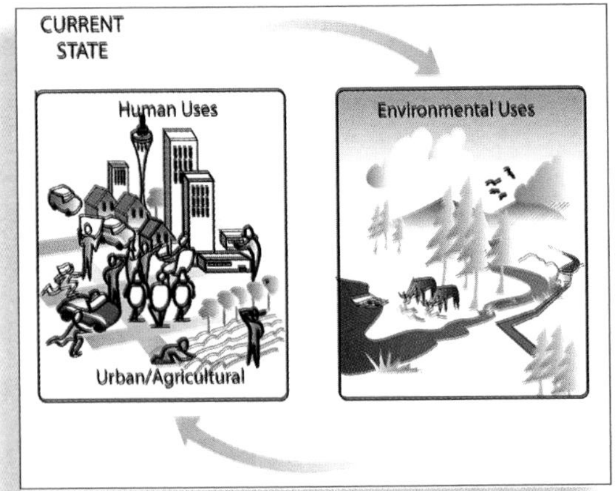

Tools You Can Use

Let's step back from our story for a bit to look at the tools I was using that you can already begin to think about putting in your visual consulting toolkit.

- ❑ **Written agendas**
- ❑ **Circular & "U" shapes** for meeting, visually suggesting equality of the voices
- ❑ **Small groups** generating their ideas on sticky notes.
- ❑ **A big wall** to post and cluster sticky notes
- ❑ **Written reports** afterwards (an Ag Innovations staffer took notes throughout)
- ❑ **Visual summaries** in the form of diagrams representing the key ideas
- ❑ **Concept graphics** to provide common, systems-level language

These are approaches you can use right from the start in consulting. If you are more experienced you may be realizing that you are already working visually, since most consultants would invariably use PowerPoint and flip charts. The key is being conscious of the impacts.

Involving a Graphics Professional

The CRWFS knew it was heading toward publishing a new report on the connectivity principle they were developing, so our attention was on

Figure 1.8

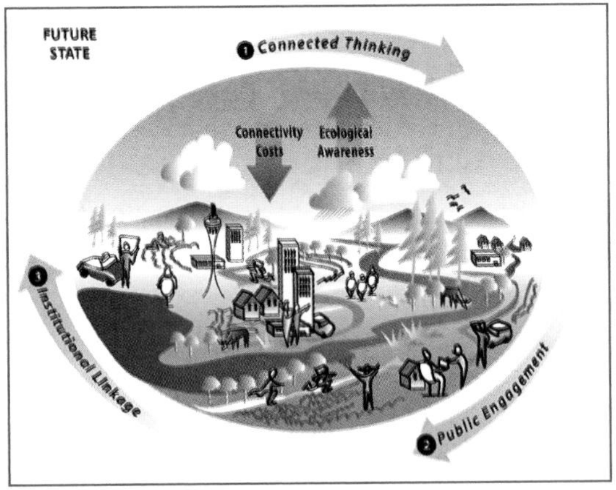

Figure 1.9

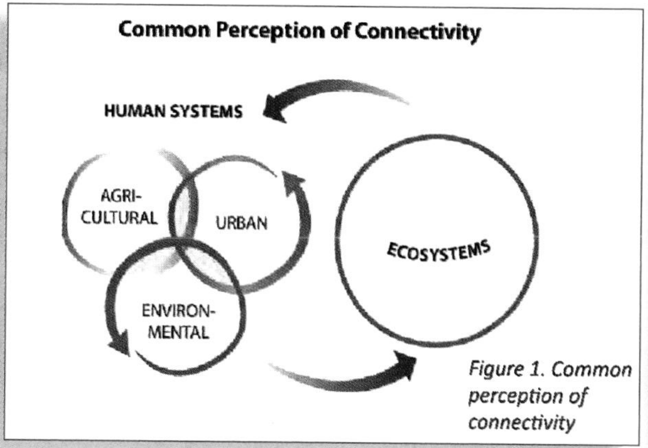

Figure 1.10

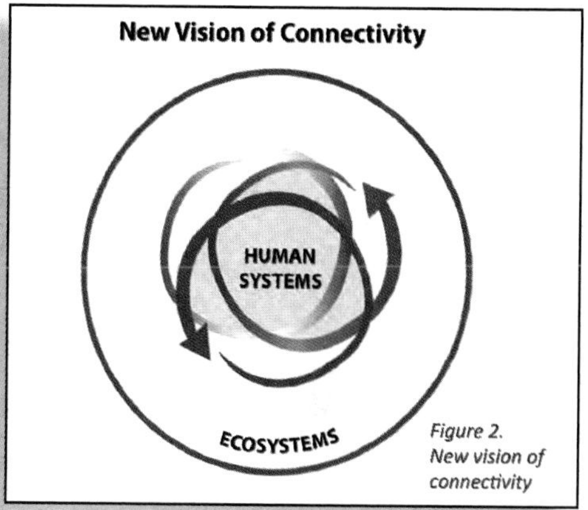

describing and illustrating these emerging ideas in as interesting a way as possible, avoiding visual cliques.

At this point I reached out to David. He has a long history of helping develop conceptual illustrations. He explained to me that there are two kinds of visuals for this kind of purpose. One is detailed enough to be self-explanatory. The other is to create a visual puzzle that pulls out inquiry and asks the viewer to fill in details. He sketched out both possibilities in his journal at the time (Figure 1.6) and then developed two more concepts in detail (Figures 1.7 and 1.8).

When I presented these refined versions to the Roundtable we got it wrong again! Beautiful!. They said the detailed image that showed the shift from current perception to a proposed future perception was actually MUCH more complex in reality. Others said the environmental image (Figure 1.8) looked like a state of nature and water cycles that preceded European settlement and that the environment doesn't actually look that nice anymore. There are not water-related uses shown in the urban picture others said. As David pointed out after I debriefed the meeting with him, over explicit metaphors can run into these kinds of problems by triggering viewer disagreements.

The Roundtable agreed that maybe they shouldn't use the detailed pictures, but just show what needs to connect and we began to develop the more abstract diagrams (Figures 1.9 and 1.10). These images emerged and were used in the report. Colors were used to indicate the different uses, and intentionally dynamic arrows pointed toward the complexity of each area.

Resolution of a Connectivity Model

This depiction of the human systems embedded in the ecosystems represented the distilled essence of many hours-long dialogue over months. In full color these diagrams really caught the eye.

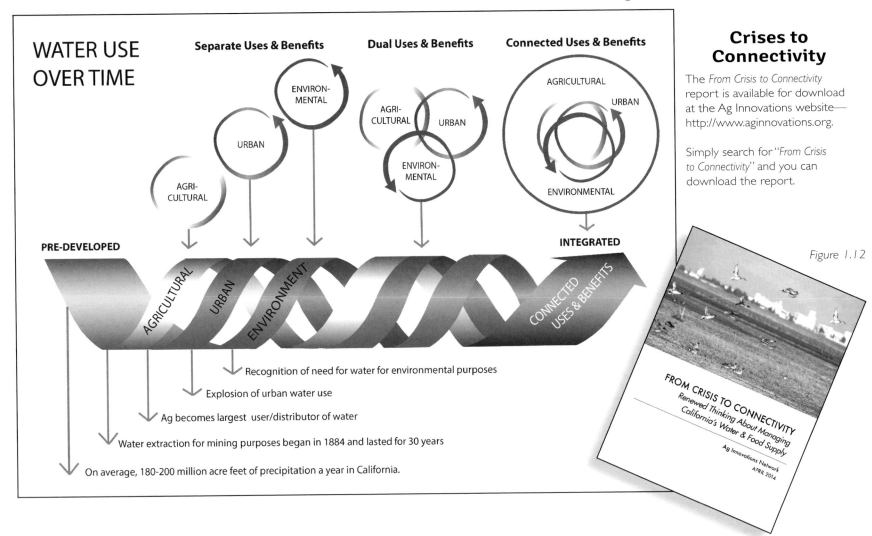

Figure 1.11

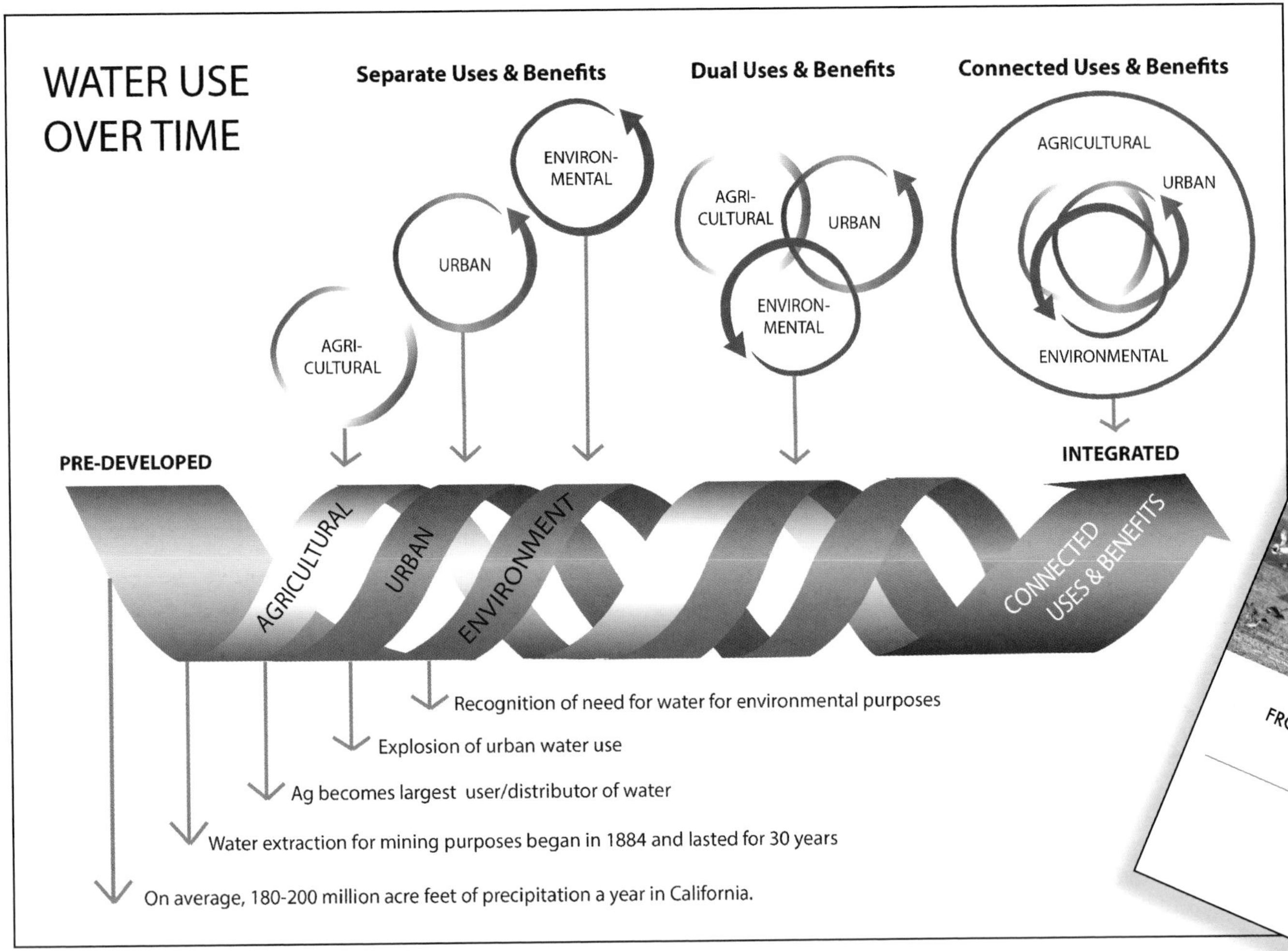

Crises to Connectivity

The *From Crisis to Connectivity* report is available for download at the Ag Innovations website—http://www.aginnovations.org.

Simply search for "*From Crisis to Connectivity*" and you can download the report.

Figure 1.12

FROM CRISIS TO CONNECTIVITY
Renewed Thinking About Managing California's Water & Food Supply
Ag Innovations Network
APRIL 2014

Illustrating the History

In parallel with our visualization of connectivity, we worked on looking at the three water uses in California over time: urban, agricultural, and environmental. This visual also clarified the historical progression from single to dual to connected uses and benefits (Figure 1.11)—another breakthrough in how to approach developing systemic solutions.

Humans Think in Maps and Itineraries

David pointed out during our sketching session, that humans want to think about systems and connections and also want to think about time. This divides graphics into two big categories—map-like images and journey or itinerary images. The final full illustration is shown in Figure 1.11. The result of the dialogue using drafts of images crystallized and confirmed for the Roundtable that the human systems need to be seen as a subset of the ecosystem, forming one interrelated system. This visualization of the two systems reduces the contradiction between the two and generates new ways of perceiving solutions.

It is important to appreciate that a critical part of the process of writing the consensual report was dialogic, supported by powerful visuals and careful note taking... The fact that our sustained dialogue led to understanding and alignment among such a diverse group of stakeholders who were often at odds, lent the report unusual credibility.

Patiently Getting Consensus

Getting consensus on the *From Crisis to Connectivity* report (Figure 1.12) was a breakthrough for the Roundtable. It was an effort to capture the emerging shift in their fundamental thinking about water in California, at the paradigm level.

It is important to appreciate that a critical part of the process of writing the consensual report was dialogic, supported by powerful visuals and careful note taking. The project was running long, yet as the project began to move toward convergence several members were not comfortable with some of the language and points of view. Through dozens and dozens of individual conversations and more group meetings, I insisted that they hear each voice respectfully. With this level of care, the group did come to consensus. The fact that our

Figure 1.13

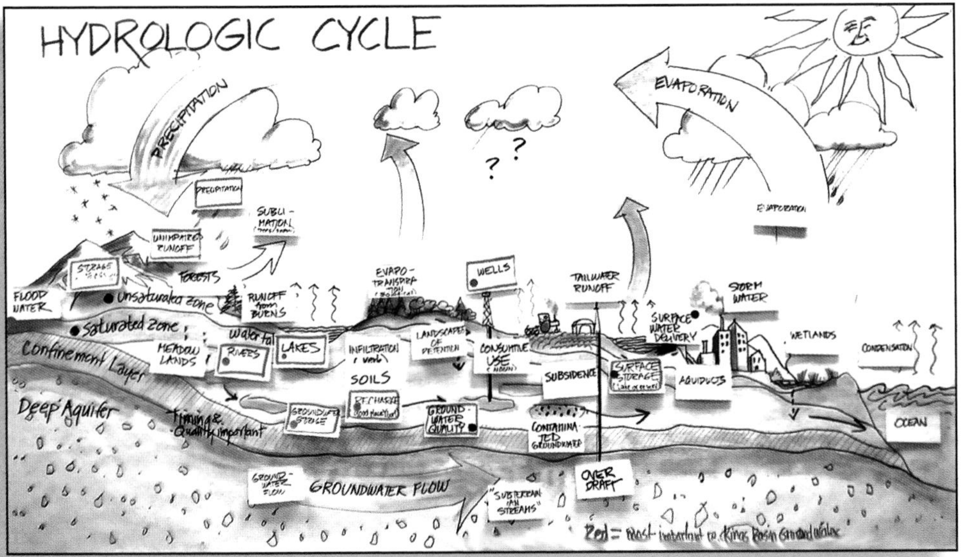

sustained dialogue led to understanding and alignment among such a diverse group of stakeholders who were often at odds, lent the report unusual credibility. As a result of this alignment, the report has been widely circulated amongst top leaders in the water world in California.

Moving to Implementation and Change

After the report was published, the issue of groundwater was moving to the front of the Roundtable's attention, as years of drought in California were pulling policy makers toward policies that would respond to the problem. The Roundtable decided to look at specific cases through their new framework. The success we had in using visualization to focus consensus and dialogue in our report led me to reach out again to David and ask if he could support our conversation with visual facilitation. I asked him to help co-facilitate the next meeting.

The challenge in addressing groundwater across sectoral lines stems from the fact that farmers, hydrologists, politicians, regulators, environmentalists, and urban water users all have slightly different conceptions of how it all works. To even engage the issue in a systemic way the roundtable needed to develop some common language. We decided to use mapping to address this problem directly.

The strategy was to draw a picture of the hydrologic cycle, which is well visualized in many sources. David found one online that was at the right level of generality and created the large (4'x8') framework shown in Figure 1.13.

The Language of the Hydrologic Cycle

The CRWFS participants had a rigorous discussion about all this language, identifying and adding sticky notes to the general ones we provided. One of the challenges of cross-sector stakeholder groups is the great diversity in meaning for what sound like common English words.

We decided to intentionally leave off most of the labeling, except for the basic layers. These we put on sticky notes. The session involved having the group as a whole determine which labels were used for which part of the system, seen as an integrated whole, and adding labels we hadn't uncovered. Our hope was that the hour or so that the group spent wrestling with the map, they would come to an aligned view of the whole system before starting their discussion about what to do in a specific California region. This happened!

The group went on to analyze a Kings Canyon groundwater case and the decision systems around it. This part of the work is confidential. Everyone found the process very helpful.

We shared this story to demonstrate how an internal consultant who is experienced in dialogue, can partner with an experienced, external, visual consultant. The fact that we are both experienced facilitators allowed us to understand each other and work the synergies. Our success with this pairing of dialogue and visualization in the context of change work led us to do other longer term projects where organizational change was the agenda. One of those, the Visioning and Change Alignment Process at the University of California at Merced will provide an integrative case later in the book.

Practices for Getting Started

Draw Out Your Own Case:

1. Pick a change or consulting project you have participated in.
2. Diagram out all the steps you took on a large sheet of paper.
3. Identify all the specific tools and practices you applied, a bit like we did here in this chapter.

Scan books on Visual Meetings, Visual Teams, & Visual Leaders
It will be quite helpful to "see what we mean" by looking at the prior books. They are all designed to be read like magazines, as well as books. You'll find some of the underlying concepts helpful in extending the usefulness of this book.

How Can You Begin Developing Visual Consulting Capability?

- ❑ **Start with what you know already.** Gisela is not a visual consultant but she understands the power of visual thinking and combining visual tools with dialogue. David came to this integration from the other direction, understanding visual facilitation and then learning more about the power of dialogue. Start where you are.

- ❑ **Collaborate**. You may be an experienced change consultant looking for visualization help or a visual practitioner interested in change work. Both fields are well developed as separate fields, as is the field of dialogic practice. We've concluded that in change work, separating these fields is a handicap that can be overcome

Summary of Visual Facilitation Tools

Stepping back again from the story reveals a set of visualization tools and some regarding change and dialogue.

- ☐ **Circular & "U" shapes** for meeting, visually suggesting equality of the voices
- ☐ **Visualized agendas** on flip charts
- ☐ **Small groups** generating their ideas on sticky notes and a big wall to post and cluster them
- ☐ **Visual summaries** in the form of diagrams representing the key ideas
- ☐ **Written summaries** of verbal conversation
- ☐ **Concept graphics** to provide common, systems level language
- ☐ **Mapping** on graphic wall templates to get alignment on systemic views and language
- ☐ **Exploring cases** with visual facilitation
- ☐ **Using explicit versions** to get consensus
- ☐ **Continuing dialogue,** sustained long enough to hear all voices and surface underlying beliefs and assumptions
- ☐ **Show change over time** through visual histories
- ☐ **Consensus-based, well-written, and highly visual final reports**

with awareness and collaboration. Our consulting work almost always benefits from collaboration, as we will consistently point out as we go along.

- ☐ **Take what resonates and practice.** It's tempting to offer a "paint-by-numbers" set of suggestions, but we know from our experience that this would not create a strong foundation for you. What we can do is share what we have found works in our experience in a way that you can see the potential or the approach, and then invite you to take what resonates and customize it to your circumstances, and skip what isn't relevant. Practicing using different tools and approaches is essential to your development (SideStory 1.1).

We've chosen to focus on the consulting challenge of designing and leading change as the vehicle for this book, knowing that all consulting engagements have an implicit agreement to help change something for the better. We know that what "better" means is, of course, something your client will have a lot to say about, and that there are as many different kinds of "better" as there are different kinds of clients.

But bringing something into existence that wasn't present before you began consulting is the generic purpose of any consulting engagement. The change arena is one needing critical competency development across the boards as the scale and complexity of our current organizational, community, and environmental challenges increase. We have identified seven challenges of change, the understanding of which will help prepare you for a strong consulting practice. We know from experience that each of the challenges can be met creatively, bringing visualization, dialogic practice, and change methodology together through an understanding of process leadership and its principles and practices.

Now we will turn to looking at the consulting process step by step, beginning with the basics.

2. What Kind of Consultant Are You?

A Collaborative Engagement Framework

Before moving further into what it takes to be a visual consultant, we want to back up and think about consulting itself. This is a term that is used to cover a wide variety of engagements with clients. This chapter explores some classic reasons people engage consultants, and distinctions between types of consulting approaches and the key interpersonal dynamics that underlie each type. Knowing what approach you plan to take when first meeting with clients is important. This chapter will help you understand why collaboration and mutual regard are so critical and how to work across these approaches. If you are already an experienced consultant and more interested in visual practices, you might skim quickly and jump to Part II on responding to the challenges of change.

Types of Change That Consulting Can Help With

We distinguish three types of change for which you might be asked to get involved as a consultant—developmental, volitional and situational. Each has different dynamics and makes different demands on a consultant. Before reading about the choices you have for consulting roles, think about the kinds of change processes you've already been involved with (Sidestory 2.1). This will provide useful context as you read on. Also review the following descriptions of types of change. Which have you experienced?

❑ **Developmental changes** are those provoked by the life cycles of individuals, organizations, and communities (Figure 2.1). You might be asked to help a leader or manager move through a career shift. An organization might involve you because its getting mature and needs to renew. An HR department might want to bring in new skills but the workers aren't at that stage and they need help working this through. Deep developmental changes often involve a shift in identity. Getting a new office can signal a real shift in power and responsibility. Mergers and spin-offs provoke culture change that may be transformational. One of the assumptions we make about

SideStory 2.1

Reflect on Your Own Experience

Take a moment to reflect on a consulting engagement you've experienced that felt collaborative and mutually respectful. This can be a situation in which you were the consultant, the client, or you could have been in some other kind of role.

1. What was the situation?
2. Where was your role?
3. How would you describe the consulting approach that was used?
4. What did people do that showed mutual respect?
5. What made it truly collaborative? Was there anything unusual about the situation?

Figure 2.1

Types of Change

Figure 2.2

developmental changes is that often the point of entry is only the surface of much deeper systemic changes that need to take place. In developmental change internal drivers arise from the nature of the work, the age of the organization, or the stages of maturity of the people.

- ❑ **Volitional changes** are changes that people choose to make (Figure 2.2). Leadership in organizations may initiate visioning and strategy processes that are motivated by aspiration. Managers trying to improve performance may realize a different culture is required, and perhaps initiate efforts to create a more customer centric workforce. New constituencies in a nonprofit may dream up new programs to attract funding and then have to make shifts in hiring policies to have the capacity to implement the ideas. A community may decide it wishes to attract new industries, or become more sustainable. People in an organization that has become routine may need to reconnect with purpose and meaning to be more attractive to younger people. Volitional changes are driven by this sense of purpose, intention, and aspiration.
- ❑ **Situational changes** are those required by forces beyond of our control (Figure 2.3). Many communities, for instance, are being impacted by volatile weather events like hurricanes and drought-fueled fires and need to recover, change, or move on. Economic shifts catalyzed by panics, or trade wars can overturn old assumptions and precipitate change. Perhaps social change is needed to bring disenfranchised groups needed basic services and opportunities.

We can't hope to characterize all the kinds of projects and causes you could get involved with, but we can generalize about the generic kinds of help that clients often ask for across these different kinds of change. In this book we will be following the case of our work at the University of California at Merced, which was largely a developmental kind of change driven by the need to double in size to be economically viable. But our initial engagement was with the School of Engineering that volitionally wanted to create a new vision. Let's look at this story as a bridge to thinking about the role you would take in any kind of request to help with change.

Figure 2.3

Type of Change

Visual Consulting at the UC Merced School of Engineering

Erik Rolland, interim dean at the School of Engineering (SoE) at University of California at Merced, wanted to have a clear vision for the school in advance of recruiting a permanent dean. He wanted to collaborate with some process-oriented consultants on this challenge. But he also had some functional relationship issues that needed attention from a team develop perspective. Erik expected us to help design a process where the SoE themselves could find solutions to both of their challenges in an integrated process.

I, Gisela, had direct experience working with organizational development issues and experience as a tenure track professor directing a master's program in OD at Sonoma State University. This qualified as some real expertise. I, David, had facilitated dozens of strategic visioning processes helping management teams align on major change and was, in addition, an expert information designer. We both think of ourselves as process consultants and were not being approached as "expert consultants" expected to provide answers. Erik himself was a tenured professor in business and was experienced in strategic processes and understood our approach, so the collaboration was a fruitful one.

But we are already using terms that might not be familiar to you. Let's look at how people in the consulting world have traditionally thought about all this, and then return to this story at the end of the chapter to see how we followed through by taking on different consulting roles.

Process consultation is...a kind of relationship where the consultant isn't coming in with answers, but instead focuses on helping design and facilitate a process where the organization itself could develop its own solutions in a way that is specific to the needs and capabilities of the organization.

Classic Consulting Distinctions

There are some classic approaches to consulting that it will help to appreciate (Sidestory 2.2). Historically consultants were people who offered their services as experts and were hired to give answers to questions the client might have and provide guidance and direction. Working with overhead slides, industry reports, and conceptual models, consultants would establish their authority, diagnose, and recommend. This expert approach is still used widely, especially by consultants that sell industry expertise.

In the United States, the assumption that consultants had to be experts began to shift in the 1960s. MIT organizational researcher Edgar Schein wrote a book called *Process Consultation* and gave voice to a new model. This book has been a classic in the field of organization development (OD) for decades. It describes a new kind of relationship where the consultant isn't coming in with answers, but instead focuses on helping design and facilitate a process where the organization itself can develop its own solutions in a way that is specific to the needs and capabilities of the organization. Schein called this approach "process consulting." He compared it to expert consulting and the doctor-patient model of helping others as a way of highlighting how process consultations differ from these other expertise-centered approaches.

In 1978 Peter Block identified yet another approach in his book *Flawless Consulting*, which also became a classic in the field of organization development (and was updated in 2000 and 2011). He added the idea of a "pair-of-hands" model to the three outlined by Schein. Block was foresighted in seeing the trend toward a gig economy and expanding "free agent" roles. Many contract employees call themselves consultants.

And the approaches are still evolving. Some of our colleagues in Germany are staying away from the term consulting altogether to avoid being caught in the original meaning implying someone telling others what to do. They are choosing different terms like "facilitation" to reflect a more collaborative and mutually respectful approach to working with the kind of change processes we are writing about in this book.

Visualization Integrates with Process Consultation

As process consulting became established, dialogue and visualization became a part of its repertoire. Marv Weisbord, another thought leader in the field and developer of the Future Search methodology, integrated breakout groups and visualization to achieve results (he gives credit to The Grove Consultant International for some of his graphic inspiration). More recently, Appreciative Inquiry, another process-oriented way of visioning and planning, has incorporated graphics extensively with the help of Diane Arsenian, a former Grove art director. The World Café, yet another process methodology, had Tomi Nagai Rothe, a Grove visual practitioner at its first Café at Juanita Brown and David Isaacs' home. "Graphic harvesting"of cafe conversations has become a cornerstone practice.

At the same time, fueled by technologically inspired re-engineering projects in the 1990s, big consulting firms began incorporating visual designers and facilitators as well as process-oriented consultants. Around this time, at Anderson Worldwide, Gisela helped design a program and train consultants in the Arthur Anderson Business Consulting Unit how to become process consultants. Today, with the explosion in new visualization technologies, working with visual media has become almost a requirement.

In actual practice, visual consultants combine the classic roles of expert and pair-of-hands with a primary emphasis on process consulting. But before you can understand the combinations, it will help to really understand the differences—"What is process consulting versus the expert, doctor-patient, and pair-of-hands approaches?" And "What are the benefits and risks of each?"

SideStory 2.2

Which Types of Consulting Do You Know About?

The following pages describe the different kinds of consultants—experts, doctor-patient, pair-of-hands and expert.

Following these suggestions:

1. Complete the little questionnaire on the first page of this chapter.
2. Check off the benefits and risks of each type that you are familiar with from your own experience.
3. Feel free to add some of your own ideas in the space below the lists.
4. Bear in mind that in actual practice you may use a combination of approaches in various sequences of activity.

I. The Expert Consulting Model

With this choice, **your client defines a need and concludes that the organization does not have the expertise to fulfill that need**. As a consultant you bring relevant experience and know-how related to this specific need (Sidestory 2.3).

Some of the types of expertise related to visual consulting would be information design, proper display formats for strategic and other forms of planning, technical expertise in interaction software and tools, video and other visual documentation technologies, data analytic expertise, or specific industry expertise if you have worked deeply in one sector or another.

Underlying Assumptions

1. Your client knows what kind of service or information she or he needs, and is able to communicate that need correctly to you.
2. Your client has accurately assessed your expertise as a consultant.
3. Your client has thought through the impact of having you, the consultant, provide your expertise in their organization instead of relying on internal resources.

SideStory 2.3

Benefits	Risks
☐ Most prevalent model, hence easily understood by client. ☐ Consultant's contribution is relatively easy to define and measure. ☐ Real expertise usually commands respect from the client. ☐ Helpful in shaping new thinking in the client organization.	❑ The client may have incorrectly diagnosed the organization's needs. ❑ The client may not communicate these needs correctly or completely to you. ❑ The client may incorrectly assess your capability to provide the information or service. ❑ The client may not have thought through the consequences of implementing changes resulting from an outside source. ❑ Implementation is likely to be resisted by members of the organization.

2. The Doctor-Patient Model

In this choice (SideStory 2.4), which we consider a subset of the expert approach, **your client brings you in to "check the organization over" to see if there are possible areas that need improvement.**

Or...

Your client may have detected symptoms of ill health, such as dropping sales, quality problems, or social conflict, but does not know how to accurately diagnose the cause of the problem. You as a consultant are expected to assess what is wrong and then to prescribe remedial measures.

For visual consultants this kind of work might be available to those people with assessment experience and deep expertise in organizational dynamics, using their skills to present solutions. There are also experts in satellite, scientific, and data visualization who can diagnose from visual material.

Underlying Assumptions

1. Your client has accurately identified the person, unit, or organization that is "sick" or threatened.
2. The information the "patient" will reveal to you, or the data already gathered will be accurate.
3. Your "patient" will believe and accept your expert diagnosis, and will accept and implement the prescription.

SideStory 2.4

Benefits	Risks
☐ Approach is motivated by an interest in improving the organization. ☐ Puts a great deal of power into the hands of the consultant. ☐ Is efficient if your involvement provides the critical expertise needed.	❑ Members of an organization defined as "sick" or problematical may be reluctant to reveal the kind of information needed by the consultant to make an accurate diagnosis. ❑ Depending on the organizational climate, interviewees may hide, distort, or exaggerate data about problems. ❑ Because the interpretive frames of reference aren't developed collaboratively, the client/patient may not believe the diagnosis provided, and reject the prescription offered by the consultant.

3. The Pair-of-Hands Model

In this choice (SideStory 2.5), the **client identifies needs and tasks and concludes that the organization has neither the resources nor the time to fulfill that need itself.** In this role as a consultant/contractor, you would be hired to fulfill that need.

In visual consulting—which involves a good bit of logistical support before, during, and after highly visual meetings—many clients will want you to carry on as, essentially, staff. This also may be the case in preparing reports and processing all the information, pictures, video, and other media that a change process can generate. In change work, especially, with a flow of many meetings, your client might want you to do the scheduling and even the participant logistical and travel support. Following are some of the assumptions you can make about this role and its benefits and risks.

Underlying Assumptions:

1. Your client knows what kind of service or information she or he needs, and communicates that need correctly to you.
2. Your client has accurately assessed your capabilities as a consultant/contractor.
3. Your client knows that the organization has the capacity to provide direction to you as the consultant/contractor and will help integrate the outcome that you produce.

SideStory 2.5

Benefits	Risks
☐ Works well when scope of work is clear and can easily be delegated. ☐ Addresses potential personnel bottlenecks and delays in the client system. ☐ Can add additional billing to your client services if you are an external consultant and you want to do the work.	❑ Without needed client supervision the services rendered do not meet the client's objectives or timelines. ❑ The work rendered may be more difficult to effectively integrate into the client system. ❑ Your skill set may not be what the client needs.

4. The Process Consultation Model

In this choice (SideStory 2.6), the **client contracts with you, the consultant, to facilitate the organization to perceive, understand, and develop the organization's business and human processes, in order for the client to improve the situation themselves,** as they define it.

Visual facilitation developed out of application of this model. The focus is on accurately reflecting the thinking of the group and organization itself, not your own.

Underlying Assumptions

1. Your client has an intent to improve the organization, but may not know exactly how to determine what is wrong, or what kind of help is needed, but wants to participate.
2. Your client organization can be more effective when it learns how to assess and manage its own strengths and weaknesses.
3. Joint assessment will ensure that potential remedies are grounded in the client organization's culture, and will be considered as more appropriate and acceptable by the persons who will need to implement these remedies.
4. Your client can continue independently to improve the organization if you can pass on your skills of assessment and improvement (visual consulting is a great help here).

SideStory 2.6

Benefits	Risks
☐ The consultant does not need to be an expert in the technical aspects of the client's problem.	❑ The model may be inappropriately applied, when the situation actually calls for specific expertise.
☐ Emphasizes joint assessment and problem-solving.	❑ The consultant's role is often less clear, especially to clients who are used to the other two models.
☐ The consultant is less likely to present a premature, incorrect, or unacceptable recommendation.	❑ The consultant must work harder to develop clear mutual expectations, at the start and throughout.
☐ Problems will be solved more effectively and permanently, avoiding recurrence.	❑ The client may agree to a process consulting approach, but later get anxious and dependent and press the consultant for recommendations or to become a pair-of-hands to help implement their personal thinking.

Figure 2.4

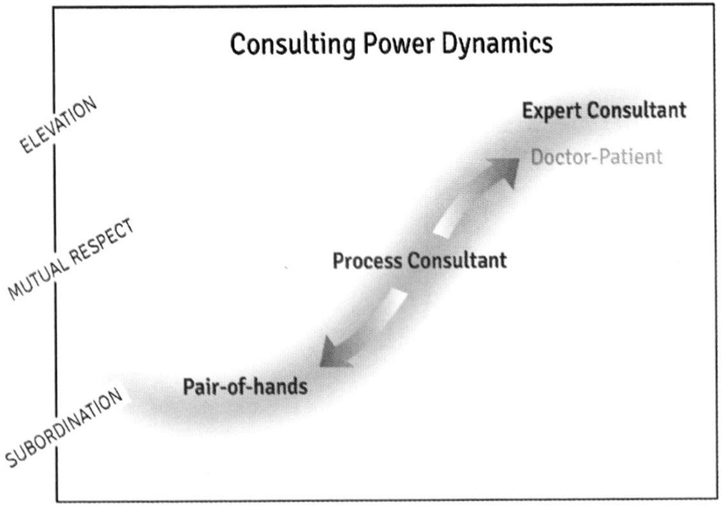

Power Dynamics

The usual differences between the four consulting approaches can be illustrated on a simple curve showing some of the power dynamics, with the process consultant being able to move either way.

More often than not the expert consultant (combined with the doctor-patient model) diagnoses and tells the client what to do, and is elevated. The pair-of-hands consultant/contractor does what the client wants and is often subordinated. But as we will show later, these power dynamics don't have to get in the way of creating respectful and mutually empowering relationships.

Be Clear About Your Role When You Contract for Work

When contracting with a client for your role it is important to be able to communicate about how you work and what you do and not do. If you think of yourself as a pair-of-hands consultant, that is very different from thinking of yourself as one of the other types of consultants. Also, each approach has embedded within it very different relational dynamics. The dynamics can become traps if you are not conscious of them. If you do recognize them you can work on changing them so that you and your client feel more empowered by the relationship and you can both better support the project. Let's look at these.

Illustrating the Key Relational Dynamics Between the Consultant and Client

We created a visual to show that often the doctor-patient and expert are elevated in importance and the pair-of-hands subordinated (Figure 2.4). As process consultants, the relationship we want to have with our clients is one of mutuality where we do not put ourselves above or below the client, and we began to wonder about it and sketched out a framework that helped us see what the possibilities are. We call it the consulting framework for "respectful engagement."

Our visualization (Figure 2.5) suggests that all three types can be collaborative, and that elevation and subordination can happen in all three as well. As we will see, elevation and subordination are not necessarily a problem, but there can be traps.

What is Elevation?

Elevation means that you assume that you or your status are somehow more important or above that of your client.

Or...

The client projects on you that you are more important or your status is somehow higher than theirs.

Here is an example of how unexamined elevation can play out. The expert consultant thinks "I know what is going on here, I have seen other executive teams struggle with this before, and this new direction I'm describing will work so much better than moving forward with your current direction." The client thinks "She is the expert in this area and I should trust what she is saying even though I don't fully understand where she is coming from. After all I am paying her for her expertise."

In visual consulting many clients will defer to superior visualization skills. This can be helpful in getting the work in the first place. But if this manifests in the visualizer projecting their imagery on the client and not listening to the symbols and metaphors that have deep meaning in the client culture, this can be a problem.

A similar elevation dynamic can emerge when a process consult is overidentified with his or her

Figure 2.5

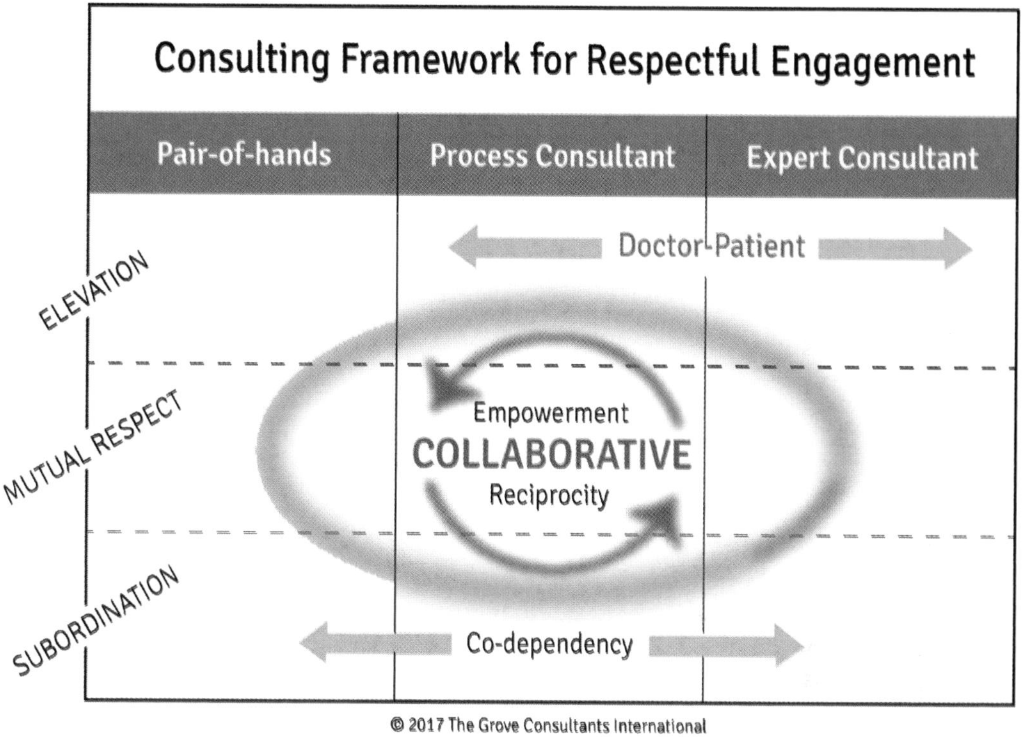

A Consulting Framework

In the visual framework shown here you can see the four consulting models along the top and the key interpersonal dynamics—elevation, mutual respect, subordination—on the left with co-dependency on the bottom. The "sweet spot," of the collaboration between you and your client, from a process consulting point of view, is in the center. This is where you and your client feels fully empowered and supported by your reciprocity.

SideStory 2.7

Humble Consulting

Since Edgar Schein first published the book *Process Consulting* in the 1960s, he has contributed many books to the field on similar themes. In his latest iteration, *Humble Consulting*, he proposes a deliberately subordinated role for the consultant.

He suggests that the essence underlying process consulting is humility—in the face of the complexity of the problems and in the relationship with the clients. He says he is there to empathetically honor the difficulties that the client faces and to focus on the client and his or her situation, not his own needs to sell himself, his skills, and his insights. Humble consulting can be characterized by commitment to helping, caring for the client, and above all, curiosity.

Other aspects of humble consulting emphasize the personal relationships with the client; listening and responding skills, being open, authentic, and innovative in the relationships. For humble consulting to work, conversations need to become a dialogue.

specific kind of process, and tries to impose their approach rather than working with the client to create something mutually workable.

What Is Subordination?

Subordination means that you assume that you and your status are somehow less important or below that of client

Or...

The client projects on you that you are less important or your status is somehow lower than theirs.

In the case of visual consultants, being expected to do the processing work related to visual reports and the like is subordinating your role in a way, but this is appropriate. On the other hand it sometimes happens that a visual facilitator will be treated like an artist or "meeting decorator" rather than a real facilitator, and is being asked primarily to create pictures that show evidence of work being completed. From a change consultant's point of view, creating a beautiful meeting artifact for a process that really isn't working well might be helping paper over something that deserves to break down to break through. If you get subordinated to an extent you can't collaborate well, this may get in the way of being able to provide good support. For instance, a lead consultant might make a decision without consulting with the visualizer and lead both into an awkward situation in front of the client.

Mutual Respect

Mutual respect is the experience of both you and your client holding each other in high regard, especially around unique differences. In this case both you, as consultant, and your client appreciate the specific capabilities, know-how, and perspectives the other brings without attributing more or less worth or status to the other than to oneself.

Figure 2.6

When a client recognizes your experience in visualization, dialogue, and change and collaborates on creating the agendas and roadmaps, the results are stronger for both parties. A person asked to do pair-of-hands work can also be respected and listened to for what they are picking up and seeing from their hands-on perspective. By the same token an expert consultant can stay humble about their limited knowledge of the nuances of an organization or community, (since by definition consultants are usually not part of the group being consulted to) and invite input from others (SideStory 2.7).

The key dynamics of elevation and subordination that we are describing can be present across all four consulting approaches, but they are more likely to occur in one than the others. For example, a pair-of-hands consultant/contractor is more likely to feel subordinated then an expert consultant. Clients are more likely to feel subordinated to the expert than to a process consultant. A process consultant's aim is to establish and maintain a mutually respectful relationship where he or she neither tells the client what to do nor does the client tell the consultant what to do but partners to find a way forward on behalf of the bigger project you are working on.

Response at an Organization Development (OD) Conference

Gisela asked two overarching questions when we presented this framework to an annual OD Conference in Portland, Oregon (Figure 2.6). The first one was **"Is this applicable to your experience?"**

It quickly became apparent that most of the practitioners found themselves being in a

Testing the Model

In 2015, we presented this framework to the Organization Development (OD) Network at their annual conference in Portland, co-sponsored with the International OD Association (IODA). We called it the Respectful Engagement Framework at the time. The room was packed with 120 people from many different countries, all very interested. We asked everyone to share their experiences with each type of consulting and the key dynamics.

Figure 2.7

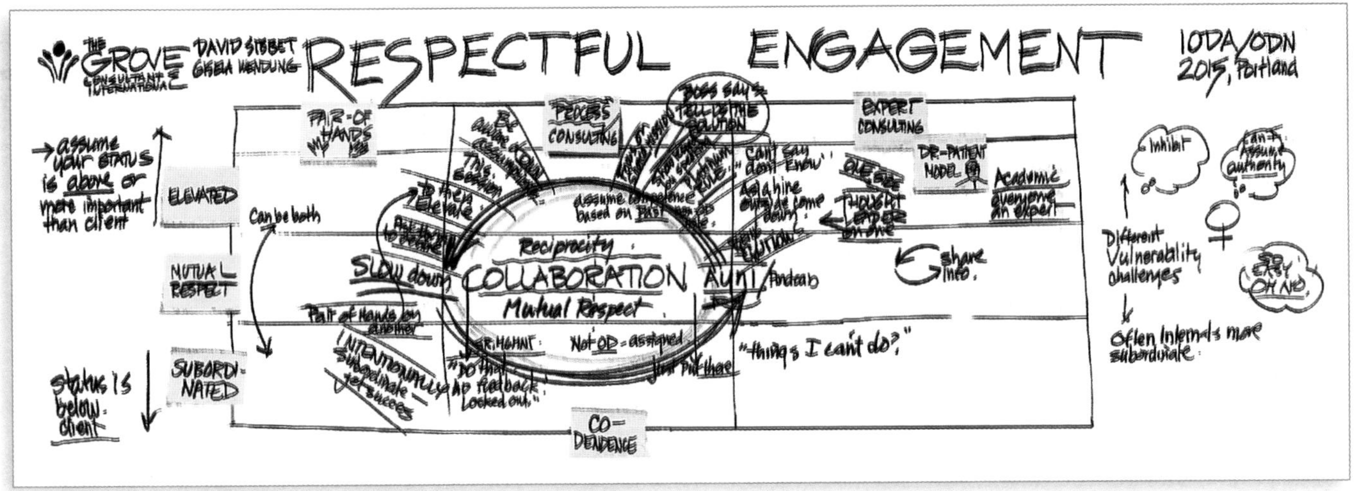

combination of these roles and often shifted across levels, especially over the course of a longer consulting engagement. (See Figure 2.7) For instance, when your expertise is in change and in designing and facilitating processes, the client will probably tend to defer to you in that regard, especially in the beginning. However, when you are actually designing the process with the client, and partnering with them, you will adjust your way of thinking and the models you use to the context your client is in, the unique situation they are facing, their culture, their prior experiences with change, and the language they use, etc. All the while helping them to see their situation and the potential for change from a new perspective. After key events you may well fill a more subordinate, pair-of-hands role, perhaps taking on project management tasks the organization could not do themselves until you are in the lead again as a process facilitator in another setting.

Gisela went on to ask the second question, appreciating the international diversity of the audience. **"Is this framework applicable across cultures?"**

We took away very important insights from this question. Just because there is hierarchy, feeling subordinated or elevated does not mean it has to get in the way of mutual respect and productive collaboration, some observed. For example, a hierarchical culture, like the

Mapping a Dialogue About Respectful Engagement

As people at the IODA/OD Conference responded, David mapped their comments into this large version of the framework. Gisela and David facilitated by directing attention to the various areas and asking questions. By writing with large letters, and keeping pace with the group, it was able to hold the focus of most of the 120 people in the room. It modeled how panoramic visualization supports large group dialogue.

Japanese culture, requires that you observe the protocol of that structure when engaging with a client. A consultant from Singapore pointed out that she often enters into a consulting engagement intentionally subordinate, then wins respect and sometimes moves into an expert role when trust is strong.

Understanding one's place in a subordination and elevation protocol is the prerequisite to developing a trusting and mutually respectful relationship. None of these dynamics are inherently better or worse than others, but being unaware of them and becoming trapped in relationships that aren't serving the organization are the pitfalls to avoid. A good habit is to stay open to learning what social dynamics and norms are and how they operate and unfold differently from client to client, industry to industry, and country to country, and to not to take them for granted. Mutual empowerment from one context to another might look quite different. You should not assume that a process-consulting approach in the United States will look like a process consulting approach in another country. In cultures quite different from ours, the more answers we already have about "right" process, the more likely we are to overlook how to make a deeply empowering and collaborative process work.

In any of the different consulting approaches, the client's expertise about their situation, their industry, and related trends, is critical to designing a change process that works. In the end, it is their change....

In any of the different consulting approaches, the client's own expertise about their situation, their industry, and related trends is critical to designing a change process that works. In the end, it is their change, their decisions, and their responsibility to grow the capacity to implement it that supports success.

Our Approach at the School of Engineering

Here is how our understanding of the approaches described in this chapter played out with Erik at the School of Engineering. The entire process was framed as strategic visioning, combining the best of traditional strategic planning approaches with forward-looking visioning. But embedded within this was attention being paid to the organizational issues

Figure 2.8

The Shadow Sides of Elevation & Subordination

	Pair-of-hands	Process Consultant	Expert Consultant
ELEVATION	*Know-it-all helpers*	*Process ramrods*	*Condescending thought leaders*
MUTUAL RESPECT	*Proactive assistants who listen*	*True collaborators*	*Patient teachers*
SUBORDINATION	*Passive order takers*	*Go alongs*	*Spinners*

Shadow Side Roles

The names for these elevated and subordinated roles purposely point to the shadow side examples and call out what the middle way of mutual respect might be called. Remember that there are also quite useful versions of all of these.

on the staff side—a team development and culture change challenge, really. Our common understanding of process design allowed a blend of these two goals in one process.

To handle the staff issues I, Gisela, operated as a lead facilitator, helping lead sensitive and ultimately effective dialogue with staff about their issues. While I was not being hired as an expert on university organization, my actual experience as an academic program administrator was invaluable.

I, David, brought in my long experience with strategy work, and particularly, visual facilitation, and led some of the history reviews and mapping sessions, with Gisela again facilitating the dialogue that made sense of this work. Neither of us were being engaged as a pair-of-hands, but there were aspects of the work that had that quality. Erik wanted well-done visual reports with pictures of the charts and work groups so he could feed forward the work to the incoming dean. He also wanted to encourage faculty who attended the group meetings to brief others who couldn't come with these same reports.

Shadow Side Applications

When we first developed the Consulting Framework we wanted to highlight the problems that arise when elevation and subordination become dysfunctional, and we wanted to explore what practicing mutual respect can look like across the different consulting models. We've touched on some of these problems already, but here is a chart of what we called the shadow side aspects of these dynamics with some names that characterize the dysfunctions (Figure 2.8).

A complex issue to write about is the trap that both external and internal consultants can get into becoming, in effect, co-dependents for irresponsible leaders who are neglecting people issues and asking the HR and other "people" functions to compensate. If attractive contracts are keeping you in this kind of bind it might be worth digging into your underlying values and connect with what you want to be supporting.

The Promise of Mutual Regard

One of our colleagues, Mary Gelinas, has been studying cognitive sciences and neuropsychology, commented that historically people survived by bonding with others like themselves in bands and tribes. But today our survival may well depend on learning how to collaborate with people who are different. The scale of challenges we face required partnerships, teams, and collaborative network. This is the hope of finding frameworks that support mutual regard.

Later on we will share more about the preventions you can put into place to help you and your client navigate these relational dynamics. We have heard from consultants who have participated in our workshops, and have taken this framework to their initial client meetings to show and illustrate to their clients how they plan to approach their work.

Our main hope with this chapter is that you can become aware of the approach you are using at any one point in time and the dynamics that come with that approach. Ultimately, as we will stress throughout this book, you will want to come to your own style and approach that express the value you want to bring forward to clients.

SideStory 2.8

Map Your Own Experience

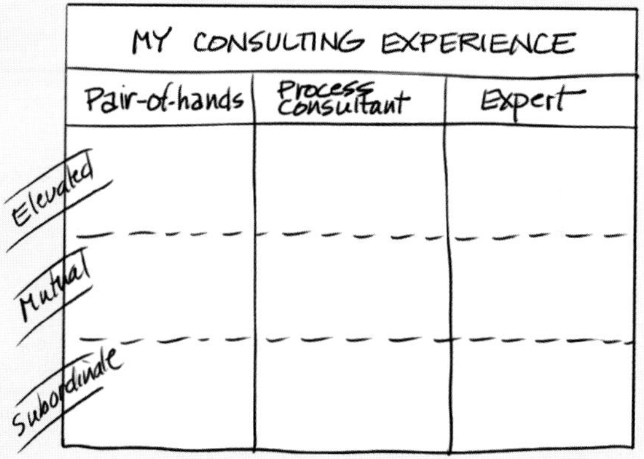

1. Take a large sheet of paper and draw out the framework.
2. Then write into the different boxes experiences you have had with each type of consulting and experiences with elevation, subordination, and mutual respect and codependency.
3. Bear in mind as you do this, that a single engagement might involve combining approaches.

Summary

- ☐ There are **four approaches to consulting** that apply to visual consulting.
- ☐ Traditional consulting roles for consultants is as an **expert** or **doctor-patient.**
- ☐ **Process consultation** emerged as a concept in the 1960s and focused on guiding processes that allow clients to participate in solution finding.
- ☐ **Pair-of-hands** consulting is another approach, and increasing in a free-agent economy.
- ☐ **Each approach has benefits and risks.** The point is to become aware of how you are approaching your consulting clients.
- ☐ **We are concerned about the consequences of the unexamined elevation** of consultants because of the accompanying devaluing of internal expertise and sense of "ownership" within a client system. This can happen with all three types.
- ☐ We **are also concerned about** the way in which process oriented consultants, many of whom are in HR as internal consultants, become the **co-dependent enablers** of power oriented, insensitive, and undisciplined managers. (It can be a tough decision to maintain your independent point of view or what you believe is needed for success when it means you could lose your contract or your job.) If you cannot talk about issues you have with your client you probably do not have a mutually respectful relationship.

Draw Your Own Consulting Portrait

1. Hang up a large sheet of paper.
2. Draw out the graphic template shown here. (It doesn't have to be pretty.)
3. Brainstorm your different capabilities.
4. **KNOWLEDGE** would be areas where you would be confident helping your client understand something.
5. **SKILLS** are things you know how to do in practice.
6. **TOOLS** in this case would be literal tools, like computer programs, visualization technologies, visualizing tools, etc.
7. **FUNCTIONAL ROLES** are jobs you've had where you would understand someone in a roughly similar role.
8. **INNER CAPABILITIES** would be emotional capabilities, levels of awareness, self discipline, etc.

3. Capabilities You'll Need
Focus on the Fundamentals

In Chapters 5 and 6 we will introduce you to two visual frameworks that have helped us organize our thinking about what would help a visual consultant to succeed when supporting a change process. Both frameworks will help you focus your attention on specific things to address while keeping the whole system in mind. They can also help explain to clients how you are approaching your work.

The first is the *Liminal Pathways Change Framework.* It illustrates the archetypal pattern that is part of any kind of transformational change (Figure 3.1). The second one identifies seven predictable challenges of change that we have identified to be a part of any kind of larger consulting process aimed at systemic change. It also identifies practices associated with each challenge (Figure 3.2).

In earlier books in the Wiley Visual Facilitation series, David explored the skills and competencies needed for visual meetings, visual teams, and visual leaders in some detail. Here we will describe visual facilitation capabilities that relate to consulting. We are also convinced that adding the capabilities of a good dialogue facilitator and change consultant are the differences that make a difference, to borrow a phrase from Gregory Bateson.

As we described in the introduction, we have tested the *Seven Challenges of Change* framework extensively with our colleagues in the GLEN (Global Learning & Exchange Network) in a series of online Exchanges.

Working with Visual Frameworks

Both frameworks and the GLEN conversations made us realize that a great split in attention in our times needs to be healed, and that is between what we know and do in the outer, sometimes called "objective"world, and what we know and are in our interiority—our selves. It's an aspect of the split our culture sustains between objective and subjective realities. Graphically the Four Flows illustrated in SideStory 3.1 intentionally integrate the

Figure 3.1

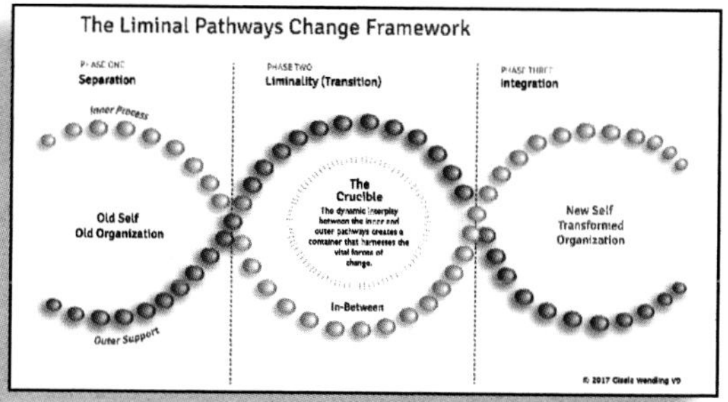

Basic Pattern of Change

The *Liminal Pathways Change Framework* portrays the archetypal pattern of transformational change, emphasizing the interdependence between the inner dynamics and the outer support structures. Chapter 5 will explain this in detail.

Figure 3.2

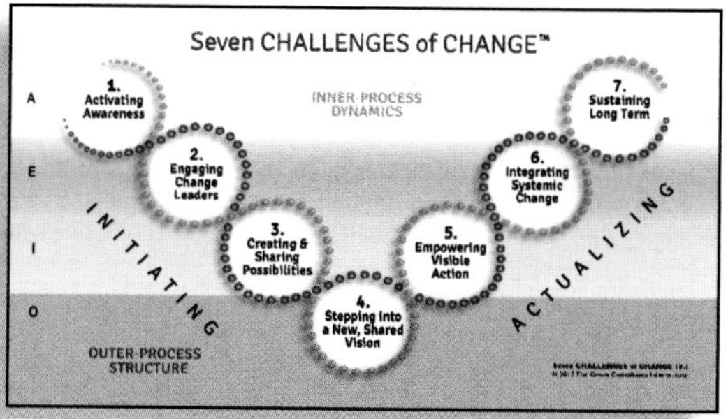

Seven Challenges of Change

This framework shows how the basic pattern of change plays out over predicable stages in a longer process.This will be explained in Chapter 6, and provide a structure for the practices chapters.

SideStory 3.1

Four Flows of Process

These process flows are common to visual facilitation, dialogue, and change. Understanding them is a place to start building capability.

I. Attention
This is the quality of inner awareness that guides what you and groups are paying attention to at any given time. It can also include what the system as a whole is paying aspirational attention to—top line.

II. Energy
This is the emotional field you and the group are immersed in and includes movement, pacing, feelings, and expressive communications. You sense group feelings by paying attention to your own.

III. Information
This is the flow of symbolic communication, in text, graphics, numbers, and all the forms of media. Translations and interpretations are higher forms of information, and include knowledge at even higher levels of understanding.

IV. Operations
This is the bottom line flow of decisions that use infrastructure and other mechanisms to control the material plane of our lives. Operations pays attention to all the tangible resources needed in this work—tools, supplies, food, equipment., and support staff.

top line (or more inner aspects) with the objective, bottom line (or outer) aspects of the work.

Working Holistically

As you think about the four flows, imagine your self dancing among them. Among our mentors are Edie and Charlie Seashore, leaders of the National Training Labs (NTL). Since its beginning in the 1960s, NTL has significantly helped shape the field of organizational development (OD). Charlie and Edie were convinced that learning to use your self as an instrument of change was essential for good practice, as essential as understanding open systems, working with valid data, and other practices of OD. They believed in working holistically in a systemic way.

Integrative Thinking

So what is the dance floor of change? The Grove Consultants International's grounding in Arthur M. Young's Theory of Process has been a decades-long effort to create tools and process models that integrate all aspects of the human experience and see the integration of objective ways of knowing with inner consciousness. In common language this means seeing our spiritual, soulful, mental, and physical lives not as separate things, but aspects of a connected human experience with different practices for working with each. Young's theory rests on the insight that it is the way things move—the process of life—that embodies universal unifying patterns. Process awareness is indeed what connects the three fields we are bringing together in visual consulting (Figure 3.3).

Visual Consulting Capabilities and the Four Flows of Process

The Grove has been training process consultants for many years with the Four Flows framework, and has evolved principles and practices for each of them. We also appreciate

Attentional Flow

This whole spread illustrates the levels you can attend to. Our consciousness is what has the freedom to move in all the dimensions of awareness.

that the capabilities connected with visual facilitation, dialogue, and change each play out on all these levels, with biases in practice (see SideStory 3.3).

The Four Flows framework describes process patterns that are universal in nature and have been described in different ways throughout history. In everyday language you may have heard people talk about spirit, soul, mind, and body as all being important. Common diagnostic tools looking at personal preference, like the Meyers Briggs assessment, based on the work of Carl Jung, distinguish intuition, feelings, thinking, and sensing. Even cartoonists have figured out how to represent these levels in their visual vocabulary (see illustration in Figure 3.5).

While life is always happening on all these four levels, we don't pay attention to all four consciously at the same time. Understanding where your clients and groups are focusing themselves is, however, a fundamental concept in process consulting. We are going to describe each flow, and invite you to bring your own understanding into the process.

Being Aware of Attention

A useful metaphor is to think of your attention like a flashlight. You can have a narrow or broad focus, and can point it inward at yourself or outward toward your surroundings. And your attention can move up and down these flows (SideStory 3.1). We argue for developing flexibility in this regard, and knowing how to pick up the clues of what your client is paying attention to.

Awareness is more inclusive than attention. And what is included in our field of awareness predetermines what we pay attention to. Some think of awareness as the "witness" or the "watcher." While impossible to define clearly, it does exist. Expanding our awareness helps

Figure 3.3

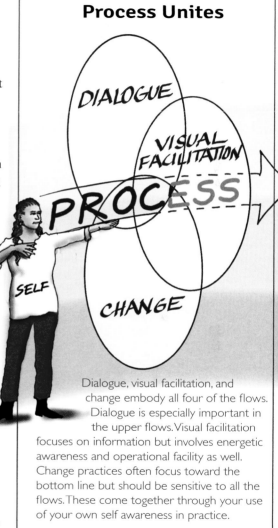

Process Unites

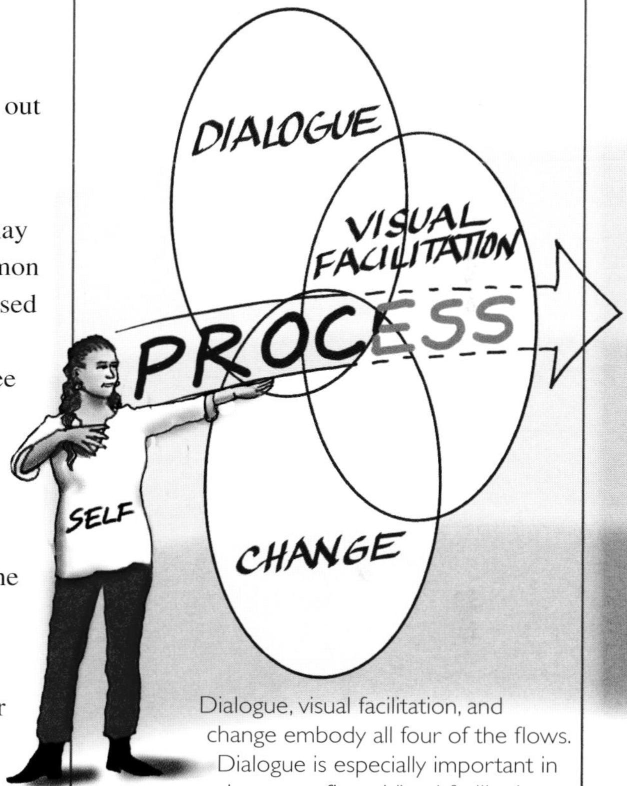

Dialogue, visual facilitation, and change embody all four of the flows. Dialogue is especially important in the upper flows. Visual facilitation focuses on information but involves energetic awareness and operational facility as well. Change practices often focus toward the bottom line but should be sensitive to all the flows. These come together through your use of your own self awareness in practice.

us see more of the whole and helps us see where we need to put our attention.

Attention is more accessible and can be observed. There are some clues, like where people's eyes are focused, how their bodies are being held, and where they are showing up physically and in virtual space and where they are not showing up. Remember that your understanding will always be a guess, and you need to stay in inquiry.

While attention is mapped into the top line flow, the awareness that underlies it plays a part in all the other flows as well. We pay attention to feelings and movement. We pay attention to information. And we pay attention to operations. But being aware of how you pay attention is an inner process.

When facilitating meetings, attention is managed through practices like:

- ❑ Framing potential outcomes with a story or image.
- ❑ Preparing your self through mindfulness practices to be centered and aware.
- ❑ Distinguishing inner intention from overtly stated goals.

Figure 3.4

Energetic Flow

Music is a wonderful metaphor for understanding the process flow in groups, and especially the energetic level of process.

Tuning into the Energetic Flow

The dynamic process of feeling and experiencing what is happening in a group process is metaphorically like listening to music (Figure 3.4), participating in a dance, or feeling the flow of the water when you are kayaking. In visual consulting it involves the following:

- ❑ Noticing the pacing and speed of activities.
- ❑ Tracking the pulse between converging and diverging.
- ❑ Feeling times when something is threatening people, and they are closing up.
- ❑ Listening for what has heart and meaning when people talk.

- ❑ Staying aware of your movements as an energetic factor.
- ❑ Understanding the difference between "pushing" a group and "pulling" them out.

Emotions, according to neuroscientists, aren't objects, but names for various energy movements in our body states. Movement has direction and intensity, can be felt directly. Emotions and experiences are rich and thin, strong and weak, accelerating and slowing, and ebbing and waning. This is why being at home in your energetic, feeling body is so important in this work. It is the "tool" by which you track this flow.

In visual facilitation your own body is both a sensor and a sender of signals to the group. It is important to keep in mind that...

- ❑ The physical miming of what you are hearing can be as important as what goes on the chart.
- ❑ Where you as a consultant stand and move in relation to a graphic recorder directly affects the field of attention.
- ❑ Your tone of voice may have more impact than the content of what you say.
- ❑ Setting a trustworthy rhythm is fundamental to change. The overall shape and flow of a change process is a bit like an opera or a musical performance. The pacing and rhythm, intervals and textures are as important as the words and concepts represented in the songs and librettos.

Understanding the Information Flow

Information points at our human ability to represent the world through symbols and representations—in graphics, text, and numbers most often. This is the material our rational, conscious minds use to "make sense" out of the world. Visualization is one, enormous part of this flow, as the map to the world of visualization in Figure 3.6 shows.

Figure 3.5

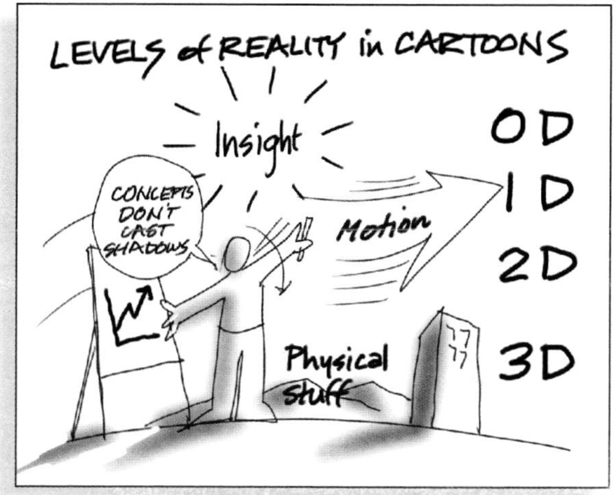

Information Flow

Cartoonists aspire to communicate across cultures and communities. They all show the operational physical world using shadows, size, and overlapping to indicate our 3Dimensional world. They use flat, 2D talk balloons and diagrams to indicate informational reality. Colors indicating intensity and 1D action lines indicate energy and movement. Our attention—which is imaginary—is just pointed at by little lines, and really has no dimensionality.

(For further understanding of the universal nature of this four-level way of thinking, look to the appendix dealing with the Theory of Process.)

Figure 3.7

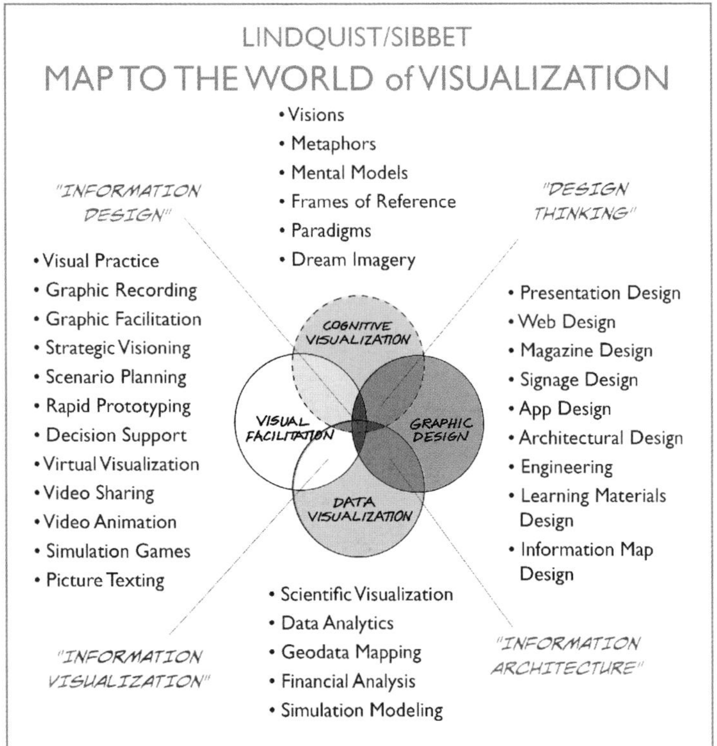

This diagram is a collaboration between Evert Lindquist, director and professor of the School of Public Administration, University of Victoria, Canada, and myself. Bear in mind that terms and boundaries are fluid and under continual evolution and debate.

Mapping Information

Maps are not the territory, but they help us orient and navigate. Here is one, first published in *Visual Leaders*, exploring the world of visualization.

Information technically is data that is "in a form" of some sort—textual, graphic, or numeric. In visual work, the forms are actually display formats or graphic templates, pictographs and ideographs. In text and language, the forms are grammatical structures, like subject-verb-object. In numbers, the forms can be charts and graphs, sequences, and formulas. Cartoonists know these forms and represent the four flows with them (see Figure 3.5) as we noted before.

Learning to be aware of and manage the flow of information also includes seeing deeper patterns of meaning, and understanding how humans make higher order sense out of the information in our conscious minds. This would include understanding patterns of discourse that advance or subordinate certain ways of thinking, with discourse including what is okay to talk about, write about, propose about, and acknowledge in reward systems. The information flow would include the kind of systems level awareness supported by big picture thinking on large wall charts.

What is true of any form of representations, no matter how specific or general is that these representations are not the material world itself, but representations of it. The symbols themselves aren't energetic patterns, unless they are embedded in vocal or performed speech. And these symbols aren't the same as what we are paying attention to though they provide clues. This is the reason it's helpful to see all models, no matter how complex, as different kinds of "maps," whose validity has a lot to do with how well they represent the "territory" of whatever they are pointing toward.

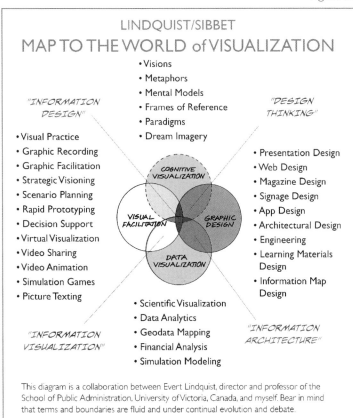

From an interior point of view, these maps and models are metaphorically sometimes called "lenses" or "filters" when they are embedded in our conscious mind. Understanding these is essential to being a good visual consultant, and for helping clients with the many confusions that arise from people becoming overattached to their representations and ignoring the real territory they represent. We will return again and again to this idea as we begin to work through actual practices. The fact that different representations of how to deal with change have arisen in the fields of visual facilitation, dialog, and change is one of the confusions we are attempting to rise above through some careful connection-making and visual representation in our frameworks.

Managing Operations

Operations concern the physically manifest world of real tools, mechanisms, resources, and infrastructures. This is the "body" level of group process (Figure 3.7). These all have existence in material form. Included at this level, for consultants and facilitators, are decisions that operate on these mechanisms to achieve results. Because physical tools and mechanisms are objective and subject to the laws of cause and effect, these can be learned and managed to achieve real control at this level. For visual consulting it includes arranging for and managing things like:

- ❑ Collaboration backbones, including staff and technology.
- ❑ Visualization tools—pens, paper, chart stands, sticky notes, and tablets.
- ❑ Digital equipment for documenting and reproducing visual material.
- ❑ Communications technology, including video conferencing, mobile, and projection technologies.
- ❑ Sound technology.
- ❑ Meeting environments, including tables, chairs, dividers, and charts.

Figure 3.7

Operational Flow

Operations concern the physically manifest world of real tools, mechanisms, resources, and infrastructures. This is the "body" level of group process.

Figure 3.8

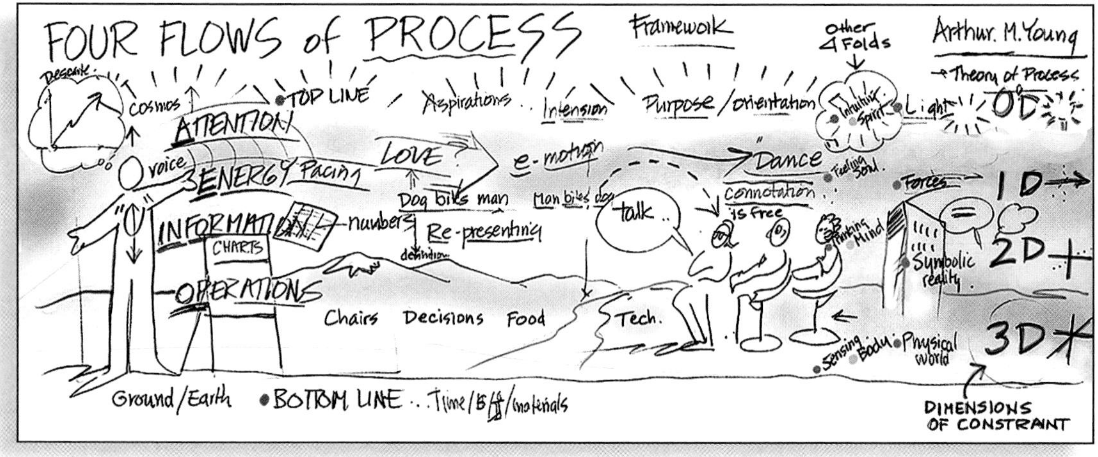

Four Flows SketchTalk

This large 4'×10' chart was created in real-time by David to explain the Four Flows to a Leading Change program. As he explained the distinctions, participants identified aspects of process work that resonated with each flow.

This kind of process, where a clear, large-scale framework is presented and then filled out with group interaction and contribution is a powerful educational tool for visual consulting.

- ❑ Budgeting for change projects
- ❑ Reproducing large charts
- ❑ Shipping of supplies
- ❑ Room setups
- ❑ Food arrangements and impacts

You can add to this list, because the real, material world is where we live and work. Change is inevitably reflected there too.

What About YOU?

You may be wondering about the "U" in the familiar AEIOU set of vowels. It's not a level. We suggest the "U" is YOU, appreciating and moving along through all these other levels! Appreciating this is a key to learning to use yourself as a factor in your work. Whatever capabilities you develop or practices you learn will be filtered through your own understanding and shaped by who you are. Making friends with your own style and adapting tools and methods is part of the process of becoming a visual consultant.

In the early stages of change people may be dealing with surprise and shock on the one hand, or perhaps hopefulness. As a change team begins to form, and people realize something is going to shift, there will be a lot of uncertainty but also excitement. As change begins to become more real and possible actions are being explored, resistance will surface and people will be assuming lots of things. In all these cases it is possible to take things personally. This is part of your capability challenge. Being aware of what you are feeling and how you might be being triggered is important in discerning what course of action to take. Areas in your own life that you are afraid to look at will be blind spots.

As people actually begin stepping into a new vision and making big decisions you will be challenged to hold the complexity during the struggle to come to agreement. You will get involved in helping people let go of the old and open to the new. All of this will at some level be supported or constrained by your own ability to do this (SideStory 3.2).

Here are some of the capabilities for using yourself that deserve special attention:

- ❏ **Active imagination:** An experienced visual consultant can look at an empty room and see images of how it might be arranged, where charts would hang, and what the flow of activity might be like, even though none are present. They can look at a blank piece of paper and project a framework of organization—choosing among formats like listing and clustering. They can imagine walking in the shoes of their clients and sense what might be possible. These capabilities involve paying attention to the imagery that emerges in your mind when you hear people speak that might provide doorways into understanding how they organize their inner minds. Imagination grows as you use it more. In change consulting, it will involve the capacity of holding contradictory scenarios in your awareness until an aligned story emerges that galvanizes action.

- ❏ **Framing:** This competency involves paying attention to the metaphors you and your clients use to organize thinking, and the ways in which you and your clients introduce needs and requests. Frames, like those on paintings and pictures, provide a clue at the attentional level of how to value the content. The same dynamic is true with spoken words, where people will set up a point with a story. Even if not explicit, your point-of-view (often called a frame of reference) will shape what everyone is paying attention to. It takes some practice to become aware of these, and more to use new ones adeptly—but this capability makes a huge difference in your being able to communicate. In visual consulting this application of your sense of things can become explicit as you choose titles and display formats for displays and visual presentations.

SideStory 3.2

Seeing Whole Systems

Mathias Weitbrecht is founder of Visual Facilitators, a firm of several dozen operating out of Hamburg, Germany. He is helping to lead the European explosion of interest in visual facilitation.

In his words, "We operate from the perspective of a systemic totality, and from the attitude of awareness, observation, methodical intervention, feedback/building of awareness, self-organization and adaptation to change.

We are excited when moving forward in a process – when a new structure presents itself, where the values, goals and vision come to life, and the entire system works together. In the field of visualization, we listen well, are able to process large amounts of information creatively, recognize patterns, and integrate perspectives and meta-views into the work. We convey complex issues in a comprehensible way through simple tools."

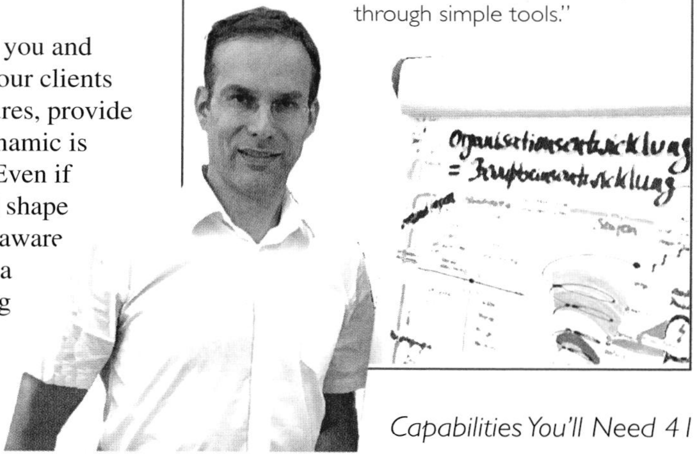

Figure 3.9

Making Visual What Touches You

Reinhard Kuchenmüller and **Dr. Marianne Stifel** literally dive into meetings armed with colorful pens and little cards, capturing the essence, feelings, and underlying issues, using their intuition to reflect the process in little images and phrases. They then post the cards and facilitate wonderful dialogue around the images they reflect. Cllients often select the most resonant ones and print them in keepsake reports.

Reinhard was trained as an architect and Marianne as a psychotherapist. They arre from Germany and live in Italy. Through their company VISUELLE PROTOKOLLE® they have pioneered a unique visual consulting practice.

❑ **Connecting with feelings:** This is the capability of noticing our own feelings and body states, even if it is uncomfortable. Learning to connect with our own embodied wisdom is a never-ending area of practice. Because people attach meaning to language and metaphors, and often have strong feelings about them, any time we are working graphically with other people's symbols we need to stay aware of when our or their feelings are being triggered.

- When do people feel safe?
- When do they feel threatened?
- When are you truly mirroring what they feel and mean?

We can learn to access these perceptions through awareness of our own reactions, assuming that the human psyche can tune into energetic fields in a resonant way. The more serious the change work we are guiding, the more this capability needs attention. It means paying attention to subtle signals. It helps us know how to move with the energy of a group by moving there yourself. (See Figure 3.9)

❑ **Context awareness:** This is the ability to pay attention to the "lay of the land," which is a metaphor for imagining and being in inquiry about all the things that are surrounding a project we are setting out to do as a consultant.

- What is the background history?
- What is the emotional loading in a culture coming from its history?
- Who else is involved in the change?
- What are the resource constraints?
- What infrastructure is in place or not to support the project?
- How are decisions about finances being made?
- What are the relationship networks?
- What are other people's stake in the change?

Figure 3.10

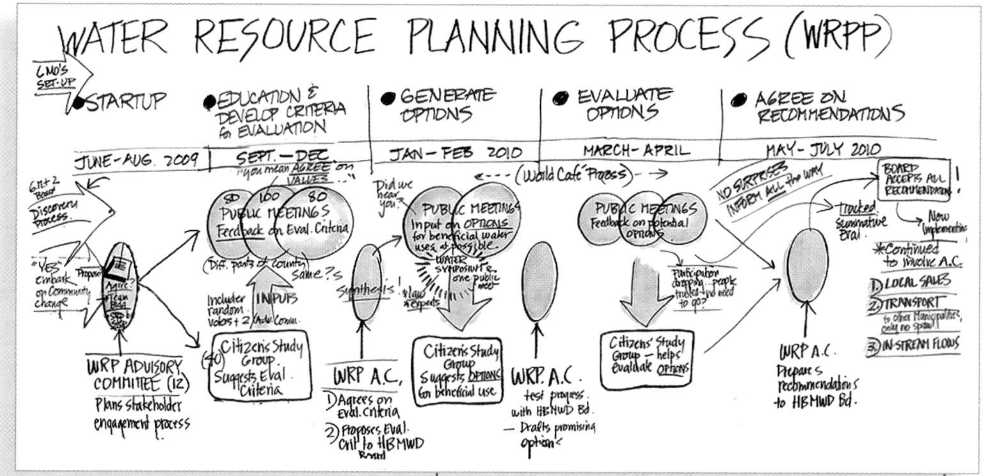

In some sense, there is no limit to what you could pay attention to when it comes to context, but there are fundamentals of what to become aware of. These are summarized in the conceptual frameworks shared in this book, which operate as high level checklists for staying aware of the larger context. Context awareness, like other competencies associated with expanding your awareness, can grow continually with experience and practice.

Senior Change Consultant

Mary V. Gelinas is an experienced organization development consultant who led an award-winning Water Resources Planning Process in Humboldt County, California. "Roadmaps create a safe space for community processes, because everyone can see and understand the big picture. When you develop them collaboratively there is even more ownership," she says. Graduates from her and Roger James' Cascadia Center for Leadership are transforming processes in rural California.

Visualization Capabilities Needing Special Attention

For those of you who are already consultants and are seeking out this book to help with the visual part, there are some personal capabilities that are worth developing even if you aren't going to learn graphic facilitation. If you are already a graphics person, but expanding your consulting facility, this will be a good checklist of which fundamental skills we think make a difference.

- ❑ **Sketching out visual frameworks**: A basic competency behind many of the suggestions in this book is being able to create large graphic frameworks that clients can write in or where you can put sticky notes and generate data. These do not have to be fancy, but you need to have an idea of what is possible. Illustrations in this book should help you. You can play with them and develop your own sense of how much space you will need for the different kinds of content you want to look at, even if you plan to work with a graphic recorder.

  Being able to sketch out big frameworks is related to the kind of sketching that you would use for "chalk talks" on flip charts when you are presenting concept or process choices to a client. A person guiding a group through change processes will

Figure 3.11

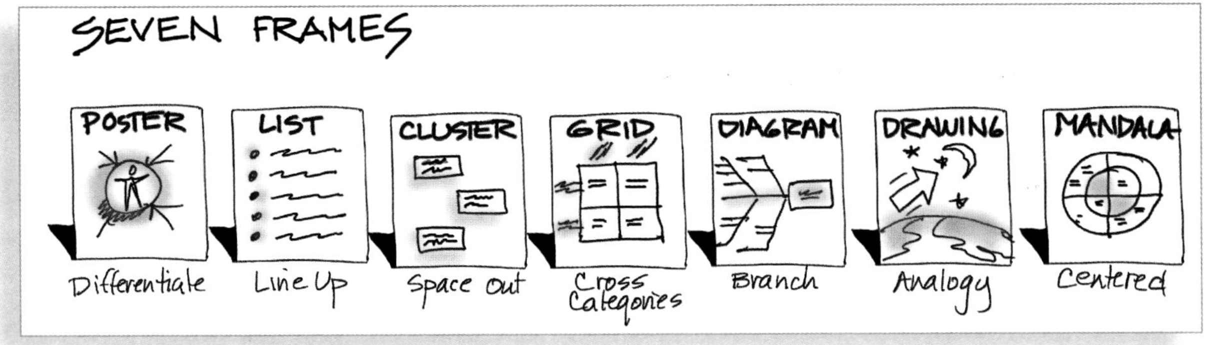

often have to sketch out the process of an activity in real time. This is more a question of knowing what to draw than being skilled at the actual rending (although clients don't mind neat charts).

The Group Graphics® Keyboard

This framework is described in detail in *Visual Meetings*, with examples of each format and their pros and cons. The Keyboard has been tested worldwide since the mid-1970s. We can say confidently, that ALL visual displays are variations or combinations of these seven basic formats. Working with these patterns in your note taking will increase your familiarity and fluidity.

In addition to being basic frames and formats for displays on the wall, the frames also points to seven different thinking processes (See SideStory 3.3).

A note for fans of the Theory of Process: This was the first framework created using ToP principles of looking at things in terms of the complexity of the process used to create the pattern, rather than the complexity of the artifact itself.

- ❏ **Understanding archetypal display formats**: The Group Graphics Keyboard illustrated in Figure 3.11 is more than just a set of choices for graphic recorders. They represent seven archetypal ways of organizing information that make it easier or harder to see patterns, and are, in fact, pointing to a spectrum of ways to think and conceptualize in general (SideStory 3.3). A visual consultant can learn to guide clients in when to use listing, clustering, gridding, diagramming, or drawing when applying these formats to PowerPoints, large wall charts, reports, and other forms of communication. (*Visual Meetings* thoroughly explains all this).
- ❏ **Visual listening**: Using visualization to reflect what other people are saying can be a very powerful, collaborative experience, and supports the social construction of meaning. Because no one recording visually on a chart can capture but a fraction of what is actually said, it becomes imperative to enroll the group in helping add in what you miss, correct what you've gotten wrong, and even better in many cases, participate in generating the visuals themselves. When practiced well, groups come to feel they are co-creating meaning. You don't have to do the recording yourself to get this effect, but you do need to know how to manage the interactive process of making sense of things, actively using the recording and mapping as a catalyst for deeper questioning and inquiry.
- ❏ **Listening for metaphors**: When people are trying to understand something they don't have experience with, they will invariably start comparing the new to what they do understand. This is metaphoric or analogical thinking. Cognitive scientists

are in agreement that these images shape not only meaning making, but perception itself. If you want an in-depth look at this competency, read *Images of Organization* by Garath Morgan. He has developed an entire consulting practices around getting organizations to explore different metaphors in depth. In this book, we will explore what it means to both listen for and draw out "generative images" that have the capacity to inspire action and create a sense of alignment in a diverse group. Generative imagery is often a metaphor. (See Figure 3.9)

- ❑ **Seeing patterns in process**: The flow and sequencing of a consulting process can be visualized. It is almost essential when it comes to designing and leading change. This practice leads to being able to actually detect flow patterns in the real time of meetings and longer processes. Our colleague, Mary Gelinas, who works in challenging multistakeholder processes, believes the visualization of the larger process provides the necessary clarity and "safety" for people who are very skeptical about participating (See Figure 3.10).
- ❑ **Using visual templates to create workbooks on the wall:** A visual consulting competency that will help you guide clients to do big picture thinking is imagining your meeting rooms and walls as giant workbook spaces, and learning how to arrange charts, wall templates, and work products around the room so everyone can see the steps and the progress. Sandra Florstedt, a colleague who worked for many years inside Hewlett Packard, started using their big ink jet printers when they first came out to do this, creating the worksheets in PowerPoint or some other graphic program, calling this a "workbook on the wall." The Grove has many graphic templates for this. It is an approach that is a key to high participation meetings. Most design thinking processes, innovation labs, and hakathons work this way.
- ❑ **Reproducing and sharing visual displays:** Digital photography has accelerated visualization possibilities like few other technologies. White boards, table size worksheets, and large charts can all be photographed and shared right

SideStory 3.3

Visual Cognition

Seven cognitive processes are reinforced by the patterns illustrated in the Group Graphics® Keyboard.

1. **Focusing (posters)** Can you maintain concentrated attention amidst a richness of choices?
2. **Flowing (lists)** Can you move your awareness in a line of thinking?
3. **Juxtaposing (clusters)** Can you think of sets of elements and play with different affinities?
4. **Categorizing (grids)** Can you clearly define aspects of what you want to analyze and cross-compare with other distinctions?
5. **Following connections (diagrams)** Can you pursue branching possibilities and remember the connections?
6. **Analogizing (drawings)** Can you systematically compare one familiar thing to something else?
7. **Perceiving wholeness (mandalas)** Can you see the unities under a diversity of perceptions?

Visual language, the tight integration of words and images, now works across all the different platforms people use to communicate.

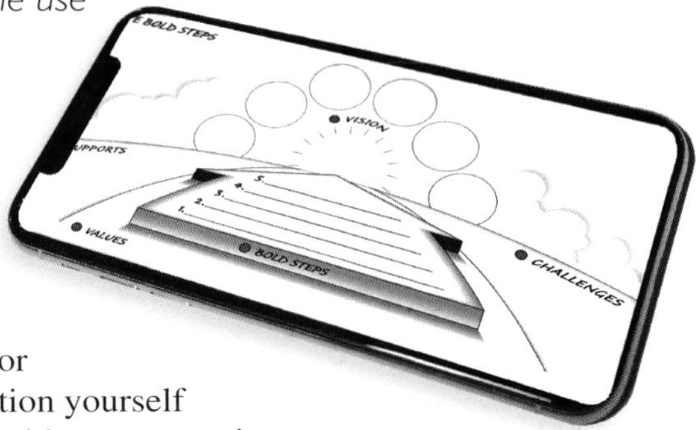

away digitally. However, it helps a lot to understand some of the technical basics, and makes a difference when the reproductions are clear on how to take clear pictures and clean them up afterward. There are apps that help with this. Whether or not you are doing the drawing and visualization yourself you need to understand what is possible to guide your associates.

- **Linking work outputs over time:** Documenting, storing, and referencing key documents in well-organized ways is part of what we will describe as a "collaboration backbone." It includes your digitalized charts, text documents, indexes, and online platforms that allow easy access in a distributed way. It includes thinking carefully about the frequency and pacing of communications. When people receive the same graphic diagrams and chart they help generate during planning, everyone can remember more and literally see what has been accomplished.

- **Taking a holistic view of human cognition**: Contemporary brain research provides overwhelming evidence that "thinking" happens throughout our entire body. Our heart and gut have as many neurotransmitters as our brains, so the common-sense idea of following your heart or following your gut has some validation. A big-picture view of human cognition will help immensely as you work to understand the inner dynamics of change, because having plans, visions, and new direction be truly meaningful means that they make sense to the whole person, not just the rational part. For change work, having a holistic view of how humans operate is critical.

SUMMARY

1. Visual consulting draws from the fields of **visualization, dialogic practice,** and **change.**

2. The expression of these competencies happens across four levels, called the **Four Flows of Process—attention, energy, information and operations.** These basic levels also relate to our spiritual, emotional, thoughtful, and physical selves.

3. **Capabilities always express themselves through YOU.** Helping you learn to become aware of and use yourself as an active ingredient in consulting is one of the goals of this book.

4. **There are special practices that form the fields** of visualization, dialogue, and change that all consultants would benefit from developing. These are summarized in the following pages, ordered roughly from attentional practices, to energetic practices, to informational practices through to operational practices. (See SideStories 3.4, 3.5, 3.6, and 3.7)

Dialogic Practices

Dialogue is a practice that focuses on the power of a group to receptively listen to diverse perspectives, suspend judgment, and explore assumptions. It can hopefully transform either/or thinking into insights and even wisdom by appreciating complexity and allowing the creative tensions of paradox to be present. The emphasis is on hearing all voices to create shared meaning. Visual facilitation can aid in many aspects of dialogue.

- ☐ **Working with intention:** Understand how the intention, yours and the group's, shapes what is seen and attended to and what not. Work to set clear intentions and visualize them.
- ☐ **Supporting readiness to share and explore:** Appreciate that sharing openly can feel risky. Understand the signs of reluctance and note when you have a "green light" to proceed. Practices range from conducting pre-interviews to suspending power difference.
- ☐ **Creating safety and nonjudgment:** Understand that feeling "triggered" happens more rapidly than responding from our executive functions. Choose environments that optimize feeling relaxed and open mindedness.
- ☐ **Making group agreements:** Create explicit "social" contracts between you and the group and between group members about optimal and disruptive behavior. Have agreements visible.
- ☐ **Listening deeply:** Other people can tell when a person is sincerely curious, receptive, and nonjudgmental. Be inquiring and ask open ended questions. Listen to your own listening.
- ☐ **Asking generative questions:** The power of dialogue is in the initiating questions and new ones that surface. Notice what kinds of questions tend to expand and deepen the inquiry.
- ☐ **Normalizing ambiguity:** Learn how to make it not only acceptable but desirable to feel uncertain and ambiguous. Feeling this is a normal response in emergent processes. Normalizing reduces anxiety.
- ☐ **Facilitating pivotal conversations and real exchange:** Not only invite different points of views but also interaction styles. Do not force resolution, invite going deeper into the exploration and hold a steady container as the heat of generative tensions rises.
- ☐ **Holding the process open for emergence:** It takes time for new ideas and insights to "emerge." Hold the process long enough or return to the dialogue at a later point. The insight might come during alone time. Support asking for reflections on ideas and insights to explore resonance.
- ☐ **Avoiding premature closure:** Resist results and problem-solving orientation long enough so that shared understanding can lead to those moments when closure becomes possible.
- ☐ **Shifting from divergent to convergent exchange:** Help the group to understand the choices they have when shifting from the divergent nature of dialogue to the convergent process of decision making.
- ☐ **Tracking collective insights verbally**: Sense when and how to verbally highlight or capture sentiments by describing the key patterns and insights the group is identifying. Our narrative and spoken-word-oriented selves need full attention in dialogic practice.

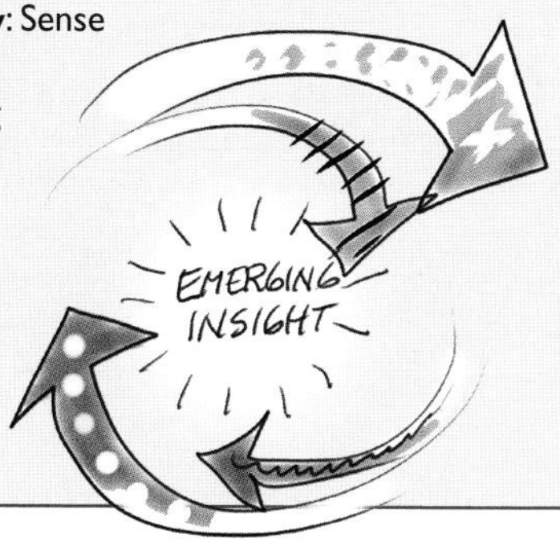

Visual Facilitation Practices

Some capabilities from visual facilitation apply to consulting, whether or not you are the person doing graphic recording in a session. A consultant who does not do a lot of active charting can work with a visual practitioner, but needs to understand the process in order to team effectively. Here are some of the practices we will explore in more depth as we go.

☐ **Framing:** Develop little stories and metaphors that set up an activity or process, and guide everyone's attention in relevant ways.

☐ **Capturing words and content:** Understand how to cluster and illustrate the flow of thinking as expressed in words. Reflecting the words people say is more important than interpreting images.

☐ **Knowing basic visual facilitation display formats:** Understand the powers and limitations of posters, lists, clusters, grids, diagrams, drawings, and mandalas. Be able to coach a recorder.

☐ **Graphic recording:** Learn how to listen visually, recording inputs on flip charts or large sheets of paper in real time (or know how to work with a recorder).

☐ **Graphic process design:** Practice using time lines and sticky notes to plan processes collaboratively with your client, translating these into agendas and roadmaps for ongoing reference during change.

☐ **Design thinking:** Appreciate how to lead a group in exploring options and scenarios, making and testing prototypes, and implementing in iterative ways.

☐ **Identifying generative insights and images:** Listen for the images and metaphors that have real energy in the group, the patterns of thinking that connect ideas, and how to capture and reinforce these as visual and verbal metaphors as you move forward.

☐ **Conceptual modeling:** Being able to show and explain change models for processes, systems perspectives, roles and other critical areas.

☐ **Graphic template design:** Understand repeating visual formats and how to design and use large, graphic wall frameworks and process maps.

☐ **Improvising:** Know how to make things up on the spot in response to surprising things emerging in a group process.

☐ **Sketch talking:** Being able to use a journal or flip chart to quickly sketch out your models and suggested activities

☐ **Using slides and video:** Understand how imagery and words work together, the impact of well-designed media, and how to use the inspirational power of rich images and video.

☐ **Versioning:** Know how to present and modify draft material in successive iterations to support alignment on current state, future state, and action options.

☐ **Staging decision rooms:** Know how to stage an information environment that optimizes a group seeing choices and patterns in their options, and how to facilitate convergence toward agreement.

☐ **Digital documentation:** Know how to take or supervise digital photography, processing, and sharing visual reports by email and the web.

Change Practices

Designing and leading change involves partnering with your client to focus on longer processes that involve many elements. It focuses on helping everyone understand changing conditions, aspirations, and development cycles through iterative consideration of visions, values, action plans, new behavioral norms, processes, and organizational forms.

- ☐ **Working with stakeholders:** Practice identifying stakeholders and their interests, and working with a diversity of people.
- ☐ **Finding sponsors:** Learn to help identify trustworthy leaders and sponsoring agencies and organizations that can champion organizational and community change.
- ☐ **Understanding levels of intervention:** Appreciate the differences between high-level paradigmatic change efforts, policy change, and action implementation to name a few different choices.
- ☐ **Organizing change teams:** Change needs a core group of process co-designers from the client or stakeholder system who can enroll others, solve problems, and be the "beating heart" of change.
- ☐ **Creating collaboration backbones:** Know how to combine communications technology, logistics staff, and reliable infrastructure to create stability in the midst of flux and change.
- ☐ **Sharing assumptions and theories of change:** A theory of change is a description of how a set of activities might lead to a specific outcome. Behind these are assumptions about how change works. Know your own assumptions and how to draw out those of your clients.
- ☐ **Setting a rhythm and pace:** Support clients and yourself setting a reliable pattern and pace for the process.
- ☐ **Working with resistance to change:** Learn the different ways people resist change, and that open resistance is usually a sign that people are beginning to engage the change. Help change leaders to respond supportively.
- ☐ **Using process archetypes and templates:** Understand models like the *Liminal Pathways framework* that describe the basic patterns of change, and have examples of tried and true frameworks for looking at the system as a whole.
- ☐ **Designing process roadmaps:** Visually lead process design teams in creating process roadmaps, and how to use generic models as springboards for customized process designs that show the specific pattern of activities, projects, and outputs over time.
- ☐ **Managing iterative processes:** Support clients using quick briefings, iterative roadmap redesign, and creative ideation to respond to changing conditions and new participants.
- ☐ **Amplifying success:** Identify and support what is working and remove blocks. Implementation needs early success models.
- ☐ **Developing leaders of change:** Partner with your client to develop change fluency and change fluidity so they can support change and change implementation in an ongoing way.

Practices for Use of Self

These are capabilities that have to do with knowing yourself and how your interact with others. It is important to understand your personal gifts and style, and to increase your interaction repertoire.

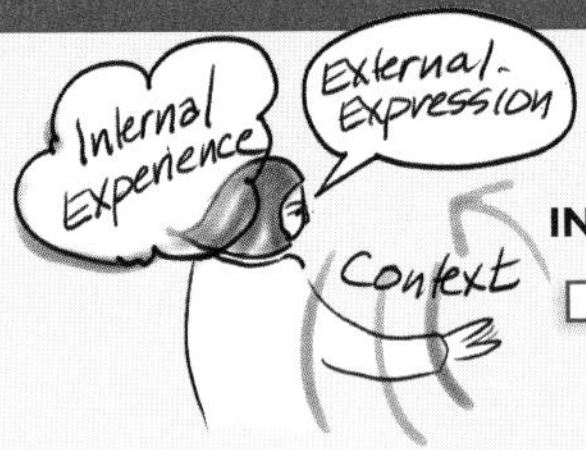

INTRAPERSONAL PRACTICES (within yourself)

- ☐ **Knowing your own beliefs about change:** Consciously identify what your assumptions are about change. Know how your beliefs and values shape your behavior.
- ☐ **Working with hunches:** Appreciate that hunches can be helpful. Practice checking them out.
- ☐ **Being Aware of attachments:** Tune into times when you are identified with a given process or solution and are having trouble listening to different perspectives and proposals.
- ☐ **Tracking your own attention:** Learn to be aware of and track what you are paying attention to at any given point at different levels.
- ☐ **Knowing personal triggers:** We can be emotionally highjacked when something triggers memories of past challenging experiences. Be aware of yours. Explore these in safe, therapeutic settings.
- ☐ **Balancing & grounding in times of tension:** Learn to center and ground yourself when you are shaken or wobbly. Practice mindfulness to find your center.
- ☐ **Knowing your learning edges & style:** Stay in touch with your own process, noticing indications you are ready to grow and learn.
- ☐ **Being aware of yourself in context:** Learn to read the energy of the group and sense how things are evolving. Imagine what is going on in peoples' interiors and the larger system.

INTERPERSONAL PRACTICES (with others)

- ☐ **Staying authentic & congruent:** Align your inner experience and outer communications to be in tune with the context you are in. Have the courage to say "it's not going well, let's talk."
- ☐ **Practicing basic interpersonal skills:** Listen, ask questions, respond, stay grounded, make process suggestions. Reach out and connect personally and at the same time maintain a separate, professional stance.
- ☐ **Imagining potential & inspiring hope:** Practice seeing and sharing your sense of the opportunities in challenges. Ask people to trust the process. Call for involvement and persistence. See and acknowledge people's gifts and contributions.
- ☐ **Distinguishing your own & client's process:** Avoid unconsciously projecting your inner process onto your clients. Know what your issues are vis-å-vis the client's.
- ☐ **Being a mirror not a magnet:** Use your physical movement and responses to reflect and shift group energy. Listen with your back if you are recording. Stimulate interaction but keep group attention on each other.
- ☐ **Holding ambiguity & complexity:** Help clients stay with ambiguity and complexity long enough to have insight emerge. Co-create crucibles, safe zones and nests where confusion and chaos can transform.
- ☐ **Understanding impacts vs. intentions:** Understand that the impact you have on others is not the same as what you might have intended. Invite feedback on your impact for your learning and encourage others to as well.
- ☐ **Making clear social contracts:** Be clear about roles, and agreements with your clients. Re-contract when your role shifts.

Part II.

Visualizing Change

Helping Clients Look Ahead

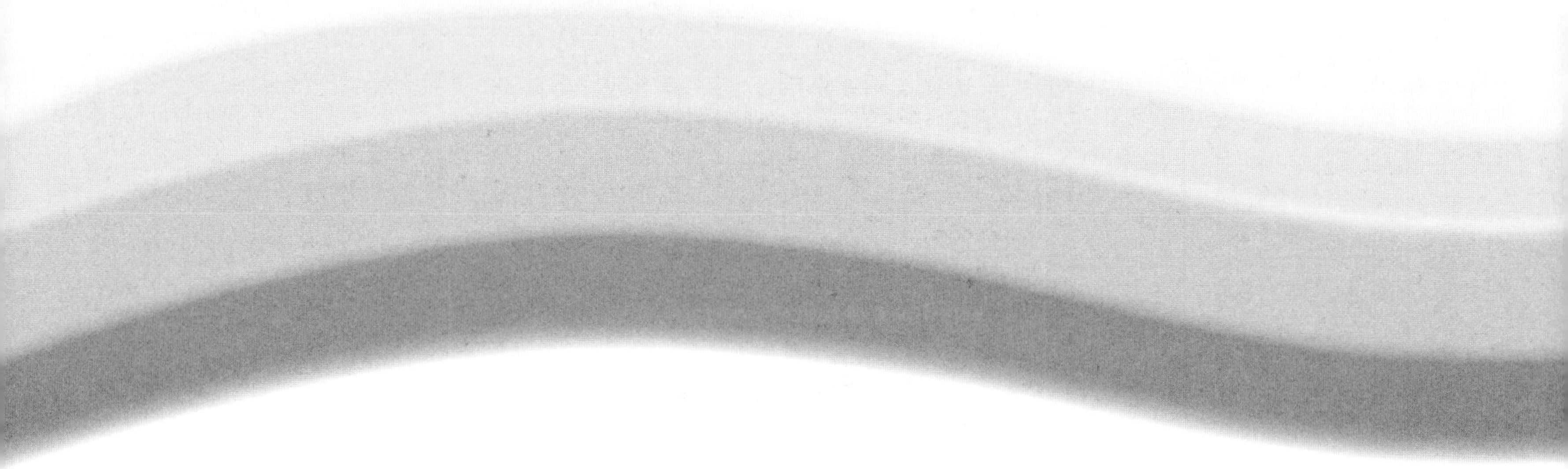

4. Finding & Contracting Clients

Succeeding at Initial Meetings

At this point in our book we are turning toward the specific kinds of practices you would use to find and begin visual consulting engagements. We'll begin with a story of how we initially engaged a client that took us through most of the challenges of change, and pull out the practices you can use. We will then explore how to find clients, set up your relationships and understand the consulting request in initial meetings, and move into contracting for a real project.

Figure 4.1

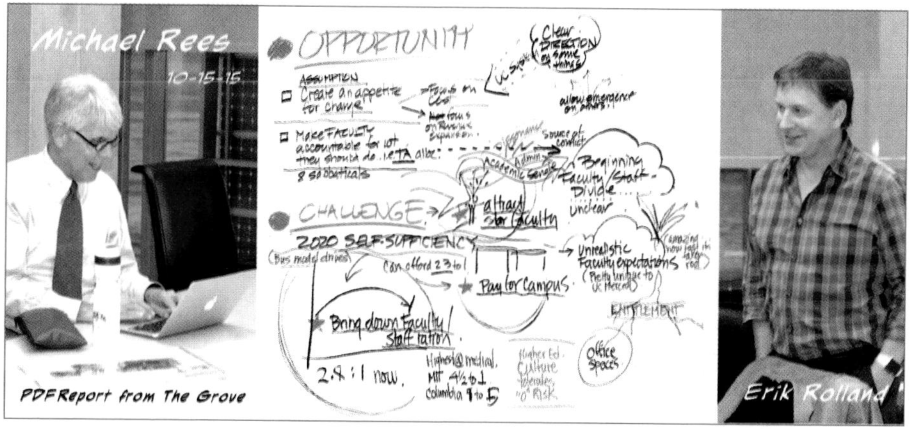

Change at University of California at Merced

In Chapter 2 we told about working with the interim dean of the University of California Merced School of Engineering, Erik Rolland, on a project aimed at both creating a new strategic vision for the department and dealing with an internal personnel crisis. The process was successful. Erik thought he should introduce us to the vice chancellor for business and administration, Michael Reese, who faced a bigger challenge (Figure 4.1).

Chancellor Dorothy Leland had just publicly committed to a 2020 vision of doubling the size of the campus in order to achieve financial viability and meet the demands for the growing student population of California. It was late fall in 2015. This meant they had four years! No less than 72 change projects sat on his desk vying for attention. Erik, from his experience at the School of Engineering, thought that our visual consulting approach might help. In this case visualization, dialogue, and action planning weren't sufficient. Michael needed a real change strategy as well. Projects of this scale have many variables and take place over many meetings and projects.

Meeting the Vice Chancellor

Erik Rolland, former interim dean of UC Merced's School of Engineering, introduced Gisela and David to Michael Reese, vice chancellor for business and administration. The change challenges were on his desk and he needed help. This is the first page of our client PDF report from that initial meeting, showing our capture of the opportunities and challenges.

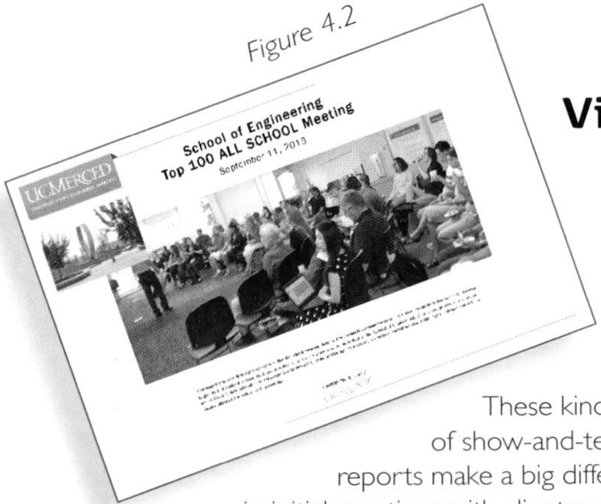

Figure 4.2

Visual Reports

These kinds of show-and-tell reports make a big difference in initial meetings with clients who are deciding if they want to work with a visual consultant (Figure 4.2). The pages below (Figure 4.3) were from the School of Engineering work with Erick.

Practices for Initial Meetings

There were five things we did in this initial meeting that are fundamental practices in visual consulting.

- ❑ **Physical introduction from a trusted associate:** Erik's physical presence in this first meeting was critical. It provided the bridge of credibility that allowed Michael, who is extremely busy, to take time to assess if we could help him.
- ❑ **Visual report**: We shared an 11"x34"visual report (Figure 4.3) from our prior work at the School of

Figure 4.3

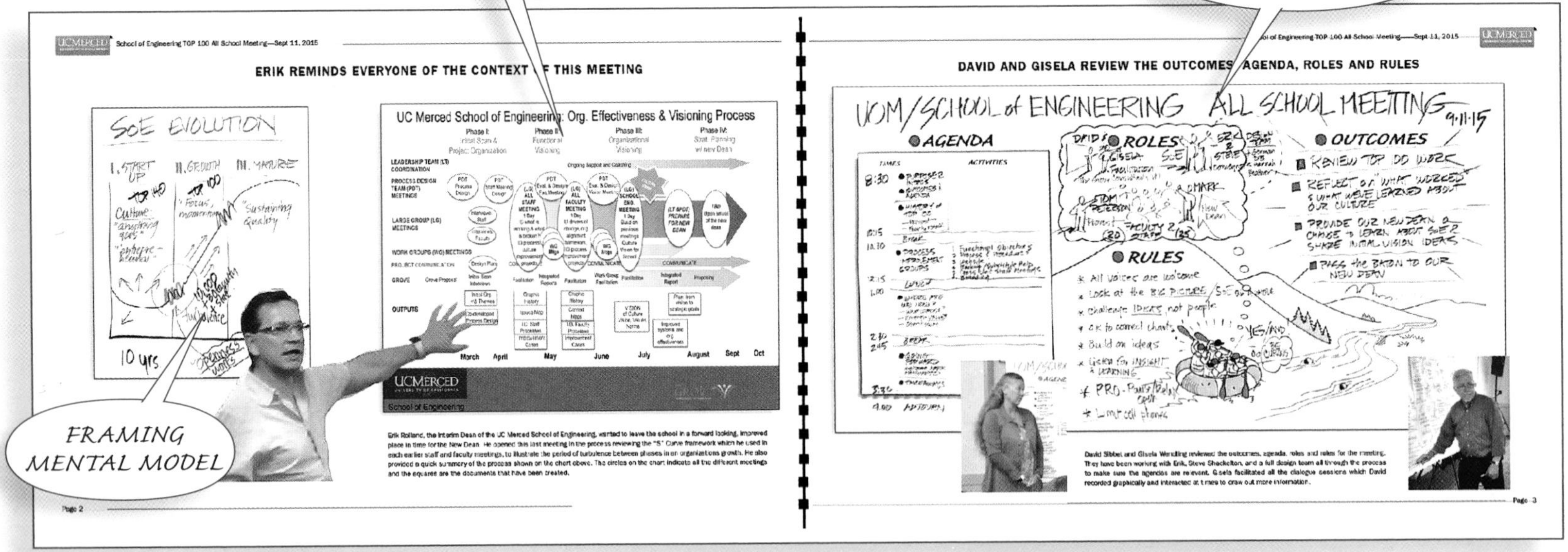

Figure 4.4

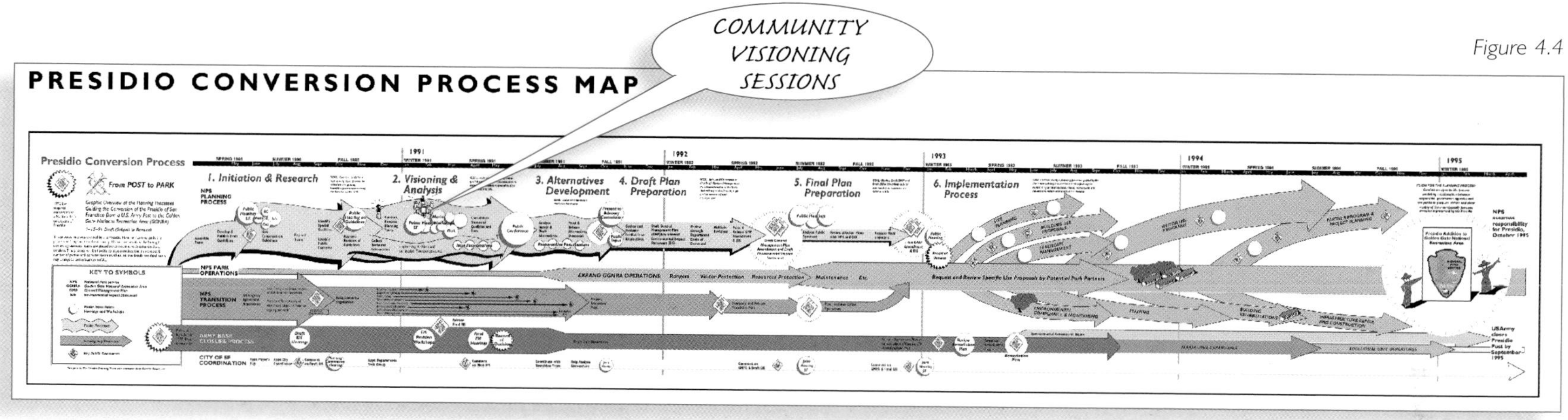

Engineering, showing tools like our framing metaphor, the process roadmap, and our graphic agenda for the meeting. (We will explain each of these as we go along).

- ❑ **Visual facilitation experience:** We provided Michael an experience of being listened to visually. He experienced the power of working this way right away as David went mapped out the big projects Michael needed to manage. (See Figure 4.5.)
- ❑ **Rapport**: We focused on the quality of the conversation and our listening, with Gisela sitting by Michael's side and staying tuned in to how he was responding—making sure the pacing of our conservation allowed plenty of space for thinking. It was clear Michael was a thinker who preferred time to respond.
- ❑ **Graphic storymap of a Change Process:** In talking about past experience, which is very important, we shared a graphic of the transition process at the Presidio of San Francisco when it changed from an army base to a national park. David had been deeply involved, and the graphic shows the entire conversion process (Figure 4.4).

"We need a big-picture strategy like that," Michael said as we briefly explained it. "We don't have a high-level strategy, and visualizing it like this would make a big difference." This conversation opened the door for a two-hour exchange about the challenges and opportunities at the university. It concluded with Michael asking for a proposal for how to initiate a change alignment process. This meeting began a nine-month vision and change alignment process with rich lessons for visual consulting.

Presidio Conversion Process

You don't need to read the detail on this chart to understand its value. There were five parallel planning processes happening around the Presidio conversion, shown as the five bands across the chart. The top was the National Park Service (NPS) planning process, which required a large amount of community-wide stakeholder engagement, illustrated as circles, which stood out in yellow on the full color map. It took less than five minutes for NPS leaders to orient people in the community vision sessions to the larger planning process using this chart, printed out 24 feet long. We as facilitators could then clearly show where the visioning sessions were happening (one-fourth of the way from the left), as well as all the other places the community could have input (the other circles).

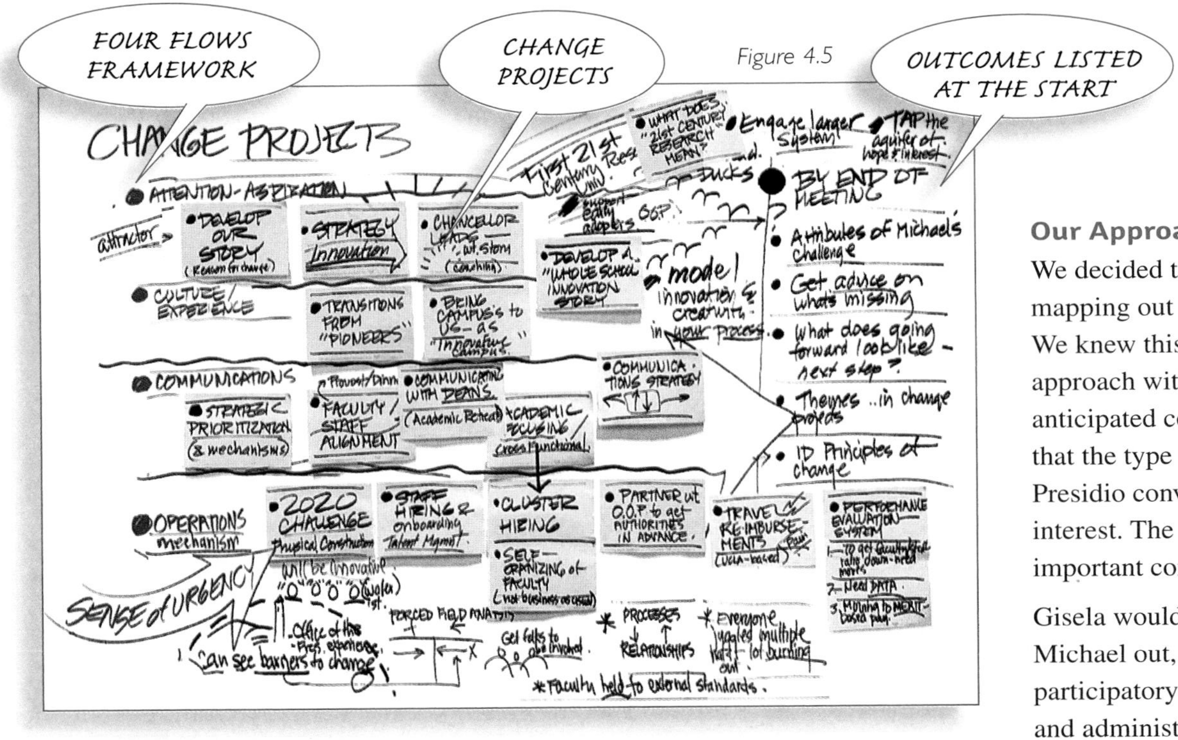

Figure 4.5

Our Approach in This First Meeting

We decided to visually facilitate this first meeting, mapping out Michael's concerns and interests. We knew this would model a process consulting approach with capability in visual listening. We anticipated correctly, from talking with Erik, that the type of storymapping represented by the Presidio conversion process map would be an interest. The Grove's expertise in this would be an important confidence builder.

Gisela would focus on facilitation and drawing Michael out, using her expertise in large-scale participatory change processes, university culture and administration, and dialogue to asking well-phrased and open-ended questions. She would model the style of collaboration and mutual respect we use in our consulting by modeling rapport, and active listening.

In addition, we were also interested in this first meeting to see if Michael had need for "pair-of-hands" help. We could create the reports from meetings but wanted to contract with them how we would handle circulating the reports, scheduling meetings, and managing other logistics. We know that if a client is understaffed it is helpful to have a conversation about their real capacity.

Mapping the Challenge

As Michael began reviewing some of the bigger projects that needed alignment, David suggested mapping them into a simple Four Flows framework labeled ATTENTION/ ASPIRATIONS, CULTURE/EXPERIENCE, COMMUNICATIONS, and OPERATIONS (for Attention, Energy, Information, and Operations). Adapting labels on frameworks to language that is clear to your client is one of the real contributions a visual consultant can make.

Moving to Preliminary Proposals

It's not necessary for you the reader to understand the substance of Michael's project overview. What is important is understanding what we did next to turn this into an actual

Figure 4.6

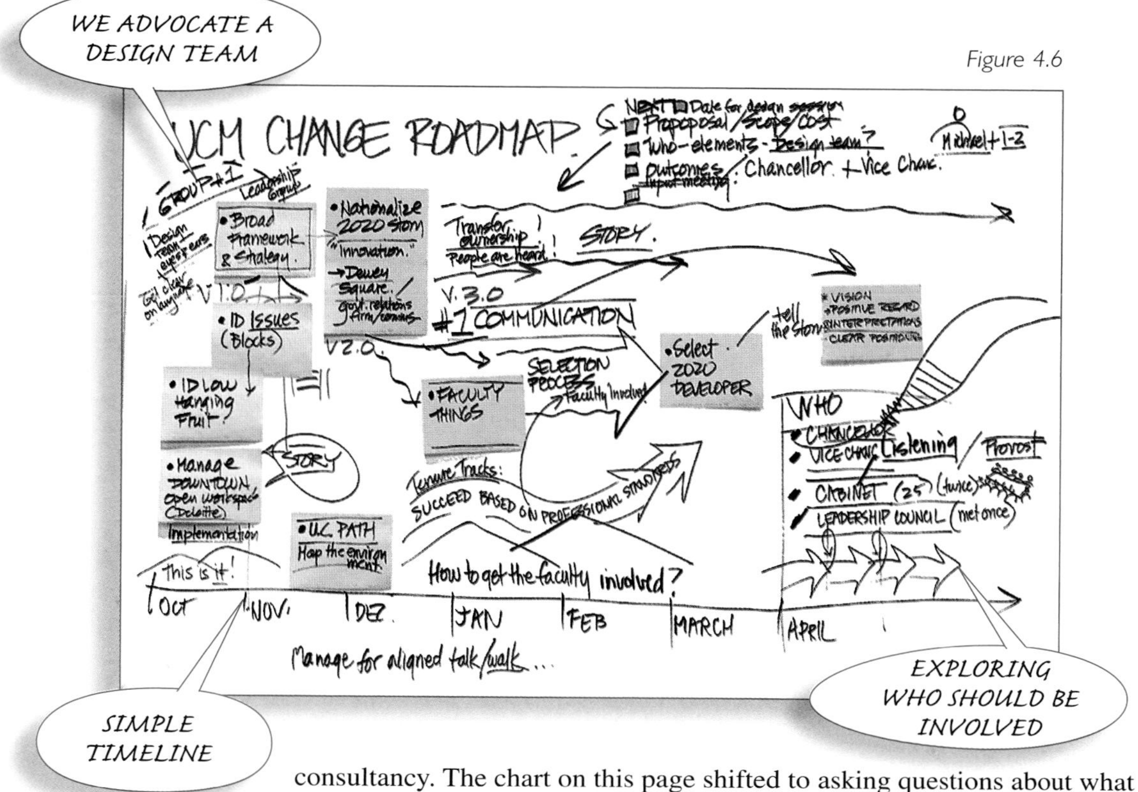

consultancy. The chart on this page shifted to asking questions about what might happen going forward. A simple time line allowed us to draft a first version of a roadmap, with sticky notes for potential steps (Figure 4.6). In a clearly consultative move, using our process design expertise, we strongly recommended selecting a design team of project leaders who would help create the project alignment map and thereby own it.

We also argued for commitments to versions of this map right from the start, because it would need to evolve, and we know that conversations about the different versions is a key to getting alignment. We explained we would convert this sketch into a proposed roadmap that would then be redesigned by the design team. When calendars came out we knew we were moving forward into the proposal stage (SideStory 4.1).

SideStory 4.1

Value of Simple Charting

The charts shown in Figures 4.5-4.6 were drawn on 4' wide plotter paper taped to a basic white board in a small conference room. We started by overlaying three sheets, like a large flip chart, and moved them to the left when they were completed. Overdoing the graphics at this point would have been distracting. Michael was focused on the content, and the most important thing was getting it clear, accurate, and organized simply enough so he could look up and see his thinking reflected in the process. The charts were colorful with yellow sticky notes and red bullets to guide the eye, but that was it.

Gisela sat next to Michael and was able to ask questions in a sensitive way that sometimes probed for deeper insight into dynamics we might eventually find challenging. Here we are checking calendars. It turned out time was of the essence.

SideStory 4.2

Create a Customer-Centric Value Proposition

Rob Eskridge of Growth Management Center is a management and strategy consultant who began to work visually in the 1980s after attending some Group Graphics workshops. He doesn't do the visual recording himself, but has mastered doing quick diagrams in his journal and on flip charts that communicate the value he can bring to clients. His long experience in marketing has taught him that communicating your value from a customer perspective is the key. In a recent Global Learning & Exchange Network Exchange on the topic, he shared four criteria for a customer-centric value proposition.

1. Clear description of your target audience in terms they understand.
2. Clear value promise. "We will help you do..."
3. Show how you will deliver this value.
4. Describe your uniqueness.

Finding Clients

How Do You Find Clients for Visual Consulting?

The story we just related about the UC Merced Vision & Change Alignment Project is a very familiar pattern of how we at The Grove find out about and start client projects. Drawing from decades of experience there are some pretty standards pathways to real work (See also SideStory 4.2).

- ❑ **Referrals**: Far and away, the most projects come from people who have seen us work and refer someone. If they are former successful clients like Erik, all the better of course. If you are beginning, you need to spend time cultivating people who know managers and others looking for help with a change project. Having these people supplied with reports like the one shown about UC Merced, if you have permission to share, or other samples of your work makes a big difference.
- ❑ **Partner with more experienced consultants**: If you are a consultant who wants to add more visual skills, partner with another consultant so you can focus on that element. If you are a visual practitioner going into more consulting, partner with an experienced consultant. In this second approach, consultants with big projects that want to add the visual component might be a primary client for you when getting started.
- ❑ **Volunteer for meaningful projects:** In order to get started and generate examples of your work and approach, take on some projects at no fee and really focus on what you care about. If this involves partnering with more experienced consultants, even better. You can learn fast by actually having to design and lead a change process.
- ❑ **Workshop follow-up**: Offering workshops at conferences or offering public workshops through an organization with a good reputation is another way to demonstrate your abilities. Again, having visual samples of roadmaps, visions, and other outputs from processes helps people remember to give you a call. Your following up will make a difference.

HELLO, THIS IS GLORIA'S ASSISTANT. WE ARE LOOKING FOR A VISUAL FACILITATOR FOR OUR BOARD MEETING

- ❑ **Expand on meeting facilitation requests**: Many change consulting projects start with a request for meeting facilitation, a perfect doorway for a process consulting relationship. The popularity of visual meetings with good conversation and dialogue is steadily increasing, responding to the higher participation rates, high touch feel, interactivity, and creativity of this way of working. When organizations or communities are facing problems or sensing the need to change, often the first step is to have a meeting to see what to do. Get in the habit of asking ***"How important is follow-through?"*** If it is, suggest getting some key players into some process design sessions before the meeting, and perhaps a debrief. Already you have a process and not a single meeting. You might also ask ***"Would it help to share the output of this meeting with other stakeholders to increase buy-in?"*** If yes, then you again have a reason to propose a longer process.
- ❑ **Expand on expertise requests**: It might be that you are a visual practitioner and are being approached to create a graphic map or other mural as an expert at the drawing part. You can begin to ask about who is important to involve so they will support implementation. Suggest some collaborative meetings to generate the data and check your work. Explain that meaningful visualization has imagery and metaphor that is deeply resonant with the culture that will be using the maps, and that picking these images will catalyze important conversation. Perhaps suggest interviews than can help get people thinking about the ideas. In other words, focus the attention of your client on the value of a good process instead of just focusing on a visual artifact.
- ❑ **Respond to RFPs**: Requests for Proposals are the norm with government agencies and many not-for-profit clients. The goal is to get invited to an initial interview so you can then see if there is a possibility for establishing a good relationship. Getting to that step is often a matter of price, experience, and the power of your references. Having a clear, visual, and accessible application certainly helps. Change work is very customized and relationship-based. RFPs are very time intensive and have low percentage of success in our experience, so pick wisely.

Requests for help can come in different sizes and shapes. The art of getting visual consulting work is to get your potential clients to see the opportunity in a more extended process as a key to having more impact.

I HEARD THAT YOU COULD HELP US MANAGE SOME REAL CONVERSATIONS WHILE WE ARE PLANNING

SideStory 4.3

Build Credibility on Web and Tablet

Visual consultants have the advantage of showing what they do in meaningful ways. If you are an external consultant, or an internal group needing to sell your services, creating a website that shows off the kind of work and value you will bring is very helpful. It can communicate your interests, values, and capabilities—all elements in establishing credibility. Potential clients can use your website to talk to their colleagues and validate why you should be retained.

Modeling tablet recording is a good way to demonstrate both visual listening capability and virtual facilitation.

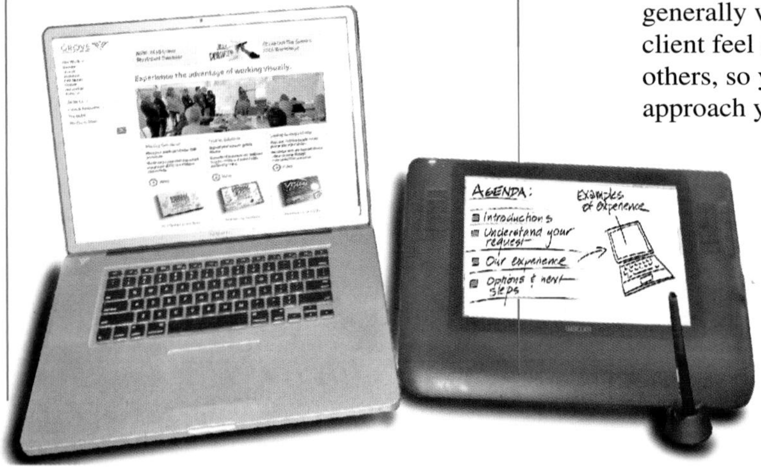

- ❏ **Say NO if there is no interest in change:** Since much of your work will come from referrals, don't take jobs that position you for future work you don't want. If you want to become a good, visually oriented, process consultant then make sure the clients you say yes to appreciate the value of involving people and getting involved themselves. Change work involves having a learning relationship with your clients so that you can respond to real, evolving conditions in a collaborative way. If you are being treated like a pizza delivery service, say no.
- ❏ **Carry a portfolio:** Visual consulting engagements generate great visual reports that can be carried on your phone or a pad. Showing people what is possible in social settings, conferences, or meals is a great way to stir up interest.
- ❏ **Create a website that includes cases and examples:** In today's organization work, in business, government, or nonprofit work, much of it is done virtually with distributed teams. While paper documentation is great for face-to-face meetings, having your capabilities evident in an online environment is critical. Your website generally won't get you the work, but it is the credibility factor in having a potential client feel solid about their choice to involve you. They will also need to convince others, so your online presence is your digital portfolio and indication of how you approach your work (SideStory 4.3).
- ❏ **Visually record initial online calls:** If you have developed some basic visual skills, demonstrating them during a video conference call will show right away the power of working this way. You can also take people on tours of your website and show examples through screen sharing, which conferencing apps provide.
- ❏ **Understand that response time is a message:** The pattern of your calls and e-mails in the initial stages is itself a message about interest, professionalism, and respect for a potential client's time. It can be the difference that counts.

The Importance of Client Relationships

Setting Up a Learning Relationship with a Client

Assume that you have made initial contact and now have arranged a first meeting to discuss possibilities. Before jumping into thinking about how to design a process, it is helpful to examine your assumptions about your potential client and how you would like to set up the relationship.

When we talk about the client, we mean the person or the leadership/management team who is actually accountable to the organization or a community for the outcome of a process. It is usually also the person who hires you and with whom you need to make clear agreements about the project.

In your first meeting you will be busy learning about the organization and the challenges and opportunities that it faces. Your client will also be learning about who you are, what you do, and the approaches you use. Unless they have worked with a visual consultant who uses process design and facilitation approaches, and has guided a successful change project before, most likely they will not actually know what you do. And, then, of course, each consultant works differently and has their favorite approaches and ways of describing their work.

In our professional field of organization development one important aspect of the client relationship is coaching the leader of change (SideStory 4.4). A vast majority of strategy and change projects fail because leaders aren't sufficiently involved and don't realize they will have to personally make changes to have things work. Having a mutual, respectful learning relationship is thus critical if you expect to support their personal challenges. If you want to include coaching the "leader of change" downstream, begin building a learning relationship as soon in the engagement as possible. Establishing a trusting relationships that allows for mutual feedback and transparency is key.

SideStory 4.4

Coaching Leaders of Change

When working on change projects, which usually involves a discovery phase, it won't take long before you have insights and information that goes well beyond what the client is aware of. Leaders can easily get insulated from what is going on at the periphery of their organizations, and change projects often involve balancing this very condition.

At times you will need to prepare leaders and other stakeholders to work with information that is new or even challenging to them. You may need to support them to fully step into their role of change leader. Initially the leaders of change may not know what this role really requires of them.

For example, it is important that a leader provides consistent and clear messaging about the change project to others in the organization, even if she or he feels the same sense of uncertainty everyone else feels. In fact, leaders are often the first ones to go through the change. Being available to coach them through this experience is helpful and is best cultivated from the beginning.

SideStory 4.5

Prepare to Make Some Early Requests

In initial meetings it is helpful to be prepared to ask for the following, especially if you are a process consultant:

- ☐ A **chance to explain your process** design approaches
- ☐ An **agreement to provide feedback** and perspectives that may be challenging
- ☐ **Permission to ask questions** to surface unexamined assumptions and beliefs
- ☐ A chance for the **client to make requests** of you in return
- ☐ **Help with organizational jargon and norms** so the language you use is familiar to them

A Collaborative Approach to Sharing Responsibility

We advocate developing a collaborative partnership with your clients. The leader will most likely not have your expertise in process design and facilitation and will be dependent on and trusting you.

This is why we began this book sharing the *Consulting Framework for Respectful Engagement* (Figure 2.5). Collaboration is based on mutual respect, empowerment, reciprocity, a sense of shared responsibility, and especially role clarity. While the client maintains "ownership" of the project because the client is accountable for achieving the organizational goals, the visual process consultant uses her or his expertise to help co-create and to facilitate an approach that supports the client organization to achieve the goals of the initiative. Tools like a visual change process roadmap can be invaluable in developing clarity. Clear agreements on mutual expectations around behavior is also key (SideStory 4.5). Clarity and trust are fundamental as you get to know the client, their change challenges, and their formal and social contracting processes.

Downstream if you as the process consultant become the driver of the project and the client begins to back off and steps back from responsibility, the collaborative approach gets out of balance. This is also true if the client begins to take over your responsibilities as the consultant and you are no longer partnering on decisions about design and approach. In both cases it will be time to revisit the agreements you have made around your roles and responsibilities. Contracting and re-contracting is part and parcel of a collaborative project, especially when they are complex and evolving, and needs to be role modeled from the initial meeting. It is helpful to advocate for regularly checking in with your clients about how it is going and giving them plenty of opportunities to bring up issues. When clients are not used to using such check-in processes this may be a big ask, but essential.

Succeeding at Initial Client Meetings

Your consulting process will have begun even before you have your first meeting. In many cases the initial request for help is communicated by an assistant or someone who knows someone. As a result, when you finally do have a meeting, there are two outcomes that are most important above all others.

1. **Developing shared understanding** of the initiating request for help and the need to be open to finding underlying issues and challenges.
2. **Establishing a reciprocal relationship** with your potential client, preferably one that is based on co-learning.

Some of the other goals for your initial meeting are shown in SideStory 4.6.

Should You Be Formal or More Informal?

Process consulting is all about engaging people, and your relationship with the lead sponsor is one of the most critical elements in success. It is also helpful to know something about the general culture of the organization and have studied up on the industry it is in, but the relationship is paramount in the initial meeting. Without falling into the trap of thinking there is only one way to conduct your first meeting, let's look at what you might attend to using the Four Flows framework we described earlier.

1. **Attention and priority interests**: It helps to be carefully tuned in to what your potential client is actually paying attention to. Is this meeting and change challenge important to them? Are they just the agent for someone else and doing their duty? Are they distracted by some other immediate challenge? Are they paying attention to the bigger picture? You won't know until you have given yourself some room for inquiry.
2. **Energy and rapport:** Rapport is largely about matching the intensity and pacing of the person you are talking to. Slow down or speed up to match their pace. Then

SideStory 4.6

What to Cover in Initial Meetings

- ☐ **Potential meeting outcomes**, starting with the client's
- ☐ **Understanding of the initiating request** (see text)
- ☐ **Simple agenda**, to get agreement on scope and time to be spent in the meeting
- ☐ **Introductions** to get to know your potential client and exhibit your capability relevant to the request
- ☐ **Client's picture of the challenge** they face and interests they have
- ☐ **Overview of the context** and issues surrounding the initiating request
- ☐ **Options** for potential beginning activities
- ☐ **Constraints**—staffing, budgets, timing, sensitivities
- ☐ **Next steps, or draft roadmap,** if the client is already engaged and confident of your services
- ☐ **Agreements** and/or takeaways

SideStory 4.7

Communicate the Value of Visualization

Dan Roam, author of bestselling *Back of the Napkin: Solving Problems & Selling Ideas with Pictures, says* "The person who creates the visual that explains complexity is the person who will win." Shortly after he had published this book, Obama was elected and tackled health care reform. Dan got upset. He knew people weren't clear on the new Health Care Act and were attacking aspects that weren't even true. "I thought I had some grasp having worked in health systems. So I convened a small, knowledgeable group and in three days we diagrammed the act with simple stick figures and other icons."

He put 46 little drawings on SlideShare and it went viral. Fox news called and asked him to present it—twice! The White House even called and had him present to the new media group. Dan believes any group can be taken to any level of complexity if you build a visual story step by step.

"Visual communications help executives make better decisions and tell better stories," he says. "Drawing the pictures isn't artistic, it's a thinking endeavor."

IN THE INTERESTS OF TIME COULD WE SUGGEST AN AGENDA?

Relationship-Building Questions to Ask

Learn to ask open-ended, invitational questions like those shown in the talk balloons on these pages.

check out if the client already has figured out how to handle the meeting, or if you can take a lead in creating a shared agenda. Imagine what they are feeling. Stay tuned to your own feelings. Risk being your authentic self. Share some appropriate personal things.

WE WANT TO MAKE SURE WE UNDERSTAND YOUR NEEDS. WOULD IT BE OKAY TO RECORD VISUALLY?

3. **Information and understanding**: A large part of your first meeting will be to learn about the client's needs and initial requests as they understand it at the current moment. Asking if they would be open to visual facilitation is a good way to support developing an initial shared understanding. The client will see visibly whether you are getting what they are saying (SideStory 4.7). The UC Merced charts are good examples of the level of interaction that tends to happen in initial meetings. If the client is forthcoming with information, that tells you one thing. If they are guarded and cautious, it will signal another. This signal might trigger you to ask a question like *"This sounds like you have some reservations talking about some of your concerns. Is there anything that I could do to make this more comfortable? Or is there something that is not working for you?"* Pay attention to how they are communicating, not just the content. People are different in how they process information. Some are highly visual and will love the charts. Others are more oriented to what you say audibly. Others might be text oriented and want to read handouts.

4. **Operations and constraints**: There are bottom-line aspects to an initial engagement with a potential client. You need to find out about givens and constraints, budget limitations, timing constraints, levels of involvement, stakeholders who need to be involved, and more.

IT SEEMS LIKE THERE IS A LOT GOING ON HERE. WOULD IT BE HELPFUL TO UNDERSTAND SOME OF THE CONTEXT?

Keeping It Light at First

CAN I SPEAK FREELY ABOUT SOME CONCERNS WE HAVE?

Figure 4.7

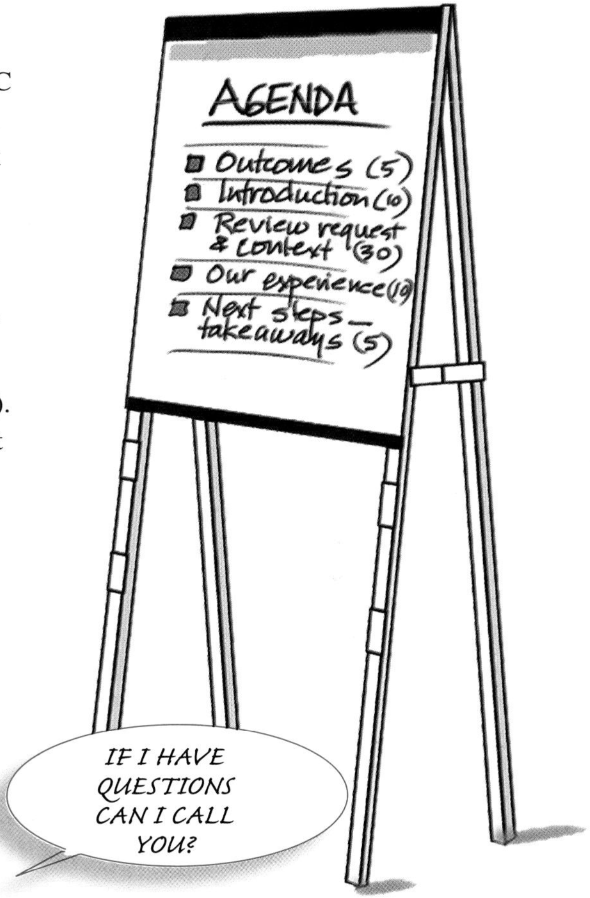

There is a lot to pay attention to. Yet it is important to learn how to keep your process focused, relevant, and relationship oriented, and not overloaded with presentation. In the UC Merced case, we started with only a list of outcomes on a blank piece of paper and handled the other items around orientation to the meeting verbally. We wanted to hear the client talk first, and most, and feel listened to.

There does come a time to respond so the client understands how you think you can help and what capabilities you bring. But much of your confidence and capability will be demonstrated by the quality of questions you ask. The questions in the talk balloons are the kind we find clients really appreciate, asked in a way that is confident, yet open.

An agenda for initial meetings can be very simple, like the one on the flip chart (Figure 4.7). As the conversation unfolds this can, of course, be elaborated on and flow to what the client seems interested in sharing. If possible, ask for the first meeting to be long enough to go a bit deeper. More information will help you create a relevant proposal.

Getting Down to Business

There comes a point at which you need to show that you understand how to design and manage a change process and have it go somewhere. If you get too caught up in trying to understand everything or over explaining your capabilities you can lose traction. Most clients will appreciate your wanting to deal with the nitty gritty aspects. This also models working across all of the four flows of process. A bridge question is to ask what kind of constraints there are. You can also ask about what parts of the process are urgent and need immediate attention. If your potential client responds it is a good sign that they are liking the relationship. End with a clear next steps process, and perhaps ask to share takeaways, if the rapport seems good.

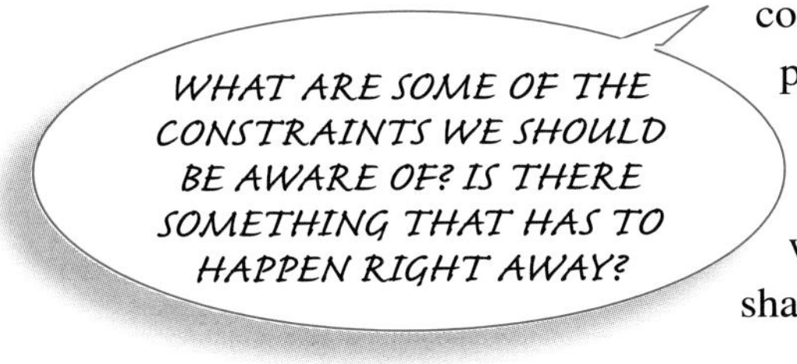
WHAT ARE SOME OF THE CONSTRAINTS WE SHOULD BE AWARE OF? IS THERE SOMETHING THAT HAS TO HAPPEN RIGHT AWAY?

Legal & Social Contracts

It is helpful to understand the meaning of contracting, both social contracts and legal contracts. Here is the important distinction.

- ❏ **Legal Contracts**: These are written, signed agreements covering financial arrangements, intellectual property, formal working agreements, deliverables, and such. Every organization has different formats for these. They are sometimes called "Scope of Work" forms or "Memos of Understanding" or just plain "Contracts." As a consultant it helps to have one that you can suggest if a client doesn't have one.
- ❏ **Social Contracts:** These are the agreements about how people want to work and behave together. Having a solid social contract when supporting and facilitating organizational change processes is important. A social contract helps you initiate, guide, and adjust your relationship with the organizational leaders who are responsible for consulting projects. At bottom it's a practice for making things as explicit as possible all the way along.

Working agreements are sometimes included in memos of understanding along with agreements on the scope of work and fees. In creating these documents check out what would work for the client.

Contracting & Proposals

When you hear the words "Can you get back to us with a proposal?" you have entered the contracting phase of engaging a client relationship. This is such a fundamental part to get right that we are going to go into some detail.

Types of Contracts

The general purpose of contracting is to create explicit agreements between yourself and your client about what you are going to do, why, when, how, with whom, and under what conditions (see SideStory 4.8). These agreements are usually captured in documents such as a memorandum of understanding or proposals that become signed contracts. The agreements usually include the goals, scope, time frame of the change initiative, roles, expectations, and how you and the sponsor will work together.

The other kind of "contract" is the social one you make with a client around how you want to relate to each other. This starts in your initial contacts and meetings, and will continue throughout a consulting process. In the rest of this chapter we want to explore the agreements you need to have at the proposal stage. In Chapter 8 we look at forming a process design team to help with change, and expand on the idea of social contracting.

Formal Consulting Proposals: Consultants and process leaders who do change facilitation generally work with proposals and memorandums or letters of understanding that are more formal, especially in the beginning stages. Proposals are documents that usually outline the desired outcomes, the work to be done, the project phases, the approaches to be used, and a fee estimate (see SideStory 4.9). Proposals can become a contract or an important part of the memorandum of understanding when both sides agree on the contents.

An outline of a typical proposal is described on the next page. In order to answer these questions you will need to do some project scoping.

What Does Scoping Involve?

The scope of a project includes a range of information about what will be included. These are the kinds of questions that you want to be able to answer.

- ❑ What is the **overall purpose of the project** as the client sees it now?
- ❑ What are the **presenting issues and opportunities**?
- ❑ How many **stakeholders** may be involved?
- ❑ Is there **critical staff** that would be good to involve?
- ❑ **How much of the process can be completed** within time constraints you've noted?
- ❑ What **resources might be available**? What are the budget constraints?
- ❑ What **specific deliverables** are expected?
- ❑ **Will re-contracting be possible** in the face of new insights and developments?

Another part of scoping is thinking about how much you will need to understand about the larger organizational context. How long of a discovery process is possible? At this point do you preliminarily understand the organization's strengths, weaknesses, opportunities, and threats (tradition SWOT questions)? Do you understand what upcoming decision points in the life of the organization or community will require alignment on change?

If the client hasn't answered these questions in your initial meeting you may need to ask if some interviews or a second meeting would be helpful. Be sure to build into your proposal a robust discovery process to activate awareness around these questions. If a client is not sure of how to proceed, perhaps you want to break the process into chunks and propose an initial discovery and process design phase and then an intention to re-contract for a longer change process informed by these activities.

Write a Consulting Proposal

Following is an outline for a typical consulting proposal. From whatever scoping you do through initial meetings, interviews, and follow-up meetings, you need to do the following:

- ☐ Describe **SCOPE** and **DESIRED OUTCOMES.**
- ☐ Briefly summarize your understanding of the **CONTEXT.**
- ☐ Describe your **RELEVANT EXPERIENCE.**
- ☐ Describe your **APPROACH** and **METHODS.** As a visual consultant you will need to explain some of the benefits (see suggestions on following pages).
- ☐ Propose a **PROJECT DESIGN** and include a sample graphic roadmap.
- ☐ Illustrate your **TIMETABLE and DELIVERABLES**, plus **COSTS** in a matrix.
- ☐ Outline your **ENGAGEMENT PRINCIPLES**—agreements on confidentiality, Intellectual Property, and how changes can be made in the agreements.

SideStory 4.10

Be Up-Front About Your Wants & Needs

As visual process consultants you too have wants and needs you'll need met to do your best work. In your initial meetings with a client make sure you share these as well. Which ones belong in your proposal depends on how you see your job and the type of relationship you want. You might ask about:

- ☐ What to do when meetings are rescheduled
- ☐ Topics to address in person
- ☐ Not making major process decisions without your input\
- ☐ Access to relevant research and prior work
- ☐ Keeping you updated on developments related to the project
- ☐ Support you need from the organization

It is very helpful to deal with anything you might consider a real challenge during initial meetings, rather than waiting for an incident to require engagement. In regards to support, you might want to explore what is available for meetings. It's possible you might need some help with scheduling from an executive assistant who knows how things work. You will need to figure out operational things like reproduction, access to any shared collaboration platforms, and adequate meeting locations.

Reflect Client Interests in Their Language

Your proposal should reflect what you have learned from your potential client in their language. These are some things you might need to find out either in the initial meeting or subsequent calls and meetings.

- ❑ **What would success look like** to the client? What are their hopes?
- ❑ **What would take things in a wrong direction**? What are their concerns?
- ❑ **Are there particular favorite elements** of your particular approach that are especially important? (In Michael's case it was having a big map of their aligned change strategy.)
- ❑ **How would your client like to be involved** in the process?

Visual Consulting Approaches

We have been addressing generic consulting practices so far in regard to proposal making. As a visual consultant you will benefit from drawing more explicit pictures of what is possible, literally. Here are some of the component capabilities you might think about either providing or partnering to provide in a more complex project, written in the kind of language you would use in a proposal.

1. **Collaborative process design**: We work with a process design team including formal and informal leaders from across functions and levels of the organization, as well as other relevant stakeholders. They collaboratively co-design the change process with the consultant. This educates and involves key leaders, both formal and informal, and works to create ownership for the process across the board.
2. **Visual facilitation/design thinking**: Visualization is a doorway to foster the types of engagement and dialogue that people need to form understanding and respect

Figure 4.8

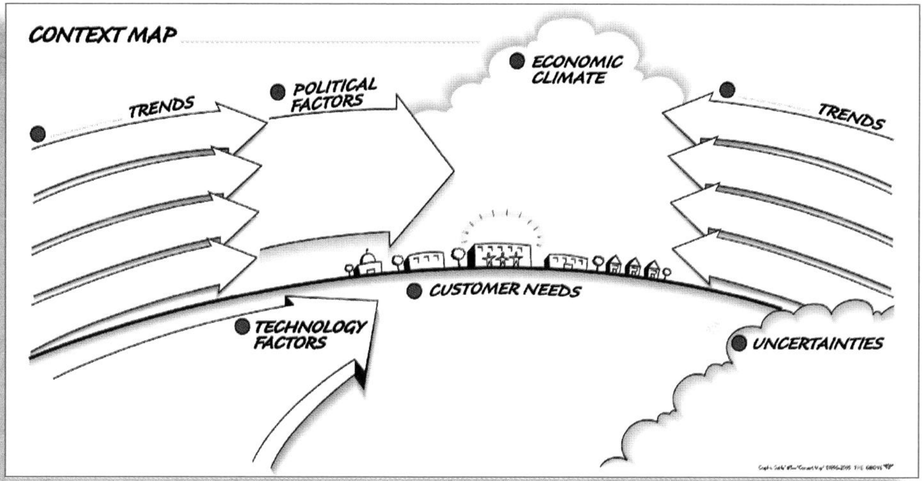

across differences and to do the learning that results in larger cross-organizational and social change. It involves graphically illustrating what people say in key meetings in real time, so that people know they have been heard. Proceedings are captured digitally and fed back in the form of reports that greatly extend the retention period of key agreements. Understanding and insights that have been mapped creatively are sometimes developed further in the iterative conceptualization involved in "design thinking." (See the last page in this chapter for an example.)

3. **Strategic vision maps**: Change work is greatly facilitated by creating large, visual maps of the group's ideas about why it needs to change, what choices it has, and what preferred futures look like. These maps can serve as a roadmap for change, such as the map created for the Presidio transition process. The iterative process of involving stakeholders in initial concepts and versions creates both alignment and buy-in. These images set the high-level direction for change processes. The template in Figure 4.8 can be shared with clients to illustrate what one might look like.

4. **Group dialogue**: Dialogue is about developing shared understanding that leads to coherent thinking and coherent action. Research on change indicates that people engage in innovative thinking and problem solving across previously unresolved differences when (1) They experience real relationships in which they can express their true concerns and cares; (2) Ideas are built on, and everyone's expertise is appreciated and not discounted; and (3) Everyone is supported to listen with an open mind. Dialogue is helpfully supported by visualization, but goes beyond visual facilitation as people experience sharing their personal truths eye-to-eye. Dialogue fosters the kind of reflective awareness and insight that is a key catalyst for both

Structured Graphic Templates

Use structured graphic templates that allow large numbers of stakeholders to collaborate in scoping the environment of strategy and change projects. This Context Map Graphic Guide® from Grove Tools, Inc. is a simple clustering of trends and other factors in a light landscape metaphor. The categories can be adjusted to include aspects relevant to your engagement. The resulting visual dialogue supports clients connecting with the drivers of change, and as a dividend, helps create a collaborative, teaming atmosphere since everyone would have something to add to this kind of chart.

SideStory 4.11

Electronic Brainstorming

Combining interactive electronic brainstorming with large-scale visualization is an interesting combination to suggest to clients. Groups of three work on a tablet or laptop and answer key questions pushed out to the group. Answers stream back into a "theme team" of leaders who propose themes that the group as a whole then discuss in town hall type exchanges.

Covision has been a leader in this kind of support. Together we have managed many large change projects. This was the process we used at UC Merced to engage off-campus staff, faculty, and students in the visioning component of the change process. We will share how this was designed in Chapter 9.

individual and group alignment and transformation. (See Chapters 7 and 8.)

5. **Getting the whole system in the room:** Large change processes benefit from "getting the whole system in the room," either literally or virtually, and having diverse stakeholder voices represented in a process sometimes called "max-mix." There are collaboration technologies that allow large numbers of people to have meaningful discourse in meetings and come to see the range of ideas reflected in the system as a whole. Some of these tools involve electronic brainstorming, polling, and grouping tools (see sidebar). Some involve breakout groups supported with graphic wall templates. Open Space and World Café methods, as well as simulations, experiential games and such help people explore human-systems dynamics.
6. **Appreciative inquiry and amplifying embedded solutions**: These are two methods receiving increased attention in systems-change work. Both methods start with the principle that the answers to a system's challenges are probably already present in the system. These are often latent, sometimes unappreciated, and if amplified, provide the most promising path to change because they are "native" to the system. Appreciative inquiry focuses on what's working rather than problem solving, as a general bias. It requires a good deal of what is called "system sensing." Both approaches benefit from visualization support.
7. **Collaboration backbone**: It is essential, in our experience, to have a team dedicated to providing "backbone" support for a multistakeholder process. The four roles that it plays are (1) Process design and facilitation; (2) Stakeholder-relationship management and problem solving; (3) Data collection and communications via networking platforms; (4) Project administration. The amount of communications and individual attention needed cannot be underestimated.
8. **Learning and Evaluation Process**: Build a learning-and-evaluation track that leaves involved parties with key learning, methods, and practices that can be applied to future projects.

Sharing a Draft Roadmap to Change

The following seven chapters will provide some detailed, practical advice on the kinds of tools and practices already mentioned, and others indicated on the full *Seven Challenges of Change* framework shown in Figure 6.2. When you have pulled together your client input, an assessment of your own capability, and have reached out to partners and other collaborators who might be involved, the next step is to sit down and draw out a draft plan of how you might orchestrate the change step-by-step. Figure 4.9 is the one we shared with Michael Reese after our initial client meeting.

Bear in mind that The UC Merced process was a large project, but not atypical of the kind of effort it takes to actually accomplish organizational change. Community and social change projects can often take even more steps and time. But all consultants we know who are succeeding at this change work use diagrams like this to communicate what's involved.

It is important for you and the client to know that the initial map you present will need to be updated as learning expands. In fact, updating and redesigning this visual story of how you are doing change is a critical power tool in helping your clients understand and own the process. But the map is not the territory. Change is dynamic and the best path cannot possibly be fully determined after the initial meetings, no matter how experienced you are. Your draft roadmap is primarily a communication to your client about what you think is important, not what will actually happen. What your proposal will reveal is your thinking quality. It is you that your clients are ultimately investing in, not your plan.

As we will show in our further description of the UC Merced project, one of the first things that happened with our design team was a complete reworking of the roadmap (Figure 4.9). It is this co-creative process that activates the awareness of what is needed to change. Without the draft material to work with it would be much harder to get going.

SUMMARY

Following are some key things you should take away from this chapter.

- ☐ **Model your competencies in initial meetings.** Actively visualize, share visual reports, establish rapport, ask clear questions, be clear about next steps and actions.
- ☐ **Find clients** by referral, partnering, volunteering, conferencing, workshops, and good website portfolios.
- ☐ **Set up a collaborative, learning relationship.** Be prepared to coach leaders of change.
- ☐ **Plan your initial meetings to cover relevant background information,** client interests and needs, your interests and needs, and prepare good, open-ended questions.
- ☐ **Invite and write a consulting proposal.** Cover scope, context, outcomes, approach, design (visual), timetable, deliverables, costs, and engagement principles.
- ☐ **Respond to clients in their language.**
- ☐ **Use visual tools** like context maps, roadmaps, vision maps, and visual process models.
- ☐ **Demonstrate competence with a draft roadmap to change.**

Figure 4.9

UC Merced Change Alignment Roadmap

This draft roadmap was included in our initial proposal to Michael Reese at UC Merced. The scope was to align the change program by creating a big strategy map. It shows a leadership track, change council and communication meetings as circles, Grove activities, calls (stars), and output documents (the rectangles). The project did not happen this way. The evolution of this map will show you how using these kinds of visual support change. These kinds of drafts .primarily demonstrate competency and the quality of your thinking.

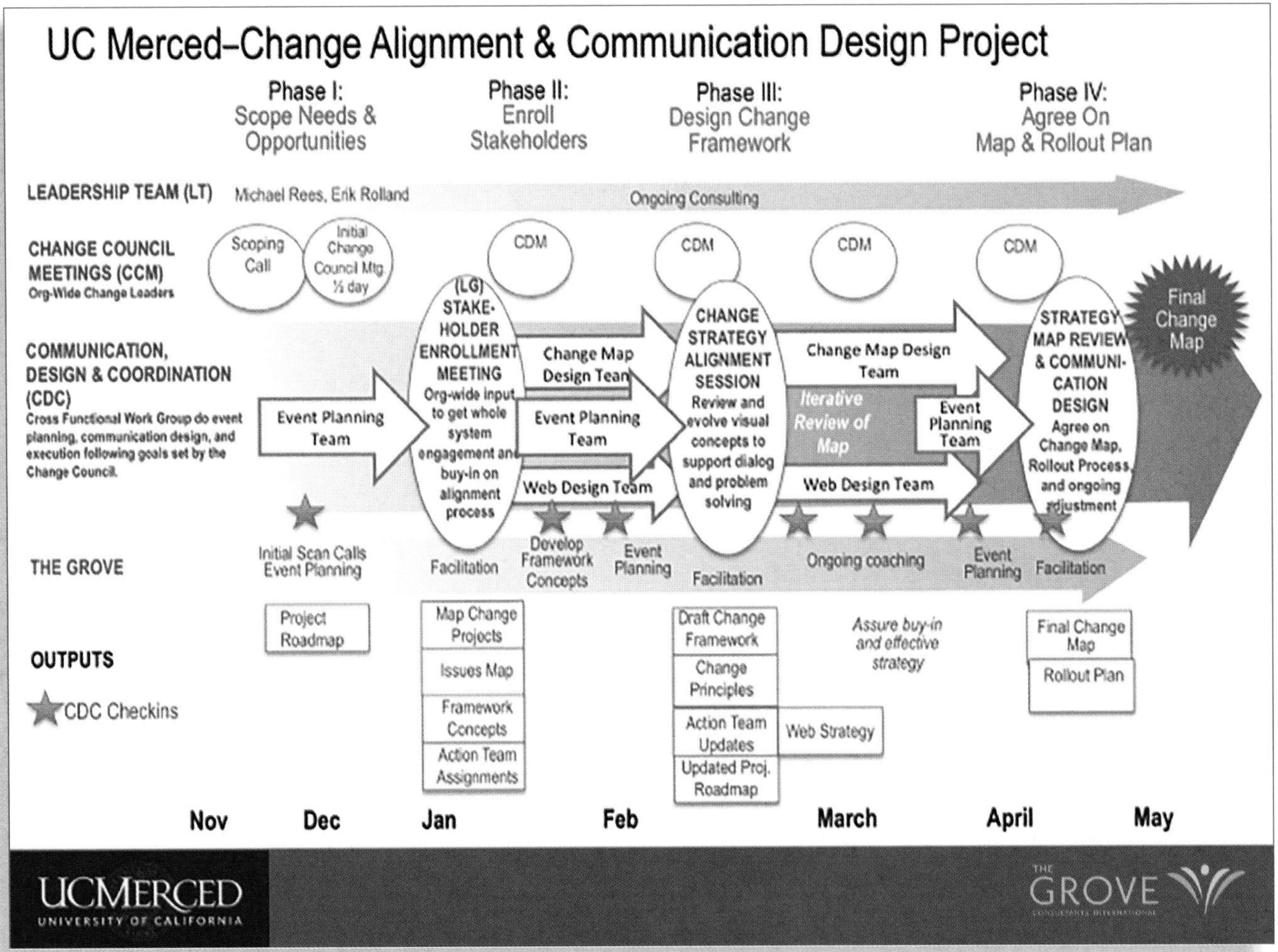

5. Basic Patterns of Change

Navigating Between Old & New

Assuming you now have a client, it is time to prepare yourself to engage the client system and understand what lies ahead for both you and the people who will become involved. Let's take some time to think about change. Here we will describe a visual framework that reflects archetypal or universal patterns that are part of any change process. These patterns are also foundational elements in the *Seven Challenges of Change*.

Change is fundamental to the human experience. For eons people have made sense out of, coped with, and supported change. We are sharing here an adaptation of these traditional approaches. It will introduce you to the basic phases of change, the inner process of moving through change, and the outer structure that supports the forward movement. It also emphasizes what it means to navigate through uncertainty of change. We believe a visual consultant should understand these basic patterns to capably design and facilitate effective change processes. Interestingly, the framework we are using is archetypal—meaning universally applicable—and will resonate quickly with clients and colleagues.

Finding the Patterns of Change

I, Gisela, spent years exploring these ideas during my doctoral research, directing the master's program in Organization Development at Sonoma State University, and subsequent work with government, private, and nonprofit clients. Once I tested these patterns of change, so much else about designing and leading change became clear, for clients too!

I find that there is an observable and steadily growing interest in indigenous wisdom traditions, supported by what I perceive of as a collective mind-set shift toward a more systemic, connected, (SideStory 5.1) and holistic paradigm. The framework that we are introducing here arises out of these traditional perspectives. It focuses on a phased approach that emphasizes working with the inner process and outer structure of change and invites visual consultants to work in a more holistic and connected manner.

SideStory 5.1

Research on Change

The material presented here arises from Gisela's lifelong interest in transformative processes. Her research crosses many fields, including creativity (existentialism), human potential (humanistic & transpersonal), vision (mysticism), individuation & alchemy (Jungian), and change (organization development) as well as indigenous perspectives, including their spiritual healing traditions, rites of passages, and ceremonial practices.

Research includes field experiences with the Qeros in the Peruvian Andes, the Kalahari bushmen in Southern Africa, and the Aboriginal people in the Central Desert of Australia. These experiences allowed her to learn about their spiritual healing traditions, their cosmologies, and circular knowledge processes. She also participated in their healing dances, rituals and ceremonies.

Indigenous and traditional perspectives shine light on ways of understanding and working with change that have been marginalized since the expansion of western colonization in the 1500s and the rise of mechanistic and scientific mind-sets.

SideStory 5.2

Reflect on Your Changes

Use a sketchbook or journal, and have a simple pen, colored pencils, or markers ready.

1. Make a list of the changes that you are currently experiencing in your life.
2. Select one change that seems particularly present to you right now. Which one has the most energy for you?
3. Reflect on the change and notice the thoughts, feelings, or images that are evoked.
4. Ask yourself, "Is there a moment, a sensation, an image, or a metaphor that stands out about this change?"
5. Take a few minutes to draw these images and associated feelings or sensation.

Change Is Fundamental

Let me share some of my thoughts on what I have come to hold as the fundamentals of change. Change can affect every aspect of our lives. It can put us on an emotional roller coaster ride—no matter if a change is about moving from one phase to the next phase of our lives, a decision we are making, or if we are impacted by a change initiated by someone or something else. Some changes deeply impact us. Others not. Some change we wholeheartedly embrace and some change we resist. And still, change can be exciting and frightening, sometimes simultaneously.

When I first began my studies in organization development, Saul Eisen, one of my early mentors mentioned, "It is not so much that people don't like change; it is they don't like being changed." What I realized then is how important it is to be an empowered participant in the process, no matter if the change is developmental, volitional, or situational.

What I also realized, and my fuller understanding about this came over time, is that real change, whether we are excited about it or not, confronts us with the unknown. **Entering the territory of the unknown is essential for change to occur.** It is out of the unknown, no matter how well we manage the change, that the new emerges. Keeping this in mind we have to ask some fundamental questions about change.

- What can we do to help us navigate this inevitable uncertainty?
- What does crossing a threshold of change feel like?
- If it is so fundamental to change, how do we best work with uncertainty or the unknown in a real change project?

Take a few minutes to do the activity outlined here (SideStory 5.2). Tuning in to your own experience with change will greatly enrich your understanding of what is to follow. After you have spent some time reflecting, put your journal aside and turn your attention back here to the research describing the ways traditional cultures have dealt with change.

Traditional Rites of Passages (RoP)

Folklorist, **Arnold Van Gennep**, first introduced the term "rites of passage" in the early 1900s. He shares from his observations that traditional cultures describe change in three phases, and each is accompanied with specific rites. He points out that rites of passages are cultural practices that are designed to transport individuals and communities across the uncertain waters of important or cyclical transitions. This can include moving from one season to another, dealing with the uncertain weather conditions that each season can bring, or ritualizing other significant changes such as readying for and returning from war, observing ritual practices associated with spiritual traditions, and more.

Classical rites of passages also mark all of the significant transitions across a lifespan—including conception rites, rites for moving into adulthood, eldership or other more official communal positions, and burial rites. The focus of these rites is to support these transitions by cultivating, harnessing, and anchoring the energy that is inherent in each process for the sake of the individuals and the communities. The goal of these rites of passages is to have the individuals and the community come through the transition well and whole and ready for what is next, rather than feeling disconnected or fragmented or left behind or stuck. While rites can address the specific needs of individuals, traditionally they are communal processes.

Victor Turner, also an anthropologist, studied both indigenous communities as well as contemporary western culture and built on Van Gennep's work. For several decades Turner researched the threshold zone and how that unfolds in this phase for the individual,

What Is Liminality?

Liminal comes from the Latin word limen and means threshold and margin—a place where we are no longer the old and not yet the new. A threshold is sometimes seen as a place of no return. A margin, on the other hand, points to the territory that is near a boundary or border—the space on either side of the threshold.

Victor Turner, an Anthropologist who wrote extensively about Rites of Passages, says that moving through the liminal phase is often experienced more like a tunnel than a simple doorway. Profound changes often require some kind of descent into the unknown, where things are not so clear, visible or known, or recognizable, where we are somehow in the dark for a while.

Learning how to create and hold a process container for people to stay long enough in this state to have something new happen is one of the fundamental challenges of change.

SideStory 5.4

Look Again at Your Change

Before we go any further into understanding the framework, focus back on yourself, the practitioner. If you took some time to reflect on a personal experience of change (see activity in SideStory 5.2), get ready to look at it now through the lenses of the change archetype shown on the next page. Keep these questions in mind as you read further:

1. How do the complex dynamics of change relate to you as a person and to the "human side" of change in your organization or community?
2. Can you recognize how the inner process and the outer structure of change are interdependent?
3. Can you become aware of the ways in which change is fundamentally a systemic and relational effort, best done by involving other people? They may be at the center of your change, and even your community.

small groups, and communities as well as in the much larger social and cultural change processes. He described this as "liminal space." (See SideStory 5.3.)

These researchers have concluded that rites of passages are invented to cultivate and harness the power of the transformative forces of change for an individual or community. When the inherent energy in change is stagnant it can be activated, when the energy is chaotic it can be calmed down. Rites of passages guide the energy of change. Turner also highlighted that traditional rites of passages in some way enact the death and birth cycle that is part of any change that is ultimately transformative. For a change to occur, something has to come to an end before something new can begin. A well-timed ritual activity can support transformation to come to full fruition.

Turner proposed that the phases of rites of passages are not limited to just supporting culturally defined crises and transition points with the accompanying rituals. He suggested that these phases **may accompany any change** from one state to another independent of cultural practices that may be in place to support these transitions. He also suggested that the three phases may be present for any type of change that occurs from one status to another. This means, even if there is an absence of culturally recognized practices, the underlying pattern is still there. This is what makes understanding rites of passages so powerful for us now.

Spend some time here with your own change, focusing on the questions to the left in SideStory 5.4. Grounding your answers in your own experience will then help you to share this framework with clients. If they are open, you can draw them in to see how the change they face will inevitably flow through these phases. Just having a language for all this provides a doorway to exploration and understanding, especially for the difficult challenges of the liminal phase.

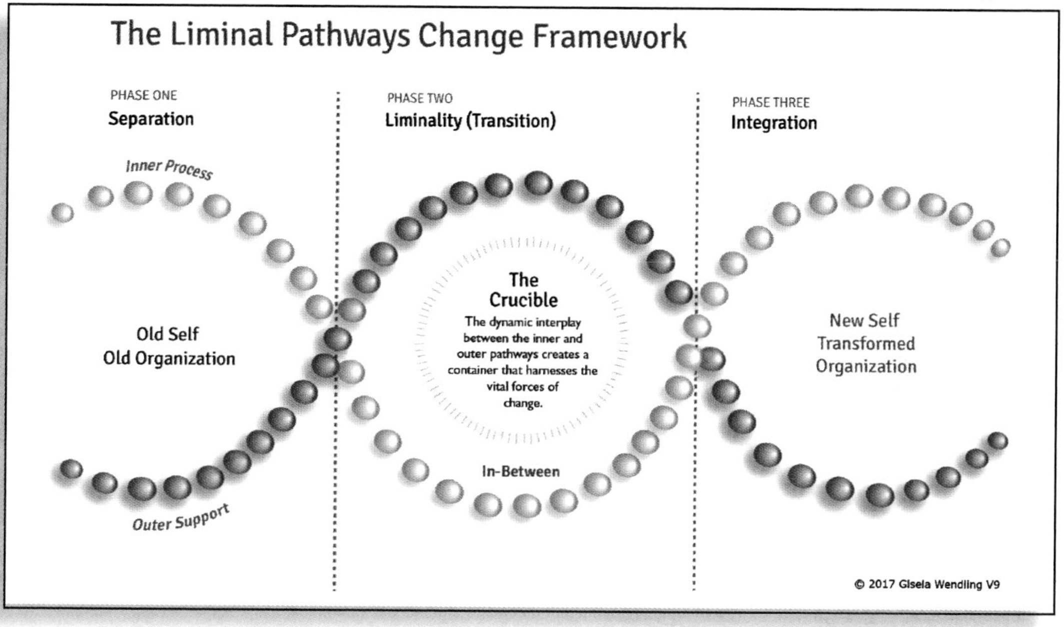

Figure 5.1

The Liminal Pathways Change Framework

The framework presented here (Figure 5.1) focuses on the personal and social aspects of change, depicting an inner process as well as supportive outer structures that help move the change forward. In this sense Liminal Pathways is a human systems change framework, and has applicability beyond traditional cultures.

William Bridges in the 1980s and 90s shared a three-phase framework for working with transitions in personal and organizational contexts, making a reference to Von Gennep's research. He defined transitions as the psychological process of adapting to change. While the *Liminal Pathways Change Framework* also addresses these intra-personal aspects of the change process, it gives more emphasis to the interplay between the inner (intra-personal) process and the outer structure (the human systems design) of change and the challenging and generative tensions of the "crucible experience" in the liminal phase. Like a real crucible used to heat and recombine metals, this phase can be very rich and challenging, especially in changes that are transformational.

We have found in our practices as change consultants that it is not difficult for people to identify which phase of change they are in. Take a moment to identify where you are in your change (SideStory 5.5). Several graduates from our Designing & Leading Change Intensive, where we have them do this exercise, say that the framework is so helpful that

Supporting Inner and Outer Process

We illustrated the *Liminal Pathways Change Framework* in a way that would make it visually clear how the inner and outer processes support each other over the three phases of change, and to emphasize the crucible experience in the liminal phase.

SideStory 5.5

Imagine This Pattern as You Read On

As you read about the three phases of change, as reflected in the *Liminal Pathways Change Framework,* imagine how each applies to some of the changes you have experienced at work or in your personal life. Do the general characteristics of each phase ring true for 00ikpoo0 you?

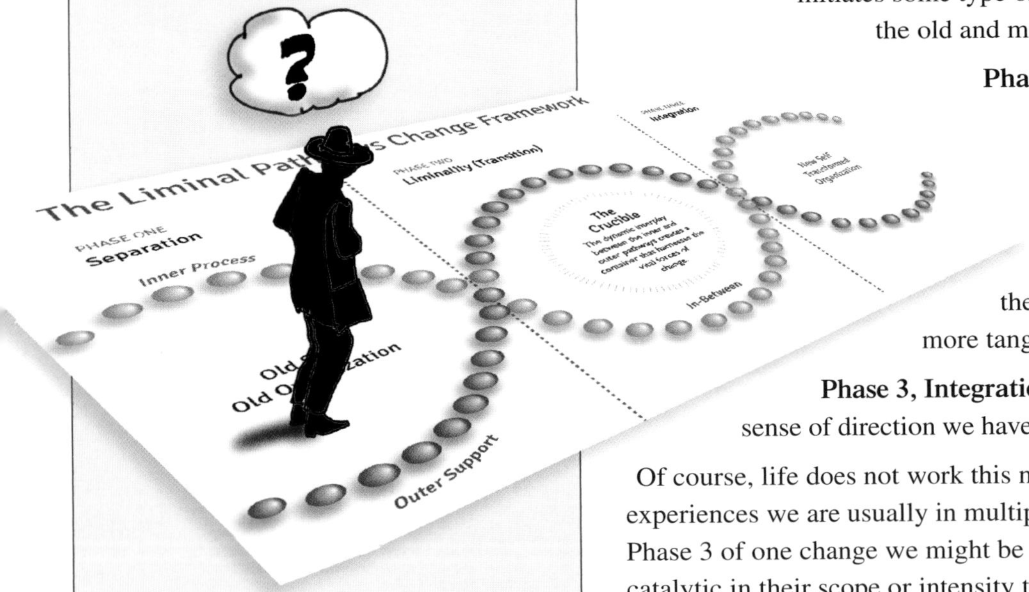

they are using the visual with their clients to help them understand that change is a process and to help them determine what is needed given the phase they are in (see SideStory 5.6).

The Three Phases of Change

The three phases of change describe the journey of change—for an individual, a group, a community, or an organization.

Phase I, Separation, is when a change is set in motion by some precipitating event that initiates some type of separation from the past. Phase 1 is about leaving the old and moving toward something else.

Phase 2, Liminality, is when we navigate the uncertain waters of change, when we feel betwixt or between. Harrison Owen analogizes that it is like a trapeze artist who is suspended in mid-air having let go of one trapeze but not yet caught the other one. This is the phase within which the new emerges as something more tangible—something truly new.

Phase 3, Integration, is the new beginning when the insights, clarity, and sense of direction we have gained during the liminal phase start to be realized.

Of course, life does not work this neatly or sequentially. We know from our personal experiences we are usually in multiple changes at once. It might be that while we are in Phase 3 of one change we might be in Phase 2 in another. However, some changes are so catalytic in their scope or intensity that they become a kind of "lead goose" for the rest of the changes. As you read, stay with the one change you have chosen.

Phase 1: Separation

A change can be initiated by all kinds of events – challenging or exciting, big or small, dramatic or subtle. We might have applied for a new job and gotten it. We decide to move across the country. Our kids go off to college, we lose a job, we are promoted, move offices, someone in the family dies, we choose a new career, our parents suddenly become dependent, and so on. Some impact us more than others, and not all changes leave us transformed. It is those that move through all three stages that are deep or transformative changes.

"To know yourself, CHANGE!!"

—Cyberneticist and systems thinker Heinz von Forester

As we described in Chapter 2, there are three types of change – developmental, volitional, and situational. Each is initiated by a different set of forces. Let's look at these from a more personal point of view.

"To understand the whole of us and the world, we have to participate with the whole of us. Specially, the bringing together of verbal and nonverbal forms of knowledge, rational and intuitive, is necessary."

—Francisco Varela

- ❑ **Developmental changes** are those that are a part of moving from one phase of life to another as we mentioned before. The life of a young adult is different from that of the teenager. Stepping into the responsibilities of an adult is another significant change. The life of a parent demands another shift again. Organizations and communities also move through developmental changes.

  In deep developmental changes there are shifts in identity. We are somehow transformed and carrying a new sense of self. Mothers experience this. But even smaller changes that don't look like transformation at first can trigger a much more profound change. What constitutes a change and whether it is transformational or not varies from person to person.

- ❑ **Volitional changes** are changes we choose, like getting married or taking on a new position. They most likely initiate a deeper emotional process, even if the change

A Meaningful Framework for People

Kevin Souza is the associate dean for Medical Education at UCSF. He came to visual consulting through using The Grove's Strategic Visioning Graphic Guides, to facilitate a strategy for educational IT in two days! He caught people's attention, and others began asking him to facilitate strategies all over the organization. Now he's focusing on change, and writes:

"Visual consulting came together for me when I went through the Designing & Leading Change workshop led by Gisela and David. What was really interesting is that I had taken 30 hours of change management coursework prior to Grove. At UCSF, a traditional change model is prevalent. Universities are very top down, and traditional models rarely include a focus on people. You learn there are early adopters and laggards. You're told to work on the laggards, but not spend too much energy on them and even force them if you have to. I have seen this backfire too many times. You not only lose people in that change effort, but lose them forever. As an internal consultant you live with the consequences for the rest of your career.

When I learned the *Liminal Pathways Change Framework*, it was the first time I'd seen anyone really marry the concept of phases of change with how to make change meaningful for people. Now when I teach about change I always talk about the *Liminal Pathways* model and the concept that true change leadership is being able to empathize how people are experiencing change and to construct an environment where their energies around that change can be transformed to focus on positive goals. This is true leadership. It's not about forcing them or telling them how to change but recognize where they are and creating the right structure for them. It really resonates."

is one we have chosen. Visioning processes in organizations that are motivated by aspiration more than necessity are also volitional.

- ❑ **Situational changes** are initiated by something else outside of your control. These changes, especially if they are dramatic and unexpected or threatening, can put us on an emotional roller coaster where we want to put on the brakes and resist. Circumstances in personal health, economic shifts, reorganizations, or catastrophes can all initiate change.

Any of these three types can be simple or a transformative change. They can trigger real shifts in identity, behaviors, and values. We emerge a somewhat different person. What may on the surface seem like a simple change can have a deep impact. No matter what the initiating source of the change, it begins a transformative process that starts to moves us through the three phases of change.

A wide array of emotions is usually associated with the separation phase ranging from fear, denial, anger, sadness, disorientation, frustration, uncertainty, and a sense of loss (Bridges). But there can also be excitement about the opportunities that lie ahead and hope for the future. A sense of loss and need for further letting go might come later. Change can be quiet enlivening at the get go, if it is something we are choosing or welcoming. As you will see, we often have a mix of feelings from the start.

Phase 2: Liminality

Earlier we eluded to the fact that when we are in this middle phase we are betwixt and between— when we are no longer the old and not yet the new. There are some predictable characteristics (See also SideStory 5.6).

- ❑ **Uncertainty**: Liminality is the place of ambiguity and uncertainty, the place of the unknown. This phase has no resemblance to the past or the future. And, how could you possibly have a full grasp of the journey through change and the future you are heading into? You can't really develop an accurate vision looking from the past. Like Einstein so famously said, we cannot solve problems at the level at which they were created. We need to be uncertain to discover. We need to be uncertain to learn. Your expertise can, in fact, get in the way during this time. It can be a time when we will confront our basic beliefs and assumptions. This is why it is so important to be exploratory throughout this phase. The promise of being in an uncertain space is that something new will eventually come your way—something that is ready to emerge in response to your beckoning. Holding the intention that this is possible helps to catalyze this process. But it is challenging.
- ❑ **Vulnerability** is one of the hallmarks of liminality. When you are uncertain and what you know is no longer useful, you might feel exposed, or naked even. You suddenly feel you could get hurt. You might feel disoriented. The typical markers on the road you normally rely on are gone.
- ❑ **Emptiness**: A feeling of emptiness can also accompany this liminal phase. If a change initiates a shift in status, you might experience a loss of power. This feeling may also arise when a change causes the need to let go of old relationships.

"Human life is not possible and worth living without some degree of stability, meaning and sense of home. Liminality is indeed a source of renewal, a restoration of meaning and the pouring of fresh wine into an old bottle. But if there are no proper 'bottles,' the fermenting power is diluted and lost. If everything is constantly changing, then things always remain the same."

—Arpad Szakolczai

SideStory 5.7

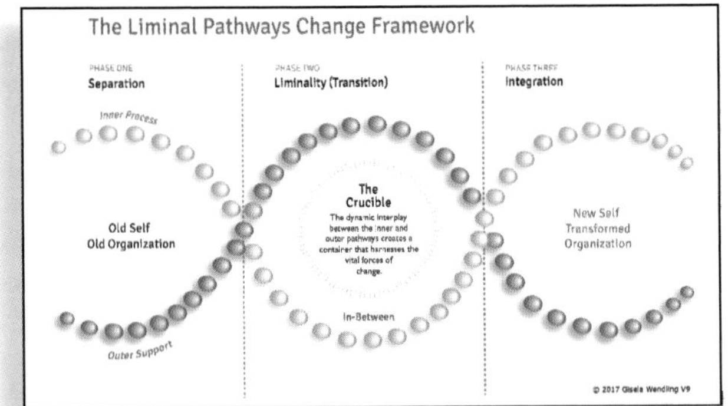

Where Are You in the Change Process?

Here is the *Liminal Pathways Framework* again. Use it to answer the questions posed here.

1. Considering the change, you identified earlier, what phase of the rites of passage framework are you in?
2. What is it like for you to be in this place/ phase?
3. What characteristics about this phase stand out to you?
4. What insights might you be gaining about yourself and the change you are in?

Sometimes people who were at the center of our lives in the past will not be the people at the center of our lives in the future.

- ❑ **Loss of Identity:** Separating from old jobs, old relationships, or former homes can all leave us without a clear identity and feeling invisible for a while. Who do you say you are? The new hasn't come yet.
- ❑ **Excitement:** The liminal phase can also be quite exciting. Bursting into the new, and anticipating it can be quite a thrill. While you might feel uncertain or challenged, you might also feel unusually alive and vibrant. Victor Turner, in his exploration of the liminal, emphasizes that threshold moments are also those when we receive "sacred knowledge." This is knowledge that was not there before. It comes from somewhere other than the usual places. You may come to recognize this special knowledge, the insight or vision, as the real seed's of your new self, new life, or future. Liminality takes us to a threshold—a word related to threshing, which means beating the husks away from the grain—separating the old to expose the gold beneath (Scharmer). This is interesting. A new change can initiate a profound inner journey in which you are confronted with the most existential questions such as, who am I, what is mine to do, what is the purpose of my life? (See SideStory 5.7)

And, what do you think it is like for a change leader? What might be their personal experience of moving through the change that they are responsible for? In what ways does their experience of change influence their capacity to guide a change and work with you on that change? How much do you think you need to be aware of and actively work with as a visual consultant? Working with the leader of change on all aspects of change is often an essential part of the work of change consulting.

In many traditional cultures, personal rites that are intended to initiate a big change, include a symbolic processes of dismemberment. These rites symbolize that our ego attachments, our need to cling to our usual sense of self, and the familiar and known, can get in the way of a change. It is this shedding of the familiar, stepping into the unknown, and feeling a loss of power and status that prepares us to be open to receive the new. Something has to come to an end. Something needs to die first. And being this open and vulnerable is not easy and yet, beneath these layers is the gold.

Liminality Can Be a Crucible

David and I have come to refer to the crux point of liminality as the "crucible." (see Figure 5.9) The crucible is a metaphor for something that can hold the intensity of the challenging and creative tensions that can be part of a personal and an organizational change process. Fear, caution and resistance are usually involved—and hope and anticipation. But these tensions are also the energy that lead to breakthrough moments and the birth of the new.

The liminal phase, including being in the crucible, can also be quite exciting. Bursting into the new, and anticipating it can be quite a thrill. While you might feel uncertain or challenged, you can also feel unusually alive and vibrant. Victor Turner in his exploration emphasizes that threshold moments are also those where we receive new knowledge that was not available to us before. It is like when we come to new insights and ideas during times of great creativity and innovation. Often the felt sense is that we are in touch with an unusual source—perhaps some transpersonal place. Something comes to us that becomes "the difference that makes the difference," to borrow a phrase by Gregory Bateson.

Implications for Visual Consulting

In the coming chapters we will explore ways in which visual consultants can use process maps, charters, stakeholder maps, and other shared visuals to help strengthen conceptual

SideStory 5.8

What Is a Crucible?

A crucible is a container that can withstand very high temperatures to melt something before it can be put into a different form. Crucibles are used for glass, metal, and pigment production. This process of heating things up is the condition for initiating a transformation.

The crucible image has too strong an emotional resonance with some people. You may choose to call the holding structure for the liminal process a container, a more general metaphor.

SideStory 5.9

Support Is Important

Facing the challenges of a liminal journey does not need to be a time without support. In traditional cultures, helpers and guides in the form of elders, medicine women or men, and others usually support individuals and the community through their transition. They conduct the rites of passages and offer guidance. In our contemporary lives these supporters are counselors, coaches, consultants, and others.

Persons going through change can also turn to inner resources such as imaginal guides or inner spiritual guidance. Deep change often is a profoundly personal process and may make us turn to our mindfulness and other practices for additional support, perhaps even more so when the change is deeply destabilizing.

containers to support continuity in the change process and visual crucibles that support moving through threshold points. Process roadmaps, for example, help to hold the process steady and help you set up visual decision rooms to support crucible experiences during critical agreements on direction and resourcing. Because deep emotional shifts need to attend this phase in change, it's also possible for visualization and graphics to get in the way if used without awareness of the stages of change. We will return to this idea later.

Phase 3: Integration

During the final phase, called integration, it is time to consolidate what you have learned and gained in the liminal phase and to adapt to the requirements of the new place or status you are in. You are at the beginning of a new path ahead. While new, we come to it with a sense of clarity, focus, and determination that was not present in the liminal phase. In time and with experience you grow more comfortable and can take full advantage of what this change has to offer. You know more about what is expected of you and what you expect of yourselves. More and more you will experience being fully recognized in your new role and who you have become.

The Inner Process and Outer Structure of Change

The contribution of the *Liminal Pathways Change Framework* is that it emphasizes that not only are rites of passages about personal change journeys but also that change is always a relational process. Is there a transformational change you can think of that does not somehow impact or involve others? Perhaps you can but it is certainly not the norm.

In traditional cultures, community members play an important role when supporting those who are going through a change. Their involvement traditionally invites us to consider how important it is to actively think about the larger human systems we are part of and the role and the tasks members of those systems can take on (SideStory 5.9).

Figure 5.2

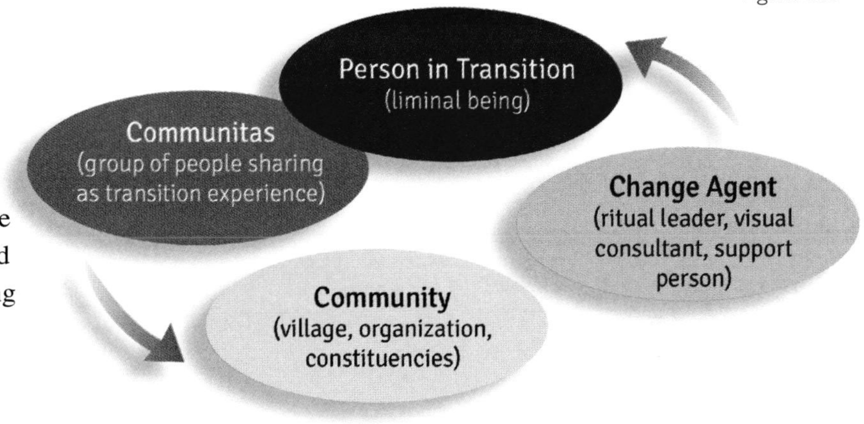

Four Traditional Roles in Rites of Passages

These are the four traditional roles in rites of passages, as described by Victor Turner.

In the *Liminal Pathways Change Framework*, we call the collective function of the combined roles the "outer structure." It is represented by one of the beaded strings. The "inner process" of the person going through a change experiences is represented by the other beaded string. When a purposeful outer structure supports the inner process of a person or group going through change, it creates the ideal conditions for a deep change to come to fruition.

We know it is harder for an individual to work through a big change on their own. We know this is equally true for any change that involves multiple individuals or multiple groups of stakeholders—in organizations, communities, and beyond. It is when the inner process is being held by the outer structures that the container becomes strong enough for transformational change. Let's turn our attention to the roles that contribute to this outer structure as a system during a guided change process (Figure 5.2). Following is a description of each role and the tasks they fill.

*The Role of the **Person** in Transition*

The person in transition embodies the inner process, meaning full engagement in all aspects of the rites of passage process—experiencing separation, the liminal phase of unknowing and potential crucible experiences, and moving into integration.

She or he separates from the familiar and known, including aspects of the old self, vocation, life purpose, status, and social relationships.

Tasks

- ❑ **Willing to be vulnerable**, engage the cycle of endings and new beginnings (death/birth), open to new and unexpected insights, knowledge, and vision.

Figure 5.3

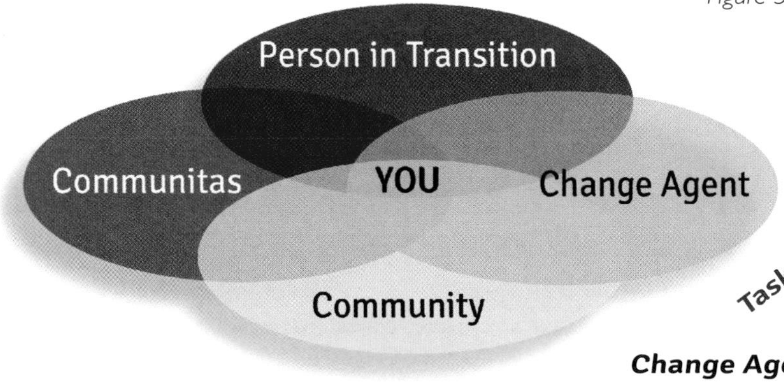

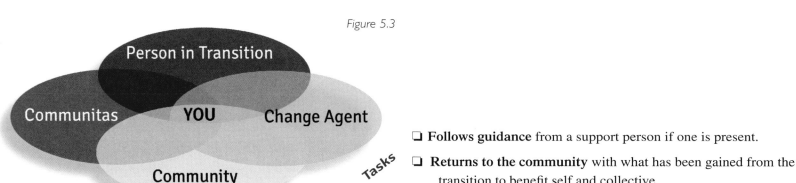

Change Agents Play Multiple Roles

The diagram here emphasizes that you as a change agent participate in change in all the dimensions that these clusters represent. It is important for change agents to support each other. We can't do this kind of work alone. The change leaders in indigenous cultures have always gathered to tell stories, share learning, and keep each other balanced and in good health and humor.

Tasks

- ❑ **Follows guidance** from a support person if one is present.
- ❑ **Returns to the community** with what has been gained from the transition to benefit self and collective.

Change Agent's Role

The change agent guides others through all phases of the rites of passage. People in this role are usually seen as having self-evident authority within the cultural tradition they function. Among traditional people, they were known as wise old man or woman, prophets, priests and priestesses, gurus, Magus (master of esoteric knowledge), or shamans. In our contemporary culture they can function within roles and professions such as psychotherapists, teachers, coaches, and consultants who incorporate the spiritual (transpersonal) dimensions of transformative processes (See also Figure 5.3).

Tasks

- ❑ **Knows the functions and responsibility** to be a trusted guide.
- ❑ **Knows how to design** or energetically evoke and facilitate transformative space and processes.
- ❑ **Challenges and helps protect** the person in transition when they are the most vulnerable.
- ❑ **Guides** and works with the community to support ritual process.

Community (Village, Organization) Role

The larger social systems that we belong to, such as our families, communities, or the organization we work for can be effected by a change we are in and can play a role in supporting or hindering us moving through that change. In traditional cultures, they often function as an extension of the ritual leader and support ritual process. They either already know what their specific contribution can be to supporting the change, or are instructed on what to do. What is the role of a parent when attending a college graduation? It is not only to celebrate the success of their daughter or son, but it is also to "see" them as the adults they are becoming and to begin to hold them to the social expectations that are now required of them.

Tasks

- ❑ **To support** the individual to let go of their old self.
- ❑ **Help with the ritual preparations**, ceremonies and gatherings that are part of the rites of passage.
- ❑ **Welcome the initiate back** as witness of the person they have become in their new role, status, and sense of self and not expect them to be who they were.

Communitas (Group of People Sharing a Transition Experience) Role: The term communitas refers to the experience of a special kind of togetherness that is experienced by those going through a change together—even if they are not close in other contexts. They form a special bond as they understand and empathize with what each is going through. Together they feel set apart from the rest of the community, and experience a sense of being marginal or marginalized. Members of this group usually function outside of the structure and classifications, such as rank and status of the larger more conventional community or society. We have observed that change teams or design teams when working on organizational change can take on some of the characteristics of being a communitas. Understanding this dynamic is important, as the goal of the change team is to help design and guide the organizational change process, and they usually are the first ones in the organization going through the change, often operating in organizational white space.

SideStory 5.10

Role and Tasks in Your Change

Going back to reflections on the phase of change you are in, answer the questions below about the role you are playing.

1. Given the phase of change you are in, how would you define your role? What new insights do you have about your role?
2. What would you identify as the most important tasks for you?
3. What might be the most important tasks of the "change agent," "village," and "communitas" at this time, given the change you are working with?
4. Whom might you ask for support and what would you ask them to do?

SideStory 5.11

Higher Learning

Almost three decades ago Harrison Owen, the originator of Open Space work, shared with us his understanding of the difference between what he called Normal Learning and Higher Learning.

Normal Learning is the kind of learning we engage to become really good at what is required to sustain a certain status quo.

Higher Learning on the other hand is the kind of transformational learning required to shift from one paradigm to another. Normal learning takes over again as we integrate the shifts.

The *Liminal Pathways Framework* is a map to understanding and supporting transformational learning processes for individuals, organizations, and communities and points in the direction of the capabilities needed to do so.

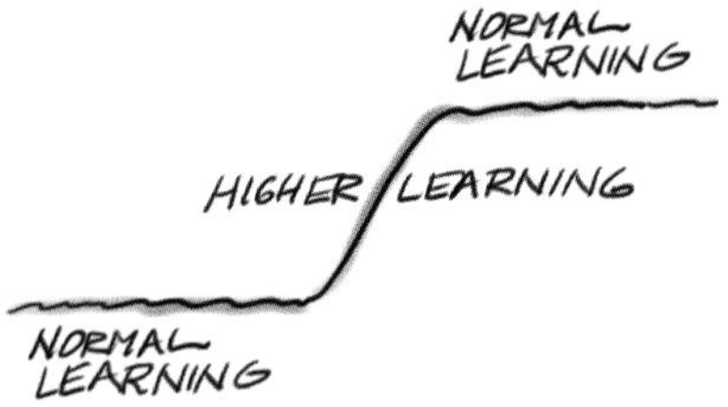

Tasks

- ❑ **Share the burden of their tasks** and responsibilities through egalitarianism and comradeship.
- ❑ **Available to open and more direct dialogue** and encounters as they share their experience of change together.
- ❑ **Recognize how they are the same as people in transition**, carrying similar hopes and burdens such as marginality, humility, and invisibility.

The Role of Consultants in Supporting the Ambiguity of Change

Most of us are habituated to recognize others only when they fit into typical definitions and classifications. When someone does not fit these definitions, the person may become and/or feel invisible or marginalized. The person or the group of people (the communitas) who are experiencing a rite of passage are neither who they were nor who they are becoming. Because of this ambiguous position they can become "invisible" to the larger community or organization. There is power and danger in this place. While stepping outside "business as usual" and the normal way of doing things is a necessary step in a meaningful process of change, if people become disconnected or invisible for too long, reconnecting might become increasingly challenging.

You as a consultant and your change teams have to remain enough like the system not to be rejected and enough unlike the system to be able to step into a liminal space to begin the work of change, including the work of designing and guiding change. Holding this creative tension is part of the inner work of a visual consultant.

Becoming Masters of Liminal Space

Change consultants are in a double role of mastering changes in their own lives while at the same time supporting their clients to master their change processes. Reflecting on your personal experience is critical to the learning process and is an important source of knowledge when working with clients on the more challenging aspects of their inner process, especially during crucible moments. Perhaps you would also benefit from being supported when going through your own deeper change processes and growing increasingly more comfortable with uncertainty and the time it takes for the new to emerge. We recommend that consultants, and especially those who work visually, develop two fundamental capabilities. They are:

Change Fluency: This is about being fluent in the language of change. It includes understanding conceptual frameworks that provide a map to the territory of change as well as knowing your beliefs and assumptions about change. What do you believe about how change works? What is your theory of change? Fluency means knowing conceptual frameworks like the *Liminal Pathways Change Framework*, the *Seven Challenges of Change*, and other models and how to share them with clients in simple sketch talks. You can build up your repertoire over time. So, this fluency is learnable (See SideStory 5.11).

Change Fluidity: This capability speaks to the emotional agility that is needed when moving in and out of change processes in your own life while also attending to those of your clients, and being impacted by the changes that are going on around you. Just how many liminal spaces can you navigate without becoming too drained? How can you discern between what is going on for you versus what is going on for the client system? How do you stay aware? There is a kind of fluidity that is needed to navigate between so many liminal processes. As you learn to accept and transcend the tensions inherent in change work, you'll experience more ease in your work, and learn to remain dynamic, alive, and nondogmatic. We believe this kind of change fluidity can be cultivated through practice. What are the personal practices that help you stay present and grounded?

Dealing with Permanent In-Betweenness

We are in a world that is increasingly complex and rapidly changing. Change processes are often interrupted, not fully engaged, and left incomplete, adding to our sense of ambiguity. and in-betweenness. The world is getting "smaller" and more interconnected but at the same time we are increasingly disconnected from traditional sense of belonging to place, home, and community.

It seems we are in a state of almost permanent liminality, caught "in between" most of the time. How can we respond?

- **Recognize permanent in-betweenness.** Accept the fact that the tensions of permanent in-betweenness (in rapid, discontinuous, and complex change) are intense and can become overwhelming, counterproductive, even numbing.
- **Galvanize and focus your energy** on one particular change. Identify and work with the most vital change taking place and fully engage each phase of the change.
- **Shift and open up limiting patterns** by doing something different. Do the unexpected. Transformative frameworks are designed to guide you to the inspired and creative threshold that breaks us open to something new.

Visual Consulting Suggestions for Using the Liminal Pathways Change Framework

Here is a summary of some of the ways you can work with the basic patterns of change reflected in the *Liminal Pathways Change Framework.*

- ☐ **Share a poster** of the *Liminal Pathways Change Framework* and invite clients to explore which current change they are in that harbors the most energy or (creative or difficult) tension for them. Are they at the separation, in-between or incorporation phase of the change? Remember the tasks of each phase.
- ☐ **Choose one change** to work with.
- ☐ **Visually create a chart of the initial conditions** and the ways they are impacting you and your client.
- ☐ **Be aware of your pace.** Slow the process down if changes are happening too quickly or speed up your pace to match or exceed the pace of the change if necessary. Resist being "caught and stuck" in the overwhelming amount and speed of change.
- ☐ **Plan to allow the experience of each phase to fully unfold** as you design change processes. When in the process, support you and others noticing, being moved, grieving, and getting excited. Don't be afraid to feel the movements and emotions of change. Don't overfocus on being clear and visual in crucible moments. Stay with the feelings.
- ☐ **Confront the death and birth cycle** and encourage "letting go"; this is necessary to transform the "form" of who you are. Re-visualizing your vision, plans, and roles is a way to make this process explicit.
- ☐ **Use crazy wisdom** to trick yourself and clients into a different perspective, through creative action and improvised expression. Drawing and visualizing activities often have this quality. Rather than calming down and meditating, get excited. Do the unexpected.
- ☐ **Consider the external resources you have available.** Is there a group of friends, colleagues, or a support community whom you and your client can ask for help? Are there trusted advisors to guide you through each phase that can help? Remember the role and tasks of the "village" and the "ritual leader."
- ☐ **When the new begins to take form, commemorate it with new narratives and generative images** drawn from the process. Creating large, original murals of co-created visions can help the new stories take root, and will help a much wider range of people share the same story.

6. Seven Challenges of Change
Seeing Repeating Patterns

Wouldn't you like to know the challenges you will face as a process-oriented consultant? We've already explored some of the fundamental orientations regarding thinking about your role. We've reviewed basic capabilities, and learned about the deep pattern in change revealed through the lens of traditional rites of passages. But ultimately, there is the task of gaining the client's respect and helping guide them through their unique challenge of designing and leading change for their specific organization or community. This chapter will introduce you to seven predictable challenges you can prepare for and work with. Each challenge will be explored in more detail in the following chapters.

The problem of navigating change is analogous to the challenges faced by a river guide (Figure 6.1). Rivers are never the same from one season to the next, and differ a lot from one to another. How does a guide develop competency? How can you, as a person who wants to be a competent visual consultant know what to suggest?

Integrating Liminal Pathways & The Grove Organization Change Model

Over the past four years we authors have been working to identify these repeating patterns for human systems change processes, harvesting over 70 years of collective experience. We are finding that the seven challenges we have identified will apply to any consulting project that requires new ways of thinking, real behavior change, and new organizational processes. To capture our full understanding, we have visually integrated the archetypal perspective reflected in the *Liminal Pathways Change Framework* with The Grove's model for looking at organization change. We have called the new framework the *Seven Challenges of Change* because it describes big patterns that we find to be present in many change projects, especially those that use high engagement approaches. We also involved a core group of colleagues who work cross-sector and globally to test this framework against their experiences. As with other Grove work, it is also supported by Arthur M. Young's

Figure 6.1

Change Is Like a River

For river guides every run is unique, but there are repeating patterns. Practices develop to handle each of these but are applied only after the guides scout the river and see which of the common challenges will be showing up. Holes, the swirl behind big rocks, appear and disappear depending on how high the water is running. The same is true in change process for the "crucible" moments we wrote about in Chapter 5.

Figure 6.2

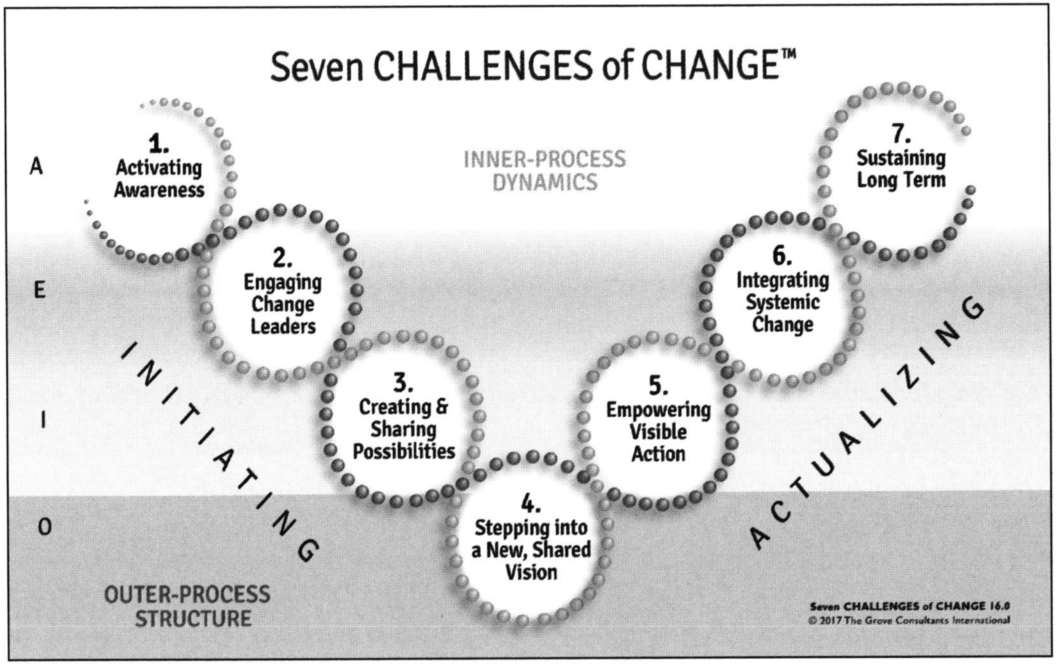

Theory of Process (see Appendix). Figure 6.2 is our graphic representation of these challenges, illustrating the interplay between inner-process dynamics and outer-process structures, and mapping them on the four flows of process.

Look at the seven challenges as two groups. One includes the challenges involved in initiating change leading up to what, in the Theory of Process, is called "the turn." The second is related to realizing the change, building on what has been initiated so far, and what has emerged from moving through the turning point.

Bouncing Ball Pattern

Readers familiar with the widely used *Drexler/Sibbet Team Performance Model* will immediately see the familiar "bouncing ball" pattern used to illustrate the essential dynamics of teamwork. The same underlying process patterns apply to organizational and community changes that you can support as a consultant.

Challenge 1: Activating Awareness

Waking up to the need to change is always the starting point in a change process. This is about activating your own awareness during initial meetings and scoping talks and understanding the current awareness of the need to change within the client system. What are you paying attention to? What does the client think is needed? What is driving this change? Like being on a river that changes, this challenge is informed a lot depending on whether the need to change is activated by external circumstances, like the fires that are challenging the western United States, or by developmental needs, like the need for UC Merced to double in size to handle the economics of a large university, or volitional as in our creating the GLEN. In most cases usually only a few people are fully awake to the need to change. But even in a full-scale catastrophe that affects everyone, people will first shut down in shock and not be open to how much has to change. Regardless of the circumstances, the first challenge is raising both your own and your client's awareness as Chapter 7 will show.

Challenge 2: Engaging Change Leaders

Early on, the primary focus is to bring together a group of leaders, formal and informal, to be the designers and the catalysts of the change process. A process consultant partners with these leaders to put into a place a change process that empowers the organization or community to stay in charge of the change and minimizes the dependency on the consultant in ultimately realizing the change. Putting in place a change team or a process design team early on is helpful. Even an expert who is supporting a change initiative usually depends on partnering with internal champions. The discovery that a change may push up against the leader's inner sense of bandwidth, capability or sense of adequacy, and reservations, along with a variety of strong feelings, expressed or not, are often present during this time. Chapter 8 will deal with the practices to boost and direct the momentum of change by identifying the needed leaders, the formation of process design teams, stakeholder mapping and enrollment, and ways to address the deeper personal concerns.

Challenge 3: Creating & Sharing Possibilities

It's tempting to think you can plan your way through change as though it is a construction project. Some are, but in our testing of this challenge with colleagues, everyone agreed that after engaging a group of leaders, the next challenge is more often than not actually trying out possibilities. It's a phase that is active, and uncertain, and exciting. It involves visioning, prototyping, linking in new participants, exploring assumptions, embracing

Looking at Visual Models

As you look at the *Seven Challenges of Change* framework in its simplest form, ask yourself the following questions:

1. Why is it called "Challenges of Change"? What does this metaphor call up right away?
2. Two strings of beads intertwine. What does this remind you of? Is there a graphic metaphor beyond "inner" and "outer" that is embedded here that might be relevant?
3. The numbered challenges tell a story. At this level of reading does it ring true with your experience? Where do you experience little disagreements vis-å-vis what you already know about change?
4. What are the little letters to the left? They seem to refer to four bands underlying the model. Why might this be important?
5. Let your own experience both resonate with and clash with what is represented here. Both interactions are important to understand.
6. Is it clear to you that all flat maps are distorted? These built-in biases are important. What is the bias in this presentation?

SideStory 6.2

Looking at Visual Models

Here are our answers to the questions in SideStory 6.1:

1. Why "Challenges of Change"?—Challenges invite responses, and are difficult. Facing challenges can transform them into opportunities.
2. DNA is a two-stringed molecule that can replicate. Good support structures in one change process can repeat in others.
3. What resonates with you depends on your experience, not ours. You'll have to answer this one.
4. AEIO refers to the four flows of process and stands for Awareness, Energy, Information, and Operations. All four levels need to be managed in every challenge. Different challenges have centers of focus on different levels.
5. Maps are not the territory, and these frameworks are more like piano or computer keyboards than little blueprints. Remember both your agreements and disagreements.
6. The bias in this framework, expressed in the arc, is to amplify the idea that you have to connect your high-level aspirations for change with the ground of where people really live and work before you can turn people toward lasting change.

resistance, refining purpose and goals, and continuing to activate awareness in the larger system. Visual consultants are finding their tools and methods full of potential for responding to this challenge (see SideStories 6.1 and 6.2). Here is where big-picture thinking is invaluable. Chapter 9 will introduce many tried and true approaches.

Challenge 4: Stepping into a New, Shared Vision

You may appreciate, if you have had some experience consulting, that the first three challenges may need to be revisited several times before you reach a threshold stage when a critical mass is willing to step into a new way of working and leave the old behind. We call this stepping in to a "shared" vision. Challenge 3 is more permissive, from a process standpoint. It's exploratory and divergent at times. Challenge 4 requires converging while simultaneously holding a great amount of complexity. Reconnecting with the deeper purpose is helpful as big decisions and trade-offs are made, and as budgets, personnel, and power shifts. Chapter 10 addresses principles and practices related to this challenge. Visualization is again a powerful tool, but attention to the inner dynamics is crucial at this point. There may have been "crucible moments" in earlier stages, but this entire challenge is a big crucible. It's the challenge of choosing a path from which there is usually no turning back.

Challenge 5: Empowering Visible Actions

In any organizational or community system, having a core group step into change doesn't mean that the whole system shifts right away. Without truly visible actions being taken that support the change, resistance and habit can start compromising forward progress. Supporting what emerges at this stage is crucial for sustaining momentum, and learning from new experiences helps you stay on track and can help amplify what is working.

It involves empowering new leaders, supporting new key initiatives, and adopting new measures of success. Making these moves visible throughout the system is critical after stepping into big commitments. So are communication campaigns and supporting new collaborations. Chapter 11 will explore these practices.

Challenge 6: Integrating Systemic Change

Visible actions, good communications, learning and amplifying early wins as well as persistence will eventually move the system to change. But now integrating new communities of practice and developing and embedding needed processes and norms throughout the system becomes the work of culture change. This is about embodying the change day-to-day such that the "new" is the way things are done. It means changing technical and other work processes, reward structures, employee development, as well as understanding how to measure success, power and mobility in the new system. In communities it may involve new laws and policies. This challenge draws on the patience and stamina of the leaders of change and requires empowerment of the organizational units to experiment and make the change their own. Chapter 12 will explore the practices involved in amplifying successes in ways that replicate throughout a system. It requires continuing awareness of how the larger system actually works and gets in the way.

With a focus on mechanization for efficiency, we have lost touch with the value of traditional methods and rituals that create a rich, cultural fabric, energizing the organization with a sense of connectivity, well-honed processes, and purpose. Many large business organizations, in their desire to be more efficient, are inadvertently taking away core rituals and activities that were historic sources of renewal, inspiration, and "glue" for employees.

Challenge 7: Sustaining Long Term

Sustaining change long term is a challenge that involves developing change fluency and change fluidity. With your support, the capabilities of designing, leading and then sustaining a change can be a focus of the organization and become deeply embedded in the culture. Traditional cultures evolved their rituals as finely tuned ways of cultivating, harnessing, and focusing the energy of change, as well as stabilizing the change into

Figure 6.3

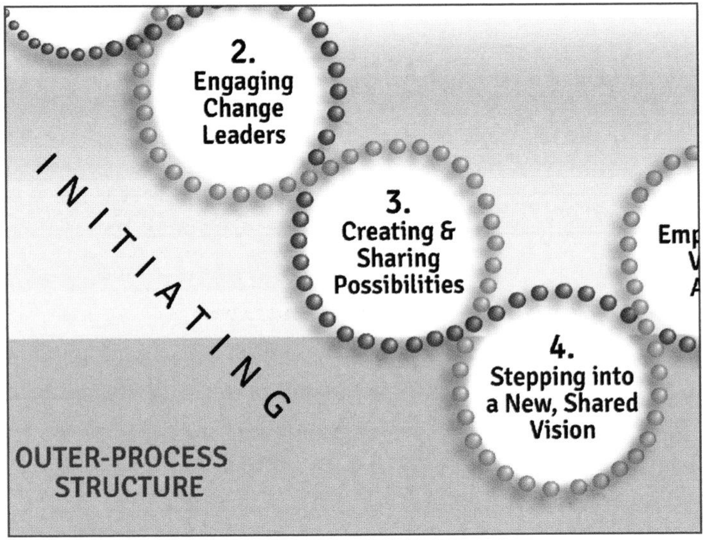

practices that then sustained the community culture. With a focus on mechanization for efficiency, we have lost touch with the value of traditional methods and rituals that create a rich, cultural fabric energizing the organization with a sense of connectivity, well-honed processes, and purpose. Many large business organizations, in their desire to be more efficient, are inadvertently taking away core rituals and activities that were historic sources of renewal, inspiration, and "glue" for employees. Understanding culture and how it evolves has widespread attention in our organizational work today. But the challenge of having new practices become embedded rituals that are alive, meaningful, and adaptive is not easy. They can easily be overdone or undone by unaware leaders. Chapter 13 will deal with the possibilities these responses to sustaining the change.

The Change Archetype Repeats

Each challenge in a change process presents an opportunity for a "crucible experience" where the inner process and outer structure allow people to break through to something really new. They vary in intensity, with Challenge 4 bringing the most "heat" to the process. Rites of passage can happen in all these transitions from challenge to challenge.

Unpacking the Visual Framework

Understanding how we have visualized these seven change patterns as a whole system is another layer of value for you as a visual consultant, for you may want to share it with clients as a way of generating some change literacy or fluency.

You will probably notice that the same double strand idea we used to visualize rites of passages repeats here (Figure 6.3). This is because all change, and each challenge you will encounter in your consulting work, will have some kind of outer-process structures that you and your client will put in place to support change, and there will be some kind of inner-process dynamics that both you and your clients will experience. Both need to be appreciated and attended. This dance between inner and outer is ongoing. (One of the reasons many change processes fail arises from under appreciating and not taking time for the inner process.)

Why the Bouncing Balls?

You will probably notice that this framework visualizes change as a process that isn't a straight line or a closed circle (two popular visualizations). In the *Seven Challenges of Change* depiction, the initiating stages go down toward the bottom of the page and then turn back toward the top. Arthur Young called this pattern "the ARC" of process, and felt it was universal. In applied terms, it points to how all process starts with nothing but potential, often beginning with something people imagine or feel as a hunch, and then materializing into plans and projects and eventually budgets, structure, behavior change, and some other kinds of tangible results.

If you think of the top of the page as the "top line" and the bottom of the page as the "bottom line," and think about experiences you have had where aspirations and visions are in creative tension with real-world constraints and resources, then this picturing of change will make sense (Figure 6.4). At some level, integrating our inner purposes and aspirations with the real world is the fundamental challenge of any change project or consultancy. When this integration is successful, a "turn" toward actualization can occur with energy and direction.

Theory "U" used this graphic representation of going down to go up in its signature graphic but represents it as a smooth arc. Young insisted this shift isn't smooth but represents a real flipping of attention and preferred the right angle.

Visualizing the shift in direction as a "turn" creates a metaphor that a different direction is possible during change. This two-fold nature of process is characterized repeatedly in the literature on consulting. Some like to call this the movement between divergence and convergence. "Divergence" means expanding out, adding more ideas, including more people, getting more understanding, etc. "Convergence" is about synthesizing, harvesting,

Figure 6.4

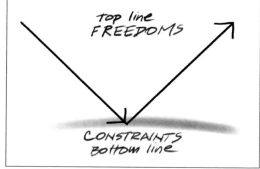

Freedom Through Mastery of Constraint

Visually it's easy to represent creative tension between aspirations and material world constraints as one arrow going to the bottom line and one going to the top line. This pattern repeats through each of the challenges in addition to being reflected in the larger process.

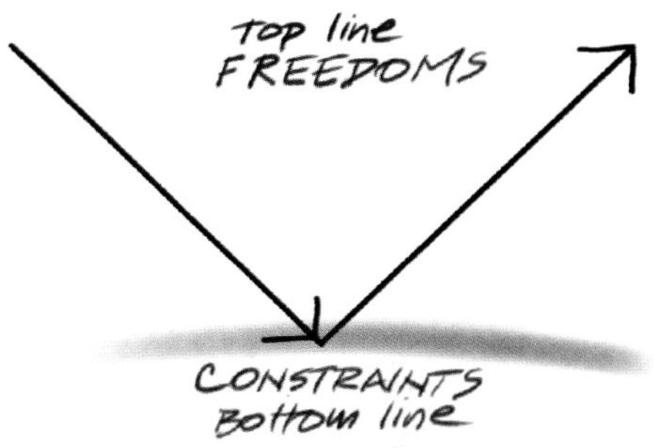

Nested Process

All processes, like music, have multiple layers. The four flows are always present whether or not we are paying attention to them. Patterns and themes persist and reappear, nesting into the later ones. For instance, becoming aware and staying awake doesn't just happen in the beginning. It persists at every stage.

Engaging leaders of change is the focus when you create the change teams and find sponsors and leaders, but continues all through the actualizing phases.

Creating and testing possibilities gets a lot of attention early on before full commitment, but the practices associated with this will continue to be important as you empower visible action, and initiative teams work to refine what they are doing.

As we write about the practices associated with each challenge we have chosen to place them with the challenge where they first appear in their fullest form.

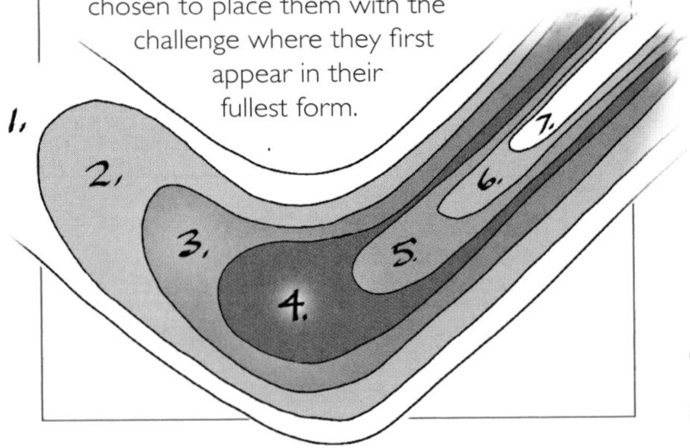

and making decisions. Sometimes visual consultants visualize this as an accordion process, with a continuous fluctuation of convergence and divergence. Both the inner-outer dynamic, and this movement between divergence and convergence accompanies whatever processes you adopt in responding to any of the seven challenges. If the challenges are like chord structures and keys a musician chooses for a piece of music, the dance between inner and outer is like paying attention to the intervals and timing that bring these chords and keys to life (Sidestory 6.3). Paying attention to the divergent and convergent pattern is paying attention to increasing tensions and complexity and then resolutions.

What About the Flows of A-E-I-O and U ?

We have illustrated the seven challenges of change as patterns in process with each having an affinity for a certain level as illustrated in the four flows. .

1. Initially **attention** is centered on "Activating Awareness" and getting attention on the need to change. Eventually attention focuses on "Sustaining the Change."
2. It soon involves people's **energy,** emotions, and relatedness as you begin "Engaging Change Leaders." Energy is also a main part of "Integrating Systemic Change."
3. Sharing and exploring **information** is central to "Creating and Sharing Possibilities," as ideas emerge in different ways—literally coming to life "in" form. Later the job is to "Empower Visible Action," having the forms show up as observable results.
4. Bottom line, "Stepping into a New, Shared Vision" is about actual embodiment personally and in the **operational** "body" of the organization or community.

The "U" is not a level, but "YOU," as we've pointed out, and represents all the intentions, styles, skills, and preferences that shape your way of working and through which your

Figure 6.5

application of practices will filter. The guide for how to be "YOU" must come from within. Self-awareness and being open to feedback and mindfulness practices help. Mentors help. Success models help. But ultimately is comes back to self-acceptance.

Learning Your Way into Using the Full Framework

Figure 6.6 is a version of the *Seven Challenges of Change* framework that includes bullet points for likely inner dynamics and the outer support structures than can help support change at each phase. At first glance it many seem overwhelming, but all these factors can come into play. This map has been our guide in developing the next seven chapters about how you can, as a visual process consultant, meet these challenges. It is a map you may use to prepare for doing actual work.

As we turn our attention to actually finding clients for change and engaging them around scoping the project and making proposals, it helps to have a big-picture sense of what is involved as you go into initial interviews. It helps to know that change processes always go through crucible moments at some point. That is why we chose to explore the underlying patterns of change before getting into detailed practices.

As you can probably anticipate from your own experience, gaining command of all the capabilities we referred to in Chapter 3 and the inner process dynamics and outer support structures listed on the big *Seven Challenges of Change* map is a long process of trying things, reflecting, learning some more, adding some practices, trying some more, checking back with the big maps to see if you missed anything, and diving in again. We have come to understand this process is never completed. Developing mastery comes out of the commitment to being a life-long learner, appreciating the adventure of learning alongside and with your clients and trusted colleagues. With openness and a will to learn, useful perspectives and advice often arrive just when you need them.

Developing mastery comes out of the commitment to being a lifelong learner, (and running the river of change many times). This kind of learning you cannot do alone. As we will point out in our last chapter, Towards Mastery, being a visual consultant working on change is an adventure of learning alongside and with your clients and trusted colleagues.

Figure 6.6

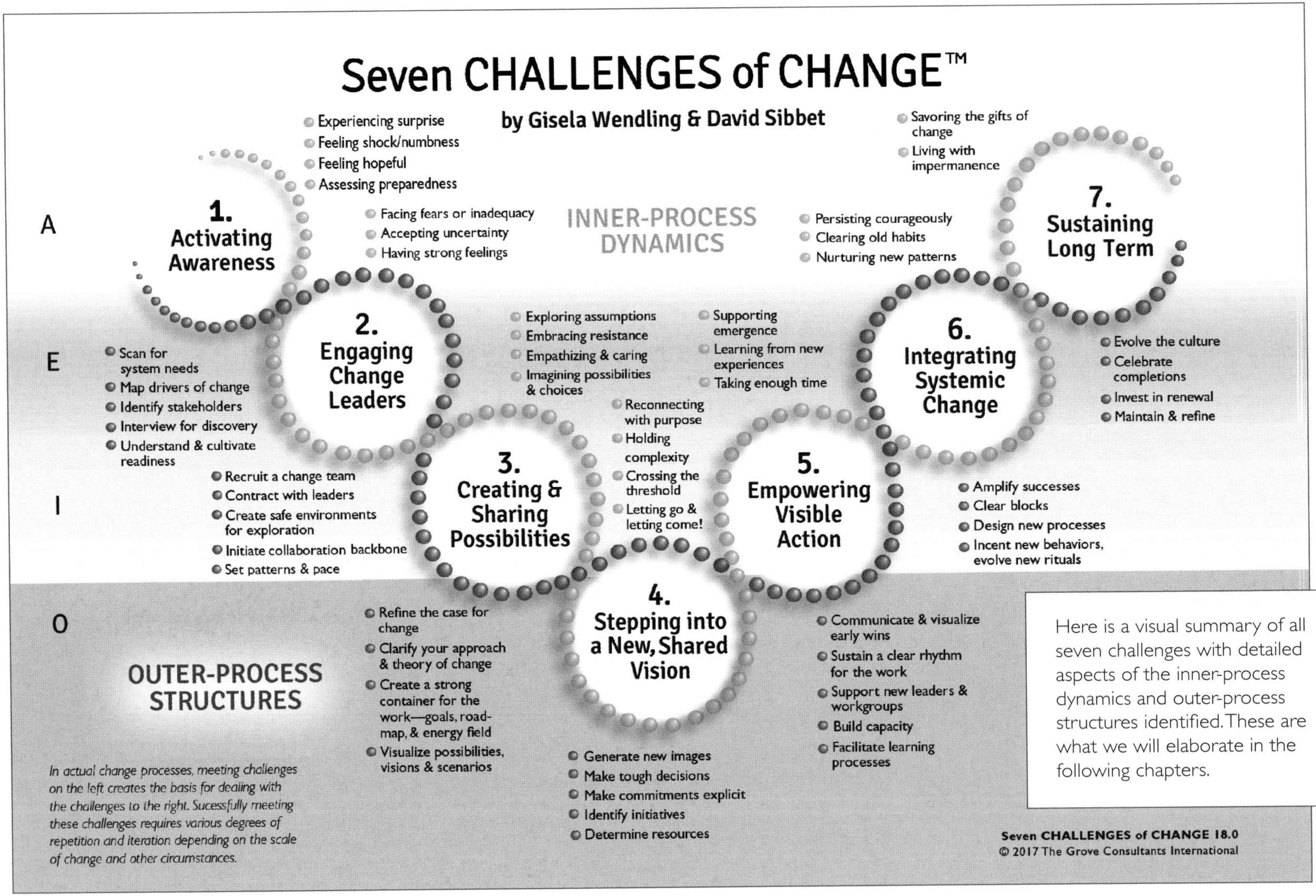

Here is a visual summary of all seven challenges with detailed aspects of the inner-process dynamics and outer-process structures identified. These are what we will elaborate in the following chapters.

Part III. Visual Consulting Practices

Responding to the Challenges of Change

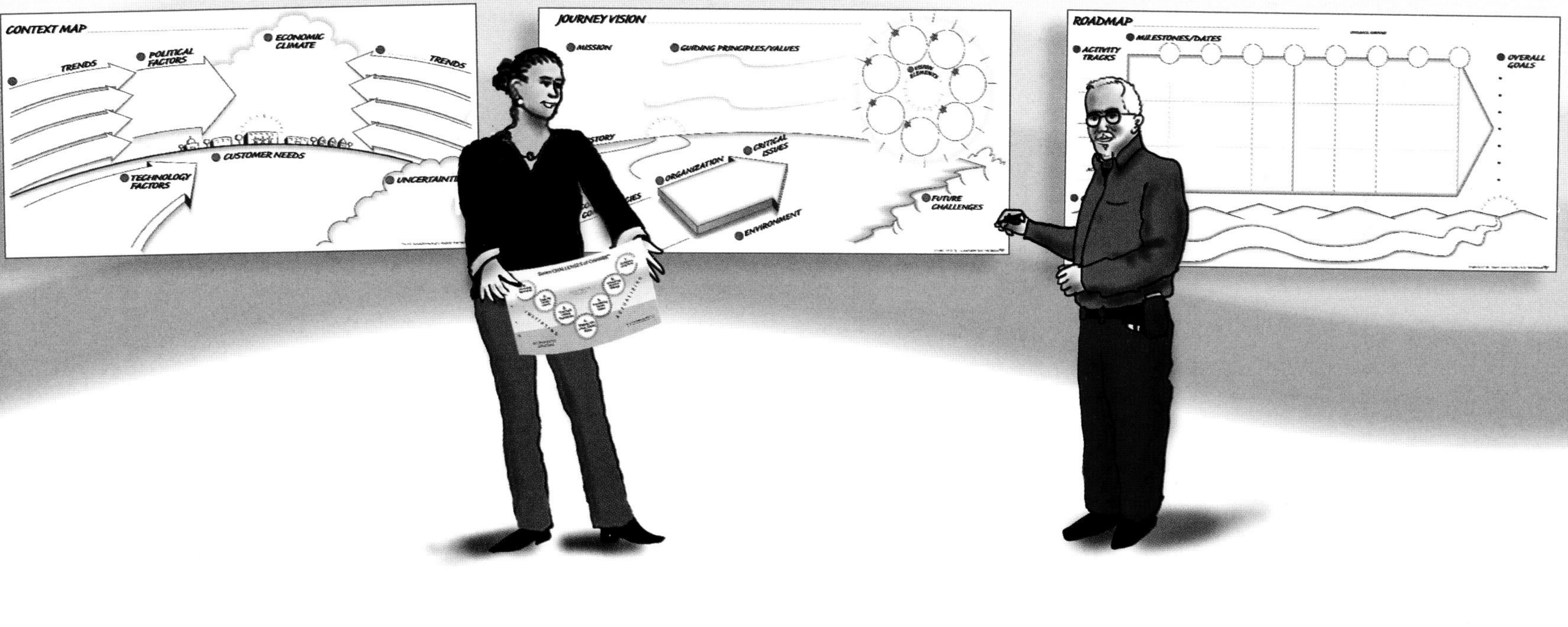

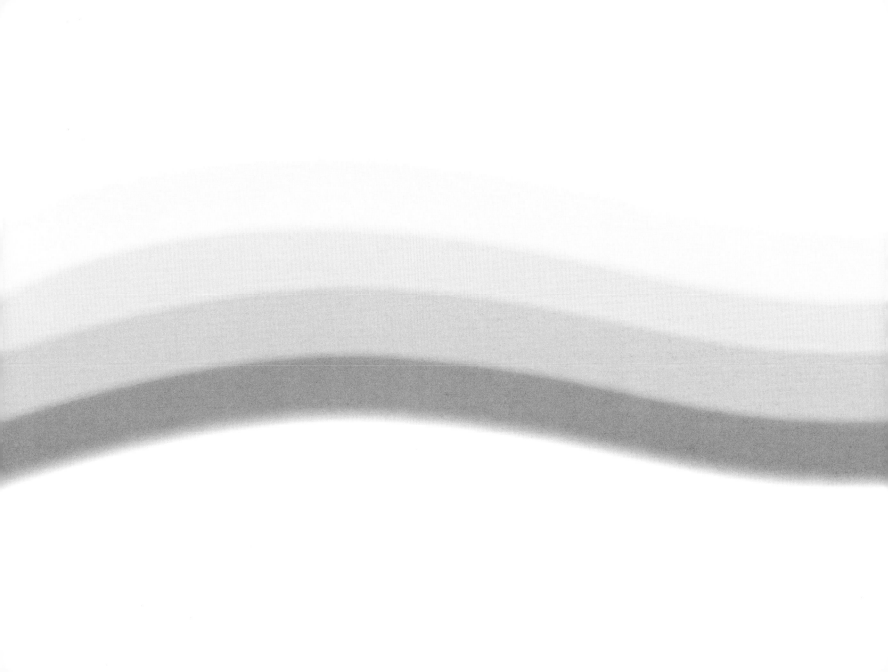

7. Activating Awareness
Recognizing the Need to Change

The challenge of Activating Awareness was most likely present before you and your client first talked. Your initial client meetings and your proposal already helped bring the need to change to a formal level and the agreement to hire you signals further that a change process is afoot (Figure 7.1).

Figure 7.1

Activating Awareness implies that during the initial phase of a change process you will begin actively increasing your client's and your own understanding of the change. As a process consultant you will want to support initiative or project team leads, gaining the information needed to begin designing the process approach to the change.

But, Activating Awareness goes beyond working with the organizational change leader. Learning and commitment will need to grow until the process becomes more and more "owned" as people become involved across the organization, community, or stakeholder groups. You will return to meeting this challenge again and again in every phase of the change. It will take place as you use the tried-and-true practice of interviewing. It will continue as you begin recruiting a formal change team. And continue again as you organize group processes, large or small, that involve members from across the organization and stakeholder groups to develop and test new thinking. Eventually the continuing activation in prototyping sessions and visioning will move toward widespread agreement about the new directions.

Activating Awareness goes beyond working with the organizational change leader. Learning and commitment will need to grow until the process becomes more and more "owned" as people become involved across the organization, community, or stakeholder groups.

Assessing Where You Are in the Change

Right here at the beginning of your involvement it is helpful to be keenly aware that the request your client has made and the approach you are beginning to articulate are not the same as the change your client system might actually be experiencing. The outer process structure you are developing is something that will be imposed upon a change that is already unfolding–however early it might be in the process–in order to effectively work

Figure 7.2

ACMP Community Conversation: How To Talk about Change Management?
PDF Report from The Grove—4.14.15

What Is Change Management?

In 2015 the rapidly growing Association of Change Management Professionals asked us, Gisela and David, to facilitate a community conversation around "What Is Change Management?" in a plenary session that involved 800 people for an hour. The point was to step back and activate everyone's awareness of this exploding field.

with it. And often the change has already been under way for some time. In the world we live in today, change is pervasive and going on all the time at different levels, with multiple types of changes interacting. Stepping back will help you be more fully aware of all the influences and forces that will impact your approach. Here are some questions to ask.

- ❑ Is the change needed to continue and make the current status quo more effective?
- ❑ Is your client leaning into something more radical, deeper, perhaps transformational?
- ❑ Has change been going on for a while and your client is just catching up and needs a change process to more effectively guide and channel it?
- ❑ Is your client system or community experiencing a catastrophe that is a true breaking point in a system that had been developing unnoticed for years?
- ❑ Have people entered a true crucible time and is someone needed to steadily hold the container where truly new solutions emerge?
- ❑ Are there multiple changes with cross-conflicting forces and tensions?

You can probably think of more possibilities. The point is to spend time really thinking

Figure 7.3

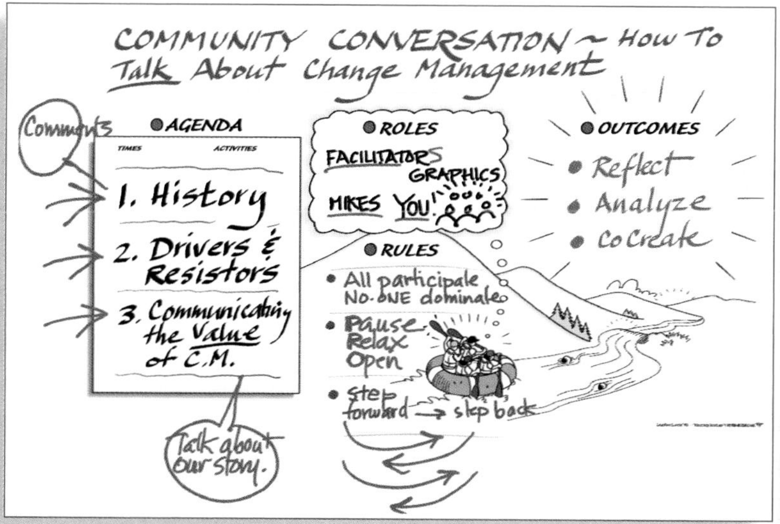

Figure 7.4

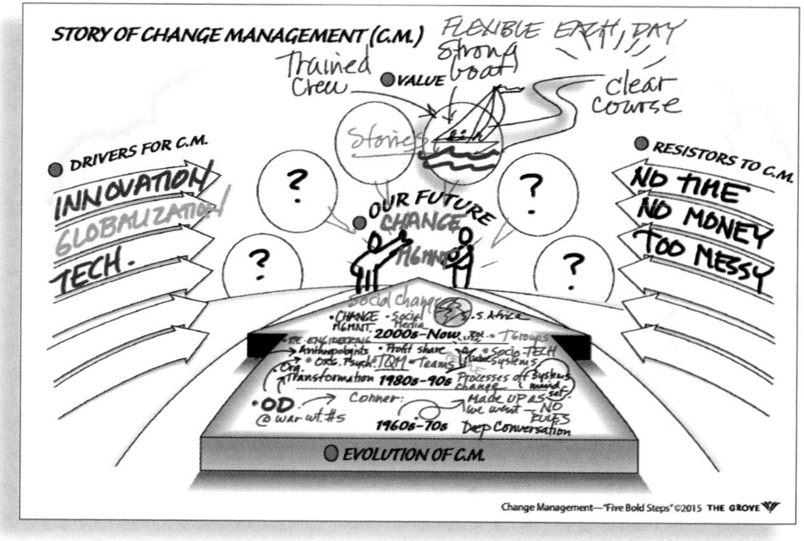

about the change you are stepping into, because it might be bigger than your scoped project, and may well interconnect with related change that are going on.

What Is Change Management?

At our Community Conversation session at the ACMP Conference (see Figure 7.2) our approach was designed to provide three conversations at table rounds in a big hotel ballroom. We used a tablet and projector to record visually. Gisela facilitated and David scribed. The agenda (Figure 7.3) was to take them first through a conversation about the history of the field, then second about what drives organizational leaders to want change management and why they resist, and third about communicating the value of change management (Figure 7.4).

After each conversation at their tables, Gisela invited participants to reflect and David noted answers on a simple template he had on his tablet. The session culminated in a town

Tablet Recordings

These are reproductions of the full-color charts used at the ACMP conference, created on a tablet and projected so 800 people could see them. The one on the left is a Grove Meeting Startup Guide® that we filled out with the agenda. The one on the right is an adaptation of the Five Bold Steps Graphic Guide®. Both are available from Grove Tools, Inc.

Figure 7.5

hall-style sharing of metaphors arising from the table conversation, which David mapped (Figure 7.5).

Metaphors for Framing Change

The ACMP client wanted to explore how their members could easily engage clients in thinking about change management. Our assumption is that how the topic is "framed" is as important as the specific content. If you think change is like a water slide without water you will see different things than someone who sees change management as a birth process. But either could be a great doorway into talking about it further. A visual consultant is one who should be aware of the metaphors they use, those the client uses, and those that might in fact wake people up to looking at something differently.

Change Management Is Like a...

Participants in the ACMP Conference took turns at the microphone to share their metaphors of change, and to raise awareness of the wide range of ways people think about change. The participants were largely internal change managers in larger organizations and not focused on transformational change, but still the differences were striking. The biggest laugh came when someone compared change management to sliding down a water slide without the water. Clearly there is a lot more going on when managing change than clear and orderly processes.

Practice With Your Own Reflections

A useful exercise for activating your own awareness is to work out with the change metaphors on SideStory 7.1, using each as a kind of "frame" through which you look at your client situation. Appreciate that a metaphor does not "work" unless you and the persons you are communicating with both have experience with the metaphor. Some of these may not be meaningful to you or your clients. This itself is important to pay attention to. It is especially important working cross-culturally. Europeans know American's have shown up when they start using sports metaphors. People may not relate to abstract comparisons if the metaphors are drawn from significantly different cultures and knowledge processes. We've brainstormed some common metaphors and associated them with the three kinds of change described in this chapter. You can call these lenses if you

Working Consciously with Metaphors

Pick a couple metaphors from each list and see what you perceive about your change looking through these frames

Circumstantial Change

- ☐ Riding a water slide
- ☐ Greasing the wheels
- ☐ Climbing a mountain
- ☐ Riding waves
- ☐ Seeing crisis as opportunity
- ☐ Funneling the energy
- ☐ Recovering from a heart attack
- ☐ Rising from the ashes
- ☐ Getting back on your feet

Developmental Change

- ☐ Experience the "S" curve from startup to growth to mature forms of organization
- ☐ Organization life spans
- ☐ Birth process
- ☐ Death process
- ☐ Weather cycles
- ☐ Caterpillar to butterfly
- ☐ Ecosystem change
- ☐ Planting, watering, harvesting cycle

Volitional Change

- ☐ Great voyage, journey
- ☐ Seeding a change
- ☐ Having a vision
- ☐ Building a railroad
- ☐ Setting the stage
- ☐ Throwing a big party
- ☐ Winning at the Olympics
- ☐ Traveling to the moon
- ☐ Winning an Oscar

want to use another metaphor. (One of the best resources for understanding metaphors is to read cognitive scientist George Lakoff's classic book, *The Metaphors We Live By*).

Where Are You Stepping In?

We wrote earlier about the three types of change that can initiate a major process. Each type could be at different stages when you are engaged.

Circumstantial change like disasters, deaths, collapses, fragmentation and other events that happen outside your organization or community can have long histories. It might be you are coming into an implementation stage long past when the change was initiated. High-impact circumstantial change can be transformational and the work is about integrating the change over time.

Developmental change happens more slowly, but can be accompanied by jumps in urgency.

Freezing—Unfreezing?

In a time when things are constantly moving and changing, Carl Weick, author of *Making Sense of the Organization*, argues we have to temporarily 'freeze' what is going on so that we can change it and then unfreeze it again. This is a re-frame of a classic OD metaphor used in the late 1940s by the father of social psychology and force-field analysis Kurt Lewin. He argued that to move through change we begin with being in a more frozen state, and unfreeze to change and then refreeze. You decide.

SideStory 7.2

Mapping Your Change Challenge

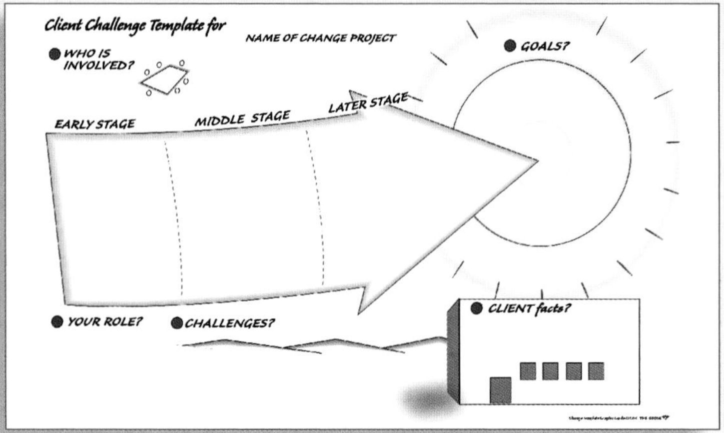

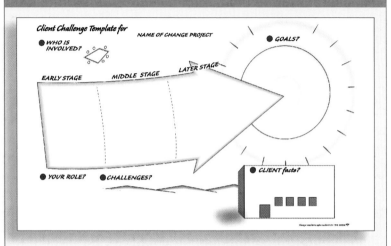

Create a map of what you know about the change you are stepping into in which your project is a part. The framework shown here is an example of what you might create.

1. Identify who you will be working with directly.
2. Identify specific goals for the change drawing from your client talks and proposal.
3. What client facts are relevant?
4. Think through your role here at the beginning.
5. What are the challenges?
6. Map out what you know about the change process already. If it's just beginning you won't have much beyond the early stage. If you are jumping in the middle then there will be more data to map.

UC Merced's need to rapidly grow was developmental. It was moving from a start-up to the high growth staged needed to achieve financial viability and response to a growing number of students. The new direction had already been announced when we began working with Michael Reese (Chapter 4).

Volitional change can be a surprise when leaders announce new aspirations. It may be a change people have worked toward for a while and is just gaining traction with more people needing to be brought along.

It is important to understand what you are stepping into because the change most likely is already under way, and your task as a consultant is paradoxical at this point (SideStory 7.2). It is to work with your client to design a process that moves the change forward and at the same time backtrack sufficiently to be able to set up the outer process structures and all the related activities that are needed to support the engagements and approaches that can bring about lasting change.

Inner Process Dynamics of Activating Awareness

What you know so far about your change project may be biased toward what is visible, talked about, or clear from your direct observation and some research. In the *Seven Challenges of Change* framework we identify some characteristic inner dynamics that may be going on with your client as an organization or community that are important to be aware of and begin working with at this stage. These characteristics, mapped here at the beginning of a change, can continue to be present in subsequent stages as people become aware of and involved in the change

There are several potential inner dynamics that your clients may be experiencing at the start of a change process (Figure 7.6).

- ❑ **Experiencing surprise:** A person's first response to any really new thing that invites change can often be a surprise that throws them off balance. Think about the first time you heard leaders announce that some new direction is being taken in your organization or community. Remember a time when a critical accident happened that ultimately changed everything. People taken by surprise need some time to recover!
- ❑ **Feeling shock/numbness:** If initiating circumstances are threatening in some way, our bodies can shut down in self-defense. This is actually a healthy response in times of overwhelm. Repeated shocks can lead to numbness and disassociation. Be on alert for people or parts of the system that seem to be having this reaction. It takes some time to soften and open up to change. It starts with accepting that this response and having these feelings is normal and even healthy.
- ❑ **Feeling hopeful:** Sometimes new conditions and forces that are inviting change will be welcomed and trigger hopefulness. People might feel excited and perhaps guilty about it. Some might be moving too quickly to imagining "solutions" as a form of denial and a way to bypass the important work that needs to happen during the letting go and in-between stages.
- ❑ **Assessing preparedness**: Some part of us will be thinking about whether or not we are ready for a real change. Do I have the capacity or energy to deal with this change? Do I have the skills to handle this one? Will it be better than the current state? What other options do I have? This kind of self-assessment can occupy a lot of attention.

Figure 7.6

Inner Process Dynamics

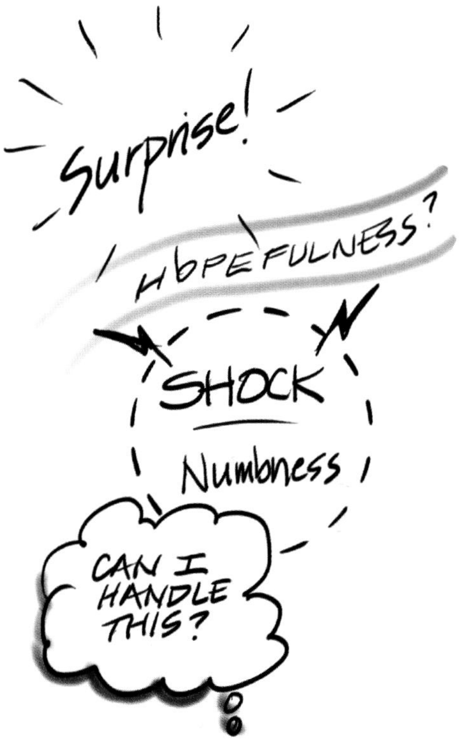

In the beginning when people are just becoming aware of the need to change, they are also stepping into a process of separating from what is familiar and dependable, which includes routines, roles, and sense of self.

Outer Structures Needed for Activating Awareness

In addition to paying attention to potential inner dynamics it is also time to put into play some of the outer structures that can "hold" people during this stage of becoming more aware of the need to change. If you remember our review earlier, traditional rites of passages provide very sophisticated outer structures of support. In any change that your client hopes will be transformational and lasting, this outer structure support is essential and something you will need to ask for. This is a big part of your value as a process consultant.

In the beginning when people are just becoming aware of the need to change, they are also stepping into a process of separating from what is familiar and dependable, which includes routines, roles, and sense of self. Letting go and stepping into the less known and uncertain often challenges people.

You can help by creating environments in which it is safe to express personal concerns. At the same time you'll engage in activities that are part of setting up the outer process structures. Here are some of the fundamental process activities:

1. **Scan for system needs**: It is essential you have some organizational frameworks to draw from that inform how you will explore the change the organization is wrestling with. We will introduce some. (Also see Figure 7.7)

2. **Map the drivers of change:** A change is initiated or influenced by drivers that are internal and external to the organization. Understanding how these act upon the current situation can indicate the direction the change might be unfolding.

3. **Identify stakeholders**: Change needs champions and leaders of change. With your client you need to begin finding out who those people might be, thinking beyond

Figure 7.7

Use Systems Models to Scan

When you are heading into the unknown, using whatever maps you have available can help sharpen your questions and perceptions, as long as you remember that the map is not the territory.

formal leadership to the informal leaders that everyone knows are the experts, gatekeepers, and networkers in the organization. You will do more of this during later challenges, but begin early to get your bearings.

4. **Interview for discovery**: Your initial meeting with the leader provides a single perspective. Scanning expands beyond this by including stakeholder perspectives from across the community or organization, not only functions but often also levels. Including interviews with people who have experiences on the ground can be especially helpful since the leaders of change often do not have that perspective.

5. **Understand and cultivate readiness**: Do people have their attention on the change? Is there energy and motivation? What do they know about what is actually driving the need to change? What resources are available for training or coaching? Are there other projects competing for attention, energy, information, and operational resources.

Tried-and-True Practices for Supporting Activating Awareness

Now lets elaborate each of these structure opportunities with some tried-and-true facilitation and dialogic practices for activating change awareness:

1. Scan for System Needs

You will invariably need more information beyond the initial analysis that informed your proposal. You and the leaders will want to determine the on-the-ground work required and enroll the people who are needed to bring about real change. It is important to step back a bit in order to offset any tendency to lock in too early on your own and the client's biases. If you have a team where your role is one of several consultants, it's also critical to develop a shared understanding of the current situation and what might be possible. In large

Figure 7.8

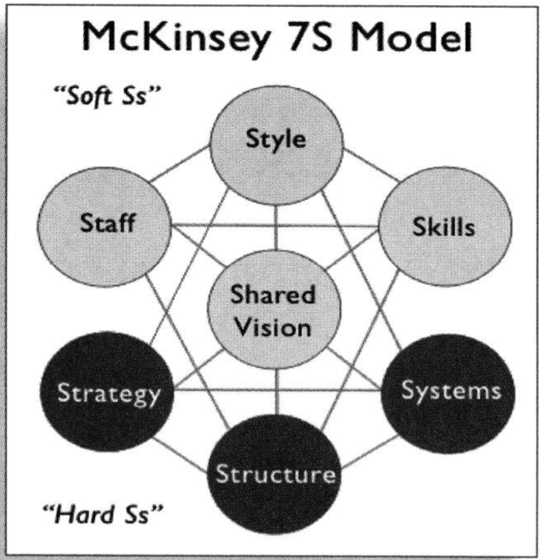

This framework guided the interviews that led to writing *In Search of Excellence* by Tom Peters and Robert Waterman at McKinsey & Company. Another widely used framework is the STAR model. You will notice the features are very similar to the 7S model. Go online to explore these.

Figure 7.9

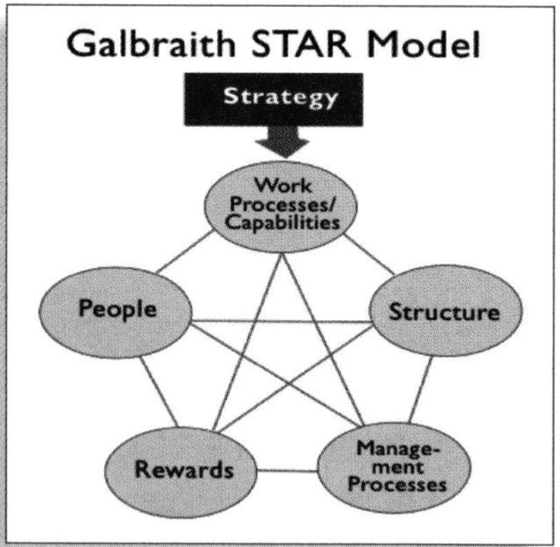

Map Your Issues to a Whole-Systems Framework

1. Draw out one of these frameworks on a large sheet of paper.
2. Go online and see if you can find out more about the distinctions used in the models.
3. Use sticky notes to map out where you think the issues are, drawing insights from early meetings and interviews.

stakeholder processes there might be a much larger group at the beginning that is willing to meet and help with this.

At UC Merced we began identifying issues in the very first meeting with Michael and mapped them out. We continued this process as others became involved in subsequent meetings once we had a contract. While we used the four-flow model to map the types of change projects in the initial meetings, we also drew on other organizational frameworks to understand the needs on a more systemic level. In Figure 7.8, 7.9, 7.10 and 7.11 we identify a few of the classic organizational frameworks. You can use these to generate questions when doing exercises outlined later in the chapter—especially in history telling sessions and context map sessions.

Frameworks for Understanding Organizations

Most consultants have a systems-level framework for asking questions about key aspects of an organization. These insure that one looks at the most relevant and important aspects. Looking at your organization through these more elaborated frames helps you develop a systemic view. Each has their biases, so having a couple of choices is helpful.

Figure 7.10

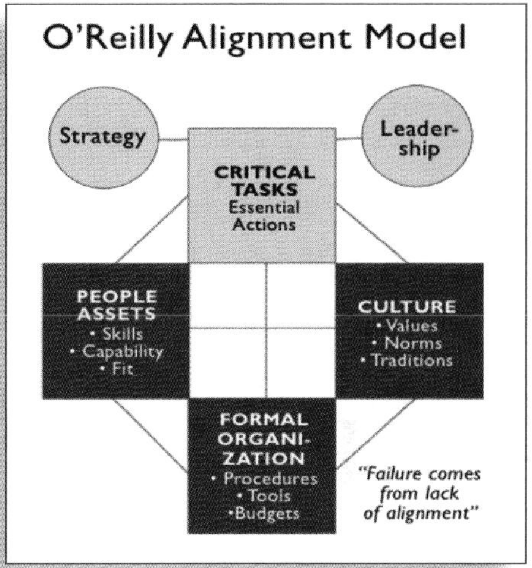

In Search of Excellence was written by Tom Peters and Will Waterman in 1982 and is considered the book that ignited business publishing. The authors used an organizing framework, now called the **7S Model**, to look at three "hard" Ss—strategy, structure, and systems—and three "soft" Ss,—staff, style and skills—with shared vision integrating the elements (see Figure 7.8). You could use these distinctions to guide questions about where issues might exist, or what you know and don't know about the elements. Different organizations prefer different words for these elements. Some organizations prefers the widely used **STAR Model** (Figure 7.9).

Each of these frameworks is an abstract conceptual map. The territory is MUCH more complex and interconnected, but having a light structure will help you frame questions more clearly. You can share the model with a person you are interviewing as well.

Charles O'Reilly, a Stanford Business School professor, emphasizes the problem of non-alignment in his **Alignment Model** (Figure 7.10), which concentrates on the importance of culture. It is leadership's job to identify the most critical tasks and initiatives, using their vision and strategic ideas as a guide. He argues that the biggest reason initiatives (think change processes) fail is that the three dark items don't align to support the critical tasks. "Cultural norms trump strategy," he is fond of saying.

Don Fletcher, the founder of the Coro Center for Leadership in San Francisco, heard from his engineering friends at Stanford that they could completely understand any machine if they answered four questions—what is the load, design, working parts, and fuel? (Figure 7.11). Fletcher applied the **LDWP&F Model** to organizations and it has become a core tool for training young leaders in public affairs to activate their own awareness about organizational dynamics. It includes nonobjective elements like purpose and motivation.

Here are two more frameworks for looking at organizational as whole systems.

Figure 7.11

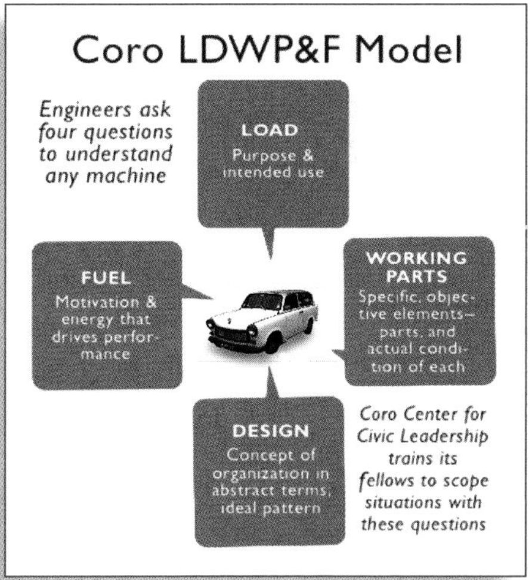

Mapping Driving Forces of Change

Here is a bottoms-up process you can use to begin your discovery process in small groups.

1. Gather some people in the organization you are going to work with and simply ask them what the driving concerns are right now.
2. Put up a piece of paper and get everyone to call out all the key issues (or work on sticky notes—then cluster and arrange them to see patterns).
3. Have people use sticky dots or markers to identify the most important drivers and bring them visually to the foreground.

2. Map Drivers of Change

In any situation there are usually conditions that have people's attention. Sometimes these are called driving forces. The most urgent ones might be called "burning platforms." Other times people will refer to them as "crossroad issues." Crossroads are places in the future that need an agreement on direction in order to decide what to do, like being at a crossroads when traveling. They are different than operational issues that may be big, and even one of the "burning platforms," but not involve a choice about overall direction.

Mapping drivers of change can be done in a number of settings in a number of ways.

- ❑ You can do it **on your own** after initial conversations with organizational leaders.
- ❑ You might visually facilitate a session **with the leader.**
- ❑ Do it as a **structured and facilitated process** with an initial group of stakeholders you might be meeting with (see SideStory 7.3).
- ❑ **Repeat it** in each of these settings and beyond to develop an increasingly fuller picture, which in turn also creates ownership by those becoming involved in the early stages of the change.

A large sticky note wall is the most direct way to identify driving issues, as we described in the California Roundtable on Water & Food Supply case earlier.

Context Mapping

A bit more structured approach than sticky notes is to create a context map of what you know about the relevant environment, working with categories of trends and factors driving change. The Grove Graphic Guide in Figure has been a standard in Strategic Visioning processes and is very flexible. Context mapping is useful early on, and it is also a powerful tool later on in larger meetings where breakout groups can brainstorm and

Figure 7.15

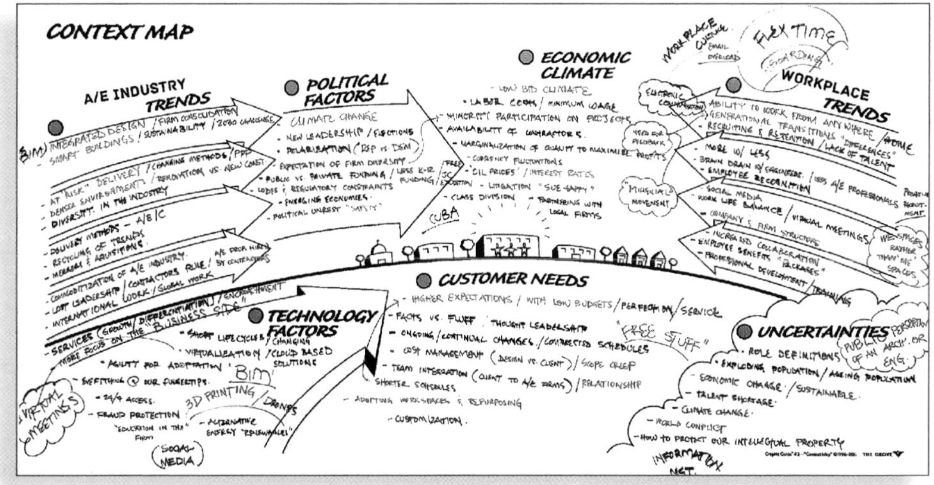

An architectural firm's leaders developed this context map of driving factors and forces.

find themes, coming to their own conclusions about the need to change. Data from this chart becomes input for creating the organization's "case for change," which will then become an important part of communications all the way along.

3. Identify Stakeholders

Another way to begin building a more systemic, cross-functional and cross-level understanding of the change is to do one-on-one or small group interviews. To build a truly systemic picture of change it is important to hear from stakeholders in all the relevant parts of the system. Understanding them will be relevant to setting up your change team and identifying early champions of the change. And the better you understand stakeholders the more you will know when and how to involve them in the change process. So this part of setting up the outer process design is really important.

Creating a stakeholder map is a direct, visual way to do this (see SideStory 7.5). You can create this kind of visual map for yourself to get oriented and think through who is involved in the larger system. Then you could repeat the process during your initial meetings with the primary client and then return to it again and complete it in more detail with the change team. You may work on it yet again as the process grows larger and your understanding evolves.

Following is the description of a way to begin creating your own stakeholder map from what you already know or have discovered in initial meetings with your client. A simple graphic template and process are explained in the exercise.

SideStory 7.4

How to Map the Relevant Context

1. Begin by determining the relevant categories for each area of the map. (The arrows aren't meant to connect with each other but just provide groups of containers for notes.)
2. Write the categories on yellow sticky notes and place them over the categories shown here.
3. Brainstorm issues that relate to the different categories.
4. Have a flip chart nearby so you can add additional categories.

Stakeholder Mapping

To identify people you might interview during a discovery phase of change, create a map of who is involved in this change, like the one here showing stakeholders involved in a regional council planning process.

1. Put the overarching **GOAL** of the project in the center
2. Identify the persons or groups of people who have a stake in the change and write names in the circles.
3. Map their **"INTERESTS"** (stake) on the outside of the circle. Interests could be hopes for gain or concerns about impacts.
4. Map between the circle and the center near the arrows what stakeholders might **CONTRIBUTE** to support the change.

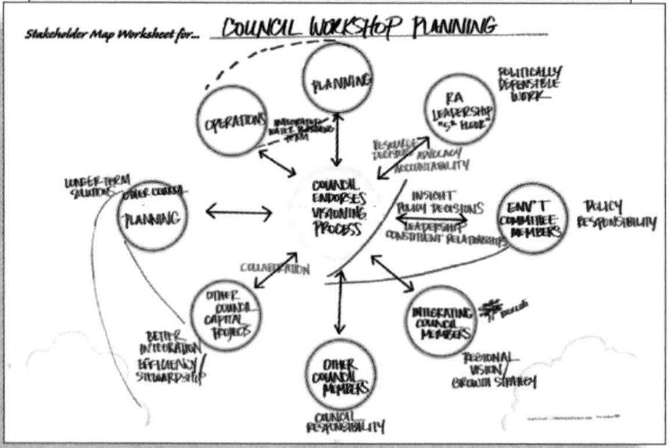

4. Interview for Discovery

Once stakeholders have been identified and you and your client have agreed on who to interview, it is time to prepare for the interviews (see SideStories 7.6 and 7.7). The interviews can achieve several outcomes.

Potential Interview Outcomes

1. **Educating yourself** and those who are involved in this early phase of the change about the client's situation, context, and other issues.
2. **Cultivating readiness** of individuals and the organization.
3. **Beginning the change.** Interviewing initiates the change. You can't begin interviewing without people noticing and talking. The kinds of questions you ask and your way of being with others helps create the kind of relationships that will support change in the long run.
4. **Developing early allies** and identifying potential participants in a change team.

It might be helpful to note here that interviews can be used at different stages in the change process to achieve different results. For example, the client might support you to conduct a day's worth of interviews with organizational leaders to help you become more educated about the organization and the change it is facing. We did this when we began our initial work at UC Merced. Alternatively, you might limit your initial conversation to organization leaders without conducting formal interviews, then set-up a change team and have them cast the net wide and interview a larger cross-section of the stakeholder groups to conduct a thorough organizational scan. The learning that takes place among those organizational members can be exponential and is a powerful tool for expanding perspective, seeing bigger patterns, and achieving systemic insights.

The following guidelines are based on those initially developed by Saul Eisen with his students at Sonoma State University. Saul was one of the founders and long-time directors of the master's program in Organization Development.

Helpful Guidelines for Interviewing Behaviors

Beforehand

- ❑ Arrange for an appropriate **environment**, allowing for comfortable and private conversation.
- ❑ Schedule **sufficient time** to provide opportunity to cover key questions.
- ❑ Prepare an **agenda** and key questions.

During

- ❑ **Greet interviewees with appropriate warmth** and support, appreciating the potential anxiety of the situation.
- ❑ **Clarify the purpose and agenda** for the interview and its part in the larger change process.
- ❑ **Share your role** in the interview and how you would like to be with the person you are talking with.
- ❑ **Describe how your information will be used**. Will it be summarized and presented to your client? Is it for your confidential orientation to the project you're starting? If confidentiality is important, explain that you will share information but not attributions and will not report to anyone else about specific individuals.
- ❑ **Inquire about any questions** or concerns the interviewee may have.

SideStory 7.6

Tips for Engagement During Interviews

- ☐ Engage in **brief, initial small talk** to help interviewee to arrive and connect.
- ☐ Acknowledge any **relevant emerging feelings** being experienced by interviewee, interviewers, and the team.
- ☐ **Follow along with interviewee's free associations** (for a few minutes) to uncover deeper or unexpected perspectives, even though they may not at first seem relevant to the question,
- ☐ Follow up on interviewee's statements to **surface implicit or unstated thoughts** and feelings.
- ☐ Ask interviewee to **slow down or repeat** a statement when information is coming too fast to write down.
- ☐ Periodically **summarize key points**, inviting clarification, additional detail, or correction.
- ☐ Stay with or **return to topics that remain unclear** until they are clarified.
- ☐ **Inquire about key problems** mentioned— any relevant history, and what has been tried so far.
- ☐ **Maintain a neutral stance** with respect to any controversial issues or conflicting camps.

SideStory 7.7

Interview Mistakes

- ☐ **Ignore your own intuition**, or act on it inappropriately.
- ☐ Postpone and **fail to raise clarification questions** or concerns.
- ☐ **Suggest possible problems** not mentioned by interviewee.
- ☐ **Propose possible solutions** to problems described by interviewee.
- ☐ **State or imply agreement with critical statements about others.**

Masterful Behaviors

- ☐ **Communicate relevant observations** about the interview interaction as it's happening.
- ☐ When appropriate, **inquire about incongruities** or contradictions that may lead to clarification or insight.
- ☐ **Modify your own interaction style** to match the client's preferred style of communication, interaction, or learning (e.g., Myers-Briggs preference.)
- ☐ Use the interview process to **begin developing a relationship of mutual trust** by showing congruence and empathy, and inviting the same from the client.

- ❑ **Sustain an informal, friendly tone**, encouraging conversational reflection rather than simple responses to questions.
- ❑ **Start with questions that are easy** for any interviewee to respond to confidently, such as describing the work they do day-to-day.
- ❑ **Ask open-ended questions** that identify a topic for exploration.
- ❑ **Use active listening** extensively to summarize and clarify statements, and to acknowledge stated or implied feelings, asking for validation by interviewee.
- ❑ **Take extensive notes** of interviewee's actual statements in his/her own words, using a first-person form.
- ❑ **Conclude by acknowledging the interviewee's contribution** of useful information and thank him/her for helping. Perhaps show consideration for interviewee's need to provide valid contributions to the change process.

Afterward

- ❑ **Review notes immediately**, clarify illegible writing, and fill in any missed statements or words.
- ❑ **Debrief with interview partner**(s) immediately after each interview, considering what worked well and what may need to be changed for the following interviews.
- ❑ **Send a thank-you**, potentially add some information about next steps.

5. Understand & Cultivate Readiness

Remember that one of the inner dynamics of this challenge is people wondering if they are up to the challenge of change (see SideStory 7.8). They may be wondering if they have the skills, motivation, and stamina. Your decisions about how many people to involve initially and whether you need more client meetings and informal conversations all flow from your assessment of the readiness of the system. Systems in shock or the doldrums may take a lot of time to activate. If the system is diverse you will need to explore more. In community work, early involvement of people is crucial in building a constituency for change. The same might be true in larger organizational systems. One organization that was very successful at rehabilitating neighborhoods and developing local leadership would take a year with a community organizer just to identify the people that ought to be invited to the first kickoff workshop.

Remember that all of the interviews and initial meetings you hold are chances to cultivate understanding and readiness for change and what it takes to succeed. It really helps with readiness to encourage people to think ahead and imagine what is coming. The purpose of the *Liminal Pathways* and *Seven Challenges* frameworks is to support you, the consultant, with imagining ahead of your client. Having practices to suggest is also important.

Beyond Activating Awareness

Our next chapter deals with the challenge of engaging change leaders from across the organization to continue to build the case for change, initiate a backbone infrastructure for the change, and more.

You will use the practices shared in this chapter again and again as you add people to a change process. This is how new people are activated about the change and how the core stories of how to move forward are shaped.

Visual consultants use the versions of stakeholder maps, drivers of change maps, context maps, roadmaps, and other visuals to both catalyze conversations and begin to develop a change narrative that captures the evolution and alignment of ideas. As the charts and

SideStory 7.8

DxVxA>R Change Formula

In change work a widely used mental model is the **DxVxA>R** change formula. It works well for people who want to understand where you are going in a simple story line.

The letters stand for the words **DISSATISFACTION** times **VISION** times **ACTIONS** being greater than **RESISTANCE**.

The practices in this chapter you just read will help you with the D—creating a case for change and being clear about the drivers of dissatisfaction.

But this is not enough for people to change, the formula suggests. People also need a vision of what's possible and they need a plausible action plan.

Developing a coherent story that includes these elements is what a change process can achieve in the early stages. The change team holds the process that makes this possible.

Summary of Activating Awareness

You have a dual role of raising your own awareness and activating the clients. There are things you should attend to:

- ☐ Your project is **enmeshed in larger and multilayered change**.
- ☐ **Metaphors can "frame" how you talk and think about change.** Practice with different ones to stretch your thinking.
- ☐ **Pay attention to the inner dynamics** of surprise, shock, hopefulness, and questions about readiness.
- ☐ **Support the process with these outer structures**
  1. **Scan for system needs**
  2. **Map drivers of change—use context mapping**
  3. **Identify stakeholders**
  4. **Interview for discovery**
  5. **Understand and cultivate readiness**

images go through additions and improvements, they function like a kind of social software, and become the language of the transformation. V1.0 becomes V2.0 becomes V2.5. The value of applying design thinking and doing early drafts becomes obvious. Of course there are settings and cultures where a computer metaphor would not be the correct frame at all. But the repetition and ongoing conversations that are needed will be part of any change, anywhere.

As organizational change theory increasingly focuses on the role of narratives to understand how social systems function and evolve, it has become apparent that any organization change includes at least shifting one of the organization's core narratives. Using a visual and iterative approach supports the evolution of these narratives. The new narratives may be about what the change is bringing in the future, but they also can be about how the organization is actually changing now.

8. Engaging Change Leaders

The Role of Process Design Teams

At UC Merced, Michael Reese agreed that having leaders of the 70 change projects become the process design team for the change alignment process made a lot of sense. He moved quickly and invited several dozen people. We were surprised, pleased, and concerned all at the same time. Twenty-four people is too many to involve meaningfully in a group that would be designing this change alignment process. By the same token many of the key leaders in the university were included in his suggestions.

This is the kind of challenge that will push you, as a visual consultant working on change, to be creative. We were, and the resulting formation of an advisory group in addition to the change team made a difference. But before going on with this story, let's step back and think about what we consultants might pay attention to at this stage (Figure 8.1).

Figure 8.1

The Inner Dynamics of Engaging Change Leaders

We anticipated that the different project leaders Michael requested to join would not only have a wide spectrum of capabilities but also a range of attitudes and feelings about this assignment (Figure 8.2). The leaders had a lot at stake given the urgency and competing priorities. They may not even have had time yet to recognize what was going on for them internally. The way Michael talked about the project's scale and the aggressiveness of the timeline led us to assume that a great deal of inward pondering might be going on for each one of these leaders. We knew that the people sitting around the table were themselves beginning an inner journey through change. Therefore we anticipated some inner dynamics like the following:

We knew that the people sitting around the table were themselves beginning an inner journey through change.

- ❑ **Facing fears or inadequacy:** Would anyone feel a lack of confidence in themselves or others to adequately meet the challenge? What kind of things might they be afraid would happen? Would they have the skills and bandwidths to productively contribute? Would they say what was missing from their team?

Figure 8.2

Change Leaders Meet at The Grove

The UC Merced change leaders held their first meeting at The Grove Consultants International main office in the Presidio of San Francisco. Michael and Erik were joined by key faculty, staff, and operational change project leaders. They were delighted to find a name for what we proposed as the process design team. "Let's be the Change Alignment Team or CAT." Delightfully it resonated with their school mascot, the Bobcat!

Here Gisela is facilitating Erik's sharing a bit about how he came to be working with The Grove with the rest of the group.

❑ **Accepting uncertainty**: Many things were not in place for a big change like this. Would they be ready to take the steps needed given the complexity and evolving nature of their task? Could they plan with so much in limbo? Could they come to see this ambiguity as normal in a change?

❑ **Having strong feelings:** For some this invitation to help with process design would be exciting and a "break." For others it might trigger past experiences of failure or lack of trust in teamwork and faith in the leaders. There might be relationship issues. All this and more could be going on inside and would not be immediately clear to either of us or to the other participants, but they assuredly would be there. We feel it is wise to be prepared for a wide range of inner dynamics to be present.

Ways to Support Your Team with Outer Structures

We knew we needed to create a strong container for the process. We focused on five things that we believe are fundamental in supporting engagement of change leaders.

1. **Recruit a process design team:** Not all consulting processes have a process design team or change team, as it is also sometimes referred to. John Kotter, well-known

author of *Leading Change*, calls it a guiding coalition. Regardless of your preferred name, your first job is getting people involved and finding champions.

2. **Contract with leaders**: You have a formal contract most likely, but now you need to make clear, social agreements around roles, guiding principles, and operational logistics. Think of social contracting as a way of shaping a productive relationship, one that you contract for now, and then again in later stages as the relationship and the project evolves and may require different types of engagement.
3. **Create a safe environment for exploration**: It's essential early on to dig down into what is really going on and be clear about both challenges and opportunities. You will find that there will be different levels of readiness to be open and to explore possibilities. Much of this depends on the culture you find yourself in. Some are tough and judgmental—basically unsafe. Others are wonderfully people-oriented and supportive. In either case the social contract you help develop will make it safer.
4. **Initiate a collaboration backbone**: Because process design teams and change teams working on a new initiative usually have not worked together like this before, they are actually operating in organizational white space (outside the formal structures of the organization). This means they need a new kind of infrastructure to do the things that have not been done before.
5. **Set patterns and pace**: A consulting process that happens over time with many different meetings and communications needs a cadence and pace, just like musicians who work in groups need drummers. It also needs what one of our colleagues likes to call a "liturgy." This is a predictable pattern of how meetings are handled and rituals that mark certain progressions. This can extend beyond meetings. For example, a reliable drum beat of communications going out about the change project makes others aware and stabilizes the new project in the system. It's more important to have a reliable pattern and pace than to have any one in particular. But it is critical to have one that you and the organization can sustain.

It's essential early on to dig down into what is really going on and be clear about both challenges and opportunities. You will find that there will be different levels of readiness to be open and to explore possibilities.

SideStory 8.1

Principles for Engaging a Change Team

If your consulting project requires a process over time that will involve a lot of people, having a core group to help you is essential for success. Here are some guidelines to apply:

- ☐ **Work for a diversity of perspectives,** ideally representing all relevant parts of the system the change will impact
- ☐ **Seek "voices," not representatives.** Collaborative processes jam up if people have to check with constituents before making decisions.
- ☐ **Look for strong, informal leaders.** Read about the roles Malcolm Gladwell says make a difference (SideStory 8.2)). Find the trusted people.
- ☐ **Keep formal leaders involved.** Find ways to help them own the process, provide support, and model the change.
- ☐ **Reflect the whole system.** In many cases it is critical to involve the people who are often ignored. Find ways either on the change team or during key meetings to involve them.
- ☐ **Involve people with change experience** in the system you are working with. It helps to have internal colleagues.

1. Recruit a Process Design (or Change) Team

At UC Merced, Michael jumped in right away and picked a couple dozen people to become part of the process design team. With some further discussion about its role and function, we coached Michael to choose individuals who could really dedicate themselves to the work, and it was decided to use the remainder of the group as advisors. In your consulting you could well face a variety of recruiting preferences from clients.

- ❑ Members are appointed by internal leaders
- ❑ Persons volunteer to be on the change team
- ❑ People are actively recruited
- ❑ Leadership becomes the process design team

There isn't a set formula for finding and selecting people, however we found that the principles of engagement listed in SideStory 8.1 to be helpful. In the 1990s when many organizations were re-engineering to take advantage of new technologies, technology consultants ran into the fact that behavior change can often be the more difficult part of the projects. This is when change management became more popular with its emphasis on buy-in through well-designed engagement processes.

People Make Change

Our operating belief is that for a system to change, the people need to change, and the change team will become the "beating heart." Set apart from the regular organization, it operates in the organizational white space we referred to earlier. It becomes the incubator for the new organization and can model new norms. It carries the seeds of the new organization. The more the change team is a real microcosm of the organization, the better, for its changes will ripple to the many people they are connected with.

Law of the Few

Malcolm Gladwell in *The Tipping Point* articulates what he calls "The Law of the Few." He writes, "The success of any kind of social epidemic is heavily dependent on the involvement of people with a particular and rare set of social gifts." According to Gladwell, economists call this the 80/20 Principle, which is the idea that in any situation roughly 80 percent of the "work" will be done by 20 percent of the participants. He identifies the kinds of people that usually make up this 20% in organizations. These are often informal leaders and are critical to involve in the early stages of change. They help bring along everyone else to have the change be lasting.

- **Connectors:** Networkers with large numbers of friends and contacts.
- **Mavens:** The information specialists and acknowledged experts.
- **Salespersons**: The persuaders and spokespersons.

In 2000 Malcolm Gladwell wrote *The Tipping Point: How Little Things Can Make a Difference*, a best-selling popularization of research in epidemiology, sociology, psychology, and group dynamics about change. He reflects a whole field of social network analysis where people have been using computers to map influence networks. The nodes in these networks are often not those in formal leadership roles. In organizational change work, for instance, the internal administrative assistants are critical conduits of information and access. Their networks inside are the ones that are often central to keeping everything running smoothly. In factory settings, workers who really know the machines and their foibles are essential.

2. Contract with Leaders

At UC Merced once Michael approved our formal contract, we immediately needed to get clear on the particulars of how we would work together with him and Erik. We had begun to set up a learning relationship in our initial meetings, which we described in Chapter 4, but now we needed to get specific. How would we stay connected? How much review of agendas and other communications should they have? How was Erik's role different from Michael's? How did the change team interface with the University cabinet? Where did Michael's top-level authority as vice chancellor of business administration fall?

Some of this we worked out with Michael and Erik on calls and others with the CAT team as a whole. Getting clear and communicating about what you need to do your best work is as important as hearing about your client needs (Figure 8.3). Here is what we addressed:

1. **Staying connected with the formal project leaders:** It was critical to get agreement on regular calls with Michael and Erik, especially before every CAT team meeting. Substantial progress was made in these check-in meetings as we aligning on agendas, confirmed decisions, explored options, and shared concerns about the process.

Figure 8.3

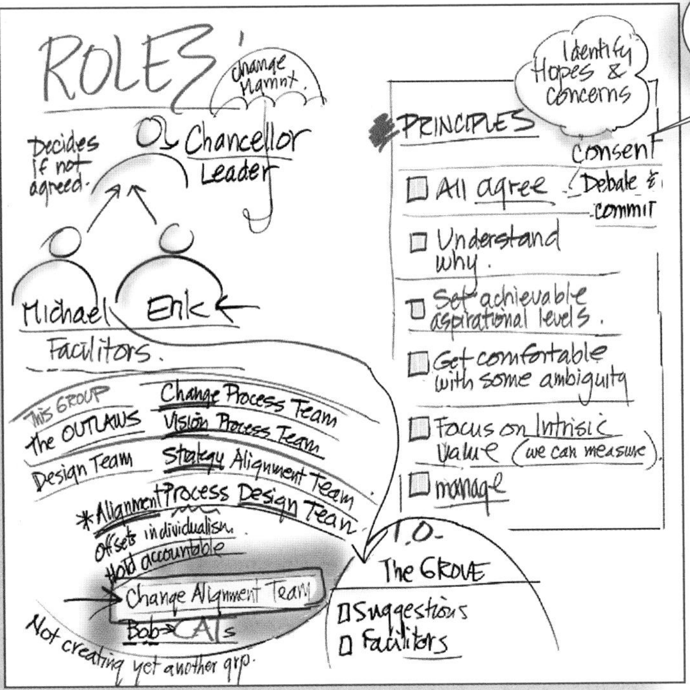

SEE FIGURE 8.4 FOR THE 2ND DRAFT OF PRINCIPLES IN THE SAME MEETING

Design Team Roles

This chart shows how David recorded the conversation about roles and our first pass at operating principles. The little diagram shows Michael and Erik directly reporting to the chancellor, and they, and then she, deciding if we couldn't agree by consensus. This chart also shows how they came up with the CAT name.

2. **Final decision authority**: We intended to work as process consultants with group consensus as the primary way of making decisions. But since time pressure was a big feature in this project, we also knew that from time to time we would need Michael and Erik to use their authority to converge on decisions. The chancellor had put them in charge of the project. When asked what would happen if they didn't agree, Michael and Erik would involve the chancellor. When so much else is uncertain in a change process, especially at the beginning, it is important to minimize uncertainty where possible. This clarity in the decision-making process was not only helpful to us but to the whole CAT team.
3. **Advisory board involvement**: We agreed with Michael that the advisory team, including the provost, stay involved as another resource for input when needed.
4. **Formal leadership role**: Within the CAT team we had a mix of Cabinet members and managers. In spite of differences in management levels the team worked by consensus.

"WOULD IT BE OKAY TO SHARE MY PERSPECTIVE ON THIS?"

5. **More than facilitative**: We consultants needed to clearly agree that while we were going to be facilitative, it would also be okay to offer our observations and suggestions, especially given that we both had extensive experience relevant to their situation. A good practice is to ask for permission when making substantiative contributions. It is a great tool for lowering resistance.

In some settings it is beneficial to write a memorandum of understanding that summarizes agreements. In the case of UC Merced we worked on our agreements during the first two meetings and included them in our reports. Getting clear how you will work together with the group adds certainty when so much else seems up for grabs. It is also useful to inquire

Figure 8.4

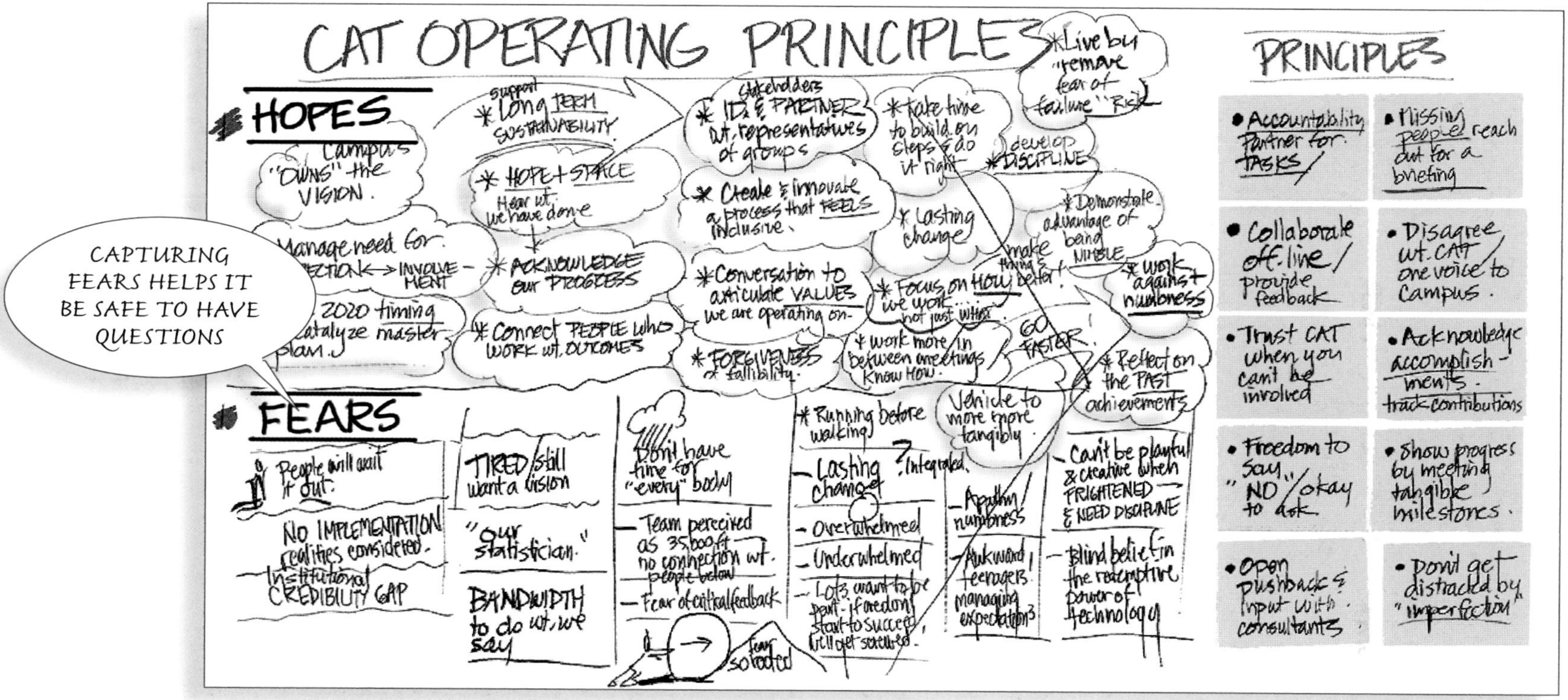

about what could go sideways and what kinds of behavior does not work in whatever culture you are entering, whether you are an external consultant, or an internal working in another function. Every organization or community is distinct. Don't assume that your way of working will automatically transfer. Ask questions. Imagine scenarios. Share hopes and fears (illustrated here in Figure 8.4). We did this with the UC Merced change team. Some powerful operating principles emerged that deepened the team's commitment. We returned again and again to these as we progressed through the process.

Operating Principles

We developed operating principles based on group members sharing their hopes and fears about their project. Once these were collected, the guidelines addressed the concerns and supported the hopes. Compare the principles on the preceding page to the ones here to see how they can evolve with dialogue and facilitation.

Figure 8.5

Group Portrait Charts

Visualizing your change team members in a seating chart is a great way to do introductions. In this one for the CAT we asked them to describe their jobs, and the number of years at UC Merced. There are many variations you can do with this. This was on a flip chart. If you work bigger you can add other information that would be useful to share. The unconscious message in this manadala format graphic is "we are unified, we are one," even if the team is just forming.

3. Create a Safe Environment for Exploration

A key part of engaging leaders of change is to make sure your initial meetings are fun, productive, and memorable, even if the challenges are big. When people understand why they are in a meeting or on a team, who they are meeting with, what they are doing, and how they will do it, they can relax a bit and enter into the work (Figure 8.5).

All the understood dynamics of teamwork come into play as you gather your process design team. David's book, *Visual Teams,* explains a team performance model and many practices that are worth studying if you are a visual consultant who works extensively with team development.

For change work where you really need to engage people in owning the process, the physical orientation of the meeting is a critical place to begin forging the agreements that will shape the team. (Are tables round or square; is there light?) It is also the place where you can begin bringing forward new norms for behavior and actually engage the process design team in taking on the role of being a microcosm of the future. They may not get this right away, but it's worth continuing to make that invitation and support its emergence.

Design Clear Processes for Your Meetings

Let us return to the UC Merced story to uncover a range of things we did that represent tried-and-true visual consulting practices. We began using a well-tested framework called OARRs, an acronym that stands for Outcome, Agenda, Roles, and Rules (see Figure 8.6). It is reinforced by the metaphor of being on a river in a boat and manning the oars to have control and fun. The format evolved from work at a large multinational company. It wanted to train all their personnel and IT people in meeting facilitation, team development, and change in a focused workshop offered by a newly created central training and development unit. The leader was very focused on being successful and wanted to know what the basic essentials were for a good meeting. We suggested four:

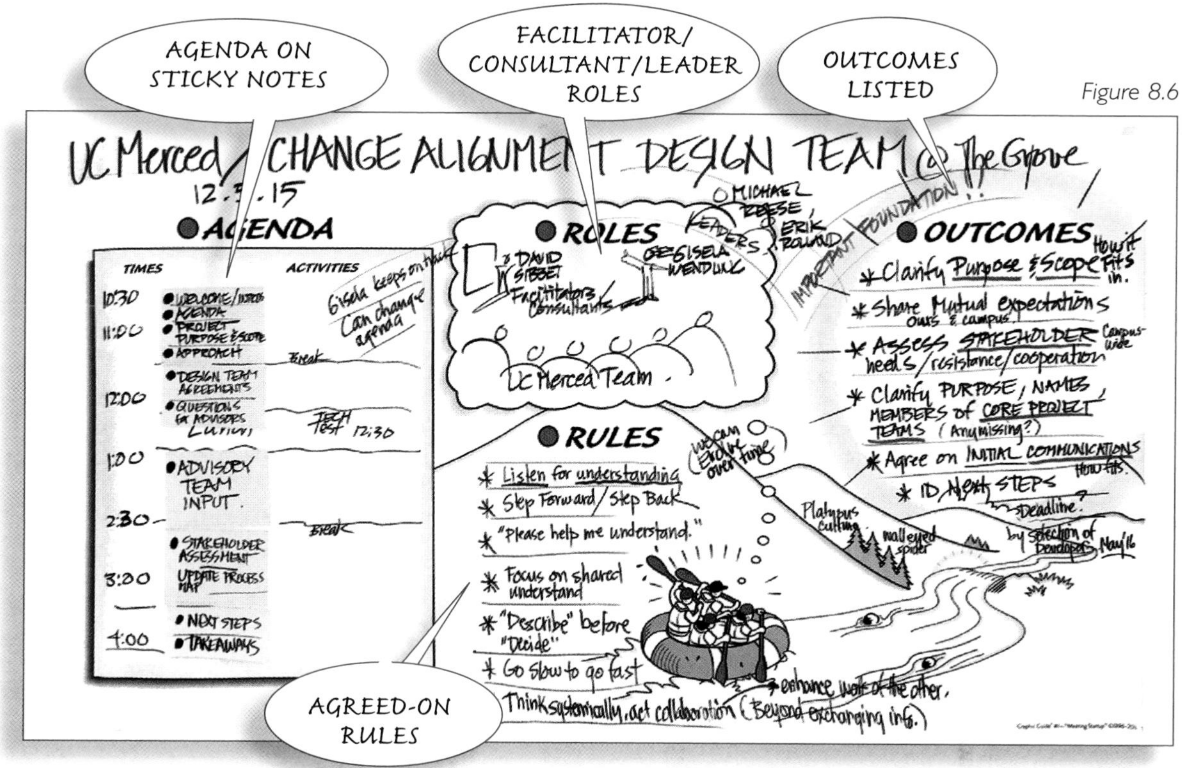

Figure 8.6

1. **Outcomes**: A clear indication of what you would like to see accomplished by the end of the meeting (horizon).
2. **Agenda:** A chart of the meeting topics and activities and times (the boat).
3. **Roles:** A summary depiction of the roles different participants will play (first oar).
4. **Rules:** Guiding principles and ground rules for handling what you anticipate to be challenges in the meeting, or behaviors that would help it succeed. These are often left blank and developed with the group (second oar).

Since its development, this framework has consistently gone viral in organizations that begin standardizing on being clear about OARRs in their meetings. At UC Merced its repeated use was one of the patterns we created that gave a sense of order to a very dynamic process. Some of the kinds of agreements on rules that will help create a safe environment are described in SideStory 8.3. It's important to frame these not only as rules but also as guiding principles and rules-of-thumb.

Meeting Start-Up Guide

This chart helped visually orient the UC Merced CAT team in their first meeting. David and Gisela jointly reviewed the items, which were worked out in preliminary agenda calls with Michael and Erik as our primary clients. This format is so popular that The Grove ended up making preprinted graphic templates called Graphic Guides® to support consultants who don't draw a lot but still work visually.

SideStory 8.3

Set Good Ground Rules for Generative Meetings

Here are a some agreements and prompts about group process that we have found to be useful over and over.

- ☐ **Listen for understanding:** If you don't ask "tell me more."
- ☐ **Check assumptions:** Keep an open mind. Ask questions and be curious.
- ☐ **Step forward/step back**: Contribute your ideas and then make room for others.
- ☐ **Challenge ideas, not people**: Practice good negotiation skills--be firm on the issues and friendly to the people.
- ☐ **Describe before deciding**: Spend time understanding before solving.
- ☐ **Take time to pause and reflect**: This is the key to our group learning.
- ☐ **All participate, no one dominate:** "If you are used to dominating, do it in the interests of listening."
- ☐ **It's okay to correct the charts** (and suggest what to write and draw).
- ☐ **For brainstorming, use the rules of improv**: Simple frame, Yes/And, 100%.
- ☐ **As we converge, make proposals.** Shift from discussion to action proposals.
- ☐ **Work by consensus**—"I can work with this."

Setting Good Ground Rules

The purpose of establishing ground rules, and at a more general level, guiding principles (like those noted earlier for the CAT) is to set up an environment where it is easier for people to explore new ideas. At the core of generative dialogue is testing assumptions, consider other perspectives, and not jumping to conclusions. You need to support having room for the possibility of divergent and bigger picture thinking.

Most managers are trained to focus on the problems right in front of them and get rewarded for having solutions. Moving from problem solving to an exploratory mode needs to be explicit and is supported by visual processes. In other kinds of settings, like community meetings, people might be used to forceful advocacy. In this case, visualization separates the points from the person and people feel heard and more willing to engage.

The facilitator helps these ground rules to come alive in the group by modeling them. So does the recorder by how openly he or she invites elaboration and correction of the charts. Process leaders should model listening, slowing down, really being inclusive, and making sure all voices are heard. Genuine curiosity, respect for the complexity of everyone's inner processing, and willingness to accept suggestions directly affects how trusting the group becomes. Seeing comments written down helps with validation, but by itself isn't enough.

Introducing "Preventions"

If you can name and talk about potential problems in advance of a real incident while setting ground rules, you can often prevent undesirable behavior. For instance, the ground rule of "all participate and no one dominate" (see SideStory 8.3) provides an opening to say something like "I don't know who of you is a natural dominator, but if you are, dominate in the direction of listening." The laughter helps the group both understanding the point and avoid the problem.

Figure 8.7

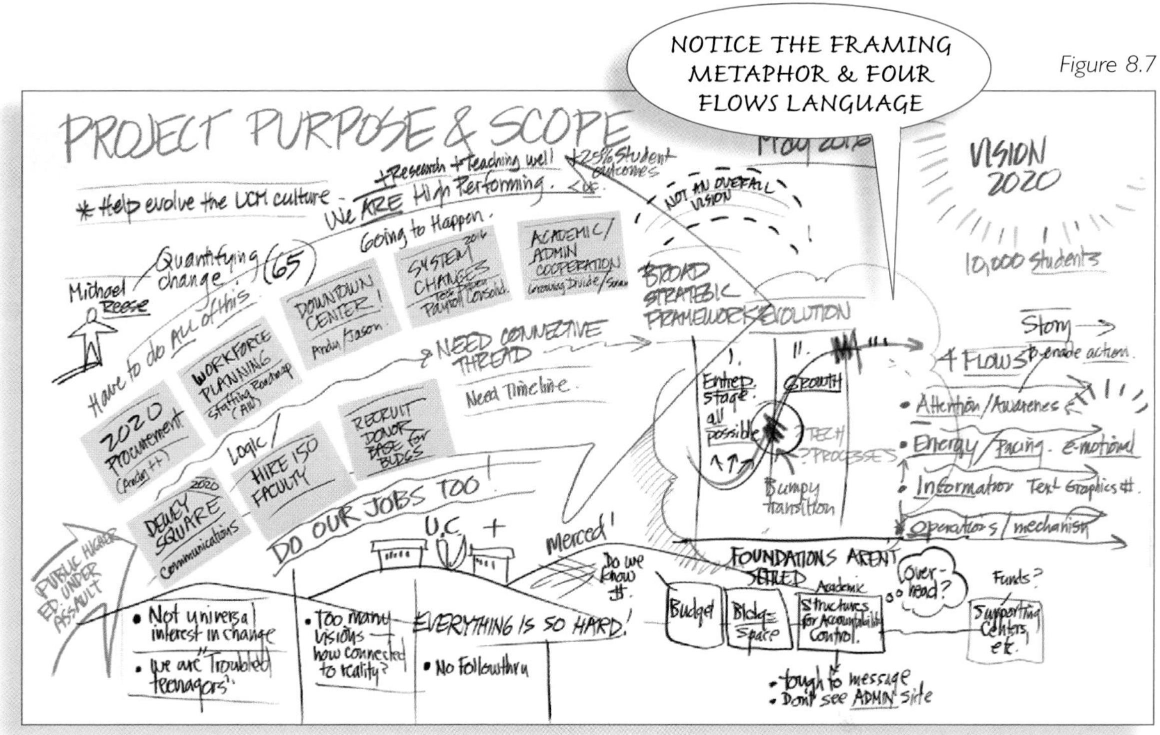

At the beginning of every meeting go over the agreements you have set and check if they need to be updated.

Clearly Frame the Purposes & Patterns of Change

Because the early stages of change can be filled with uncertainty and strong feelings, it helps a great deal to have leaders of the process take some time at the beginning to frame the issues and the overall potential of the project. In the case of UC Merced we made sure Michael and Erik led off the first meeting with the overview illustrated. This is also an excellent time to use visual facilitation. The impact of leaders sharing directly, without slides, but still having the key ideas mapped out in a memorable form, is to create both clarity and some excitement. Slides tend to reduce the energy of the group, as the look and feel is often too polished or predictable and therefore invites less engagement or a sense that something is fresh and evolving. Visual facilitation is not only active energetically, but leaves behind charts that can stay visible continuously, allowing people time to soak in their meaning.

Enactment as Modeling the Change

In this and following meetings, we continually looked for chances to turn over the orienting and sense-making parts of the meetings to the CAT team. In preparing to orient the team

Review Purpose & Scope

This chart shows Michael's review of the top-level change projects that need alignment over a landscape of challenges. Erik shared a framework of the "S" Curve to introduce the idea that UC Merced was moving from a startup to a growth culture, and the transition would be bumpy, and that the uncertainty and confusion was completely normal and part of what the change team should embrace. David also introduced the Four Flows idea to provide the group some common language for process.

in the first meeting, Michael was already thinking hard about the priorities he faced, and you can see how the story of what is most important to focus on is literally evolving. You can track this evolution if you compare the first charts (Figures 4.1 and 4.5) to the one on the previous page (Figure 8.7), and then to the later versions of the big-picture strategy map, a fulfillment of Michael's original interest. (Figure 10.17).

As you will come to understand in the later challenges of actualizing change, unless you cultivate process and change leadership from the very start, you have a good chance of seeing your work come to naught as energy wanes and no one feels responsible for ongoing work and renewal.

Every meeting has opportunities for involving people in this process..

1. **Have leaders review desired outcomes of meetings.**
2. **Draw people out to be active contributors** by asking questions.
3. **Use dyads and small groups** to generate more ideas and support diverse thinking.
4. **Encourage members to introduce new ideas** and practices for the process itself.
5. **Introduce visualization activities** that get everyone moving and thinking big-picture.

As we have been stressing all along, the critical distinction between process consulting and expert consulting is how much you insist on the client not only being involved but taking on leadership in the process. As you will come to understand in the later challenges of actualizing change, unless you cultivate process and change leadership capacity from the very start, you have a good chance of seeing your work come to naught as energy wanes and no one feels responsible for ongoing work and renewal.

The Importance of Meeting Venues

Having our first CAT meeting at The Grove's offices in the Presidio of San Francisco created a different kind of environment – inviting possibility thinking. Not only were people away from the campus and the triggers of regular work, the Presidio is a park near the ocean. The round table and natural sunlight and a room with great space of visualizing made it a wonderful environment. In later meetings at UC Merced we worked to convert regular classrooms into settings with "U" or square-shaped table set-ups to preserve a more circular feeling. Some of the new meeting rooms in a new building had wonderful glass walls for posting charts. There are always challenges around venue, but it makes a difference having a nice one that invites more open, informal behavior as people are getting to know each other. Natural light makes a huge difference if you can arrange it.

4. Initiate a Collaboration Backbone

The term "collaboration backbone" was first introduced to describe an array of activities that enable large multisector stakeholder change initiatives to be effective. This ranges from developing a guiding vision and strategy, building processes that align thinking and activities, growing will and momentum, funding, and policy development. We have come to use this term also in smaller scale settings, when a series of stakeholders work together for the first time. Learning to function in organizational white space can actually support the process design team to be freer of prevailing norms and attitudes that might prohibit creativity, boldness, and sense of safety in every-day work settings.

In direct proportion to how dynamic and even chaotic a change consulting project may be, it is important to have a clear infrastructure everyone can count on. In sailing, it is the stability of the keel of the boat that allows for flexibility in the sails. In business the strength of your accounting disciplines allows managers to plan and optimize resources. In community work, a roadmap like the Presidio Conversion Process shown in Chapter 4 assures people that there is some structure and grounding for the process. SidesStory 8.4 presents some of the elements to keep in mind.

Working Remotely

Increasingly, process design and change teams have to work remotely. With UC Merced

SideStory 8.4

Elements of a Collaboration Backbone

It is helpful to put the following elements in place as you begin a project, especially when working with many stakeholders.

- ☐ **DISTINCT VISION & STRATEGY** that provides consistent direction
- ☐ **STANDARD, REPEATING PROCESSES** that align thinking and activities.
- ☐ **ROADMAP and MILESTONES** that evolves and keeps people oriented.
- ☐ **COMMUNICATION PLATFORMS** that everyone agrees to use, including video, web, and document sharing
- ☐ **SUPPORT STAFF** than can schedule meetings, send reminders and notifications, and help coordinate documentation.
- ☐ **FACILITATION TEAM** for working meetings. If you don't facilitate a lot then team with someone who does.
- ☐ **DOCUMENTATION** protocols, storage and access.
- ☐ **WEBSITE or NEWSLETTER** for broader involvement and communication.

Figure 8.8

IT LOOKS LIKE WE MAY NEED TO WORK ON THE VISION AS WELL

we introduced having a video conference call in the very first CAT team meeting, to involve the advisory board members, and give us the opportunity to have virtual and visual meetings going forward (Figure 8.8). Part of our collaboration backbone as visual consultants is working remotely.

Graphically Recorded Video Conference

The CAT moved to The Grove's Fireplace room for this Advisory Board call. We used zoom to connect, and Smartboard to project the conference. The room is also set up for good audio.

Figure 8.9

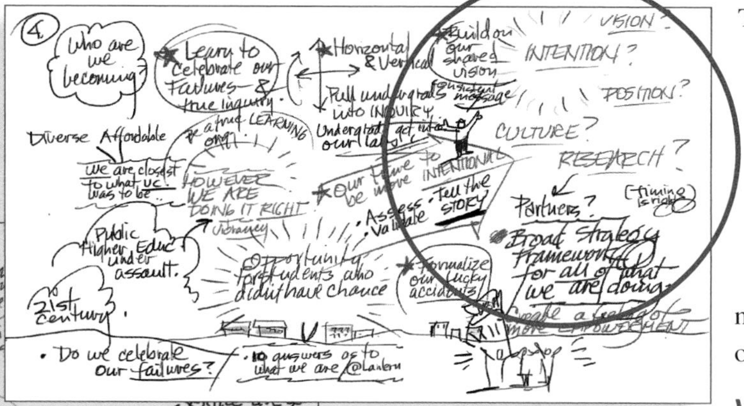

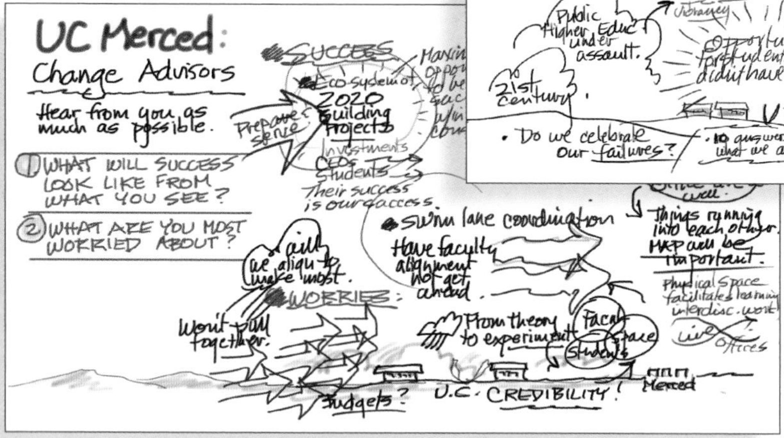

The advisory meeting graphics on this page were produced by David working on a laptop and a small graphics tablet while Gisela was facilitating. The reproductions (Figure 8.9) are from digital files produced by a sketching program. (There are now many options for making online graphic recordings.)

What About the Vision?

This initial meeting precipitated a significant shift in scope as the CAT inquired about the advisors' hopes and concerns about the change alignment project. "We also need to tell our story and build our vision," they said. It began to be clear to the CAT that if they did not have an overarching vision for the university beyond doubling its size it might be difficult to align on and prioritize the change projects. (The area circled on Figure 8.9 captured these comments.) This insight led Michael, with the support from the CAT, to invite the chancellor to a meeting with us several weeks later to explore the possibility of developing a vision of the university as essential to the developmental change they were in, and help shape the change alignment framework. (We will describe the vision process in Chapter 9.)

Roadmapping the UC Merced Project

The afternoon of the initial UC Merced CAT meeting was spent reviewing the roadmap we had included in our proposal, and helping the CAT understand that we needed to rework it based on their sense of what was really possible and needed given what they currently knew. Creating and using it as a guide for action would be one of their most important jobs, along with being those responsible for delivering a change alignment framework.

A process roadmap is not the same as a detailed plan for a project. To work well it needs to be high-level enough that it provides a framing story for the process, and communicates enough about organization and structure that people are willing to enter into the process and participate. There are three elements that tell the story in words. These are:

1. **Name of the Roadmap**: This should clearly express the purpose of the process.
2. **Title for the Phases**: These should substantively describe what is happening in three to five chunks, not more.
3. **Names of the Work Streams**: These should also seem clear and logical.

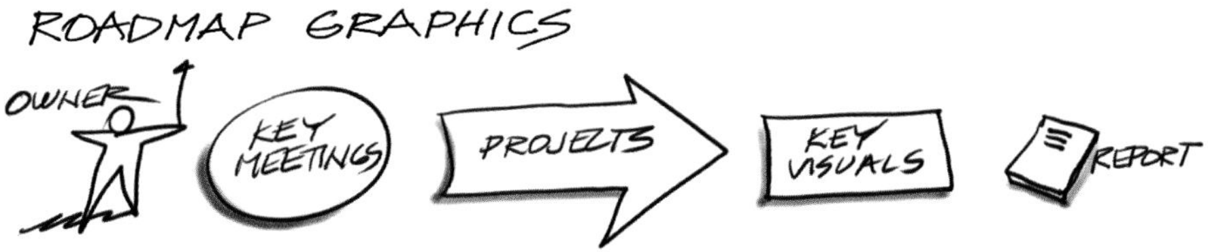

SideStory 8.5

Roadmap Elements

Designing a change project roadmap involves agreeing on several elements and combining them visually in a chart that can be posted, distributed, and used as reference framework all through the project. It needs...

- ☐ **A TIMELINE** covering a span that feels realistic, probably in weeks, and months.
- ☐ **GOALS** to be achieved by the end of the Roadmap time line.
- ☐ **PHASES** or **STAGES** that break the process into 3 to 5 parts with names that communicate a high-level story of what is going on.
- ☐ **WORK STREAMS** (sometimes called swim lanes) that break the process into flows of activity that need focused attention and leadership.
- ☐ **OWNERS** of the work streams. These would be members of the change team.
- ☐ **MILESTONE** events and deliverables. These are events, reports, or announcements that often represent public commitments and help move the process.
- ☐ Identified **CHALLENGES** that need to be overcome to succeed.

Figure 8.10

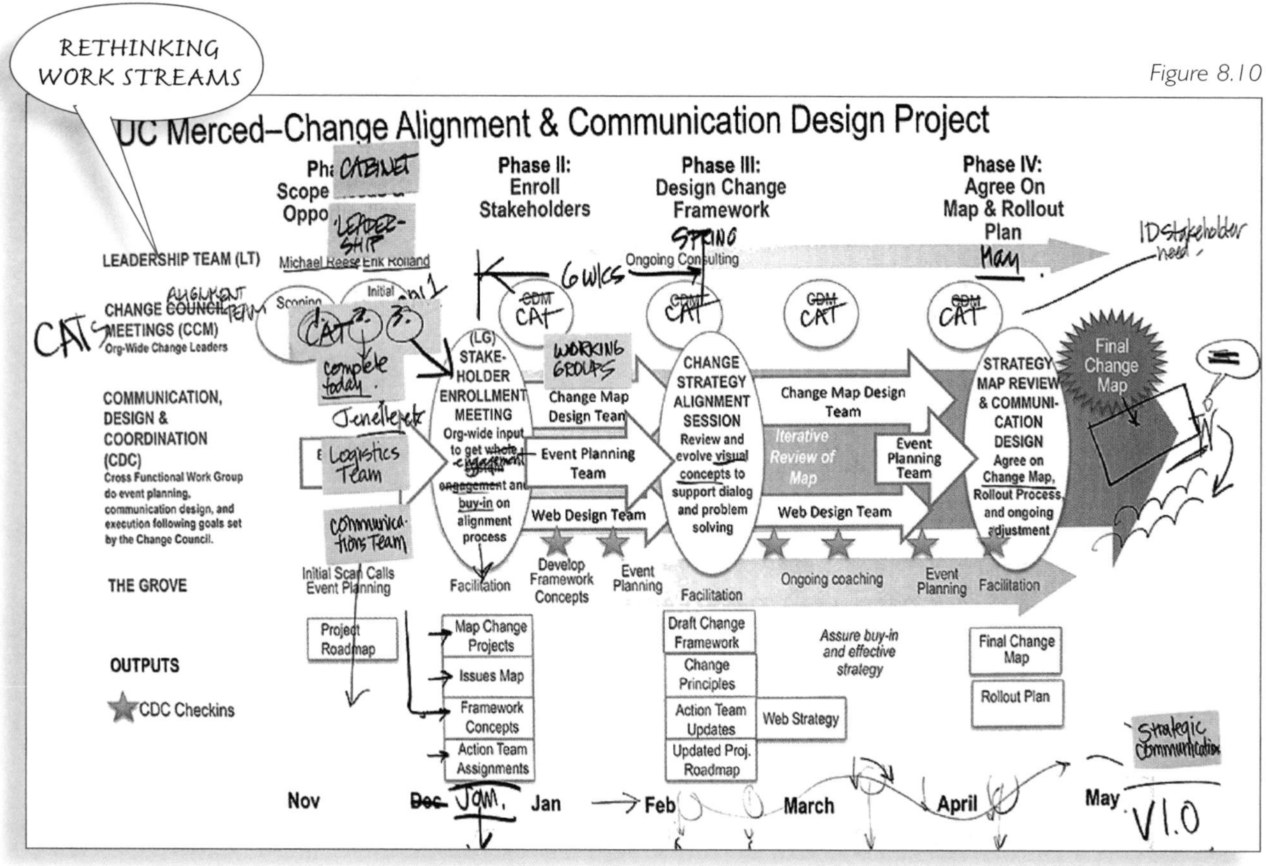

The roadmap graphic itself is a visualization that conveys the effort that will be involved. To engage the CAT we printed out a large version of our proposal roadmap and oriented them to the four phases we were proposing:

- Phase I: **Scope and Opportunities**
- Phase II: **Enroll Stakeholders**
- Phase III: **Design Change Framework**
- Phase IV: **Agree on Map & Rollout Plan**

Critiquing the Proposed Roadmap

The CAT tackled reworking the work streams right away, adding the Cabinet and seeing the CAT as being responsible for the big meetings as well as the Change Alignment Map. A logistics team and communications team were added. This reworking is essential.

We showed four work streams on the version shown in Figure 8.10. (These will change.) We assumed regular work with the **Leadership Team**, Michael and Erik. We had imagined regular meetings with a **Change Council**, which you can see was renamed the **CAT.** We assumed a central **Communication Design & Coordination** group would be doing the bulk of the work, with The GROVE supporting. Outputs are shown along the bottom. But the changes had already begun. We next hung up a fresh roadmap Graphic Guide and began to develop a new roadmap that would be fully owned by the CAT (Figure 8.11). A caution

A key at this point in roadmap development is to draw out constraints and givens. We found out there was a deadline for proposals for new 2020 building contracts. They needed to be in by March. Right away the dean's were having a meeting that could be a chance for CAT to brief them on the project.

Figure 8.11

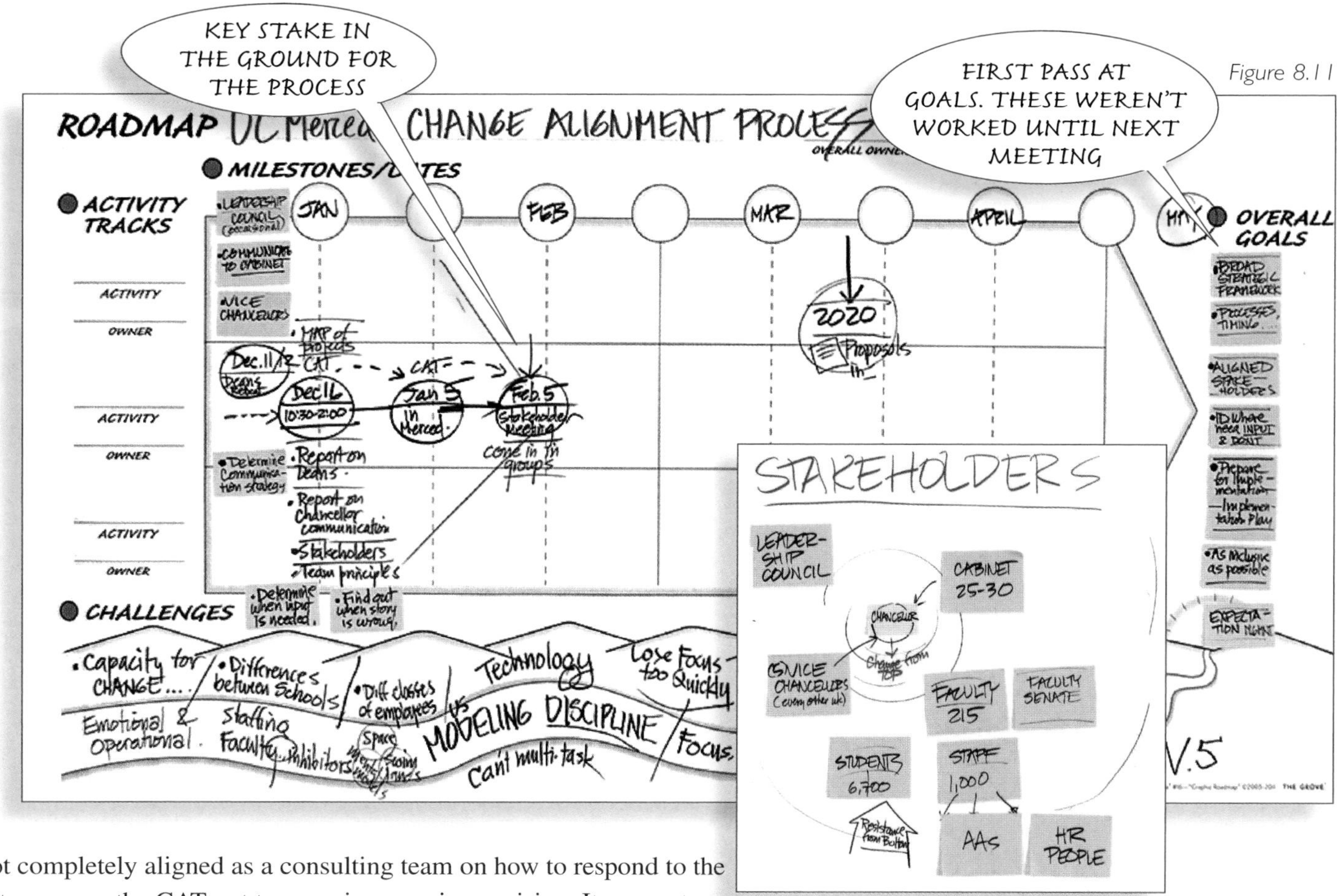

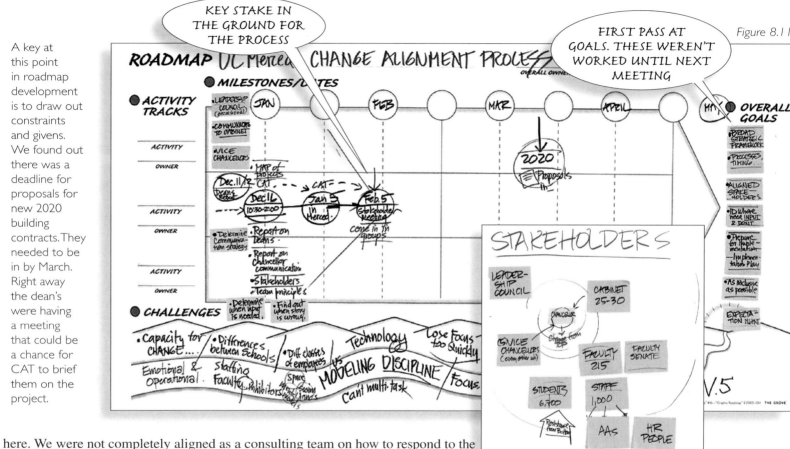

here. We were not completely aligned as a consulting team on how to respond to the change in work streams, so the CAT got to experience us improvising. It was not comfortable, but they got that this would be a collaborative effort, not just following along. What they did set was an initial Stakeholder meeting in two months, a key milestone. They also began working on goals, stakeholders, and surfaced a good number of challenges. We ended the meeting with a round of meeting evaluations and takeaways, and an agreement to meet soon online to refine goals, and analyze the stakeholders in detail.

First Stakeholder Map

This first pass at a stakeholder map was very brief. It established the importance of the larger stakeholder meeting and also underlined the need to think longer term and systemically..

SideStory 8.6

UC Merced Process Pacing

(Includes only first two thirds)

October	**1. First meeting** Scoping, agreeing to work together
November	Leader call to check scope
December	Leader call to review agenda
	2. Change Alignment Team (CAT) meeting
	Leader call to review agenda
	3. CAT video meeting
January	Leader call to review agenda
	4. CAT meeting – Goals, operating principles, roadmap
	Leader meeting to review agenda
	5. Chancellor visioning Session
	Communications Team strategy call
February	Leadership call
	6. CAT video call
	Leader call to review questions
	7. Provost Visioning Call
	Leader call to review agenda
	8. CAT meeting –Review maps & summit design
	Leader call to review agenda
	9. First Cabinet meeting: Visioning
	CAT call to create and review summit agenda
	Logistics calls
	10. Cabinet call to review Vision Map
March	**12. STAFF SUMMIT MEETING** –Visioning
	13. FACULTY SUMMIT MEETING – Visioning
	Leader call to review questions
	14. CAT debrief for insights and learning

5. Set Patterns & Pace

Every consulting project will have its own pressures and pace. What is important is to **be conscious of setting a pace and keeping it**. Your pacing establishes momentum for the project. Your pattern creates a process container. Sustaining momentum may mean slowing and increasing the pace, but always paying attention to how it connects with the work you are focusing on next.

SideStory 8.6 shows the rhythm of meetings in the first two thirds of UC Merced project (not atypical). You can see the regular cadence of meetings and calls in between. The pace was slower at first, but accelerated as the big summits drew closer.

Other Strategies for Setting Pace

- In Silicon Valley, "event-driven management" involves setting a date for a product announcement without having it completed. The event drives the process.
- Agile planning processes set smaller goals in two-22week sprints, resetting the drivers regularly.
- In community work the effort it takes to involve a wide range of stakeholders requires having commitments to key events well in advance so that people can plan in their calendars.

One of the elements that helps set the cadence is the regularity of check-ins and other small meetings and calls in between the main events. These should be part of the process planning.

The Role of Regular Communications & Staffing

Having a strong communications and staffing team as part of the collaboration backbone allows you to set patterns and pace more effectively. Every meeting and call shown in SideStory 8.6 required following a cycle of work that supported the project. And the list doesn't reflect the pattern of email and texting that surrounded each step in the process!

Every community and organizational culture has a culture of communications and tool preferences that you need to tune into as a consultant. If you are internal you need to overtly coach external resources on how to succeed. Which "channel" is used for urgent matters—email, text, voice, collaboration app notifications or other means? Does your client use video conferencing regularly and is comfortable with it? Whatever kind of communication environment you find yourself in, the objective should be establish a regular rhythm and pattern to your communications.

This repeating pattern becomes a discipline. If this pattern is choppy and inconsistent it will take energy away from the challenging conversations and exchanges that are the real work of the change.

It may also be that you want to visually brand your process, so that all email and printed materials have an identifying look and feel. The porject might deveop a logo as a brand. For community work across multistakeholder process, this kind of attention can help establish patterns where there are none.

Scheduling people and venues or securing needed vendors is a real art that administrative assistants master. There are those who can work wonders, others might be new at the job, while others might not be effectively supported (SideStory 8.7). It is very important to lobby for an array of internal help that you can work with directly if you are an external

SideStory 8.7

Logistics Checklist

When you are doing more detailed planning for your change process, these kinds of recurring logistics details need to be handled by your client project staff or you. They are part of the pattern.

- ☐ **Scheduling meeting rooms**
- ☐ **Scheduling calls**
- ☐ **Designing and sending agendas** for leader reviews and in advance for participants
- ☐ **Sending video conferencing links** in advance
- ☐ **Sending reminders** of the video conference the day of the call
- ☐ **Creating outcomes and agenda charts** for meetings (either on charts or tablets)
- ☐ **Helping set up meeting venues**
- ☐ **Arranging for supplies—**markers, paper, tape, templates
- ☐ **Arranging signage**
- ☐ **Checking technology**
- ☐ **Handling participant communications** during key meetings
- ☐ **Digitally documenting** the meetings
- ☐ **Creating and sending the reports**

Engaging Change Leaders Summary

- ☐ **Track inner dynamics.** Fear, uncertainty, questions about capability, and lots of feelings accompany this challenge.
- ☐ **Create outers support structures**

1. **Recruit** formal and informal leaders.
2. **Contract** for how to stay connected with leaders, final decision authorities, advisory groups, and your role as a consultant beyond facilitation.
3. **Create a safe environment** by designing meetings with clear OARRs-outcomes, agenda, roles, and rules; set good ground rules; select good venues.
4. **Initiate a collaboration backbone,** including vision, standard processes, roadmap, communications platforms, support staff, facilitation team, documentation, and web support.
5. **Set patterns and pace** through repeating processes and regular communications, frequency of meetings, and frequency of check-ins.

consultant. If the project is really big, partner with someone on your change team to organize the internal administrative work. Internal consultants may contract for this pair-of-hands role.

If you are an internal consultant it is equally important to have logistics help, although you may be more knowledgeable about to know how to work the system to support your process.

If your role is to be a process consultant, you may want to avoid getting pulled into an administrative role. Because the change process is often operating in the white space outside regular operations, getting attention for the meetings and process on people's calendars can be challenging. If you do have the confidence of your sponsors and strong internal design teams, you can unintentionally become a real force within the system,gaining too much control, and losing the contribution you can make as an independent facilitator.

The Challenge of Moving into Change Creatively

With leaders of change becoming engaged and having the beginnings of a solid roadmap and backbone for the project, it begins to take on a life of its own. When we reviewed the *Seven Challenges of Change* framework with peers who had been through change processes, all agreed that the change starts happening right away. There is often not a clear planning and implementation cascade, but parallel initiatives and experiments. This is where having a very resilient tool kit is an asset. This is also where really understanding how design thinking works helps. The advantage of a visual consultant is having many ways of getting people involved in finding and sharing new ideas and possibilities. We address these practices next.

9. Creating & Sharing Possibilities

Designing Approaches, Strategies, & Visions

Exploring assumptions
Embracing resistance
Empathizing & caring
Imagining possibilities & choices
3. Creating & Sharing Possibilities
Refine the case for change
Clarify your approach & theory of change
Create a strong container for the work—goals, road-map, & energy field
Visualize possibilities, visions, & scenarios

Figure 9.1

How can a small group of change leaders begin to change a larger system? Where do the new ideas come from? Should we support leaders to find and share new strategies and a vision, or work with many stakeholders to collaboratively generate them? Should we skip visioning altogether and improvise with what is emerging now? How can we involve both our innovators and our procedurally oriented stakeholders in the same process? When should we work on the design of a process and when on its substance and content?

Whether a challenge is circumstantial, like a California drought that is threatening wildlife, or developmental, like a successful company wanting to develop younger leadership, or volitional, like starting a new nonprofit to raise awareness of a social issue, ideas about what approach to take must arise from somewhere (see Figure 9.1).

Establishing Some Language for Design

We created this diagram (Figure 9.2) to help you understand this chapter. It deals with the challenge of sorting out what you are being creative about as you begin work. One aspect is designing the process itself, and choosing the methods you will use and how to construct containers and crucibles that allow something new to happen. The other part is working on the substance or content of the change—the strategies, visions, and proposals for new initiatives and solutions to problems. Your idea about how all this integrates is what we are referring to as a "theory of change" or approach, when

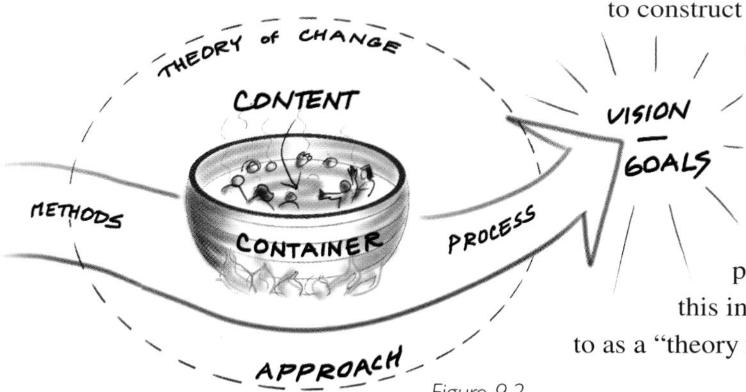

Figure 9.2

SideStory 9.1

Visual Listening

At **Hewlett Packard** a process design team guiding a visioning process in HP Labs was working on the design of a big, employee-wide gathering. Over 800 people would be involved in a big town hall meeting in a tent erected in the parking lot to share their visionary ideas.

HP Labs had been working with David to visually facilitate smaller teams in the 13 labs articulating emerging opportunities, but wanted to engage the entire organization in more general visioning. Maybe "visual listening" would work, Barbara Waugh, the HR lead for the process suggested. The idea of having David map out peoples' ideas on a huge front wall appealed to everyone. Instead of being the lead presenters, the leaders of the labs would be **leader listeners** and HP Lab employees would be the lead voices!

The generative question was to be "How Can HP Labs be the Best Corporate Lab **IN** the World?" But in one of the design meetings, someone had an insight. "It's the wrong question" they said. It should be "How Can HP Labs Be the Best Corporate Lab **FOR** the World?"

This simple shift in the question was the difference that made a difference. The opening "keynote listening" event was a huge success, as person after person rose for the mike to answer this question and see it recorded on the 10' by 40' wall in front.

it is articulated for a specific situation. Your theory is basically an explanation of why you think the approach you are developing with your client will work.

This challenge assumes you now have a process design team, or change team, if that is what you choose to call it. Ideas have already begun to surface during the process of engaging these leaders of change that may be mixtures of ideas about process and ideas about content. As a visual consultant you should be prepared with some suggestions of how to support both, and help design teams be clear about what they are working on, and help them understand that by definition a creative process has a lot of trial and error and surprise (SideStory 9.1). In this chapter we will share several cases and highlight a range of practices that will help you respond to the challenge of creating and sharing possibilities for both process and content. Here are some questions clients have faced at this stage.

- ❑ **The Environmental Defense Fund** wondered how to involve critical outside stakeholders in helping them evolve a new approach to habitat restoration in the Central Valley of California.
- ❑ **National Semiconductor** wondered how an internal change team could involve leadership in launching a Leading Change Program for all managers worldwide and create a vision map and change process that any executive could explain.
- ❑ **The DLR Group,** a large architectural and engineering firm, wanted to know how to build on a successful five-year strategic visioning process conducted by the firm's partners and extend it out to emerging leaders in the firm.
- ❑ **The Change Team at UC Merced** originally set out to create a big picture strategy map aligning change projects, but once involved needed to find a way to expand their focus and involve the entire campus in visioning at the chancellor's request
- ❑ **The Garfield Foundation** wanted to get environmental NGOs and grant makers to

collaborate on cleaning up global warming pollutants in the upper Midwest. How should the four work groups they had identified go about designing strategies for change.

It is once again helpful to step back and appreciate the kinds of inner dynamics that go on as clients head into actual ideation, solution-funding, and direction-clarifying activities. Creating space for people to deal with these inner dynamics is a big part of the design challenge (see Figure 9.3). Creating safe, open environments is so critical we will elaborate on in more depth.

Predictable Inner Dynamics of the Creative Challenge

Some of the inner challenges people face are the following.

- ❑ **Exploring assumptions:** People used to being effective are often action oriented and count on successful approaches that become habits. The way we act and the way we think about things are usually based on assumptions that we ordinarily take for granted. A change process will require becoming conscious and digging under "the way it is usually done" and potentially shifting our assumptions. This is especially critical and difficult if your change process is including new strategy development with successful managers who rely on historic success patterns.
- ❑ **Embracing resistance:** Stepping into the betwixt and between can be challenging. Changing behavior is hard work. Imagining new possibilities that might affect a person's status, identity, and power can bring us to our edge. Resistance needs to be appreciated, embraced, and understood as a completely normal part of change (See SideStory 9.2).
- ❑ **Empathizing and caring**: To come to creative solutions that cut across old boundaries and bring forward new ways of working and organizing will require everyone to begin empathizing with and caring for the larger network of stakeholders who will

Figure 9.3

Lego® Serious Play

At a recent Visual Facilitation Field Guide book sprint (a compressed writing event), Dean Meyers, a visual consultant from New York, led a small group in a Lego® Serious Play session to think about teamwork and collaboration, a feature of the book sprint process where 37 authors were collaborating on creating a new field guide.

One of the exercises, shown here, was to "think with our hands" and create some arrangements that visualized principles of teamwork that we cared about. We then shared them to pull out themes.

Resistance as Progress

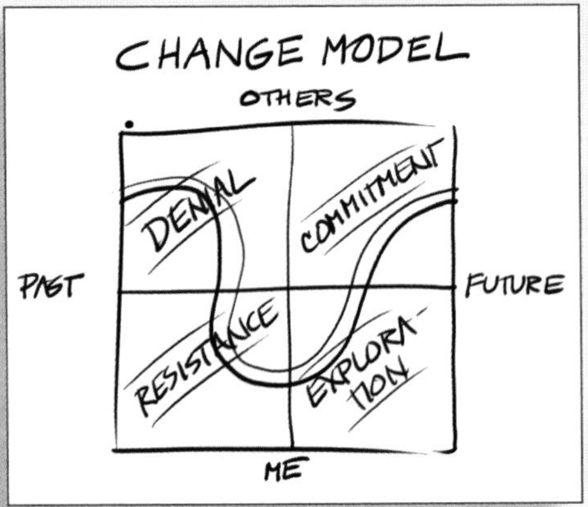

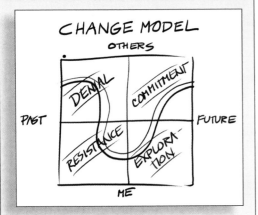

Cynthia Scott, a psychologist who worked with The Grove during a long change process at National Semiconductor, would give a quick chalk talk about how resistance is actually progress. You can add this model to your tool kit (with attribution).

1. Explain that change is moving from the past to the future, with implications for others and for you.
2. People always start by assuming most of the change will be for others.
3. As it becomes clear the change will affect them, resistance appears.
4. Thus resistance is progress! Moving out of denial.

be affected by change. These kinds of feelings are not always easy to access, and drawing them out of people who aren't used to being involved is difficult. Both time and attention to the process are required. However, active listening and working through challenging feelings is an important part of being able to progress.

❑ **Imagining possibilities & choices:** At an intellectual level, everyone in a real change will be challenged to think beyond what they already know by definition. People have different ways of processing information and different learning styles. Some love blank paper. Others will prefer light structures and ideas to push off from. It is also challenging to some when really juicy new ideas start to come alive in the organization even before you are through with planned stages. You will need to continually work to be sensitive to these inner dynamics.

Psychology, neuroscience, cognitive science, and creativity have all informed our thinking about these issues as visual consultants. Each field is extensive by itself. But they are so important we want to present several concepts in these pages for which you can find additional resources and study further. We aren't trying to be comprehensive. We do know that learning to facilitate people in the creative stages of process is as much about your own connection with creativity and your own confidence in people being able to imagine possible futures, as it is about technique. But it helps to be aware of some basics principles.

Exploring Assumptions

One of the critiques of strategic planning in the 1990s, after several decades of popularity, was it's tendency to be analytic and therefore too oriented to the past, and too tied to the assumptions and mental models that informed earlier successes. As technology and the general environment have become more complex and dynamic, consultants began moving beyond analytic planning to find methods that truly test assumptions and provide space for new strategies and visions to emerge. The Grove developed Strategic Visioning, which pairs traditional analysis with imaginative speculation about desirable futures bringing in aspiration elements, supported by visual facilitation. Design thinking arose in this time.

Consultants also increased their focus on dialogic practice as a way of uncovering buried wisdom in the group. Dialogue uses active listening and questions to surface assumptions. You invite people to suspend judgment and trust that shifting perspectives, and hearing all voices through rounds of inquiry, will reveal deeper and perhaps more holistic insights, such as seeing underlying patterns or finding generative ideas. If there is a lot of pressure to find solutions quickly, as in crises situations, this may be challenging. But without taking time to step back and reflect, there will not be space for anything new to emerge. Being willing to be uncertain is essential for learning and recognizing new insights.

Gervase Bushe and Robert Marshak have edited a collection of essays in *Dialogic Organization Development: The Theory and Practice of Transformation Change,* exploring the assumptions behind new methods in organizational development that center on conversational exchanges—World Café, Open Space, Future Search conferences, Appreciative Inquiry, the Art of Convening, the Art of Hosting, the Circle Way, and the like (see SideStory 9.3). They conclude that all these approaches provide spaces for people to discover new generative images and begin developing new narratives, based on the assumption that our inner stories and images guide behavior. New social science theories about how we, as people, collectively come to know what we know are getting more attention. The essays describe a growing understanding about how social construction shapes our notions of what is real and valuable. In addition, new research suggests that social patterns mimic the emergent properties of living systems. But Bushe also cautions OD professionals to not forget strategy development in order to remain relevant to organizational leaders. (We will return to describing these methods in more detail as we look at the outer structures that support change challenge.)

Dialogic OD Methods

Here are some of the new organization development methods that support the social construction of meaning.

1. **Art of Convening** (Neal and Neal)
2. **Art of Hosting** (artofhosting.org)
3. **Appreciative Inquiry** (Cooperrider)
4. **Charrettes** (Lennertz)
5. **Circle Way** (Baldwin)
6. **Community Learning** (Fulton)
7. **Conference Model** (Axelrod)
8. **Dynamic Facilitation** (Rough)
9. **Engaging Emergence** (Holman)
10. **Future Search** (Weisbord)
11. **Intergroup Dialogue** (Nagada, Gurin)
12. **Narrative Mediation** (Winslade & Monk)
13. **Open Space Technology** (Owen)
14. **Org Learning Conversations** (Bushe)
15. **Participative Design** (M. Emery)
16. **Polarity Management** (Johnson)
17. **Preferred Futuring** (Lippitt)
18. **Reflexive Inquiry** (Oliver)
19. **Real-Time Strategic Change** (Jacobs)
20. **Search Conference** (Emery & Emery)
21. **Six Conversations** (Block)
22. **Social Labs** (Hassan)
23. **Strategic Visioning** (Sibbet)
24. **Sustained Dialogue** (Saunders)
25. **Talking stick** (preindustrial)
26. **Technology of Participation** (Spencer)
27. **Theory U** (Scharmer)
28. **Visual Explorer** (Palus & Horth)
29. **Whole-Scale Change** (Dannemiller)
30. **Work Out** (Ashkenas)
31. **World Café** (Brown & Issacs)

Exploring Resistance

Four Types of Resistance

1. Share the four types of resistance noted here and explained in the text.
2. Have a conversation about experiences people have had with each.
3. Share practices for responding to each type.

This activity will raise everyone's awareness, acceptance, and ability to work with resistance as a natural part of change.

Embracing Resistance

In asking people to explore new ideas and look at assumptions, you will undoubtedly encounter resistance. Resistance is a natural response to change, and people have it for a good reason. A lot is at stake. It helps to appreciate that when people resist they are engaged, as distinguished from those in denial who are not responding. Resistance has energy. It is something you should expect and be ready to work with.

In our Designing & Leading Change workshops we adapted Rick Mauer's work on resistance and articulated four types, finding that they resonated with the Four Flows framework (see SideStory 9.4). When we present this model we draw out ideas of how to respond to the different types of resistance as a way of preparing to deal with them.

1. **Disagreement with purpose**: There is a kind of resistance that comes from people questioning the purpose of the change at a top line level.
2. **Emotional—fear of personal impact**: If the imagined personal impacts of the change are scary, people can have strong emotional responses.
3. **Not enough information**: People also might not be clear about what is going on from a communications perspective. They simply don't understand or have enough information.
4. **Wrong leader**: But there also might be resistance because they don't trust leaders or fellow change team members from past experiences.

Each of these types of resistance can arise as an inner dynamic of this phase of the process. Empathizing and caring through active listening and dialogic practice helps a great deal with types one and two. Giving voice to questions and fears allows people to begin to move beyond them. Visual facilitation is directly helpful when dealing with

Figure 9.4

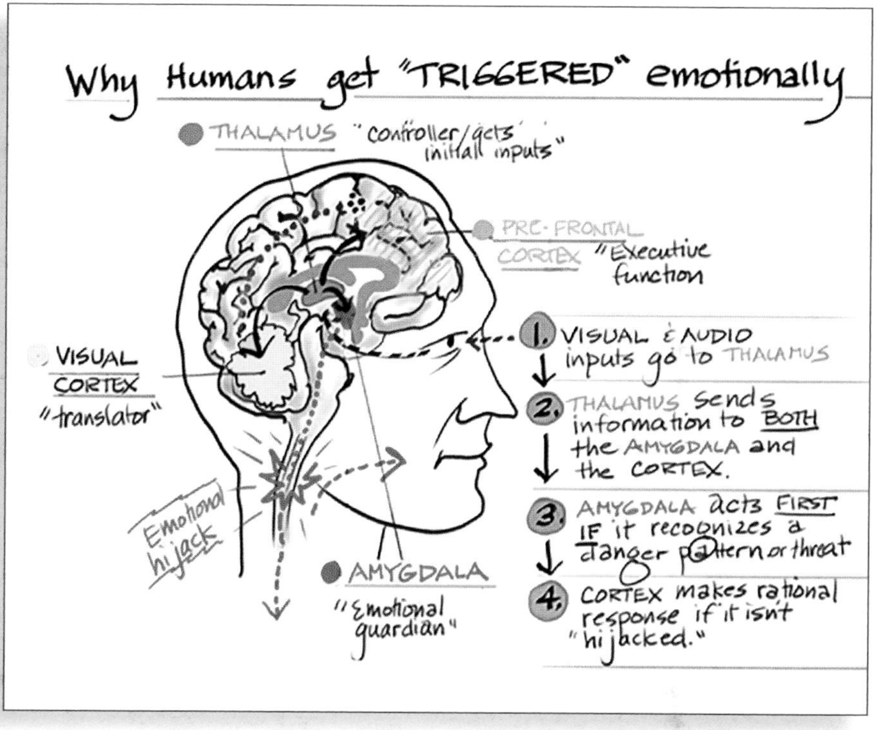

informational resistance by drawing out areas of confusion and using visualization to help make things clear. Leadership may operationally have to replace leaders who may have insurmountable historic issues. Maurer proposes that all resistance needs to be directly addressed as part of the change process, and also notes the fact that resistance may not get resolved, and can reoccur in later phases.

Empathizing & Caring

As you head into the process of getting people to open up and be creative, it is helpful to appreciate how vigilant our built-in nervous system is about these kinds of invitations. Our colleague, Mary Gelinas, has researched emerging studies in neuroscience and finds widespread agreement that when people are feeling threatened or unsafe, the cognitive functions shut down (Figures 9.4 and 9.5) making it difficult to have constructive collaboration. She's been very concerned that the Native American, ranchers, timber workers, and fishermen stakeholders she works with in Northern California are used to being discounted in public processes and can get triggered. (This is the word used to indicate a state of becoming emotionally flooded or "hijacked," with common reactions being fighting, fleeing, or shutting down.) She observes that even when there is no actual threat, people can be triggered by symbols connected with earlier experiences that were hurtful. It can also happen in the presence of unintended messages, like the symbolism of an all-white facilitation team working with ethnic minority groups.

Even in routine engagements, if a person senses any kind of threat, internal processes can

The Hijack Response

Neuroscientists know now that the amygdala, which receives incoming neurological data sooner than the executive areas in the neocortex, can trigger a hijack response. This emotional response is a guardian kind of capability built into our psyches. Have you ever been in a meeting where there are sudden outbursts of anger by someone triggered in this way? It's normal and even important for keeping us protected.

Figure 9.5

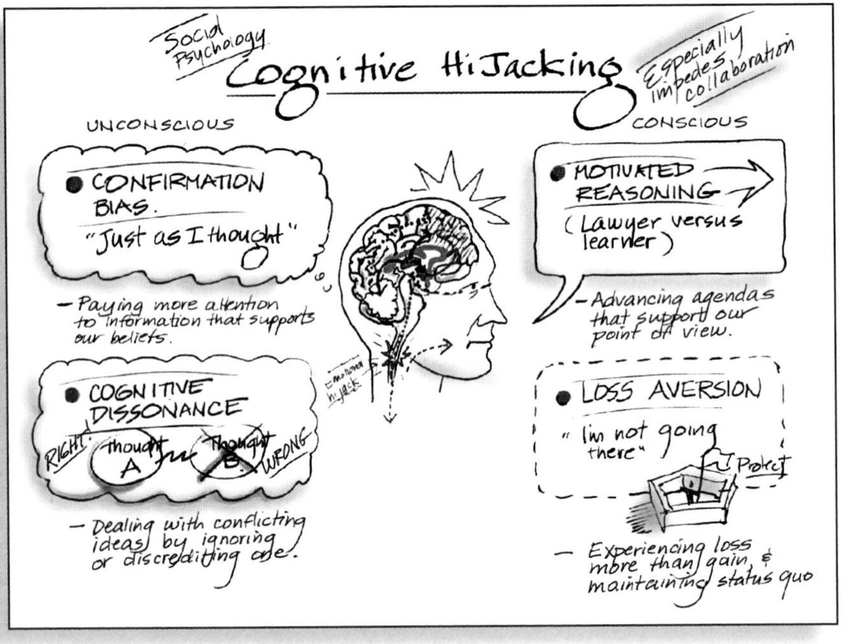

Cognitive HiJacking

Mary Gelinas, in her book *Talk Matters: Saving the World One Word at a Time*, describes how when a person feels threatened, the hijacking response can exacerbate what social psychologists have identified as common strategies for dealing with being overloaded or being strongly self interested. She has named this phenomenon "cognitive hijacking," as shown here, and identified four results; two unconscious and two conscious.

constrain curiosity and exploration. David Rock, an Australian leadership coach exploring the neuroscience of leadership has identified five factors that people find attractive and when ignored or undermined find threatening. They spell SCARF.

1. **Status**: Will my status be diminished or improved in this process? (Mauer's emotional resistance-SideStory 9.4.)
2. **Certainty**: Is it clear what we are doing or confusing and unpredictable? (Mauer's information resistance.)
3. **Autonomy**: Is my ability to control my situation going to improve or be reduced?
4. **Relatedness**: Are these other participants friends or foes? (This relates to Mauer's noting how historical mistrust can create resistance.)
5. **Fairness**: Is what we are heading into fair or unfair? Will I be treated fairly? (Mauer's emotional resistance.)

We conclude that if you want to work on your own ability to create the kind of energetic field that invites creativity, it helps to know how to manage your own reactivity. Mary has found that mindfulness training can help a person accept trigger events, and learn to leave space to re-balance and be responsive rather than being reactive. However, this capability can't be counted on in most settings and groups. She has found it is helpful in some situations to actively engage clients with sketch talks or handouts about the hijacking response, thereby making it okay to express these feelings and not be dominated by them. There is a great deal you can explore on these subjects beyond the scope of this book.

Figure 9.6

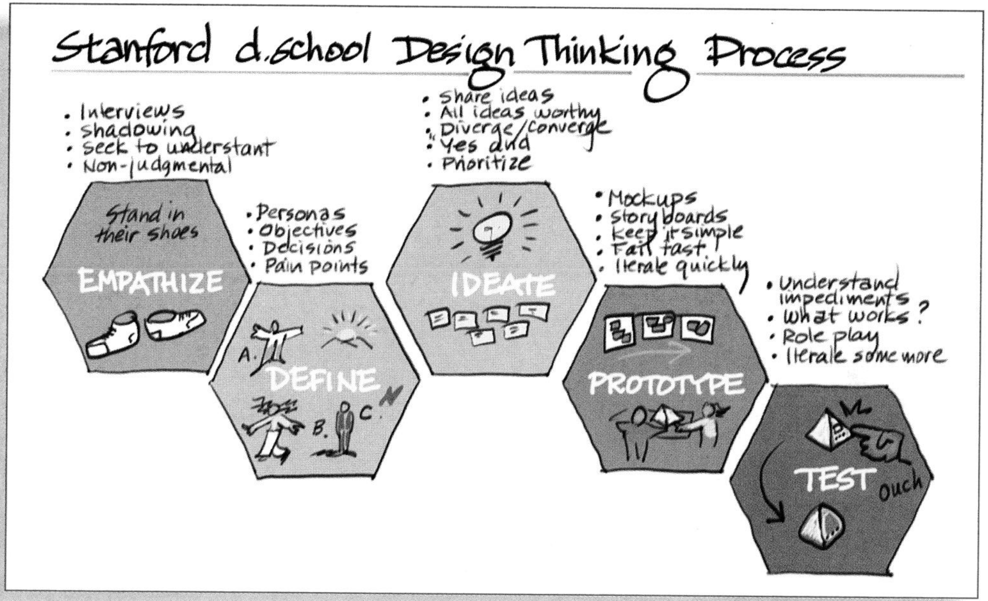

Trust that being sensitive to these kinds of inner dynamics is essential to good visual consulting.

Imagining Possibilities & Choices

On the other side of the challenges of people feeling threatened are the positive rewards of practices that help people shift into more exploratory states.

Design thinking is an increasingly productive way to do this. It clearly focuses on the value of playing with ideas and imagination visually on paper and other media. Not surprisingly, many visual practitioners embrace its methods. The term and techniques have been popularized by Tim Brown, CEO of Ideo, a leading Silicon Valley design firm, in his book *Change by Design: How Design Thinking Transforms Organizations and Inspires Innovation*. The popular d.school at Stanford University is now working with Ideo and other designers outside of regular academic disciplines and evolving these ideas (Figure 9.6). The d.school's orientation is stated first thing on its website: **"We believe everyone has the capacity to be creative."** This approach reinforces our experience that active acknowledgment of peoples' experience combined with dialogic approaches and visualization is needed for full effectiveness. Interestingly, they suggest beginning with empathy for the situation and persons for whom one is designing. Designers who want to have real breakthroughs appreciate that a purely rational approach is not the most effective way to stimulate idea formation. When the energetic level of group process is attended to in ways that respect feelings and relationship, it moves the mind the way water floats boats.

Design Thinking

The Stanford d.school is a place where people use design to develop their own creative potential. They provide an intentionally experimental, student-centered, and project-focused set of workshops and activities for students from all other disciplines. They have a simple rubric for the Design Thinking Process that David illustrated for an online GLEN exchange and is shown here.

SideStory 9.5

Why Change?

What reasons are your clients sharing for wanting to change? Here are some examples.

- ☐ Organize a **new organizational unit**
- ☐ Design a process for a **merger**
- ☐ Open a **new market**
- ☐ Design a new **sales campaign**
- ☐ Communicate a **new vision** and strategic direction
- ☐ Revitalize and **grow a nonprofit** board
- ☐ Improve **organizational effectiveness**
- ☐ **Redesign a core organizational process** like recruitment or procurement
- ☐ **Align competing change projects**
- ☐ **Align cultural** values
- ☐ Support a **culture of innovation**
- ☐ Plan a **new leadership** and/or employee development program
- ☐ Involve stakeholders in a testing and improving a **new civic plan**
- ☐ Achieve a **policy change** in environment, health, economics, etc.
- ☐ Bring **new constituents** to the table
- ☐ Achieve **peace and reconciliation**
- ☐ **Reshape a dysfunctional paradigm**

Four Kinds of Outer Structures

How can you support a change team entering creative space for either process or content design? There are four ways (take another look at Figure 9.2 at the start of this chapter):

1. **Refine a case for change**: Your change team, and eventually the whole system, needs to be fully enrolled in the need to change. This case for change is a story that combines current dissatisfactions with visions of possibility and some plausible arguments about how change might succeed. Knowing why and how a change might happen strengthens the stake people have in breaking through to new ideas. Being creative in expressing your case for change is a first step in designing change.

2. **Clarify your approach and theory of change**: An "approach" is an expression of the general way you intend to go about the change process. Under any approach are some theories about why that approach will get results. This kind of thinking can be visualized, and helps align the change team and prepare them for the work of designing a change process.

3. **Create a strong container for the work—goals, roadmap and energy field**: A container is the supportive part of the change that people will rely on as other things become more dynamic and uncertain. The container needs to provide stability for all four flows of process, with consistent attention to purpose, a strong energy field coming from leaders and consultants, a clear and accessible visual roadmap, and bottom-line logistics and resource support that can be relied upon.

4. **Visualize possibilities, visions and scenarios**: Your container will beg to have great contents. These are the strategies, concepts, versions of visions, pilot projects, experiments, solutions, generative imagery, and other material that emerges as the system heads toward full commitment to something new, and the fourth challenge of fully stepping into the new vision.

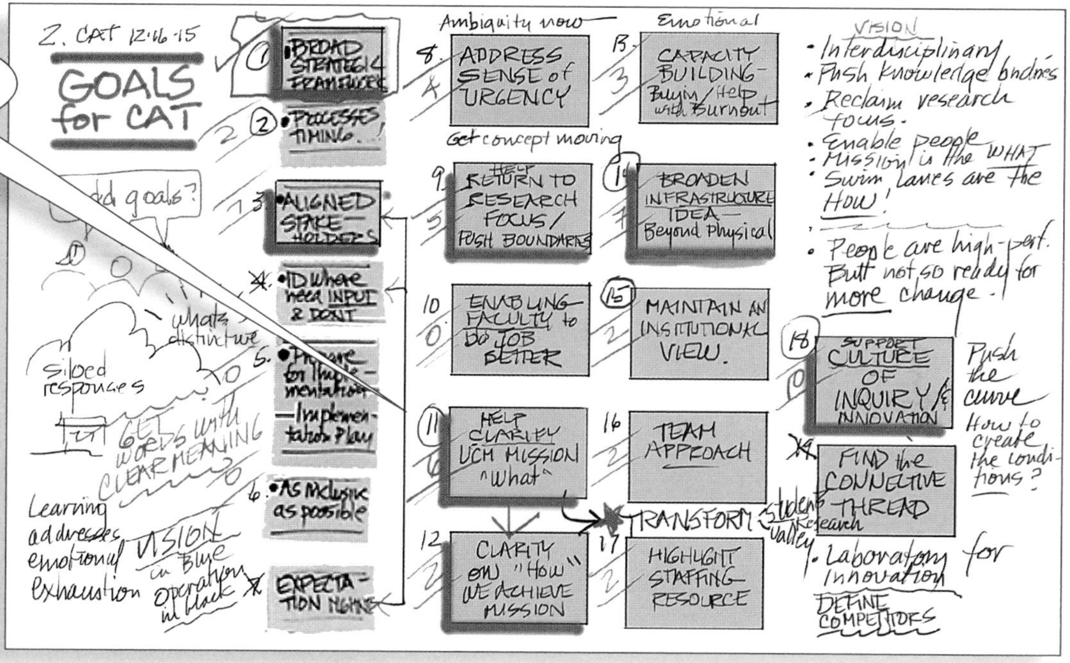

1. Refine a Case for Change

A top concern of the UC Merced CAT team was getting clear on what they were really doing. They knew the driver of the project was aligning the many change projects, but a case for change needed more. They began this part of their design process by getting clear on goals, (Figure 9.7). This revealed that they needed to add visioning to their scope.

What is an Attractive Entry Point?

As visual consultants, our entry point at UC Merced was working on aligning the many change projects connected with expansion. But you can see right away from the list of types of reasons for change (see Sidestory 9.5) that entry points can cover a very wide range of expressed needs. Some are described in terms of tangible outcomes that almost sound like solutions rather than goals. Others are very broad, leaving lots of room to the imagination. The consulting challenge at this point is to realize that the entry points your clients prefer and the goals they state are usually the tip of an iceberg of other aspects of the system as a whole that might need to change. Under each presenting interest are sets of patterns, organizational systems, and beliefs that hold the old system in place and may have to be changed to achieve results up on the surface. It is impossible to work the entire system at once, but you do need to articulate a case for change that provides a promising start. Involvement in an initial project will then, if you keep the larger system in mind,

CAT Agrees on Goals

This chart was developed on a tablet with a sketching program, simulating sticky notes. After the UC Merced CAT team surfaced all possibilities, David numbered them and Gisela guided the group to vote for their top five (giving people votes equaling to one third of whatever number of items assures noone loses their favorites). The ones getting the most votes have heavy borders. The need for a vision popped out, and even began to generate ideas of what it should include.

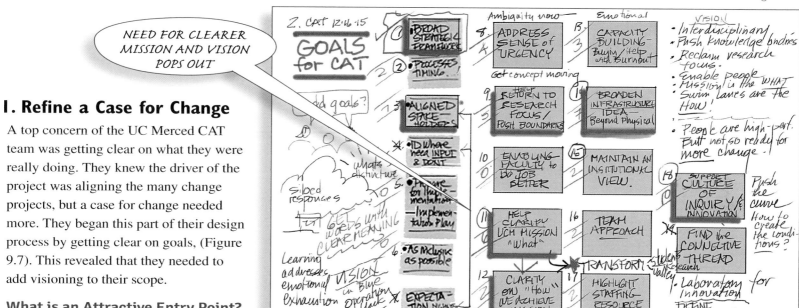

Figure 9.8

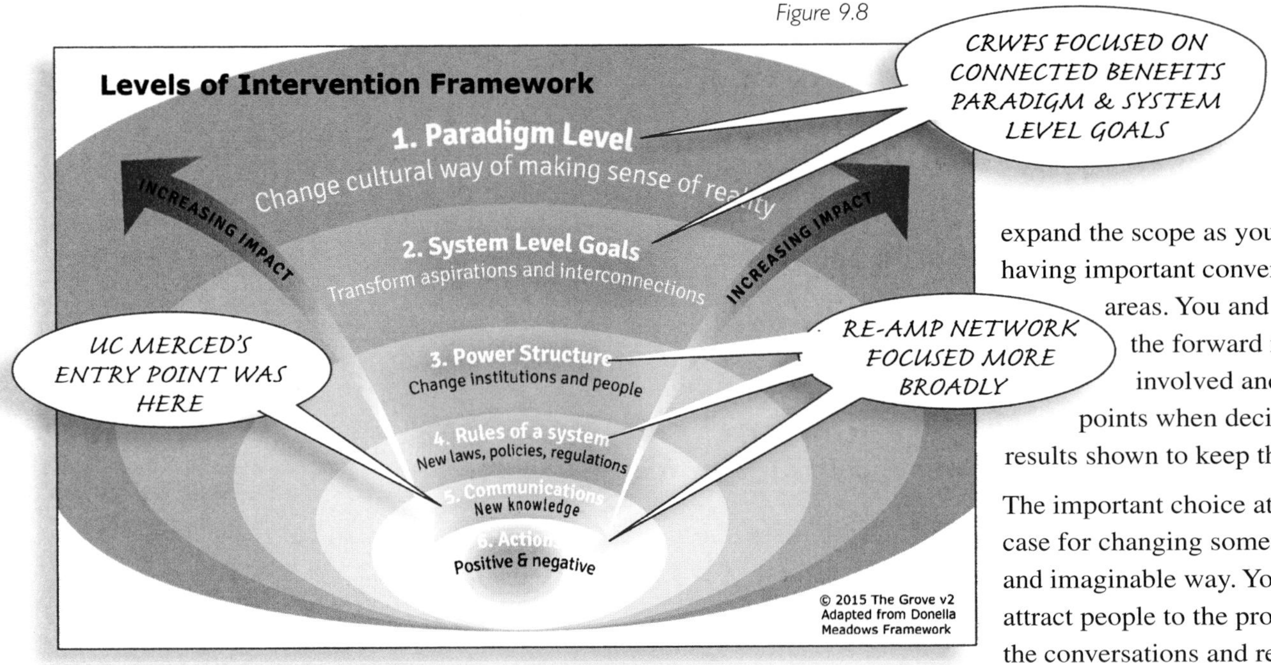

expand the scope as you make progress. People begin having important conversations about change in other areas. You and the change team can steward the forward movement, keeping everyone involved and talking, and converging at points when decisions have to be made and results shown to keep things rolling.

The important choice at this point is to agree on a case for changing something in a relatively specific and imaginable way. You want the stated goals to attract people to the process and engage them in the conversations and relationship building that will become the seedbed for new thinking, new norms, and new processes. It will take experimenting and what, in visual consulting jargon, would be called "iterating" or creating versions of ideas. If people are engaged in the process and believe in its potential, working on the different visual versions can create a powerful level of buy-in.

Levels of Intervention

Gisela adapted this framework created by Donella Meadows, a thought leader in applying systems thinking to sustainability. It shows a series of levels a group might decide to intervene in a larger system, from concrete actions at the bottom line to overall paradigm change at the broadest level. This scheme helped the California Roundtable on Water & Food Supply, described in Chapter 1, to determine their own sweet spot for making change—levels 1. and 2. The RE-AMP network, on the other hand, focused across a range of levels.

Visual Models Can Help

Visual models can provide your change team ways to think about where the best entry point might be for beginning work. Here are two that have been helpful to us.

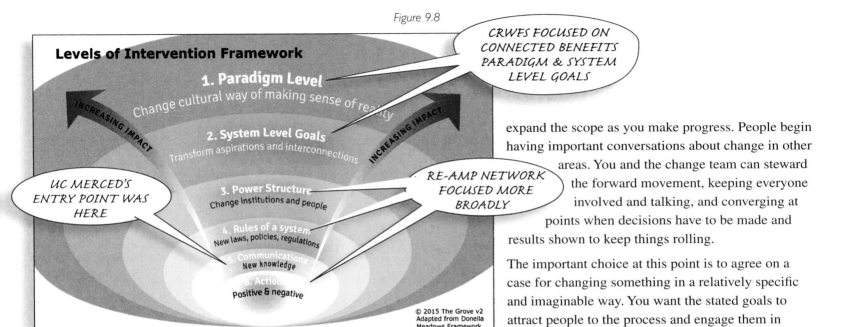

- ❑ **Levels of Intervention diagram**. Gisela adapted this model (Figure 9.8) based on the work of Donnella Meadows for the California Roundtable on Water & Food Supply (CRWFS) to help them discern and affirm where they as a type of think tank could make the greatest difference. Some in the group wanted to see more immediate behavior change, but the sweet spot was articulating a new connectivity paradigm

Figure 9.9

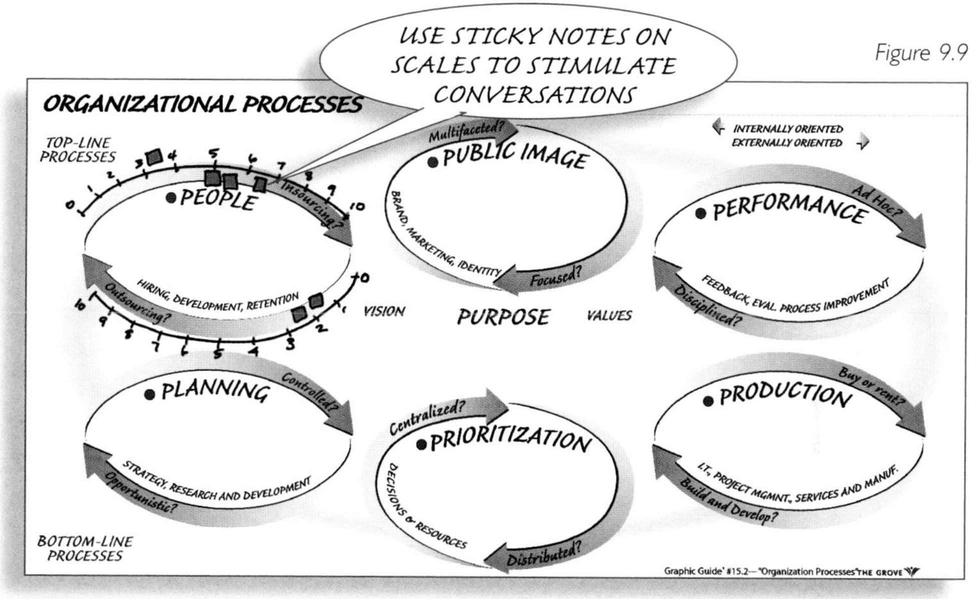

and linking institutions to set system goals. The diagram helped clarify their focus.

Garfield Foundation, on the other hand, organized a collaborative network in the upper Midwest called RE-AMP—involving 150 environmental NGOs and 15 foundations—to impact the power structure, rules of the system, communications and direct action, all guided by their ambitious goal of cleaning up global warming pollutants 50% by 2030.

UC Merced was focused on aligning communications and actions for change in its initial project. Then the visioning process shifted focus to working on system-level goals.

For whatever situation you are facing, the best point of intervention lines up purpose, capacity, and interest/passion.

Whole System Model: Changing a key process is another way to look at entry points. The Organization Processes framework (Figure 9.9) suggests that organizations are a combination of core processes. Planning, Prioritization, and Production deal with the strategy, structure, and systems in the organization. The processes for managing People, Public image, and Performance deal with staff, style, and skills. Purpose and associated vision and values integrate the whole. Each of the six core processes can have an inward-looking approach or an outward-looking approach. This model, designed by David, adapts the inner-outer idea illustrated in Tony Pascal's evolution of the Seven S model (Figure 7.8), as interpreted in *Managing on the Edge.* He suggests that there is creative tension between inward and outward looking approaches that contribute to the vitality of any organization, with fashions moving back and forth between inward and outward focus over time.

SideStory 9.6

Core Process Analysis

Use this template to both assess where your organization is focusing attention and where it would like to head in the future.

1. Make a scale on each arrow from 0 at the narrow end to 10 at the arrow tip.
2. Ask your change team to put small stickies on each one to indicate how much attention each approach is getting. (i.e. is "Insourcing PEOPLE" a "5" and "Outsourcing" a "2?")
3. Facilitate a rich discussion about how much people know about the overall focus of attention in the organization.

SideStory 9.7

Questions to Refine Your Case for Change

These questions can help your clients clarify their case for change.

SCOPE & OUTCOMES

- ☐ What is your level of dissatisfaction with the way things are now—high or low?
- ☐ Has this change been attempted before?
- ☐ What are the drivers of change and are beyond your control? Are there any parts of the current organizational strategy that would be supported by this change?
- ☐ What goals are important for real impact?

STAKEHOLDERS

- ☐ Who benefits from having things the way they are now?
- ☐ Who would benefit from a change?
- ☐ How much stake do you personally have in supporting a change?
- ☐ What is connected to the change you think is needed that we should also pay attention to?

SUPPORTS

- ☐ Is leadership in a position to fully support working on this change?
- ☐ How can we get leaders involved?
- ☐ Who might be your early supporters?

If you are relatively inexperienced in organizational thinking, it would be helpful to study one of these whole system models and visually map your understandings onto it as a workout. The most important outcome is not a precise measure of what is happening, but insights about what needs to change that arise from taking a whole systems perspective.

If you are more experienced at organizational thinking you may find the distinctions we are making about different aspects clear enough, and perhaps your learning will be to find ways to facilitate your change teams in using these kinds of visual thinking approaches themselves to look at their own organization as a whole system.

Coming to Agreement on Your Case for Change

Returning to the case we are threading through this book, the UC Merced Change Alignment Team (CAT) took a second, video conference meeting to clarify goals as we explained earlier. Aligning the 70-plus change projects was the point of entry that had already been agreed on. But identifying more explicit goals made it clear that many on the CAT and on the Advisory Board, as well as Michael and Erik, were coming to the conclusion that without some agreement on the overall vision for the University it would be nearly impossible to agree on project alignment.

This project was no longer just at the organizing, prioritizing, and communication levels, in terms of levels of intervention. Announcing the university would double in size in terms of students and faculty, and knowing that it would mean doubling the physical campus, which is what the 2020 Vision announcements described, was not the same as knowing what kind of university they wanted to be and what kinds of emphasis they would come to be known for. This expanded the focus to looking at whole systems goals, referring to the levels of intervention framework (see SideStory 9.7). The goal alignment discussion in the second CAT meeting laid the groundwork for a change in scope of our project.

Figure 9.10

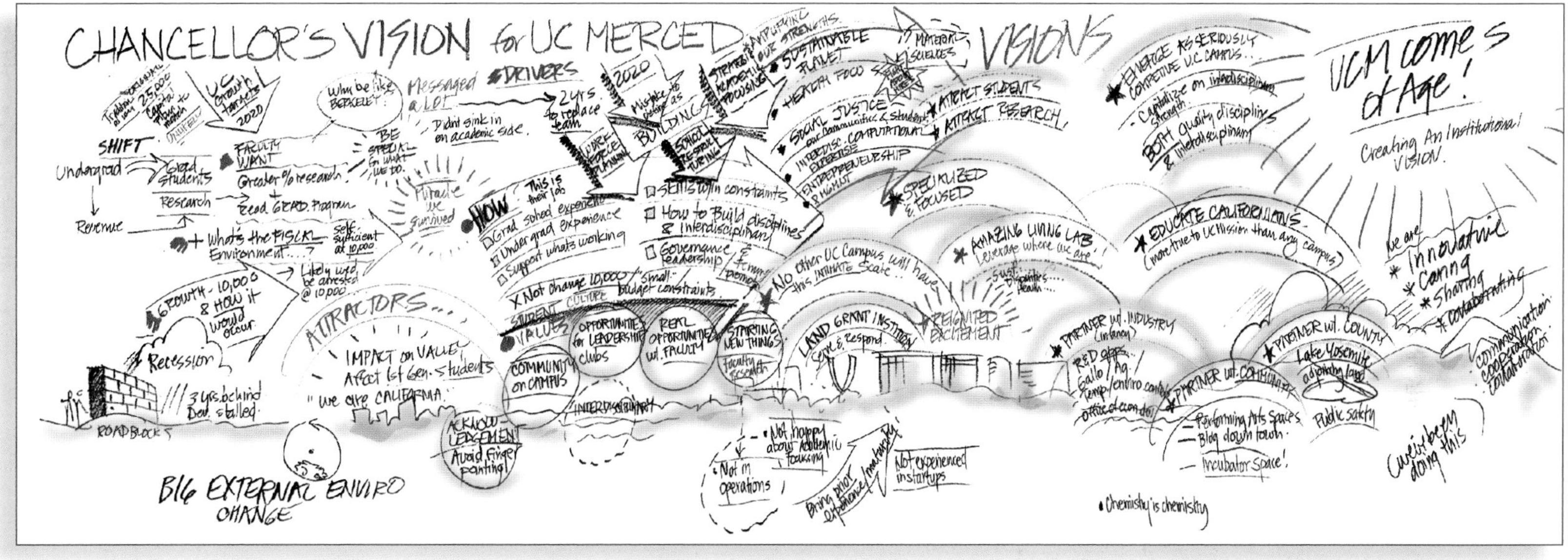

Changing Scope at UC Merced

Michael and Erik knew that we consultants would have to talk with Chancellor Dorothy Leland about her vision before we could go further. In that organization the chancellor is a key spokesperson for overall direction, and was in the final decision-making position for any visioning activity. So Michael arranged for a meeting for her to share her vision with us (see Figure 9.10). At the end of the meeting the chancellor came to the same conclusion as the change team. There had to be a visioning process. But she went a step further. "We need to involve the whole campus," she said. We were excited by her commitment and involvement, and knew the CAT would have to rethink its process design.

2. Clarify an Approach & Theory of Change

One of our assumptions was that clarifying an approach to our expanded scope at UC Merced would mean designing a strategy for getting key stakeholders in agreement on

Chancellor Leland Shares Her Vision

Michael invited Chancellor Leland to spend some time with David and Gisela and share her vision for the university. We met in the same room the CAT had been working in the day before, so their beginning roadmap was on the wall and we were able to brief the chancellor on the project's intentions. After experiencing sharing in this way, she insisted that her Cabinet have the same experience and that the entire campus be involved in the summit's we had planned.

Figure 9.11

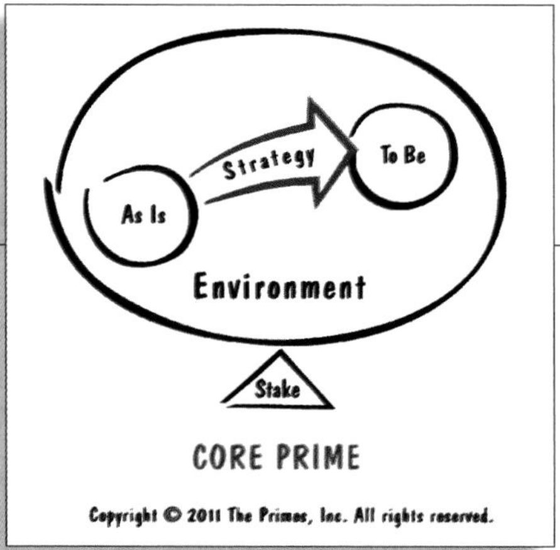

The Core Prime

Getting people to enroll in change requires a story for change whose elements are spelled out in Chris McGoff's *The Primes.* He argues that five agreements are needed to effectively engage people in change.

- ❏ Agreement on **current "As Is" state**.
- ❏ Agreement on **Environment** surrounding the challenge.
- ❏ Agreement on the **Stake** that people have in change. What degree of commitment is there to moving from the current state? What is the case for change?
- ❏ Agreement on **future "To Be" state.** What is the vision of where things are headed?
- ❏ Agreement on a **Strategy** to reach the future state.

their current state (system analysis), a desired future state (vision), and how to get from here to there (process design). The CAT knew that in their current state they needed alignment and a big-picture strategy map of priorities. Now the CAT realized that to get alignment they also needed a vision of the future state. At the Chancellor's request they would involve the University Cabinet and the larger community of students and faculty.

In thinking this through, we were guided by a theory that change is propelled by narratives that respond persuasively to all the elements of the D×V×A>R change formula (Discontent × Vision × Action is greater than Resistance) we described earlier in SideStory 7.8. But there is an additional element called "stake" and a creative visual depiction of this approach that Chris McGoff developed with Michael Doyle (one of David and Chris' mentors). Michael was co-founder of Interaction Associates, and an architect turned visual consultant who helped bring professional facilitation to the business world in the 1970s. In 2007 he worked with Chris to illustrate consulting concepts that were at the heart of their work. They called these "primes" for primary concepts. Michael unfortunately passed away just as they began work, but Chris completed the book in 2012, drawing on his own extensive experience in consulting (He is founder of The Clearing in Washington DC., a consultancy branded with visual consulting at its center). He published it as *The Primes: How Any Group Can Solve Any Problem*. Its heart was the Core Prime, diagrammed in Figure 9.11.

Change Leaders Need to Have a Stake in the Outcomes of Change

Adding stake to the concept makes a difference. Chris believes you can't get very far with change unless the core team has true stake in the process. Adding this element invites exploration of everyone's emotional connection at the energetic level, and their bottom line stake operationally, thinking in terms of the four flows. It pushes the conversation beyond just having the story be intellectually clear. At an important offsite with the heads of most of the emergency relief agencies in the United States after the Haiti earthquake and during Katrina, Chris engaged everyone with this model. The gathering challenge was to see if they could begin a process of coming up with an integrated whole-of-government response rather than independent agencies trying to cooperate ad hoc. Chris insisted that they agree on the case for change and their stake in the process before continuing.

He had the group break into three, and each was to mount their best argument for entering into a process of find a whole of government response. He then said that after the first presentation, the others were to challenge it in every way possible. Then the second group could go, of course pulling in any upgrades to their argument from the initial challenge. This continued another round. All the while I, David, was recording the arguments visually on charts. After all the best arguments that had survived their strongest criticism were assembled, Chris challenged everyone to declare who had full stake in the process. This was a big ask. There was a long reflection period. But three keys leaders stepped forward and the others followed. Only then did the group enter into creative visioning around what a whole of government process might look like.

Articulating a New Approach at UC Merced

Chancellor Leland's strong encouragement for doing a broad visioning process required a change in scope and approach on our project at UC Merced. She had also responded to the suggestion of using electronic brainstorming and live stream technologies to involve remote participants and open the process to the whole campus. This was a big change! Michael and Erik were eager for suggestions. We knew we were working to design a map for the Change Alignment Project. Would it now be the Visioning & Change Alignment Project? Probably. And if so, what would be our general recommendations on how to proceed? How could we engage people so they all had real stake? (See SideStory 9.8).

SideStory 9.8

Approach Should Include

When you describe your approach, be clear about each of these items.

- ☐ **Presenting issues:** These are the symptoms of need or sometimes called the "pains" Discontent is part of the energy of change that needs to be channeled. These are also process challenges you face.
- ☐ **Desired outcomes and goals:** This describes your change team's sense of how much they can accomplish within scope.
- ☐ **Scope:** It starts with a description of what we have been calling the entry point. How much are you taking on in this beginning period of change (assuming that things will evolve as the change work begins). The scope includes a sense of how fast you want to start seeing results.
- ☐ **Stakeholder involvement:** You need to start with some idea of how many people you will reach out to. Your approach may specify stakeholder analysis and further involvement as part of the larger process.
- ☐ **Leadership and other supports:** Who and what is supporting the change process as it begins?
- ☐ **Process methods and theory of change:** This is a description of the underlying logic of why the activities and methods you propose will achieve the stated goals.

SideStory 9.9

Common Visual Consulting Methods

In the process consulting field, common methods many people understand that are usually accompanied by visual facilitation are:

- ❑ Strategic planning
- ❑ Action planning
- ❑ Visioning
- ❑ Design thinking (charrettes and hakathons)
- ❑ Learning journeys and workshops
- ❑ Process improvement processes
- ❑ Re-engineering and organization redesign
- ❑ Large group stakeholder involvement
- ❑ Appreciative Inquiry
- ❑ Future Search conferencing
- ❑ Agile planning
- ❑ LEAN
- ❑ Values clarification

Generic Approaches to Change Processes

At Michael's request we wrote a memo outlining three possible approaches to adding a visioning process to our change alignment project.

1. **Top Down**: Here the chancellor and Cabinet would agree on and communicate a vision, engaging others in helping figure out how to implement it. This was a process used at National Semiconductor in Gil Amelio's successful turnaround of that company in the early 1990s. (We share that vision in Figure 11.7.)

2. **Bottom up**: This would involve large summit meetings of staff and faculty at UC Merced to collaboratively generate a vision, coming to some consensus, with the Cabinet and chancellor setting parameters. This bottom-up process is often used to involved very large communities of stakeholders, and was used with the College of Business Administration at Cal Poly Pomona, which we will describe in Chapter 11.

3. **Blended approach**: Here the chancellor and Cabinet would create the outlines of a new vision and engage a larger group of stakeholders in refining it and imagining the initiatives needed to implement it.

In UC Merced's case they chose the third approach, which we will describe later.

Lets look now at some of the methods you might combine into an approach that could guide you in being creative in the process design phase of your work.

Using Field-Tested Consulting Concepts

Approaches are methods that have some history, articulated processes, and practices that people may or may not have experience with. Here we list some of the common consulting methods that use visualization centrally (SideStory 9.9). Earlier we listed out methods that emphasize dialogic approaches (SideStory 9.3). In terms of change the *Liminal Pathways* and

Seven Challenges of Change frameworks are two approaches, with the latter reflecting the *Four Flows Model* of process.

One way to start a conversation with your change team about approach is to lead a graphic history review of past changes in the organization or community you are working with (SideStory 9.10). This allows everyone a chance to tune into the organization's history with change and harvest some ideas about methods that worked in the past. The methods and approaches that you use in your eventual process designs need to be understood enough by the change team that they can advocate for and support them during implementation. Anchoring in common experience when possible is helpful.

Our experience suggests that new ideas about both the process and the content of what you are working often emerge after you enter into a process and can't be completely predicted in advance. The key is to get started with your best ideas, and then follow the energetic flow and improvise, using iterations of visions and roadmaps to keep the conversations productive.

Distinctions in a Theories of Change Map

In our Designing & Leading Change workshops we set out to see if we could make sense of all the change methods that are being used. We mapped them on a big chart. A reproduction is shown in Figure 9.12.

The distinctions we used to map these methods reflect a spectrum of underlying assumptions people have about change. One spectrum shows on one end the belief that focusing on the objective problems and coming up with measurable, objective shifts in

Map out a Graphic History

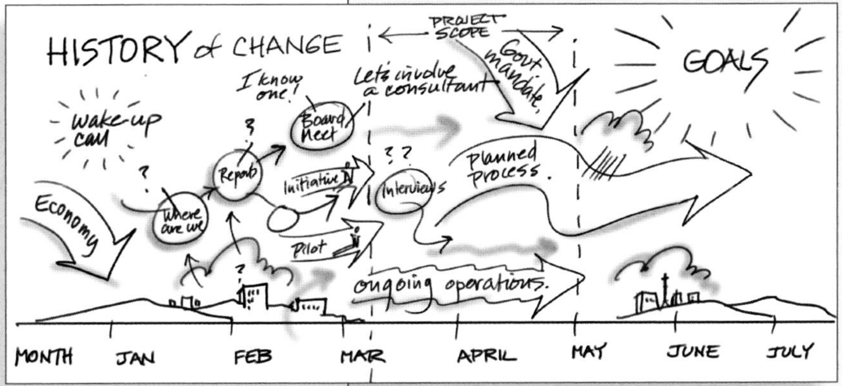

Sometimes it helps to find out what your organization knows about change from past experiences nontheoretically.

1. Post a large piece of paper and inquire about past times when similar projects have been attempted.
2. Draw out information about both external and internal factors that have given rise to the key issues.
3. You can use the Four Flows framework to guide questions.
4. Focus on the story-telling, not the picture. One advantage of the visual approach is you can hop around.
5. Do this on a wall or sit side by side with the person you are interviewing and work in a journal or on other paper.

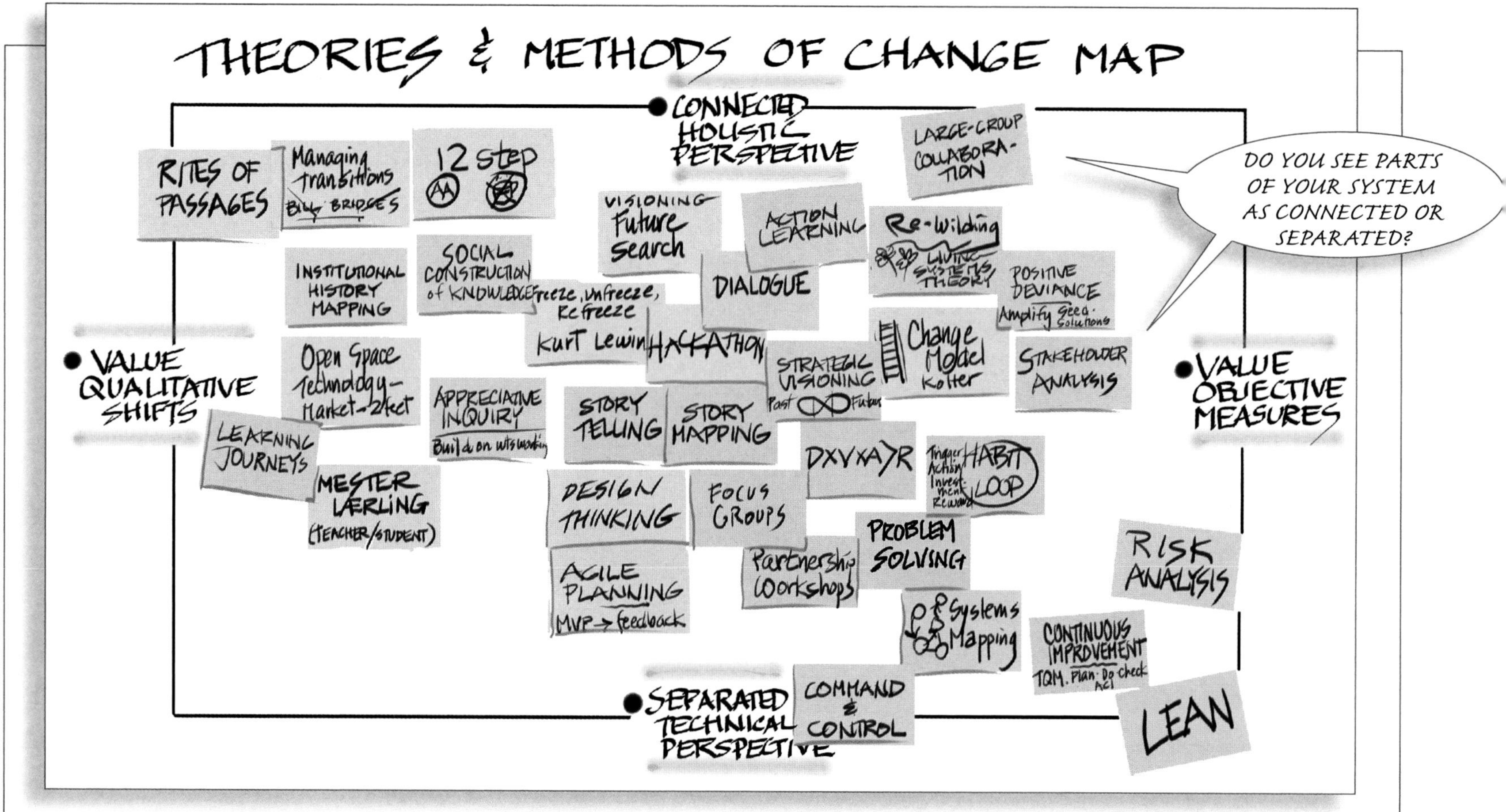

Designing & Leading Change workshop participants identified all the methods of change they were aware of, and some theories that had names, and placed them on this grid. The two spectra are really gradients—one between the value of objective measures on the one hand and qualitative shifts on the other—the other between a separated, technical view of the world and a connected holistic one. Of course in the real world these blend, and the placement of these methods is very debatable. That was the intent—to stir up awareness and conversation. Any of these theories and methods can be searched online for explanations.

performance is the way to create change. On the other end is the belief that change requires qualitative shifts in people's hearts, minds, and souls to be lasting.

The other spectrum deals with the belief that rational processes and technical systems are composed of separate elements that need to be integrated in objective ways. This, in a way, is what some call "modernism" as a school of thought. The other end of this spectrum is the belief that systems are holistic, interconnected webs of influence and fields of energy and that change happens dynamically by living into the change and holding strong intentions. This emerging perspective has many names.

While we have created a spectrum with seeming opposites, in the real world we see approaches that blend aspects of each extreme. In the field of OD, the more modernist or diagnostic approaches dominated the 1960s, 70s, and into the 80s. In more recent years, change consultants give far more weight to the social narratives that shape behavior, as Gervase and Marshak are explicating in their description of the dialogic approach. They too are careful to point out that it is a blend of diagnostic and dialogic approaches that often ends up being useful.

Identifying and placing the elements on this Theory & Methods Map sparked a wonderfully rich and inconclusive exchange in our workshop as we realized the enormous range of methods and the different scope and meaning implied by the names. As challenging as this is, it is a helpful way to become conscious of your bias, and not be locked into just one method.

Organizational change teams need enough structure and language to get engagement, and then focus on grounding the case for change in some concrete goals connected to language and experience they understand. This exploration sets the stage for designing a roadmap for change that everyone can agree on.

Figure 9.11

Leading Business Innovation

Maaike Doyer, CFO and strategy designer for Business Models Inc. (BMI), heads up their U.S. practice. Using graphic templates like the Business Model Canvas combined with Grove Graphic Guides, she inspires group creativity.

"Doing a workshop visually and encouraging participants to be visual really helps to stop the blah blah," she says. "You lose the arguing and focus on seeing the essence and core of what people want to say. We encourage participants to be visual and use sticky notes—we push them. 'Is this an arts and craft class—I thought we are doing strategy,' some say. But when you warm them up and draw yourself, they jump in and express things even their colleagues don't know about. I really love the power of templates. If you give people a blank sheet they just start talking and are all over the place. If you frame the strategic conversation you don't get distracted. I use templates plus conversation, then another template, and then visual reports!"

Maaike comes to visual consulting through BMI, designing new strategies and innovation for corporates.

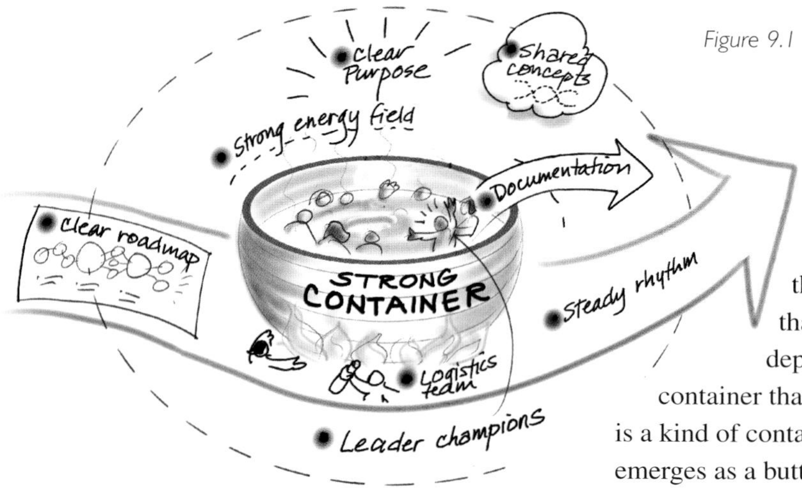

Figure 9.1

3. Designing a Strong Container for the Work

Process consultants talk about creating and maintaining "containers" for the work. This is, of course a metaphor. A container is something stable that can hold ingredients. In cooking, containers are appropriate, or not, depending on what you are setting out to cook. In metallurgy the crucible is a container that can withstand high heat so the metals recombine. In biology the chrysalis is a kind of container for the caterpillar as it turns to mush, recombines its molecules, and emerges as a butterfly. All types of containers have the characteristic of being reliable. In process work its elements and surrounding forces form a coherent whole (see Figure 9.1).

Another Way to Look at Elements of a Strong Container

Attention

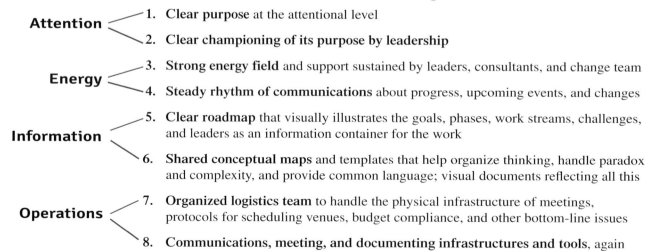

1. **Clear purpose** at the attentional level
2. **Clear championing of its purpose by leadership**

Energy

3. **Strong energy field** and support sustained by leaders, consultants, and change team
4. **Steady rhythm of communications** about progress, upcoming events, and changes

Information

5. **Clear roadmap** that visually illustrates the goals, phases, work streams, challenges, and leaders as an information container for the work
6. **Shared conceptual maps** and templates that help organize thinking, handle paradox and complexity, and provide common language; visual documents reflecting all this

Operations

7. **Organized logistics team** to handle the physical infrastructure of meetings, protocols for scheduling venues, budget compliance, and other bottom-line issues
8. **Communications, meeting, and documenting infrastructures and tools**, again providing a platform for work at the operational level

You may have proposed all these elements, but now you need to create, implement, and maintain them as a container for the work. You begin this process in Change Challenge 3, but will continue through Change Challenge 4 and into whatever handoffs you arrange.

UC Merced Roadmap

The introduction of the Visioning process to the UC Merced Change Alignment Team meant a redesign of the Roadmap. We had other elements of the strong container in place by this time, but the big agreements on number and size of meetings, participants, focus, pacing, and support all needed considerable discussion. Several meetings were required to make these decisions. We needed to figure out how to involve the Cabinet. It became clear that the CAT would continue to work on the change alignment framework, but the chancellor and Cabinet would work on the draft vision that would go to the summits for reviews. How would we move from the chancellor's vision to one that reflected the entire Cabinet? How would we review these in the summits? Would the staff and faculty meeting together or separately at the summits?

On the following page is the roadmap that sums up the results of those meetings (Figure 9.14). You do not need to understand this particular process in detail, but we include this diagram because its form has emerged in our practice as a reliably clear way to visualize an approach. (It was intentionally created in PowerPoint so the client could adapt it.)

This roadmap was subsequently used in large poster format as an orientation tool in every subsequent Cabinet, CAT, and Summit meeting throughout the rest of the process. Along with the other elements listed above, the CAT was successful in creating a strong container for the process.

Figure 9.12

Visual Strategies for Sparking Creativity

There are an endless number of visualization techniques for getting a group to be creative. Here are some practices with minimal scribing skills.

- ☐ **"Success looks like" jam sessions**: Take whatever you are wanting to explore and have small groups create a picture of what success looks like to them. Compare and harvest themes.
- ☐ **Metaphor play**: In visioning, ask triads to answer the question, "Our organization is like a..." (plant, machine, other organization). Explore each idea for what it illuminates and obscures. Harvest best ideas.
- ☐ **Visual scenario exploration:** Take classical four-box scenario options and play with how you would visualize them.
- ☐ **Theming with graphic wall templates**: Provide standard Grove Graphic Guides to small groups. Fill out, post, and harvest themes visually.
- ☐ **Three dimensional prototyping**: Use Lego blocks, clay, or other materials and ask people to express their idea three dimensionally. Exploring what the constructions mean draws out great ideas.
- ☐ **Video prototyping**: Use smart phones to make a video of your ideas.

UC Merced Roadmap Changes

In Chapter 8 we went into some detail about how to design a roadmap with your change team. As the CAT headed into the challenge of creating and sharing possibilities, we had to change the UC Merced Roadmap. Here is the final version that was used in every subsequent meeting to keep the process on track. We share it again to underline the importance of iterations.

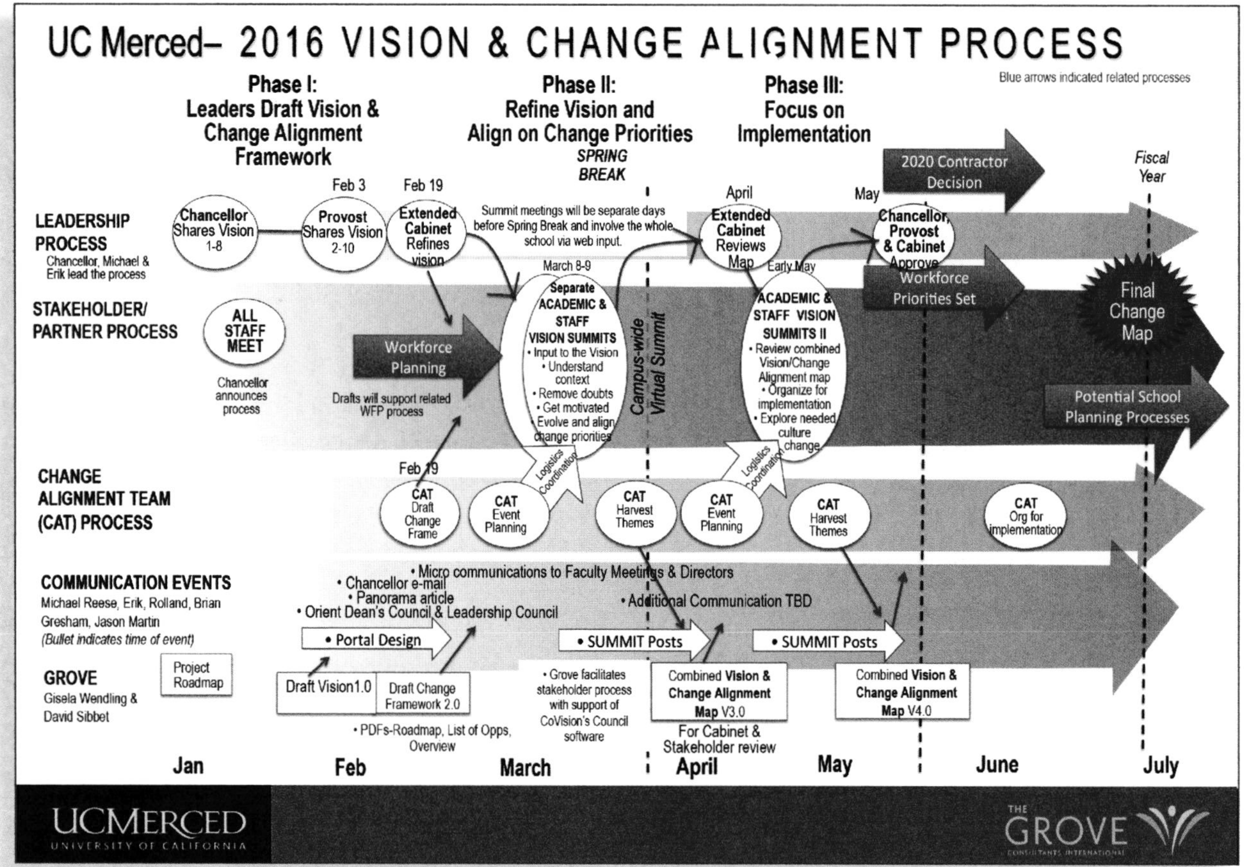

1. The overall name of the project and phases were renamed to include visioning.
2. We included the chancellor, provost, and Cabinet process at the top and the CAT change alignment work flow at the bottom as support.
3. The summits were named and expanded.
4. The expected deliverables are clearly illustrated along the bottom.
5. Other related projects are shown as darker arrows, to keep a whole-systems perspective.

Figure 9.15

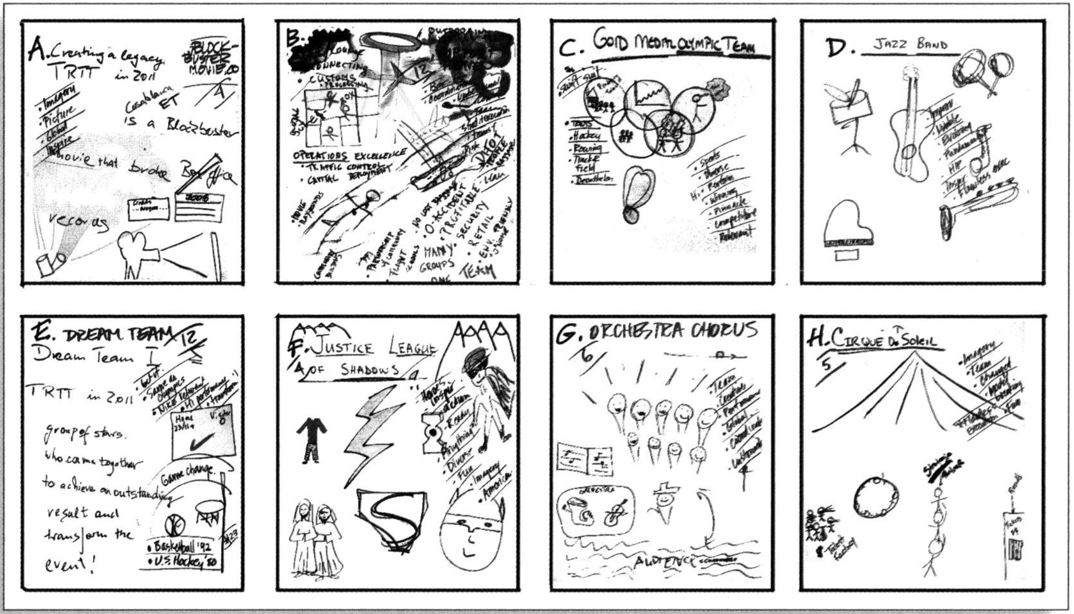

4. Visualize Possibilities

Once the change team you support has decided on its entry points, determined an approach, and created a container for the work, then your client will be involving people in the activities everyone has planned. This is when getting creative about the substance and content of the change is important. We can't in this book hope to characterize all the activity in this creative stage, but do want to share some of the types of things you can do to stimulate creativity in regards to whatever it is you need to figure out. On this page are some examples of the kinds of visualizing financial people did to envision their future organization (Figure 9.26). This kind of play is about the ideas, not the skill in rendering. The substance emerges from inquiry.

Portray Your Organization in Imagery

On vision maps, the way the organization is characterized will be a graphic metaphor that invites people to imagine what is possible. This will complement the vision statements, which are often in words. To get images that resonate, it works best to draw them out of the group. This is a terrific opportunity to have everyone think about their organization as a whole system, but in a natural, nonthreatening way. Comparing what we are working on to what we already know is a built-in kind of process for most people. If you listen, people will do this in ordinary conversation. "Oh, our organization is a real dynamo," someone

Metaphor Play

When the Treasury Department of a large, multinational company was looking for a metaphor to organize a vision for its four divisions, we asked eight pairs to generate flip chart images answering the question, "In the future, treasury is like a..." After reviewing each image for what worked about the metaphor and what didn't, they chose "C." the Olympic team as the best. It was a precise fit for that culture which cared about top performance The individual work of different units became the different sports. They were united in wanting to please their many stakeholders. And the Olympic rings became their vision elements!

SideStory 9.13

Finding the Right Metaphor

Getting a group to play with metaphors is straightforward. Here's the process.

1. Supply enough flip charts and pens for every pair to have a set.
2. Ask each pair to answer this question: ***"In _____ years, we'd like our organization to be like a..."***
3. Encourage everyone not to worry about the drawing, but sketch out their answer on a flip chart with a clear name for the metaphor at the top and maybe labels on some of the parts (see Figure 9.15).
4. Give people about 15–20 minutes.
5. Have each group share their flip chart.
6. Ask the group to identify key aspects of this comparison that they like. Note these on the flip chart.
7. Ask what this comparison doesn't show or obscures. Note these as well.
8. Step back from all the charts and invite a conversation about the metaphor that would provoke the right kind of orientation to the vision or strategy map you are creating.
9. On a large sheet, map some of the actual vision and strategy ideas on a large sketch of the metaphor.

might say. Another will say "We are like a three-ring circus." The side story in Figure 9.15 shares how one company worked with metaphors visually. SideStory 9.13 walks through how you can do it with groups that are working to visualize their plans and visions in a creative way.

Prototype Three-Dimensionally

For groups that are locked into habitual ways of thinking, getting people to share ideas through physical modeling can result in breakout conversations and insights. The **Lego Serious Play™** process developed by the company and now certified to consultants is an increasingly popular way to do this. Figure 9.3 earlier in this chapter tells how Dean Meyers is using this approach in his visual consulting practice. John Ward, a colleague called his consultancy Knead to Know, led The Grove through a series of **clay modeling** sessions to become clear about our values. Another process that has roots in Jungian therapy is **sand tray work**. In this approach hundreds of figurines are used to address a question by creating an arrangement in a tray of sand. The participants then tell stories about what the various elements mean, sometimes being asked to speak from the perspective of one of the elements.

The essence of each of these processes is to get people to tell stories about the little sculptures and arrangements, and find shared meaning in the process. To the extent that human consciousness is distributed, and for many is deeply rooted in their body knowing, this kind of approach can be the part of the change process that unlocks their participation.

Visually Work with Scenarios

A creative way to do strategy work is to develop scenarios that address a set of different possible futures. Scenarios are created by identifying the drivers of change and analyzing

Figure 9.16

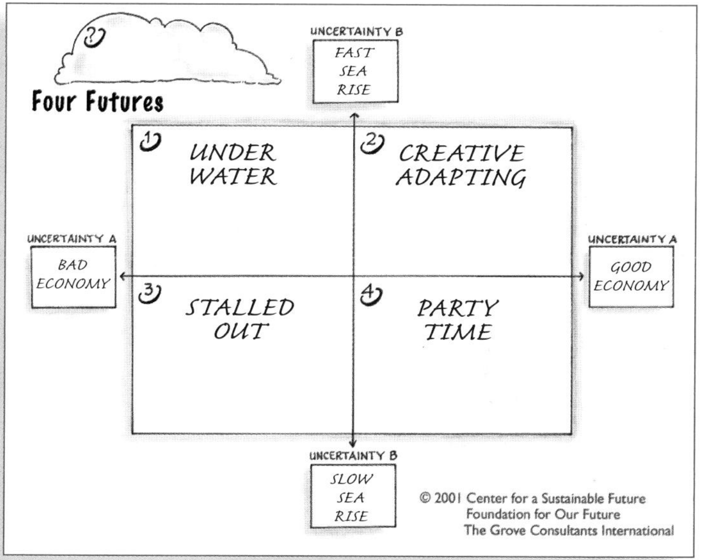

which ones will have the most impact. Then these are assessed as to which are the most unpredictable, and could have a wide range of ways of showing up. For instance, the economy could be booming or busting five years out. Weather patterns could be wet or dry. Social networking technology might be in a new period of acceptance or experiencing a backlash. One practice is to take the two most unpredictable, high-impact forces, and use them as axes on a four-by-four grid, to get four possible futures—good economy and wet; good economy and dry; bad economy and wet; bad economy and dry.

You then give the four groups imaginative names and ask groups to describe life in each one of those contexts, and come back with images and metaphors that describe the situation. (Figure 9.16). This activity invariably generates a LOT of conversation and insight.

Co-Create a Storymap of a Vision and Change

In 2014 the Environmental Defense Fund (EDF) approached us to help develop their ability to collaborate with stakeholder organizations that they hoped would support a new approach to habitat restoration in the Central Valley of California. This case is a good example of a client needing help with creating some acceptance of a new possibility of change at Challenge 3. In this case storymapping promised to provide a way for engaging people who had historically focused on regulation rather than developing innovations. By focusing on getting agreement on the map (Figure 9.17) we created a container for relationship building. Conversations surfaced important biases, and possibility thinking became more possible. By reviewing drafts of the large storymap over several meetings we were able to look at the history of habitat restoration collaboratively and agree on needs

Scenario Worksheets

Keith Wheeler and Jack Byrne of the Foundation for Our Future worked with The Grove to develop scenario worksheets for high school students to share their ideas about the future. This one takes two uncertainties that would have future impact—like climate change or the economy—and contrasts two different outcomes for each—i.e. huge sea level rise vs. small sea level rise, and expanding economy vs. collapsing economy. Students brainstorm what each quadrant would be like in the future (high seas and bad economy; high seas and good economy, etc.) The kids had no problems with this and were extremely creative.

Figure 9.17

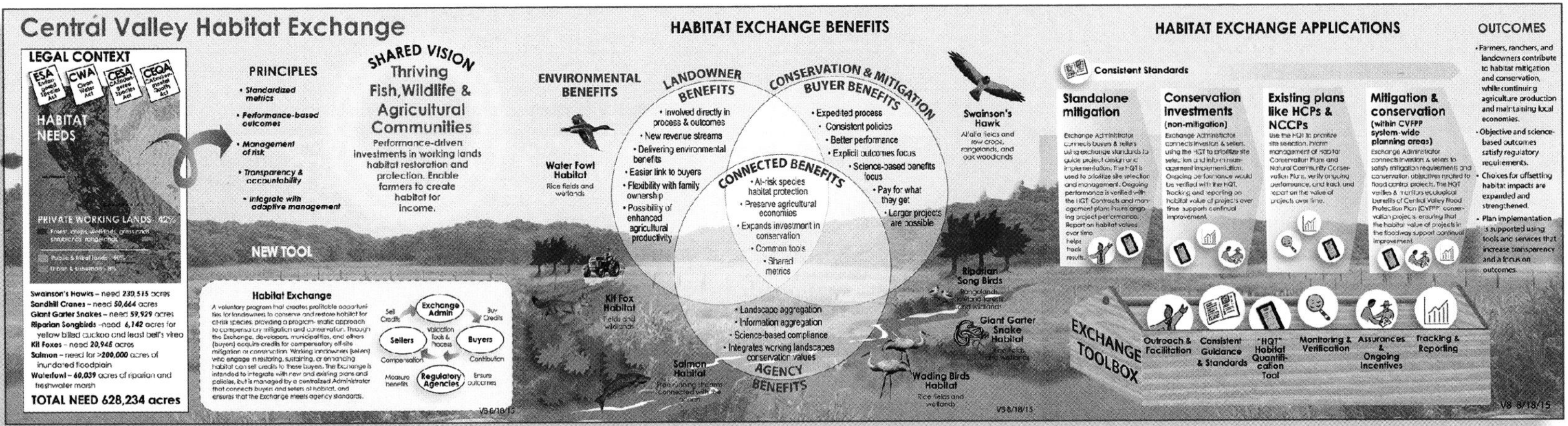

EDF Storymap

This threefold map shows the current state needs on the left, vision in the middle, and tools for action on the right.

Summary

- ☐ **Creativity is required** for process design and substantive, content generation.
- ☐ **Attend to inner dynamics** around assumptions, resistance, creating safe environments, and possibility thinking.
- ☐ **Use outer structures to foster creativity**
  1. Create a **strong case for change.**
  2. Understand your **approach.**
  3. **Build strong containers,** with scope, process, leadership, support and clear pattern and pace.
  4. **Lead your clients in creative thinking.**

and hopes across some of the differences. Visioning possibilities also provided both organizations a chance to have sensitive dialogue about concerns people had regarding the new ideas. Successive revisions and check-in meetings began building a bridge of understanding between EDF and regulatory organizations. The process had the double value of helping the EDF internal team sharpen their thinking and come to agreement on their approach and narrative.

Like many practices we have share in this book, you can use Storymapping and other methods in just one part of a larger change process.

Taking the Turn

Our next Challenge is called Stepping Into a New, Shared Vision. This is the time when the change process has reached a point where people are ready to make the big decisions that move into the new in a way that is a "no turning back phase." While this challenge of creating possibilities is divergent, the next is converging toward real commitments.

10. Stepping into a New, Shared Vision

Committing to Real Change

Figure 10.1

The *Seven Challenges of Change* model illustrates Stepping into a New, Shared Vision at the bottom of the "V" shape. Here is when aspirations meet real-world realities. Agreements and decisions on new visions couple with decisions to begin new initiatives and resource them properly. While the visual diagram looks static, when the process converges toward agreement, the intensity increases greatly. It can take many meetings and conversations, sometimes feeling more like a tunnel than a threshold. At other times it can feel like a real crucible, when the heat is high in a turning point event. When commitments come forward, the release of energy into forward movement can be palpable (Figure 10.2)—a true turn.

- At **UC Merced** the clock was ticking. Michael and the school needed to prioritize their many initiatives and move forward. They also needed to agree on a new vision in order to prioritize the change project. How much of the campus should be involved? Could they embrace new technology to do this, knowing that some of the infrastructure was still being developed?

Figure 10.2

- At the **RE-AMP network's** first cross work group gathering in Minnesota, people circled the touchy question of including nuclear energy in their working groups. Some argued there was no way to reach their goal of cleaning up global warming pollutants 80% by 2030. Others said the network would fail if it were included, because the issue was too controversial.
- At **DLR Group** the four dozen partners faced the decision to focus on becoming known as a leading design firm or stay a profitable, efficiency-oriented firm.

Figure 10.3

The Inner Dynamics of Commitment

Stepping into a new, shared vision involves some important inner dynamics. While creating and sharing possibilities is open and divergent, this challenge requires convergence and agreements, letting old things go and letting new things come. Here are some inner dynamics to watch for as groups head into this territory.

- ❑ **Reconnecting with purpose**: Most change situations are not resolvable by rationality alone. A sense of will and purpose needs to re-enter the process as it converges toward key decisions. It may mean having people spend individual, reflective time thinking about their own inner purpose before moving to action. Purpose for an organization is about its reasons for being. It is not the same as goals. It's a connection with the deeper reasons and feelings you have about why you need to change. How humans connect with purpose is a bit mysterious. It can be a feeling more than a thought. It may need space and time. But when it happens it can be like the tinder that lights the larger fire of a shared vision (Figure 10.3). While this phase of change is often the time of greatest constraint, reconnecting with a sense of purpose is the inner shift that can help pull camps out of "positions" and into consensus.

- ❑ **Holding complexity**: Challenges at this stage can range from simple, to complicated, to complex, to chaotic and may present themselves in any of these forms. You as a visual consultant and your clients will have to embrace a lot of complexity and sometimes paradox, where things don't seem to go together.

  At Procter & Gamble when A.G. Lafley was CEO, he describes a meeting where one camp was arguing for efficiency and economies to compete against the many smaller companies challenging different specific products. Another group was defending P&G's traditional orientation to quality and best-in-class, products. The efficiency folks were arguing for pulling back on expenses to be more profitable.

Lafley is reputed to have listened carefully to both arguments, and then concluded, "We have to do both." Great leaders and really masterful consultants can hold a lot of complexity and keep people from bolting from the process when it doesn't resolve easily. Your clients will have a range of capability in this regard, and you need to be prepared to help support them staying open. If you can embrace the complexity long enough, rather than moving quickly to either/or choices, it's often possible to have new and unexpected solutions arise. Once perceived they often seem like a natural development, coherent, or perhaps even elegant.

- ❑ **Crossing the threshold**: At certain points it's clear that there will be no easy turning back if certain decisions are made. In our personal lives, getting married is that kind of act. Becoming a parent is another example. Decisions to merge, divest, or enter a new market can have this quality. As much as we would like certainty, it is rare when it comes at points of major change, especially transformational change. Sooner or later it's necessary to decide and act even without complete assurances. Signing the Declaration of Independence was this kind of step for the US founding fathers. Ending apartheid was one for South Africa. Deciding to integrate all organizational data on a cross-functional platform is another. It takes time to come to this kind of resolve. But making these choices turns attention and energy in new directions, and releases energy into the process of acting and evolving going forward.
- ❑ **Letting go and letting come**: As the threshold times are reached, the inner psyche needs to continue to do the work of releasing aspects of our old identity and ways of thinking to create space for something new to come in. This phrase, "letting go and letting come" was originally coined by Robert Tannenbaum, one of the early pioneers of organization development. Your clients in this phase of change may need encouragement to let truly new ideas come in and for new intentions to emerge. This may involve getting clear about what to give up and stop doing. What is no longer serving? What needs completion? Attachments are real, especially when the past has been successful. As a result, being open to creating the new is not a path that can be

How humans connect with purpose is a bit mysterious. It can be a feeling more than a thought. It may need space and time. But when it happens it can be like the tinder that lights the larger fire of a shared vision.

Figure 10.4

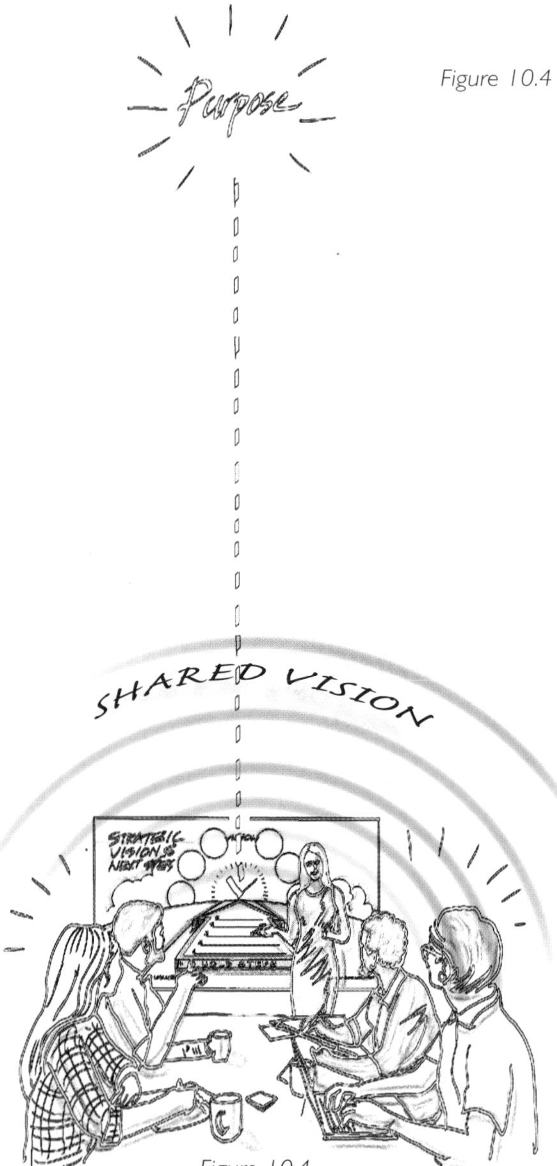

Figure 10.4

entirely known. There are always risks, and giving up what is known and familiar can be tough. As a visual consultant you may have been a strong catalyst for creating and visualizing emerging possibilities, but at this point the real shift has to be in the hearts, minds, and bodies of your clients themselves. Encouraging and creating safe spaces for reflection helps. Pushing them too hard can get in the way.

Nonobjective Aspects of Stepping into a New, Shared Vision

Groups are immersed in a field of attention and energy that are only partially observable. These fields are the context for the inner dynamics we just described. In them, people experience each other and resonate with each other like instruments in an orchestra.

When members of an organization have been in a long process—looking at their external environment, their organizational situation, their different options, and potential futures, and then find themselves approaching a big collective decision, they are in a different kind of place than what they are usually in. For some, their awareness might be exceptionally heightened. Others might feel depleted. But for the group as a whole, when approaching a real turning point in a group process, the energy shift in the room is often palpable (Figure 10.4). In this kind of context, one person might step forward and voice something that has been on the edges of people's awareness and is suddenly in the center. The rippling impact sparks others to share. Something becomes clear and compelling. A true turn is happening, and it can feel like it has a life of its own, creating a contagion of interest. This isn't something you can predict, but it can be anticipated and supported when it starts happening. Just holding space for the shift is the best practice at these times.

This kind of shift doesn't always happen in group meetings. In some settings agreements stall, with positions deepening. This may catalyzes a leader to dig deep into his or her own resolve and sense of purpose and find a way forward. However, if this happens in a context where the leader or leaders have been listening to and understanding all perspectives, and wrestling with choices respectfully, it can be a welcome shift to have some direction and commit to action. Leaders in this case need to be encouraged to stay open to additional insight. Unless everyone eventually feels a shift in their own understanding and the energy that comes from feeling aligned and sharing an emerging sense of commitment, the change process will be handicapped.

For you as a visual consultant, both tracking content, and staying open and resonant with the larger fields of energy that leave a group feeling aligned or fragmented, is truly a challenge, but a key to getting results (Figure 10.5). It takes practice to do both especially with larger organizational change projects. Collaborating with another consultant to stay fully aware of all these dimensions is good practice, especially in large scale processes.

Supportive Structures for Stepping into a New Vision

Let's turn our attention to how these kinds of inner dynamics can be supported as people enter into what is often a "crucible" kind of experience. Visual consultants have some real advantages in this regard, for images and graphic environments can create conceptual containers that allow people with diverse points of view to start seeing new patterns, literally. At the crux moments of the turn in a group process, it needs to be held, well facilitated, and not forced. The leaders, the process design team, and the facilitators need to participate in this holding. From the get-go of process design work and subsequent meetings, you will want to lay the groundwork for having leaders trust the process. You also build capability within the client group when working through smaller issues and

Figure 10.5

Feeling Energy in a Group

Whether working alone or in a team, the more you are attuned to your own internal responses as they play out in your mind, emotions, and body, the more you can discern what your own inner knowing tells you about what is needed in the group. You can learn to sense energy fields, read the group, and discern next steps to take. Remembering to notice your physical sensations, thoughts, and feelings all together is an essential self-awareness practice. This is a key aspect of what we mean by "use of self."

Figure 10.6

Power of Imagery

Adam Kahane tells the story of South African's coming to grips with apartheid in a series of scenario-planning sessions. First there were many dozens of stories of how a transformative change could take place. Then everyone met again and a dozen still seemed viable. In yet more meetings a couple of scenarios began to rise above the others, each connected with a very generative image.

One was called "Icarus" and suggested that the African National Congress, if it came to power, would move too quickly to change, over-reach, and like Icarus melt from coming too close to the sun. Another scenario was called "Flight of the Flamingos," and suggested that if everyone took off gracefully, together, they could weather the change. They aspired to the flight of the flamingos. But many say that the image of Icarus helped keep the ANC from over-reaching in those early days. -

creating more process awareness by regularly inviting reflections on what is happening. This will grow the process leadership capabilities of the group and prepare it for big turns.

When transformative change is taking place, deep cultural norms are being challenged. Culture is to the organization as identity is to the person, and a transformational process literally alters the form of each. As a result, this stage of developing and committing to a sense of the new may take some time.

Activities that Provide Outer Structure

1. **Generate new images**: Symbols and metaphors have enormous power in people's imaginations. When coming to a big turn toward a new direction, that new direction needs to be remembered at a deep level, and pointed to by generative images that suggest action and possibilities. Within organizational contexts, generating a picture of the new vision that has real resonance and buy-in provides something tangible to commit to. Keeping it high level enough that invites possibilities and actions differentiates this kind of imagery from plans with concrete steps. Agreements on the words and images create a type of conceptual space that can "hold" the converging process over many versions. We will share how UC Merced accomplished that, as the change alignment framework became a Vision & Change Alignment Map. The story about South Africa (Figure 10.6) is a powerful example of how generative images can anchor and guide a transformational change.

2. **Make tough decisions:** Convergence in a change process usually means some things have to be put aside. The RE-AMP network decided not to take on the issue of nuclear power in their initial years, in spite of the intense belief on the part of some that they could never achieve their greenhouse gas reduction goal without it. UC Merced faced a huge challenge rising from the high costs of recruiting top-level research faculty in tension with the high costs of labs and support staff. DLR

Group knew that focusing on becoming a top-level design firm might mean trading off profits for a while. Visual consulting practices for creating decision support environments help enormously in this regard. (We'll describe how the DLR decision was facilitated, later in this chapter.)

3. **Invite explicit commitments**: Stepping into a new vision requires not only an inner shift in interest but also making explicit commitments. Designing and facilitating occasions for people to arrive and express their inner sense of clarity in overt, visible ways is part of the visual consulting art. Special events and actions that show evidence of leadership commitment are helpful. At UC Merced, getting contracts for new buildings was evidence for that kind of commitment. Encouraging your clients to pay attention to how they embody commitment is an important service you can provide.
4. **Identify initiatives:** Another expression of commitment is identifying and resourcing key initiatives that will take action on the new visions and possibilities. Many strategic visioning processes end in this. Cal Poly Pomona's College of Business Administration made sure that initiative teams were in place at the same time they agreed on the overall vision by which they would start to steer. The DLR Group, which will be described later, not only empowered a series of initiatives but held a second partner meeting to create first drafts of action plans as a group, to cement everyone's intention about the new directions. There are different practices associated with this kind of process we will describe.
5. **Determine resources**: Stepping into a new vision means matching commitments to resources, otherwise you may have weakened implementation. Financial resources are important, of course, but people's time may be the more important factor that needs attention. As you will see in the next challenges, actualizing change is a long process, and requires extended support. Allocation of special resources is a key part of the "body language" that signals commitment (Figure 10.7).

SideStory 10.1

Check Your Organization's Body Language

People in large organizations expect leaders to craft messages about new initiatives in appealing ways, but before "buying-in,"often wait until there is real "body language" that demonstrates the commitment. Body language in organizational terms includes the following. Use this checklist when advising your clients.

- ☐ New leadership **appointments**
- ☐ **Budget** reallocations
- ☐ Explicit **policy shifts**
- ☐ Creation of **new organizational units**
- ☐ **New ways of measuring** progress and performance
- ☐ Making sure **key people appear at meetings**
- ☐ **Hiring** policies
- ☐ **Promotions**
- ☐ **Bonuses** matched to new directions

Organizational body language that is congruent with the vision and associated goals evokes and strengthens the commitment in those whose challenge it is to implement the change.

SideStory 10.2

Common Processes in Dialogic Approaches

In Gervase Bushe and Robert Marshak's *Dialogic Organization Development: The Theory and Practice of Transformational Change* they have identified three inherent processes that are common when organization change.

1. One of the characteristics is that the **old narrative is disrupted** some way.
2. A second is providing a space and process whereby people can **develop a new narrative.**
3. A third is the **emergence of generative images** that evoke a sense of possibility and action. These range from framing images that energize meetings to emergent images that come to symbolize entire movements, rippling out with meaning as people embrace them. Many of the examples they cite are of people coming to a new metaphor that opens their perceptions beyond previous understanding. One example they point out is the way in which the concept of "sustainability" engaged environmentalists with the building developer communities.

We propose that dialogic approaches combined with visualization support successful change.

1. Generative Images & Visions

Visual practitioners work with metaphors all the time since these lend themselves to illustration. Working visually with metaphoric representation within a visioning process provides a strong container for change to occur. Many of the capabilities that we outlined earlier for guiding change, dialogic processes, and visual practice come fully into play (SideStory 10.2). Let's return to our story about UC Merced to see, in practical terms, how visual consulting practices supported stepping into a new, shared vision.

UC Merced Articulates a Vision

Following our meeting with Chancellor Leland, where she shared her personal vision, we conducted a similar session with the provost, using a tablet on a video call. We then began a visioning process to engage the entire campus. Here is what we did.

1. We created a **draft of the chancellor and provost vision** to share with her Cabinet.
2. We facilitated a **Cabinet-level visioning session**, integrating their new ideas and interests with the chancellor and provost's ideas.
3. We created a **large, draft vision map to be shared at a staff summit** and a **faculty summit.**
4. **We held the two Summits** where staff and faculty had a chance to respond, add, and share what staff and faculty considered to be priorities. Live streaming and an electronic brainstorming platform were used to involve remote participants.
5. We created **another draft of the Vision & Change Alignment Map,** worked up by the CAT, for presentation at a second summit meeting to test the ideas and develop goals that might flow from these agreements.
6. We facilitated a **combined Staff/Faculty Summit** to agree on the vision and change alignment priorities, and the criteria for setting priorities going forward.

Figure 10.7

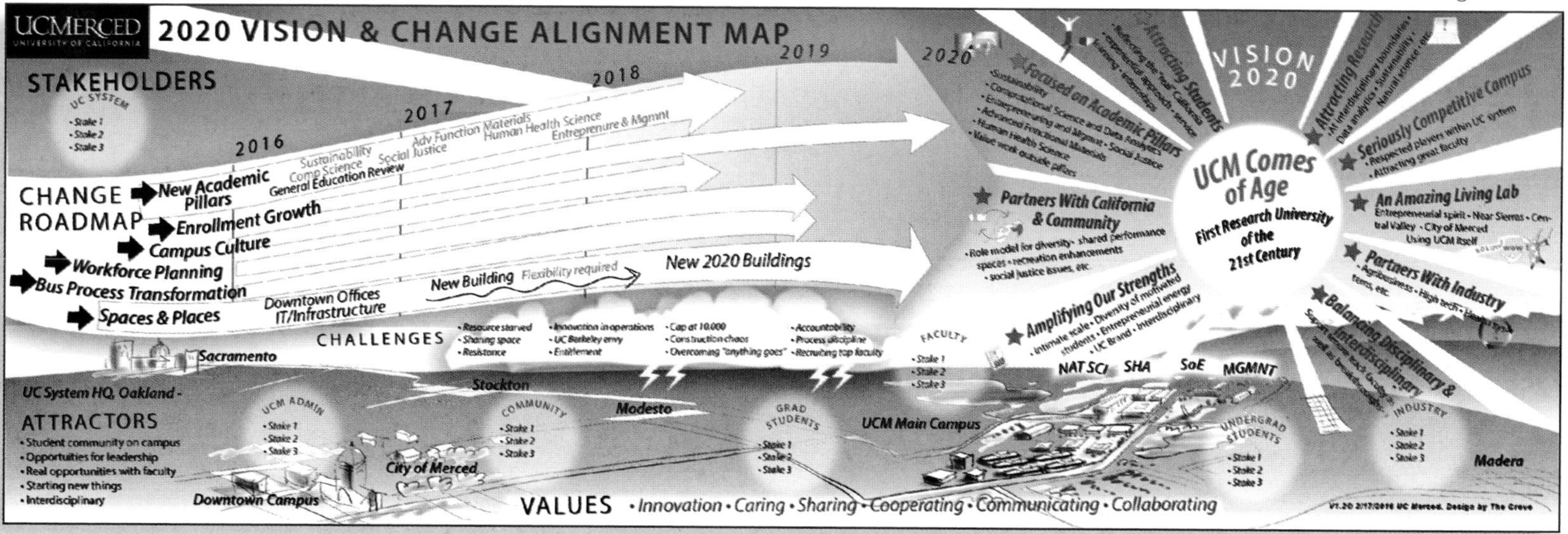

While the goal of getting an agreed-on big-picture map of the vision and change project priorities was the integrating activity in the change process, spiraling around this were numerous CAT meetings, smaller huddles, leadership conversations, and other projects all interacting and generating ideas about what needed to change. This is where the real alignment and change occurred.

Visioning with the Cabinet

In preparation for our first cabinet visioning session we prepared a translation of the chancellor/provost vision plus the CAT's initial ideas about aligning the change projects (figure 10.7). A key meeting design decision was choosing to have the Cabinet work on their vision first before seeing this map. The entire CAT was present so most of the significant leadership of the university participated. Everyone participated in a well-tested visioning process (see SideStory 10.3). One of the reasons this process works is it integrates different ways of connecting with inner knowing. Some like the quiet of their own imagination stimulated by the guided imagery questions. Others like telling a story

First Draft of a UC Merced 2020 Vision & Change Alignment Map

This was the initial draft integrating the chancellor and provost vision for the university, and the initial articulation of work streams identified by the Change Alignment Team (CAT). The CAT worked several rounds on this version before showing it to the Cabinet.

The image on the right side of the map was meant to look like the rising sun, a prominent experience in the great valley where Merced is located . The change projects moved over a landscape of challenges, stakeholders, and values.

SideStory 10.3

Visioning Process

The following is a well-tested process for catalyzing vision ideas.

1. Explain the **purpose of the visioning,** which is to "imagine a desired future."
2. Lead a **guided imagery session** that invites everyone to imagine a time five or so years in the future when a gathering is happening to celebrate being successful. (Structure general questions in the guided imagery session that don't provide any detail, but spark ideas.) Have everyone take private notes after the guided imagery session.
3. Have **pairs or triads share their visions,** giving each 4 minutes to tell the story in the past tense as though it has already happened. The others then give a couple of minutes of feedback about what was most compelling. Then shift roles and the second tells a story and so on. The full round takes 20 to 30 minutes.
4. Ask everyone to **join a second pair or triad** and repeat.
5. **Share ideas and map all themes** on a large cluster diagram(Figure 10.11).
6. **Dot vote** the most compelling.
7. **Talk about the patterns** of shared vision themes that emerge.

Figure 10.8

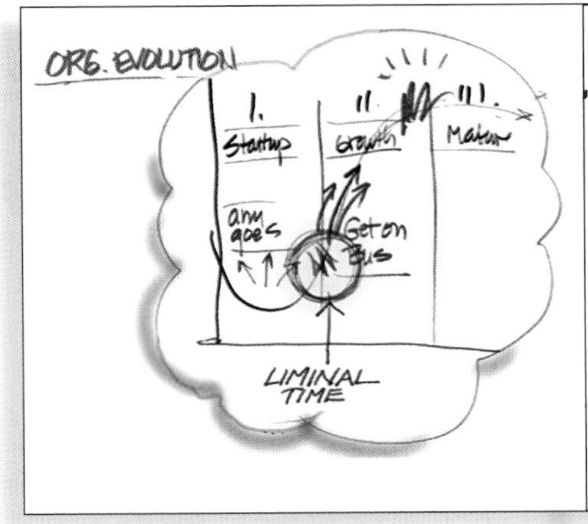

Figure 10.9

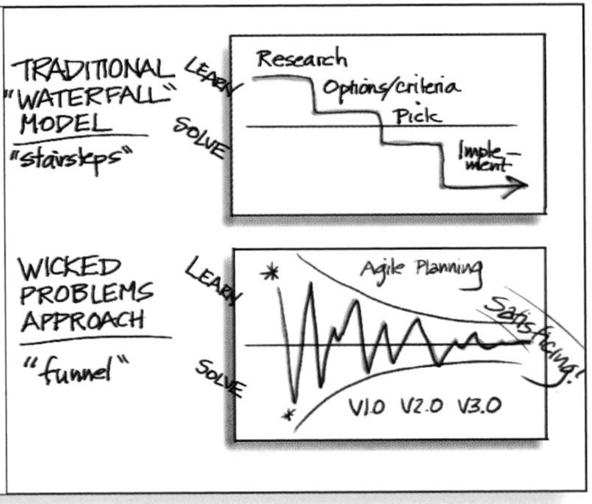

The Importance of "Framing" Metaphors

Two images were used throughout the UC Merced process that helped everyone orient to what they were doing at a big-picture level. These kinds of tools are a critical part of what a visual consultant can bring to their work.

The "S" Curve drawing was used to explain the shift UC Merced was finding itself in between start-up and growth phases in the organization's developmental change process. It is generally understood that the transition between stages is not smooth, but can be turbulent, or, appreciating this as another example of the basic pattern of change. Telling this story helped normalize the ambiguity many were feeling with the uncertainty and shifts in identity as the university began moving out of its more entrepreneurial era.

The Wicked Problems diagram was a second image used to help frame the work of the Vision & Change Alignment Project as a wicked problem with changing players, complexity, changing circumstances, and unpredictable timing. Both traditional planning and wicked problem approaches spend time both learning and solution finding. Traditional planning assumes that learning comes first and generates options, which are picked and implemented in sequence. In wicked problem solving (not unlike a design thinking process), solution finding and learning alternate with a steady funneling down toward something that will not be perfect, but will "satisfice." We wanted the academically oriented people to be prepared to support a more permissive process, avoiding arguments over details.

and tapping the power of spoken words. Others respond to the visual mapping that supports literally seeing patterns and connections. The three combined works well.

In the cabinet meeting we varied the process in a critical way. After the two rounds of triads sharing their visions, we invited Chancellor Leland to share her and the provost's, unveiling the large draft we had created (figure 10.7).

Chancellor Leland shared the content of the vision in an inspiring way, but did not like the sun image, which looked like a hub and spokes. "It looks too mechanical," she said. "Maybe it should be more of a spiral." This was a crux moment. If we had been attached to that version or argued for it because of this or that the process would have been derailed. Instead we openly explored that possibility. She and others resonated with the idea that the spiral implied an evolutionary process, and continuing unfolding. This was especially appropriate because UC Merced is a young, only 10-year-old university.

First Draft of a Shared Set of Vision Themes

After the triad work and the vision presentation, we asked everyone to pair up and connect their own visioning with what the chancellor had just presented, "What are the shared vision elements that we could all align on?" we asked. All these ideas then went on the board, creating the long, 16–foot display. We then asked the Cabinet to dot vote the most compelling items. Figure 10.11 is the final chart with all the potential shared vision themes, with the areas of most attention highlighted.

First UC Merced Cabinet Meeting

A combined Cabinet and CAT meeting was held in the chancellor's big conference room. The table doesn't move so we brought in easels and large sheets of foam core board for graphic work.

In this picture Gisela is orienting everyone to the meeting. You can't read them but the OARRs chart and the Roadmap were both on the wall and were used to orient everyone.

It's essential that when a group is accustomed to leaders chairing these kinds of meetings, make it clear you have been asked to facilitate. Have the leader explicitly introduce you and your role and their desire to participate, which is what we asked the chancellor to do.

Figure 10.14

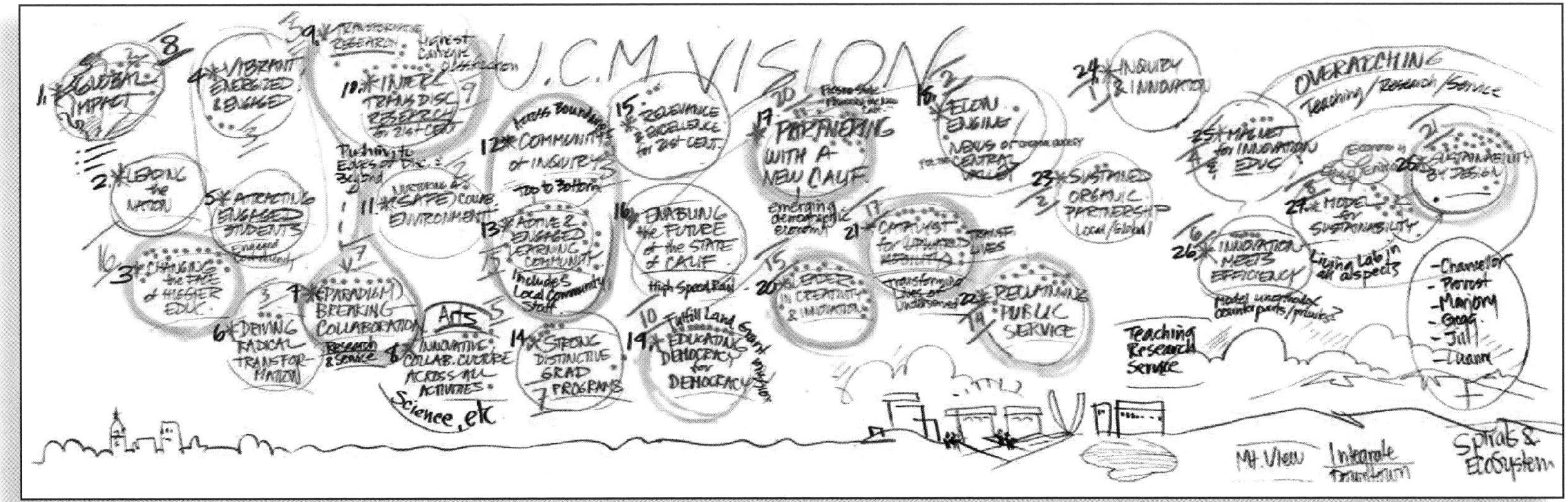

Clustering Vision Themes

Here is the chart we created of all the ideas emerging from the visioning exchanges and the chancellor and provost sharing their vision.

For this kind of activity it is important to write boldly and not confuse this kind of chart with interpretive graphics. The horizon line and simple sketch of the campus provided a grounding kind of frame. The main focus was on the content and the language that would be used in the vision. Everyone has to be able to read the chart from midroom, and during the dot-voting, which then graphically shows which items were considered most compelling.

All during visioning with the Cabinet, we stressed that these ideas would be revisited in the big summits, and we would go through this visioning again, optimizing the possibility of identifying the truly deep, emergent vision that was probably already implicit.

The Cabinet session was very well received. Since their stated role is to keep track of the big-picture vision, they appreciated having the time for a real engagement. It ended with the chancellor being explicit about wanting the Cabinet to attend the summits and participate, listening to the faculty and staff with curiosity and an open mind.

Following this and all the other meetings we published an 11"×17" report with color images of all the charts and the different group activities so people could remember the conversations, and created a revision of the large vision map for sharing at the summit. The revision process involved several meetings and calls with the client and the CAT.

Holding Big Summits to Do Large-Scale Visioning

The Summits were themselves an embodiment of the level of commitment of the chancellor and university leadership. Extending it with technology so everyone could

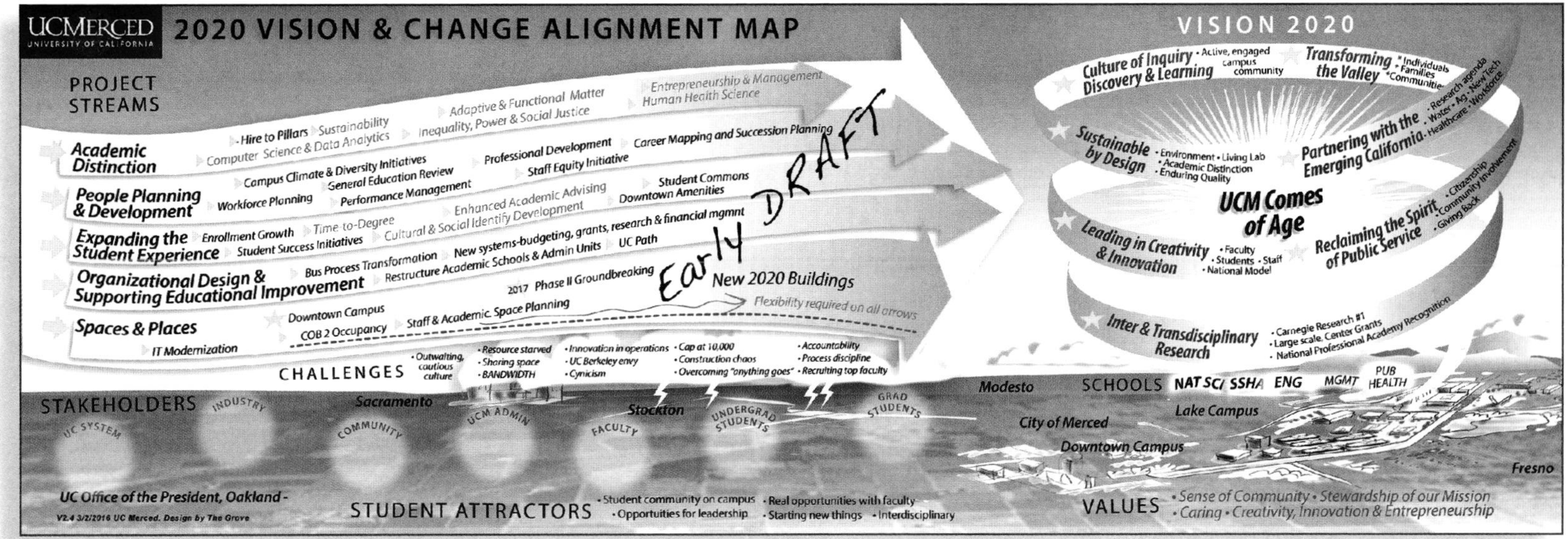

participate was an even bigger communication of intent. There are many layers we could unpack here, but we want to emphasize what we did to create a strong container.

- ❑ The Summits **blended collaboration technology** with **big-picture work**.
- ❑ **Key presentations were recorded live** on the stage boards which also held large murals of the process Roadmap and Vision & Change Alignment Map.
- ❑ The **process was also live streamed** to the campus, and projected on the large image magnification screens (see Figure 10.13).
- ❑ In addition Lenny Lind and his Covision team managed an **infrastructure of iPads and special software that allow electronic brainstorming** around key questions, voting, and ranking of elements.

Gisela was the lead facilitator for this event. David was on point for orienting the remote participants by speaking to the live stream camera, and provided the graphic recording. Several logistics people helped, including Malgosia Kostecka from The Grove.

Second Draft—2020 Vision & Change Alignment Map

On this version the vision is a spiraling up from the campus. The CAT had also worked on fleshing out the project streams and values as a draft for the Summit participants to explore. We made sure to have a big label **"Early Draft"** to keep the door open to new ideas.

Figure 10.13

A Summit Setup

At UC Merced, round tables in their gymnasium were able to hold 200+ staff, attending Cabinet members, and leadership. In front was a stage, 32 feet of foam core boards on easels for recording visually, two LCD screens on either side, and a big image magnification screen overhead. A professional crew of about 5 people managed the sequencing of images and the live streaming.

Coordinating with this team was part of the visual consulting job, making sure that the visual environment matched what we were working on. We also held a full dress rehearsal with the CAT the day before.

The Process for the Summit

The agenda for the Summit's was very carefully developed with the CAT in every detail. They would play key roles in holding the container. An even more specific facilitator agenda detailed every move, question, and all the materials that were needed at each step. The process was as follows:

1. **Orientation** by the chancellor, provost, Michael Reese, and Erik Rolland. They explained the purpose, process roadmap, and framing metaphors.
2. **Input on Current Realities**: Tables answered iPad questions—"What's special about UC Merced?; What needs to change?" Input was complemented by theming and town hall comments.
3. **UCM Draft Vision Overview**: Provost and other cabinet explained the vision map.
4. **Visioning**: Guided imagery, work on table graphics, town hall check-in, then entering key ideas into iPads, theming.

Figure 10.14a

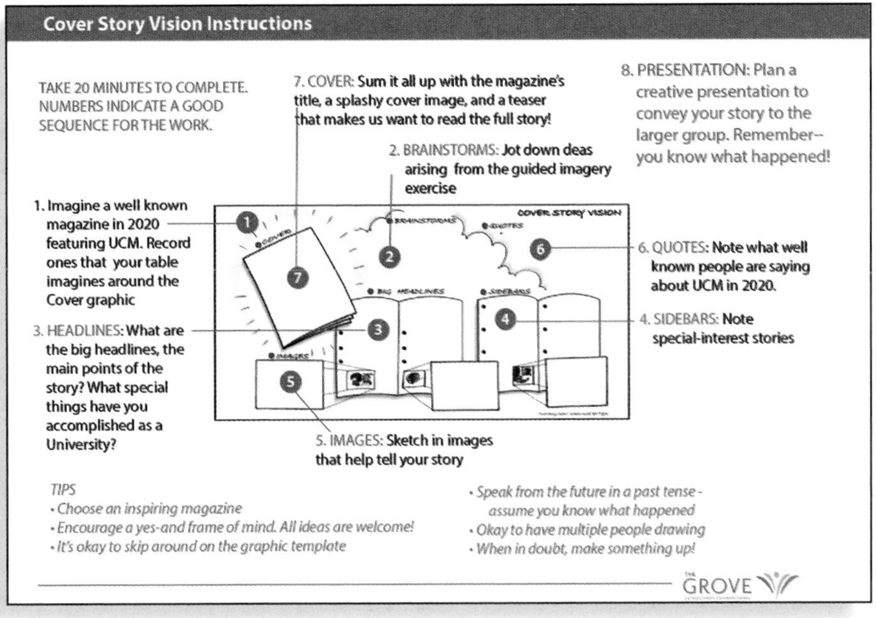

Cover Story Vision Instructions
TAKE 20 MINUTES TO COMPLETE. NUMBERS INDICATE A GOOD SEQUENCE FOR THE WORK.
7. COVER: Sum it all up with the magazine's title, a splashy cover image, and a teaser that makes us want to read the full story!
8. PRESENTATION: Plan a creative presentation to convey your story to the larger group. Remember-- you know what happened!
2. BRAINSTORMS: Jot down deas arising from the guided imagery exercise
1. Imagine a well known magazine in 2020 featuring UCM. Record ones that your table imagines around the Cover graphic
6. QUOTES: Note what well known people are saying about UCM in 2020.
4. SIDEBARS: Note special-interest stories
3. HEADLINES: What are the big headlines, the main points of the story? What special things have you accomplished as a University?
5. IMAGES: Sketch in images that help tell your story
TIPS
• Choose an inspiring magazine
• Encourage a yes-and frame of mind. All ideas are welcome!
• It's okay to skip around on the graphic template
• Speak from the future in a past tense - assume you know what happened
• Okay to have multiple people drawing
• When in doubt, make something up!
GROVE

Cover Story Visions

People can easily imagine being on the cover of an important magazine. In a guided imagery process, invite people to individually imagine getting the magazine, opening it, and seeing the big headlines and featured items, images, and quotes. Then share and record the ideas that arise.

Note the table setup below. Each had copies of the draft vision, two iPads per table, and two Cover Story Templates, as well as printed agendas.

5. **Identifying Shared Vision Themes**: Input & polls on iPads, theming on big boards.
6. **How Can We Move Toward the Vision?**: Inputs, theming, town hall.
7. **Identify Success Factors**: Inputs, theming, town hall.
8. **Takeaways**: Town hall format, roving microphone.

The successive rounds of triads, theming, and town hall open discussions pulled up the themes that really had passion and energy. Because the remote participants had access to the electronic system via browsers, they could participate in all the input sessions and polling. We hoped the spaciousness and layers of interaction would gently disrupt old narratives and provided space for new ones to emerge. In addition, the Vision Map began to become a key generative image for a new direction.

Figure 10.14b

Cover Story Visions

A key activity for the staff was getting to generate visions at their tables for the future of the university. This process used a large tabletop template with instruction cards as shown in Figures 10.14a and 10.14b. To get it started Gisela led a guided imagery activity, and then the people at the tables generated their visions

Figure 10.15

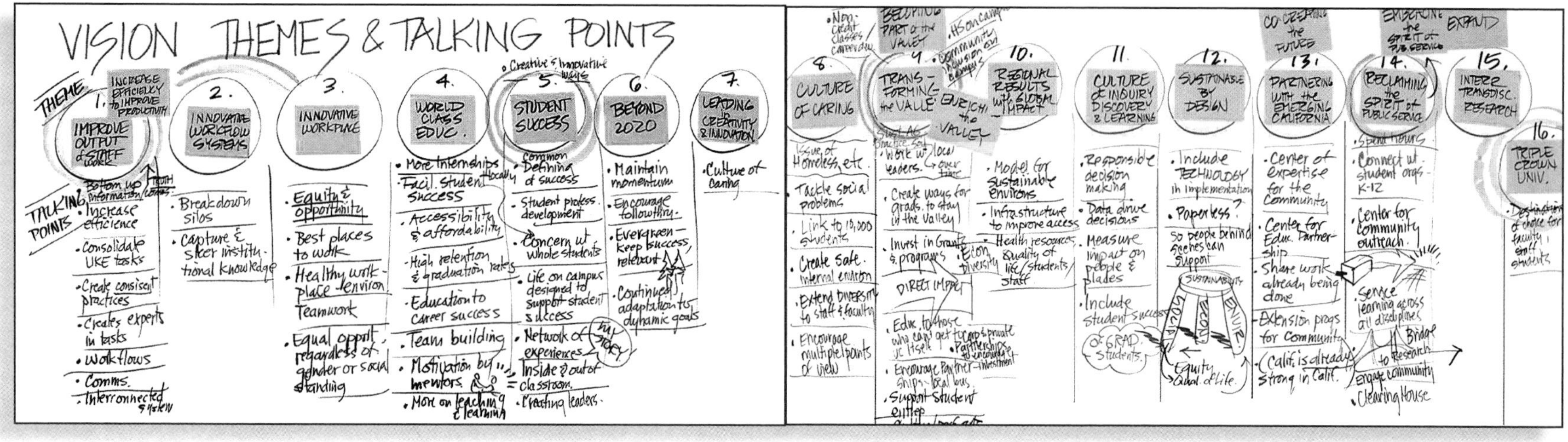

Staff Come to Draft Agreements

The final output from the Staff Summit is shown here. A robust town hall format discussion supported by traveling microphones precipitated an energized exchange.

One example was the vision element #9 on the draft regarding "Transforming the Valley." Several said this sounded almost colonial, maybe patronizing. "What about enriching the valley?" someone else proposed. Having an impact on the valley was a core driver for putting the university in Merced in the first place and remains a compelling vision. But the nuances were important. The staff were sensitive to this, and that element in the vision became "Enriching the Valley!"

on the table top cover story templates. People were asked to share a few ideas in the large group before lunch, then after lunch each table was asked to enter their most compelling vision ideas into their iPads.

These items were then themed by the theme team, and shared on the large screen and the iPads.

A second question had the tables look at the vision themes and phrase them into compelling headlines and talking points that would explain them. The headlines were called out from the tables one at a time while David created sticky notes. Gisela invited other related headlines and asked what the talking points would be. These were also recorded (see Figure 10.15). Input included the people who were participating virtually.

Staff identified sixteen vision headlines. To make it possible to rank order them, Lenny Lind also recorded them into the Covision system simultaneously. Small groups then talked and ordered the headlines on their iPads. The results were calculated immediately. David heavily circled the top ones (Figure 10.15).

As the day progressed, all of the eight or so large charts that were recorded up front were posted around the room. All of the 20 Cover Story Visions were also posted. Three large Vision & Change Alignment Maps hung on different walls. By the end of the time, the several hundred people were surrounded by their own ideas and thinking, and left from the town halls with a felt sense about what had heart and meaning for everyone.

Faculty Summit

The faculty summit was similar in structure and elements, but much smaller in size due to the fact that faculty are teaching and are also fairly distributed geographically when they aren't teaching. But several dozen participated in the entire process of visioning, and came up with a comparable set of vision elements. The focus centered on the interests and vision from the faculty perspectives allowing for a deeper, collegial discussion about the student population and the place of research and associated resource needs, tenure process, and academic direction.

The charts of vision themes from the two summits provided a very clear picture of where the staff and faculty were in agreement, and where there was different emphasis.

The Rest of the Story

In concluding the UC Merced story and showing you the final Vision Map (Figure 10.17), we want to highlight several things about working with generative imagery.

After the summits the CAT had some critical meetings making sense out of all the input. What came through loud and clear was that there were a guiding set of criteria for determining project priorities that arose in the summit exchanges. It was also proving to be impractical to try and prioritize 5 years of projects with so many variables. However, it did make sense to emphasize the criteria and focus on the next year's priorities, and check those out in the second combined summit of faculty and staff.

Figure 10.16

Collaboration Tech

To support a big meeting with video streaming, image magnification, and good audio you need an audio-visual team like this to make technology transparent.

AV can be augmented by collaboration technology like that provided by Covision, shown below. Agendas, questions, polls, and other queries are sent out to all participants who see it on their table iPads or in their browser if they are remote. Inputs are typed in and read by a "theme team," who sit in a group and develop themes from the incoming material. These themes are then shared visually and discussed in the big group.

The Final UC Merced Visioning & Change Alignment Map

Figure 10.17

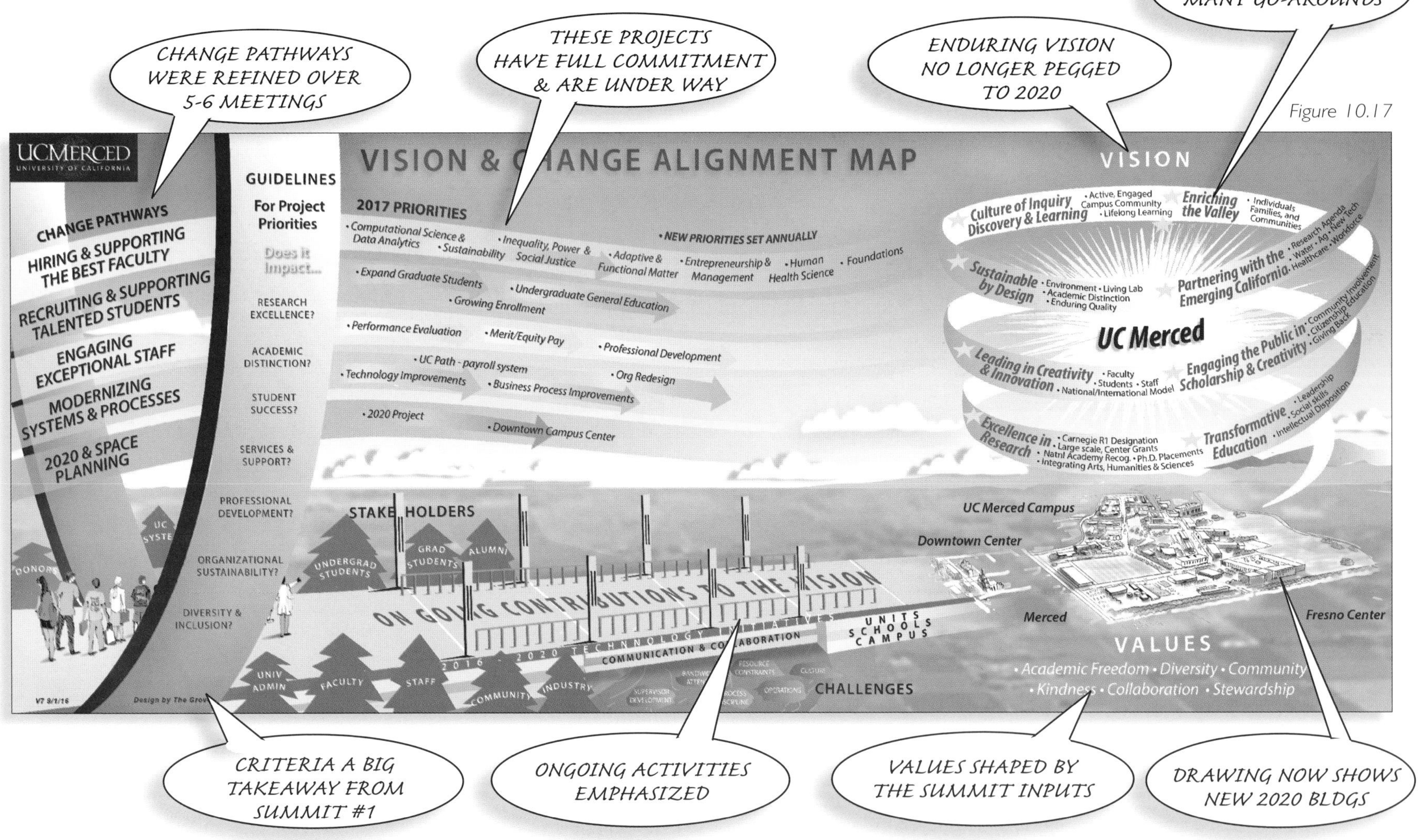

Figure 10.18

UC Merced Process Experiences a Crucible Moment

At the very end of the first faculty summit, faculty and administrators faced the tough decisions needed around staffing resources. This combined meeting was one of the first where this critical issue could be addressed constructively. Sitting close in a circular format, faculty directly addressed the criticality of more staffing. The administration was able to share its constraints and concerns. People came away feeling like this engagement was a turning point. in mutual understanding.

A breakthrough in imagery occurred when, after several different rounds, someone thought of mapping the criteria on an image of a large, central sculpture on campus called "Beginnings" that all entering student march through. It represents a large seed opening. This was perfect. You can see it on the left side of the final vision map (Figure 10.17)

A second breakthrough was having the projects moving over Scholars Bridge, a place on campus where the graduating students march. So the birthing and fulfillment of the change projects would be illustrated on this evocative imagery, with very special meaning to UC Merced. Many rounds of dialogue resulted in the images in Figure 10.17. It is now used to orient incoming students and personnel and is a live document.

2. Making Tough Decisions

Towards the end of the faculty summit, we were preparing to review the success factors, Gisela had intuitively invited everyone to pull into a closer circle to bring more presence, focus, and energy to this last activity. Then one of the faculty who had not spoken all day asked for the microphone as the first to speak. "I don't want to hijack the meeting, BUT I'm going to. We can't do any of this without more staffing and support." He went on to underline one of the really tough decision points in the UC Merced path to 2020. How would they fund both the faculty support needed to be a top-ranked research institution, one of their agreed-on visions, AND pay the kind of salaries needed to attract top new faculty and the needed labs (See Figure 10.18).

Michael and others were certainly aware of this issue, but had not had a face-to-face dialogue in a group setting with administrators and faculty together where this issue could be fully brought into the open. While the tension was high in the room at this point, the dialogue that ensued allowed both sides to express their concerns while at the same time

DLR Group Decision Room

A large architectural and engineering firm invited all partners to a two-day strategic visioning session. A decision room was staged in the hotel meeting room using large displays. In this picture you can see the graphic history in the background and large SPOT analysis charts on the right wall. A context map and visions were posted on the walls not shown. Here, they are focusing on coming to agreement on their strategic vision elements on the Five Bold Steps Graphic Guide shown on the left board.

fully, actively hearing each other. A clear shift occurred at that moment. Rather than each side being perceived by the other as mostly concerned with their own resource needs, they as a combined group began to truly see and explore together the bigger picture of overall resource constraints and the inevitable tough decisions that are required to shape a path forward. Michael came away saying that this was one of the most important exchanges yet of the work we were doing.

DLR Group Agrees on a Five-Year Plan

In visual consulting, crux points (or crucible moments) often arise in the process of working to get agreements on a final version of a key chart outlining forward directions. Because handling these points is so important, we want to dive into a little detail on how you can use graphic wall templates within a decision room environment to support this kind of process of convergence within a group when the heat is high (Figure 10.19). In this case it is the Five Bold Steps Graphic Guide, but used for a different purpose than prework and presentation. Now, the template was used **to record commitments only**. The

Figure 10.20

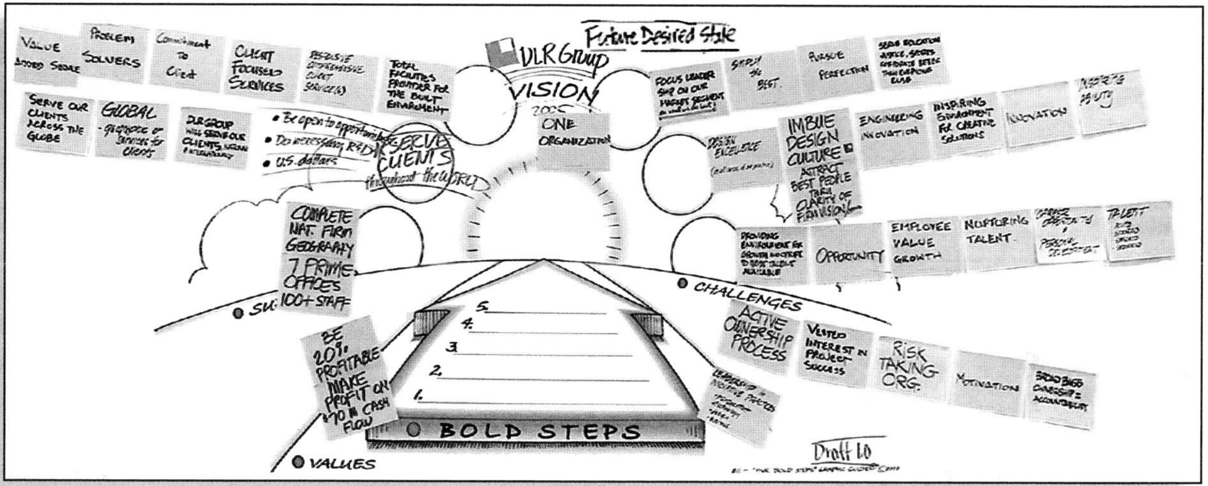

specific way in which this kind of convergence is facilitated is important to understand. It applies to any point where tough decisions are part of the process. This was a meeting that I, David, facilitated alone, and is what a visual consultant learns to do with practice. I'll describe it in the first person to let you see what I was focusing on in the process.

The two-day process was the following:

1. **Current state analysis:** The group reviewed its history, current environment, and SPOT analysis (strengths, problems, opportunities, and threats).
2. **Visioning:** Small groups, following a guided imagery session, completed Cover Story Visions and identified some themes.
3. **Harvesting vision themes:** In the afternoon of the second day, we turned to agreeing on the vision.
4. **Reviewing strategic vision elements:** The group picked one cluster to work. "What headline statement would focus your organization on the conversations you need to have," I asked. (It is important to frame the purpose of the Vision maps as "**supporting leadership to share the new narrative.**" Words can never be completely self explanatory—but they need to be compelling, inviting interest and inquiry, and brought alive by the leaders themselves sharing their understanding.)
5. **Proposing vision headlines for agreement:** Manage this kind of convergence. by

Harvesting Candidate Vision Themes

Pairs were asked to identify "candidate" vision elements from the earlier visioning work on sticky notes. Sticky notes were arrayed in clusters of similar items, boarded in long lines that rayed out from the Five Bold Steps Template as shown here. This chart shows getting agreement on the first element of "Serve Clients Through the World."

For subsequent elements we rearranged them in columns to allow room for writing talking points on the template. These kinds of chart adjustments are common and made on the spot.

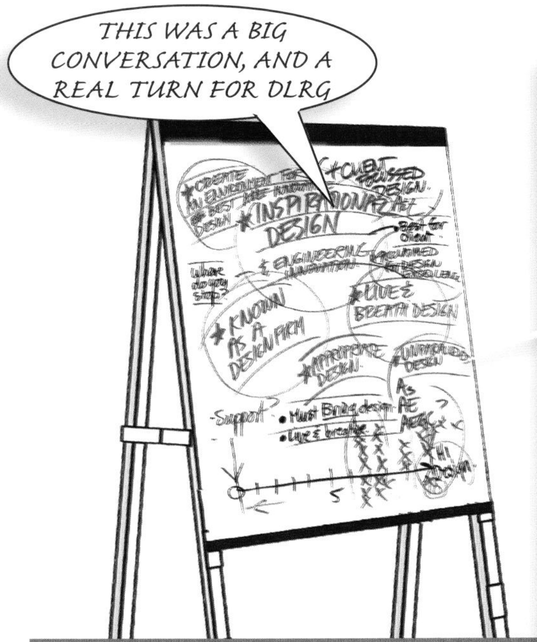

Figure 10.21

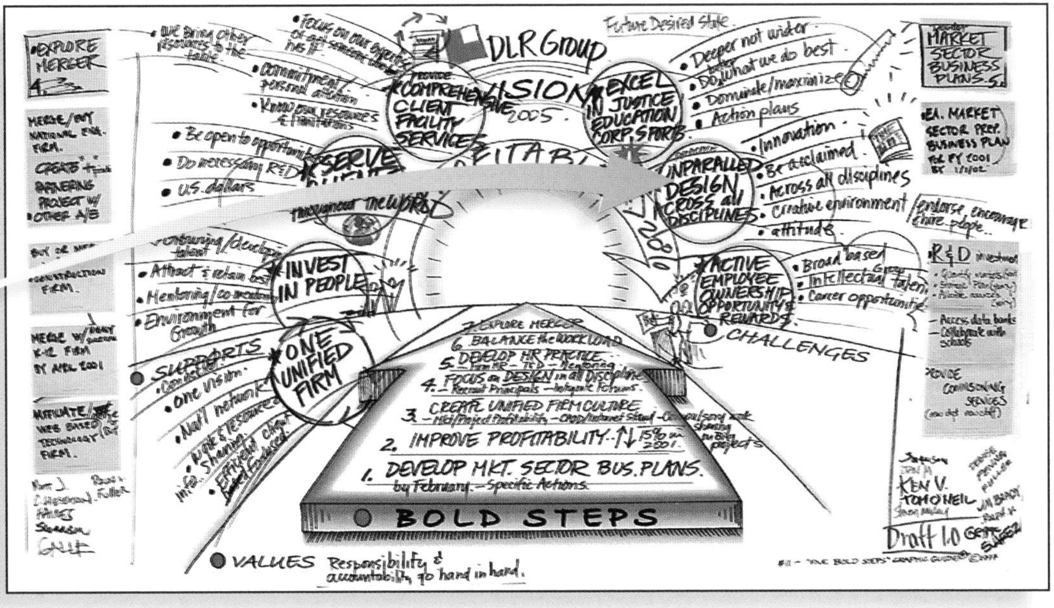

Using Templates for Commitments

Here's the process:

1. Ask, "After all your listening and talking, what's a headline that will generate the most relevant response."
2. Immediately write whatever people call out on a flip chart, boldly, and circle it.
3. Ask "Any other possibilities?" Maybe one or two others will come forward.
4. Move to agreement when a statement resonates, like a bell ringing.
5. Ask for talking points after agreement.

asking the larger group to **shift to a proposal modality**. Focus on the energetic response of the group to guide whether to push for more.

6. **Agreeing:** As proposed headlines come forward, either write them boldly as a candidate headline, or list them as a potential talking point. Explain that the headline should engage interest, and the talking points indicate more specifically what is meant. What goes in the headline versus the talking points is a judgment call the group ultimately makes—but I use my intuition to make the initial boarding. If any disagreements are voiced, even groans or other subtle signals, ask for other suggestions. At a point where all the ideas are out, pick the one that seems to have the most energy. Hold it in your right hand, invisibly, and raise it up and down, based on participant response. "Was this all the way up?" If the reaction is lukewarm, lower it or pick a second one to test. If none get a full response, ask if someone has a proposal for a headline that everyone would find compelling. If you get a strong response, test it by saying, "Going once. Going twice...pause. Three times! Agreed!"

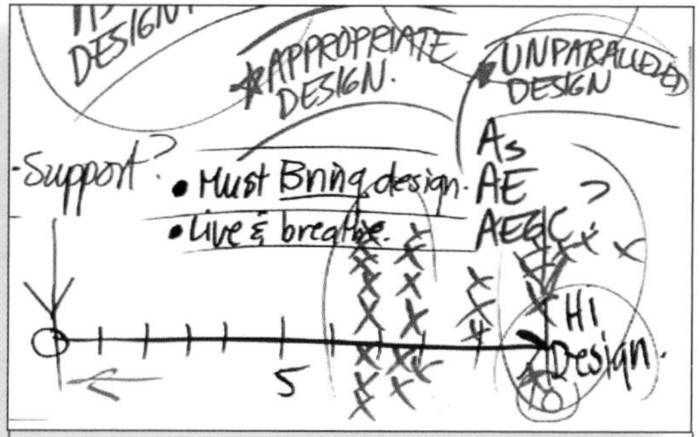

7. **Writing on the chart**: The first agreements are often slow, but when the group gets it, the energy explodes with applause. Only at this point write the headline on the Five Bold Steps chart. Ask "What talking points need to go with this?" People call them out. Write them on the big chart, even if they were on the flip charts already. Coach the group —"Let's not refine these talking points now, but come back after you've had time to soak on this vision.".
8. **Working through all the elements**: It took four hours to complete the chart in Figure 10.21. It was a wonderful, exuberance process. I was functioning like a human cursor with my pen. As a consultant I noted the energy states with my voice and movement. If the agreement didn't have energy, I wouldn't write it on the chart, but push for better proposals. Time and again this has worked to get convergence. Of course, I and the group were finely tuned by this time, and they trusted I was in service to them, not my own ideas. In addition, I encouraged leaders to be active in the converging process and they were. Their shifts and statements were critical.

DLR Group has engaged this kind of visually oriented strategic visioning process four times now, for a succession of five year plans. It has evolved to involve young leadership as part of their development. In 2012 a prominent architectural magazine voted DLR Group the top A&E design firm in the industry.

3. Invite Explicit Commitments

Our earlier points about the importance of body language in supporting the credibility of a new direction or vision comes into play here. As a visual consultant you will be involved with your design team in designing the turning point events and processes that bring things to some kind of convergence. In those moments you need to encourage the leadership that has been emerging to be very visible and overt in how they are expressing their commitments. Some of the ways you can do this are listed in SideStory 10.4.

Commitment Checks

The issue of whether to make design excellence a hallmark of DLR Group was a critical one. It would require a heavy lift from everyone. It would require a shift in mindset, hiring, and who got what kind of support. The debate on this item was passionate. But during this Five Bold Steps process they came to unanimous partner agreement that they wanted to head in that direction. Making a commitment check proved to be an important step in the process.

The intensity of the debate was such that I, David, felt it would be good to poll the group and not just trust my energy reading around commitment. So I put up a 0–10 little scale. The 10 would be "all in." A "0" would indicate complete disagreement. You can see the results here. This provided trustworthy evidence that the agreement had real commitment. A vigorous discussion followed about what it would take to have all "10s."

SideStory 10.4

Explicit Commitment Practices

- ☐ Have leaders **verbally express their commitment** at the conclusion of key summits and other meetings. Get them up on the stage doing this if you have one.
- ☐ Ask leaders to **participate in takeaway sessions** and share their commitments in a personal way.
- ☐ **Ask key emerging leaders to lead specific initiatives** flowing from strategic visioning processes.
- ☐ Have everyone **sign agreement charts.**
- ☐ **Take photos** in front of the agreements charts and post that photo on the cover of the reports that are circulated.
- ☐ **Write action agreements on a chart** and have leaders revisit them.
- ☐ **Hold a "step over the line" activity,** and physically ask people to move from one part of the room to another across an imaginary line of commitment.
- ☐ Arrange to have a **special announcement of a resource allocation decision** that supports the new vision. This might be a special appointment, creation of a new unit, or budgeting one of the agreements.
- ☐ Have leadership **announce how they intend to keep the vision fresh,** and re-turn to and update it at a future date.
- ☐ **Hold a celebration.**

The more explicitly you can mark movements in a new direction with imagery, visualization, stories, and body language the more it will stick in people's memories. Marking such thresholds and turning points with ritual-like activity, like unveiling the vision map, or holding a special event, reminds people where they are in the process and the work they have accomplished. This helps keep the momentum and focus going. In larger systems there are almost always regressions. People take two steps forward and then one back but hardly ever return to the starting point. This means successful change processes repeat things and make commitments explicit to help create the conditions for actualizing new directions (Figure 10.22). Remember—a commitment is not a plan, but a resolve. It is the point where vision and current realities come together. It can be magical.

4. Identify Initiatives

Stepping into a new, shared vision becomes even more embodied when people get involved in initiatives linked to the vision. In many cases work groups and initiatives have begun during the Creating & Sharing Possibilities phase and are then commemorated during the Stepping into the New, Shared Vision phase.

Cal Poly Business School Strategic Initiatives

After the third large-group meeting at Cal Poly Pomona's School of Business Administration, new strategic initiatives teams were formed. Each strategic initiative was headed by two members of the design team bringing the new spirit of change and collaboration to that team. We'll describe this process in more detail in the next chapter on Empowering Visible Action, but it's a great example of how a change-oriented mindset resulted in starting a critical element in the process earlier and carrying it through in later stages. Forming the initiative teams made it clear and explicit that this vision was real.

DLR Group Gameplan Session

The DLR Group, upon agreeing on their vision, concluded their two-day initial meeting determining action teams for each one of the elements on the vision. They reconvened the entire group a month later and developed action plans in parallel. They worked in a large room and were able to share and post graphic gameplans for each of the vision elements.

5. Determine Resources

In both the Cal Poly and DLR cases described above key people in the change team became the nucleus of the new working groups. There are many variations on how to handle this, depending on the context, but making sure there are real owners for agreements goes a long way toward assuring the new vision becomes a living expression of intent. SideStory 10.5 suggests ways your client might want to handle this process.

Prioritization & Portfolio Analysis

We have been emphasizing that it is important to ground a vision in bottom-line realities for it to have real traction. In the case of UC Merced, the fact that the CAT team was tasked with the change alignment part of the map, which would prioritize next year's initiatives, kept the entire process in sight of the immediate realities of workforce planning, new construction, and moving the administration groups downtown.

In other settings, as a visual consultant you might want to plan to have some sessions looking at current resources allocation and see what needs to change in light of the new strategies and vision. Rob Eskridge developed a portfolio framework embedded in the agricultural metaphor of sowing, growing, harvesting, and plowing (see Figure 10.23). This kind of framework can be used in a couple of ways. A large wall graphic is good for using large sticky notes. After determining the relevant criteria, based on the strategy or vision,

Options for Picking Initiative Leaders

Who steps up to lead new initiatives and literally step into action is a crucial aspect of embodying change. It helps to facilitate this process well. Here are some guidelines.

- ☐ Have **formal leaders pick initiative leaders**: If the formal leadership feels good about the people who will lead initiatives, they will most likely be more supportive.
- ☐ **People in the organization can volunteer**: In community initiatives, work groups are often volunteer positions. It is critical to get inclusive, facilitative leaders in these roles. This often requires identifying the natural leaders earlier in the process and encouraging them to volunteer.
- ☐ **Announce leaders later:** At DLRG, they decided not to determine initiative leaders in the first meeting, but wait until the gameplan session a month later.
- ☐ **Acknowledge change team members**: Cal Poly had members of the change team lead the initiatives. Often over the course of the change team meetings it becomes clear that certain people have the interest and capability.
- ☐ **Pick self-managing teams**: In some settings, the team themselves determine roles and how they will handle leadership and decisions.

Summary

- ☐ **Pay attention to the inner dynamics**—reconnecting with purpose, holding complexity, crossing the threshold, and letting go and letting come.
- ☐ **Support the process with outer structures**
  1. **Generate new images**: Listen for powerful, evocative metaphors that emerge from the process; guide exploration with large-scale vision maps like the one used with UC Merced; hold space for surprise.
  2. **Make tough decisions**: Look for crucible moments, create decision support rooms, shift to using wall templates for commitment rather than divergent sharing.
  3. **Invite explicit commitments**: Use visualization and organization body language to mark agreements, plan communications and events.
  4. **Identify initiatives**: Make sure the right leaders are chosen.
  5. **Determine resources**: Embody commitment with budgets and time.

of what needs to be sown, or grown, then participants identify specific products or services and place them in the proper quadrant. The harvest quadrant is for services and products that are established and might still have more life but aren't right for growing further. The plow category refers to things you would like to stop or repurpose so those resources can be used elsewhere.

This investment portfolio process can be quite analytical if you add estimates of person time required or actual monetary amounts to the sticky notes. When people are thinking concretely at this level, it truly is a "stepping into" the vision. In the case shared here, a large vision mural was shared at the beginning of each planning session to provide context.

Figure 10.23

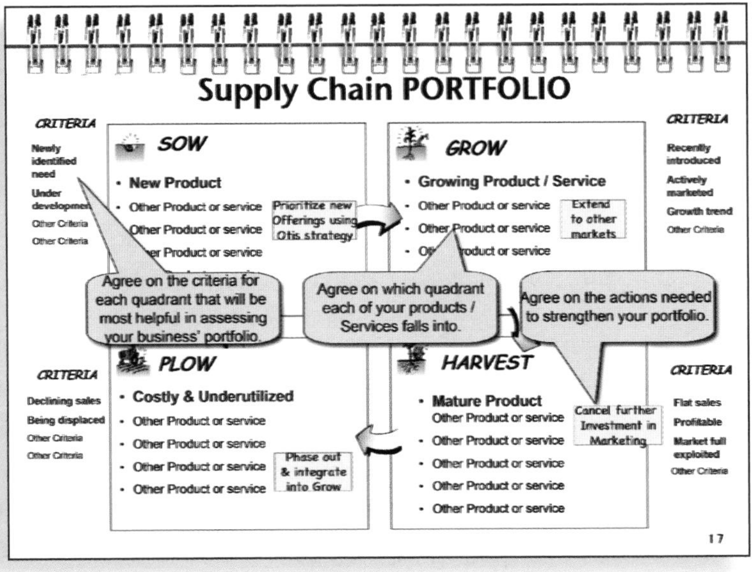

Investment Portfolios

At a national company that makes fresh baked goods, a visioning process was linked to their annual planning cycle. Every function was asked to look at its resource allocation in light of the new ideas. The team leading the process created a guidebook backed up with PowerPoint templates so that managers could come into the meeting prepared. The investment portfolio instructions are shown here. Using these worksheets, the groups then used larger wall templates to integrate their analysis, and to project, using different colored sticky notes, what they would like the future allocations to look like.

11. Empowering Visible Action

Involving New Leaders

Figure 11.1

There comes a time in change when commitments have reached critical mass guided by a new vision and direction. Attention and energy now focuses on actualizing the change. Leaders and others become intent on seeing real shifts in behavior and results. But it may be that the turn from exploration to commitment is not known throughout a system, especially if the change is in a larger organization or a community or does not involve a high engagement process. Therefore this is the time when the "new" needs to become visible, with clear organizational results and community improvements. The challenge of this stage is that part of the system may be just entering the change process. Expanding more ownership and buy-in throughout the system will be critical to long-term success.

We have already made the case that you do not necessarily encounter the seven challenges sequentially. Not only can earlier stage challenges pop up after the big commitments have been made, but you actually benefit from working on this challenge of empowering visible action back when you began planning for change in the first place (Figure 11.1) The approach you have co-designed with your client might well already foreshadow aspects of the new or changed organization. You may have encouraged your design teams to adopt practices and outlooks that could be the seeds of a new organization.

Figure 11.2

It's Time for a Baton Pass

Wherever you find yourself, after big commitments have been made, your primary task is to involve more people to support implementing the vision, goals, and related organizational processes or redesigns your clients envisioned. In some cases a clear passing of baton to your client is what is called for (Figure 11.2). In others you may need to continue for a while if they don't have capabilities in process facilitation. The client may also ask you to continue in a consulting role with the leadership team as they guide the change through the implementation phases. In all cases it helps to be ready for your client stepping forward into full ownership.

All these challenges feel very different if they are faced by people who know there is real commitment to the new direction and vision. And support grows when people who haven't been involved are invited to help shape how the change unfolds in their units.

The actual transfer of process ownership varies situationally. It is quite possible your engagement with the internal stakeholder group may begin to fade as they integrate and operationalize the change. With experience you can plan for this hand-off period and work to empower the organization to take on the implementation and be ready to maintain and evolve the outer process structures that you helped them build. You may also be very helpful suggesting useful, tangible tools and skills training that will give organizational members a new way to execute their work.

However your role evolves, the challenge of this stage is for your client to make visible and accepted changes, and to grow ownership in moving the changes forward as much as possible. There are always more people who need to be brought along, especially in lowers levels of the organization. There are setbacks. There are surprises and changing circumstances. There are hosts of problems to be solved. Many new ideas will be proposed. Caution and resistance may be part of each step and need to be embraced. But all these challenges feel very different if they are faced by people who know there is real commitment to the new direction and vision. And support grows when people who haven't been involved are invited to help shape how the change unfolds in their units.

If your process design for change already foreshadowed this challenge, by now you will have already created initiative teams and selected leaders. But now those teams need to get results. Skeptics will be watching. Leaders themselves may need more convincing. How do you help when the client begins to assume full ownership and momentum builds? There are many things you can do. That is what this chapter will describe.

Internal Dynamics of Empowering Visible Action

Let's start again by thinking about the kinds of less visible internal dynamics. As we said, this is the stage where the process needs to be clearly owned by your client. Culture change especially only comes from enactment. Here are some inner dynamics to think about.

1. **Supporting Emergence**: As soon as initiative teams start working and the organization begins to communicate its vision, new, unforeseen possibilities emerge. This can mean working with a whole new level of complexity (Figure 11.3).

   At **UC Merced** a new chief of staff was appointed just as the vision map was being finalized. He rightly had questions and wanted to make some changes.

   In the **RE-AMP** project that was cleaning up global warming pollutants in the upper Midwest, several victories in stopping coal plant permits brought attention to the network. The receptivity of several gubernatorial candidates to sustainability-oriented policies sparked members to propose a new work group focusing directly on policy formation and political support. At the second annual meeting, network members created the new Global Warming Solutions work group and began working out strategies that would be actively supported by five governors.

   At **Cal Poly Pomona** the new vision map was used creatively to raise money, something unanticipated.

   Helping prepare yourself and leaders to expect and work with what emerges is part of the consulting job. The basic pattern of change we described earlier in the *Liminal Pathways Change Framework* applies during this challenge. As new developments

Figure 11.3

What Is Emergence?

The principle of "emergence" refers to phenomenon of living systems exhibiting properties and functionality that are not predictable by the parts separately. This phenomenon is evident throughout nature.

The ripples formed by wind on the beach are emergent properties arising from the interaction of sea, sand, and wind, not from the elements themselves.

In change processes the interaction of the process itself, new initiatives, and the regular working of the organization give rise to all kinds of unanticipated developments. These can be sources of breakthrough and inspiration if your client is nimble and open to emergent solutions as an aspect of change.

SideStory 11.1

Seeing Organizations as Living Systems

As organizational development consultants we are used to thinking about organizations as living systems rather than machines. Organic mental models yield deeper insights and responses in our experience. While there are mechanical aspects to organizations that are important, to the extent they rely on people they are "alive" and living systems characteristics need to be appreciated.

Since the first waves of research on living systems became available to the organizational consulting community in the late 1980s, with such books as *Chaos: Making a New Science* by James Gleick, consultants interested in systemic change have become steadily convinced that many of the principles being uncovered about complex systems in nature apply to organizations.

These ideas are spreading. For example, businesses now regularly speak of their markets as ecosystems, increasingly appreciating that they work in value "webs" rather than value chains.

Working visually with groups to record graphic histories, context maps, and action plans is frequently an organic process where meaning and patterns of insight emerge in unpredictable ways, just by "growing" the displays through consistent contributions of the group.

arise as part of the implementation process, the change team and leaders will continue to go through new, mini-processes of change. It helps to have everyone understand that breakthroughs emerge from these in-between and emergent spaces. You can help support this being not only okay but an important aspect of this time.

2. **Learning from New Experience**: Necessary, ongoing work competes with new initiatives and especially with the need to learn while trying out new things. Culture change especially requires learning. This means taking time for reflection and "pop-up" meetings that aren't about the projects and progress but are about learning from the experiences themselves. A useful bridge role for you as a process consultant is to contract to facilitate these kinds of learning sessions. It enables you to track the process without getting re-involved with guiding the actions themselves.
3. **Taking Enough Time**: Another internal dynamic is people pressing to shortcut the actual time it takes to make change. It is so tempting for busy people to rationalize shortcuts and it's important to keep your eyes open for this. Coaching people to invest the necessary time to make real change is an important role of the consultant. When it comes to social change even more time is usually required to bring along the stakeholder groups that are involved.

Cultivating a Living System Mindset

With the challenge of empowering visible action you are moving out of a time of convergence in the previous challenge to a time of divergence as the change takes form. New ideas and creativity often begin to flourish as energy turns toward responding to what needs attention to help realize the vision. This challenge of change may be better considered an agricultural or gardening problem, where you attend to people and new initiatives the way a gardener pays attention to new plantings—watering, tending, and pruning if necessary. This means supporting initiatives that are getting results or changing the scope of ones that seem to be struggling. It often means coaching or even changing leadership. Keeping organizational attention on what is emerging and being learned, and taking the time that different initiatives need is a lot like tending and watering (SideStory 11.1).

Let's turn to look at what else you can do in an outer way to support change when it has these characteristics (SideStory 11.2)

Outer Structures That Support Visible Results

In our calls with our peers while developing this book we all agreed on five activitie that really help at this stage.

1. **Communicate and visualize early wins**: Visual consultants can help a lot by supporting initiative teams showing results using visual media. Some of the visualization is seeing real construction and physical evidence of change in three dimensions. We'll share a story about a vision map helping raise big funds.
2. **Sustain a clear rhythm for the work**: The emphasis here is on "sustain," since you have probably set a rhythm in your earlier work. But the conflicts of demanding schedules and competing schedules can break the rhythm. There needs to be regular email updates, meetings, announcements, and special events.
3. **Support new leaders and work groups**: As more people get involved with the implementation it helps to stay alert for new people who would be helpful as initiators and leaders, and work to create opportunities for them to contribute. A political consultant once told us, "if you want to get more backing and involvement, make it easy for your friends to support you."

"

System 1 & System 2

Holger Balderhaar is a visual consultant in Berlin who visited us recently and told a fascinating story about how he works with initiative teams. He took a consulting job working with a local newspaper company in Northern Germany. It was a traditional and quite hierarchical organization, but wanted to be more innovative and organic. He chose to contract in an unusual way that created space for the more innovative teams to work differently and optimize the chance for new ideas to emerge and take hold, without disrupting the main organization directly.

He told them he would not consult to the regular organization, which he called "System One." Instead he contracted to work with the innovative projects that he called "System Two." Holger explained to them that they might work in different ways with different rules in System Two, but not to confuse this with how people worked in System One. "We also set up a "System Three," he explained, drawing out this picture on a piece of paper after dinner. System Three would meet occasionally and reflect in a meta dialogue on what they were learning in both of the other systems and about the interaction between the two coexisting systems.

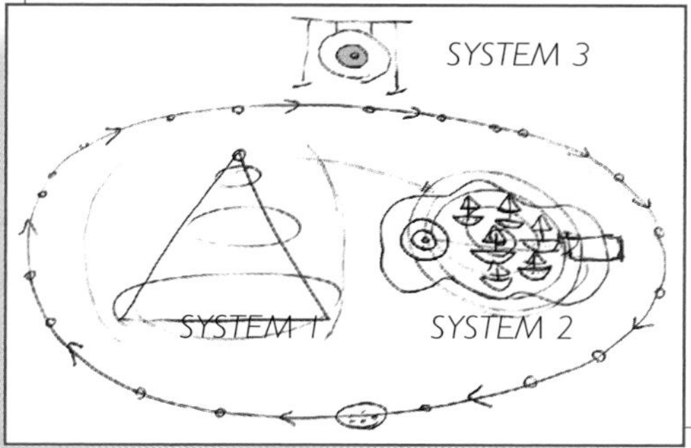

"People really adopted this language and it settled a lot of confusions," he said. The different venues and rules cued them to how to behave in each system.

SidSideStory 11.3

Exchange Toolbox

As part of the Habitat Exchange being proposed for the Central Valley of California, the Environmental Defense Fund is investing in working with ranchers and farmers to calculate habitat investments and progress using online support systems. Working with social media to amplify progress against visions is an increasingly important part of creating visible results.

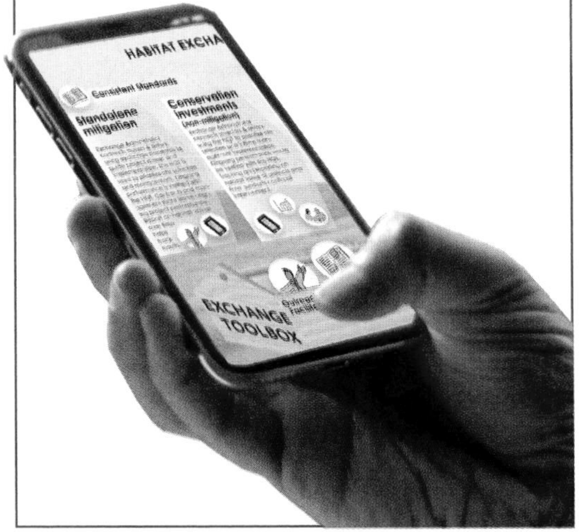

4. **Build capacity**: This is the time in change to do skills development. Trying to initiate change with training doesn't work too well. But when people have a new direction and motivation, and you've made decisions to build the processes and procedures to support change, then skill development is not only relevant but necessary. You can, as a visual consultant, be very helpful providing coaching and training in process skills, visualization, and communications.
5. **Facilitate learning processes**: There are many interesting ways to support ongoing learning. One is to link this need with capacity building by supporting people to create their own playbooks of best practices for new processes. Writing, creating, and publishing in any medium is one of the best ways to learn. Another is to propose special reflection sessions you might facilitate. And there are many more.

1. Communicate and Visualize Early Wins

I, Gisela, along with Laurie Durnell, The Grove's co-president and senior. consultant, worked on a project with the College of Business Administration at Cal Poly Pomona and explored what empowering visible action can mean in practice. While focusing on how our client took visible action in this case, I will also highlight what you can do to help the organization get ready for this challenge at earlier stages.

Need for Change at Cal Poly Pomona College of Business Administration

We were invited to help the college on two levels. One was to support the college to more fully embrace change, collaboration, and innovation, and to help them develop a strategic vision and initiatives that inspired new and bold actions that would help it stay competitive within its marketplace. There was also a need to rebuild momentum for several major procedural changes, such as moving from an academic quarter system to the two-semester system. Obstacles included a culture of silos, elaborate bureaucracies, and significant resource constraints for new initiatives—all not unusual for more mature academic

Figure 11.4

institutions. Our project was positioned as part of a true renewal process for the college which was to celebrate its fiftieth anniversary the following year.

We proposed a high engagement process, following the principle that strong employee and stakeholder engagement creates higher overall ownership of the aspired change as well as develops real solutions that are more in line with the overall interest and capacity of the college to realize them. To establish a shared sense of focus and overall direction of the project we conducted scoping interviews and shared our interview summary with the project leads, the dean, and his two associate deans.

Beginning the Culture Change with a Design Team

After some thoughtful deliberation with the dean and his associate deans, we invited individuals from across departments and units to join the design team. The dean was insistent that this design team bring together the true diversity of perspectives and interests to create an opening for future buy-in. The design team included 16 members, not all of whom participated in all the meetings. The disadvantage of a larger team like this is that it can act more like a committee. To address this we supported them to form into small action groups to accomplish the work that needed to be done.

In addition to cultivating the design team (SideStory 11.4), the dean modeled being very open to new ideas and creating an environment in which it was safe to think outside the

Seeding a Culture of Collaboration in Large Meetings

As part of the high engagement process at Cal Poly Pomona, all available faculty and staff were invited to participate in three, all-day meetings over the course of seven months and a half day all-hands meeting to kick off the new semester and present the results of the visioning and set up work on initiatives. Here is the big process design.

1. **The first meeting** focused on what was working and what needed to change (case for change).
2. **The second meeting** focused on developing a shared vision and beginning the overt focus on culture change.
3. **The third meeting** focused on discovering a shared metaphor for the core element of the vision map, vision themes, potential initiatives to realize their goals and operating principles.
4. **The fourth all-school meeting** presented the first full version of the vision map, including strategic initiatives for further fine tuning.

SidSideStory 11.4

Begin Growing a Culture of Collaboration Early

Working together to design an approach to their high engagement process was for many in the College of Business Administration their first experience of collaborating on an all college level. They were stepping together into ambiguity.

During the design meetings, they got to know each other, expressed their concerns, and challenged each other to step up to what the college needed now. They began to accept a new kind of leadership responsibility, bonded around new possibilities, and began to volunteer for action steps. They were excited and cautious. The seeds of the change were planted with them and they were living into what it meant to change, to navigate ambiguity, and to collaborate and innovate—not yet in terms of new strategic initiatives but in terms of this change process as a microcosm of the whole organization.

While they did not bond in a way that a group of initiates going through a rite of passage would, they certainly exhibited some of the characteristics of a communitas.

Together they entered the liminal zone as they collaborated on creating the future of the organization. They operated in a new organizational white space, establishing norms and ways of working together that were new and foreshadowed the culture they aspired to become.

box and test new possibilities. Members expressed hesitation at first, but as the case for change became more convincing and they experienced having room for all perspectives to be heard, the interactions became more trusting and the energy to move forward increased.

Expanding the Conversation

The design team decided, with the encouragement from the dean, to display in the college hallways some of the large graphic wall charts created during the big sessions. This promoted curiosity. Faculty, staff, and students who had not been involved entered into the conversation. For example, one of the classes took it upon itself to share with the design team a document detailing what they believed about the strategic direction of the college.

The four large group meetings (Figure 11.4) required prep work not only by the design team members but also by the various departments and units. At the same time the dean initiated cross-functional working groups to share about and propel forward initiatives that were already believed to be part of the future of the college. During the first large meetings we heard reports from the departments and units, learning about what each of the groups were doing. During meeting two and three we heard from the new cross-functional teams and the new project ideas they were working on (SideStory 11.5). This created a sense of connection and "seeing the whole" that many of them said had not experienced before.

One of the early insights emphasized the importance of streamlining each group's effort to develop strategic partnerships with industries. Another important conversation ensued about the college's unique way of providing academic excellence—especially their focus on experiential and innovative education. It was not so much that the ideas were new. It was the process of having cross-college conversations that was new, and it allowed them to clarify, ask questions, consider, make distinctions, consider new possibilities, and in a way even celebrate their hard work over the decades that the college has existed. In these meetings staff and faculty worked in max-mix tables, practicing their muscles to talk and work across functions. Energy in these meetings was high as we explored challenges and opportunities. They began to foreshadow what a culture focused on collaboration and innovation might feel and look like.

A fourth all-college meeting was held to share the first full draft of the vision map with the case for change, vision themes, and strategic initiatives. This meeting again allowed for reflection, discussion, and input. Truly insightful and unanticipated input emerged. It was clear that the vision themes could still evolve, as staff and faculty we had not heard from before shared perspectives that had not yet been considered. We synthesized all the input and integrated it into the next version of the vision map, modeling an iterative and high-engagement approach to expanding buy-in, ownership and innovation.

Empowering Visible Action

Our point in sharing this case is to underline how our client, the dean, had the foresight to support an engagement process that activated new behavior early in the process, empowering collaborative activity at a college level across and within the various departments and units. He anticipated that shifting from ideas into action, from initiating into realizing, would require more than motivation and good will. It needed agreement on the vision, driving external and internal forces, organization strengths, operating principles and initiatives, goals, AND a new experience in collaborating.

The outer process structure we used provided opportunities to model and practice what meeting this challenge can be like. The design team had evolved to become the strategic action team. As part of handing off the baton to that team and the leaders of the strategic initiatives they added a meeting on roadmapping the next phase of the project that had not been included in our original process design. In addition it would take time to reflect on

SideStory 11.5

Change Physical Spaces & Tools to Reflect New Directions

Changing physical spaces and tools is a direct way to make change visible. You can do what Cal Poly Pomona's College of Business Administration did to support new strategic initiatives teams that were formed at their third large group meeting. Each strategic initiative was headed by two members of the design team bringing the new spirit of change and collaboration to that team.

- ☐ **Provide collaboration technology**: Members of the college design team explored new collaboration technology to support their initiatives and to streamline their processes.
- ☐ **Scrum rooms:** Borrowing a term from agile planning, the college set up a scrum room where the strategic initiative leads would come together each Monday morning to report on, streamline, and integrate their efforts.
- ☐ **Large collaboration spaces:** The college redesigned the layout of one of their larger meeting spaces from auditorium style to a collaboration space.

Figure 11.5

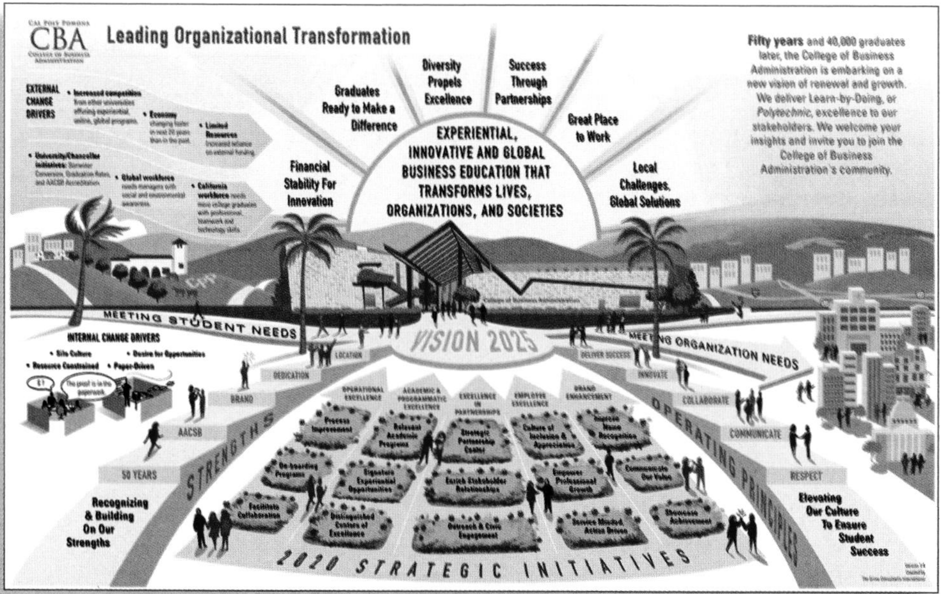

College of Business Administration Vision 2025

This vision map was co-created to reflect important symbols in the actual physical landscape. A beloved rose garden in this image holds their initiative goals. Campus walkways show the strengths and operating principles, but also reflects a central metaphor of the college being at a crossroads as it embarks on its Vision 2025, mapped on a rising sun, a real symbol in Southern California. Tiffany Forner, The Grove's art director, deserves credit for the design, which went through many iterations as it evolved.

key learnings about change in general and what they had learned about the college that could inform their work on creating results. This meeting resulted with a rough draft of the major goals and milestones for the next six months including roles and responsibilities for moving forward and a promise that they would implement all of it. Everyone was empowered by their shared understanding and agreed-on approach.

After three months we checked in with the dean to see how things were going. He had been concerned about how to maintain traction with the initiatives without actualizing early wins and bridging across the lull of a winter holiday break. He did something bold.

A Surprising Visible Result

The dean invited potential donors who were also former graduates from the college to lunch with him in a gazebo right in front of the college in full view of the beloved rose garden. While the gazebo is not depicted in the vision map, the college building and the rose garden are (Figure 11.5). The table was elegantly set along with laminated versions of the Vision 2025 map for each of the donors. Over lunch a conversation ensued about the strategic initiatives depicted on the vision map. Right there in this setting, the guests made donations of several million dollars to fund the creation of a Center for Innovative Analytics, one of their most important initiatives!

The college is now anticipating using the vision map in similar industry partner events to communicate and promote ways people can get involved in supporting the vision of the college. In the meanwhile the excitement for the new center serves as a catalyst for integrating the new vision and strategy on a wider systemic and operational level.

2. Sustaining a Clear Rhythm for the Work

We wrote earlier about the importance of setting a clear rhythm in the beginning of a change process. Sustaining a clear rhythm is another matter (SideStory 11.6). This often means extending the beat over more time than the cadences of the initial stages of change.

DLR Group's Five Year Plans

One impressive example is how the DLR Group sustained it's commitment to become a leading design firm with a decision to repeat its five-year planning process five years later, and then again each five years two more times. Each period deepened their commitment and elaborated what it meant. Their rhythm was in years, not just days.

In the third and fourth periods, DLR Group expanded the strategic visioning process to have office-wide meetings before the main partner meeting. These fed forward context maps, and SPOT (strengths, problems, opportunities, and threats) analysis charts from each location's point of view. DLR Group began to see their planning process as leadership development for young practitioners and partner leaders.

RE-AMP Institutionalizes Annual Meetings

In 2006 the RE-AMP network fully committed to a vision of reducing global warming pollutants in the upper Midwest 80% by 2050. There were four active work groups and The Grove was facilitating the development of strategic plans for each that would be shared in a cross-work group gathering. The steering committee that guided the network was skeptical about organizing a two-day meeting, because everyone was busy. The Infrastructure Team, which was responsible for process design, facilitation, and communications consulting

Can You Imagine a Band Without a Drummer?

Most music has rhythm and a beat that holds the music together. Can you image the Beatles without Ringo Starr? Yet it's easy to ignore the same need in group process. There is a rhythm set by the cadence of meetings, calls, and messages. If it is strong and reliable people learn to listen for it and follow it. At a deep level a strong rhythm inspires confidence. On the surface it makes it fun. Managing the energy flow of process means feeling and keeping the beat.

felt strongly it needed to be a two-day event to allow the network to form the personal relationships needed to sustain work over time. After considerable discussion the steering committee agreed.

The two-day meeting was a turning point. It was very energizing to see each other's work and provide cross-group input. As a result the network decided to conduct this meeting every year to review results and provide visible evidence of progress.

Figure 11.6

RE-AMP's Annual Cross-Group Meetings

RE-AMP's initial network, begun in 2004, funded by the Garfield Foundation, and involving 12 environmental NGO's, has now grown to today's network, comprised of over 160 participating organizations and 15 foundations. A pooled fund (allocated by the members of the steering committee and contributing funders) reached $2.5 million in 2014. The regular rhythm of annual meetings helped a great deal. They were all fully visualized, as you can see from this picture of David and Laurie Durnell from The Grove, facilitating a closing session at the first annual gathering.

The RE-AMP network institutionalized its annual meeting as a big base drum beat for their multiyear process. The reliability of these network-wide check-ins has contributed hugely to the network's continuing growth and influence (Figure 11.5)

3. Support New Leaders and Work Groups

Commitment brings everyone face-to-face with a host of things that need attention. New initiatives come forward regularly. Cultivating these new leaders is a critical part of getting change to become well rooted. At the first RE-AMP annual meeting one of the participants stood out as an activist around policy development to help new governors take on environmental agendas. The Infrastructure team and others encouraged him to propose a new work group. The network then formed a new Global Warming Solutions work group that he led successfully. At later conferences a transportation work group developed and the effort expanded to include Michigan.

At UC Merced a third summit meeting asked a combined group of faculty and staff to test the new vision by working out specific goals and action proposals for the agreed-on vision elements. People self-selected the vision elements they wished to work on, and table templates allowed them a place to develop their ideas. One of the CAT was a person trained a bit in organization development. He became critical to one of the key initiatives, which was to move many administrative units to a downtown office. This project became one of the priorities in the following year.

As a visual consultant it could well be that you can re-contract for specific help in regards to these kinds of follow-on projects.

4. Build Capacity

As we said in the beginning of this chapter, now is the time to train people in the new skills they need.

Leading Change at National Semiconductor

After National Semiconductor's (NSC) top management stepped into their new vision in 1990, they committed to a week-long Leading Change program that would involve all the management-level personnel in the 128,000 employee company. This was a huge commitment, but deemed necessary to achieve a real turnaround. David was facilitating the change team charged with designing this program.

Wisely, the company chose to have its change team facilitate the Leading Change program with no outside consultants in the room. Instead they asked The Grove to train them in facilitation skills as a capacity-building move. We co-created a complete training program and facilitated a training of trainers workshop just for the internal change team. The cadre of NSC internal staff that had this experience went on to facilitate internal re-engineering and strategic visioning processes throughout the company. They often worked alongside Grove consultants to learn even more. One of the key strategies in making this possible

SideStory 11.7

Why I Work Visually

Bill Bancroft of Conbrio Consulting is a visual consultant who trains leaders, facilitates strategic visioning, and helps organizations build capacity. "When I was 13 years old, I remember working with my Dad under the house to fix a plumbing leak. We were in a small space, it was dark, and it was tough to see. My job was to hold the flashlight. Dad instructed me: 'If you shine the light so you can see where I'm working you'll learn, and I'll be able to see what I'm working on too.'

When I think of visual consulting, I think of shining that light. It's why I work graphically. I'm not a recorder; my drawing is utilitarian. I incorporate sticky notes to give participants an equal voice. And I use photos cut from magazines for participants to support telling their stories. I record the gist of their stories next to their photos.

In short, I work with groups through the visuals we create together. Thoughts flow from the group to the charts on the wall and back out to the group again. I'm holding the flashlight so they can see their ideas, make sense of them, and create something even better. Without my holding the flashlight neither they nor I could see nearly as well what we're doing together."

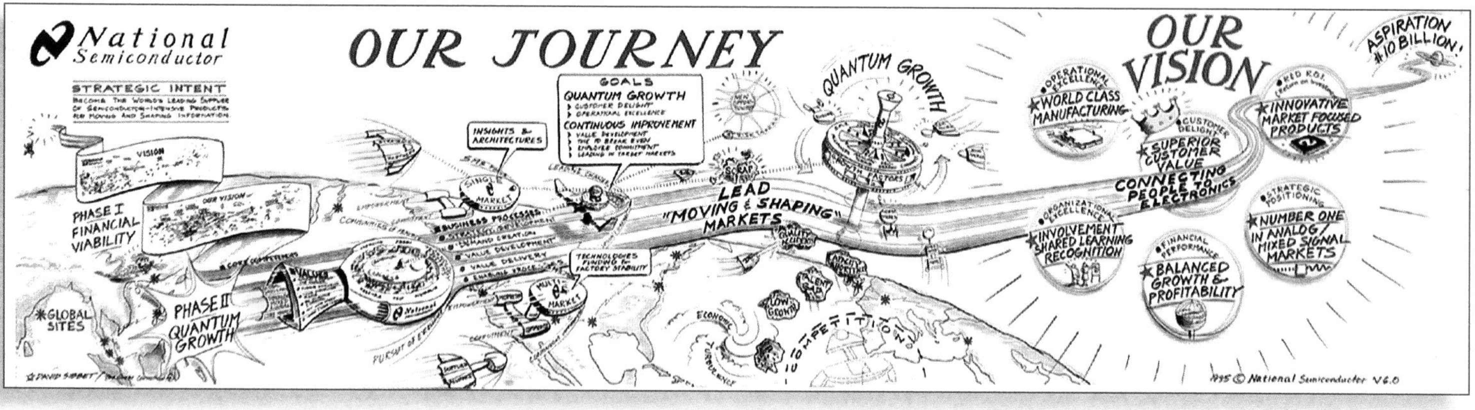

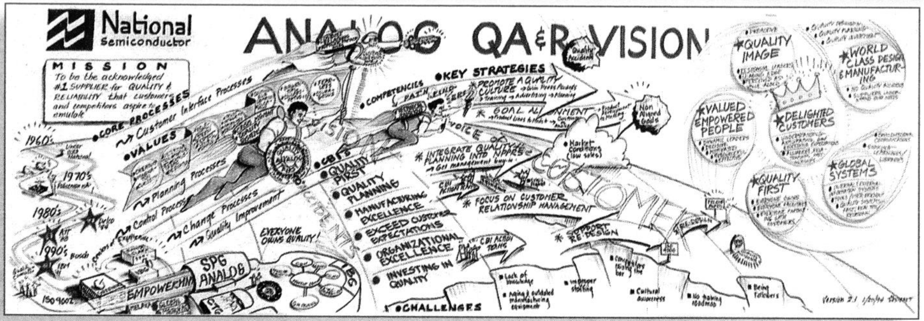

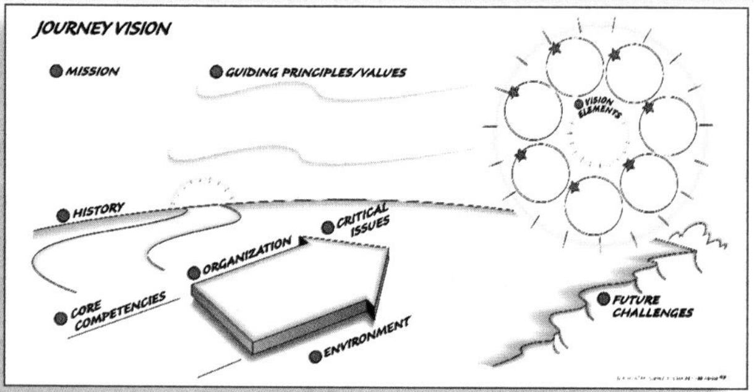

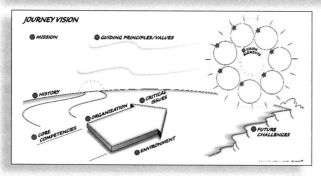

This vision for the Analog Division Quality group reflects the basic template, and links to the big NSC vision's spaceship image in the lower left. The template is now one of The Grove's Graphic Guides®

Large-Scale Visualization

The Grove's involvement with large scale visualization began at National Semiconductor (NSC) during Gil Amelio's tenure in the early 1990s. David facilitated an internal change team that not only communicated the new vision worldwide, but built internal capability in visual planning at an unusually effective scale.

The top image here is the 24-foot-long, full-color NSC vision it it's third full iteration after 4 years, reflecting its central Star Trek metaphor. By 1994 the vision had 96% recognition world wide and was being emulated by inspired graphic artists in the company.

The Storymap approach allowed leaders to tell consistent stories, and the underlying template that lay behind the vision served as a framework for strategic visioning internally. Groups would develop their responses to the different areas on the Journey Vision, and then translate their work into a unique visual, with a central metaphor for the organization they aspired to create to fulfill the vision.

was organizing the work around a template that was an abstraction from the original NSC vision map (Figure 11.7). This experience was the seedbed of The Grove's large-format visual consulting, and even though now nearly 30 years old, is still full of lessons for today's practitioners (SideStory 11.8)

Coaching Training at Headstart

A three-county Headstart program was alive with the vision of becoming a learning organization and moving away from a checklist supervisory approach. They served 1,500 families in three large rural counties. Gisela had facilitated a large-group event with 100 staff and teachers to identify the values they were wanting to embody. They examined what these values would look like in action and identified scenarios of how these would play out, concluding that it was important to empower from the bottom up, and create a coaching culture. They needed to build capacity.

A change team that had already been set up earlier took on this task, and with Gisela's guidance co-designed and created a complete coaching system that included training of staff to train trainers and redesigning the whole performance system. In addition, a peer coaching program was put into place for special subject teachers. To demonstrate their commitment, the leaders themselves engaged executive coaches. Adding capabilities like this was essential to this organization actualizing the vision. What is needed in culture change is not only skill building but also creating the conditions in which these new skills are supported and recognized.

SideStory 11.8

Useful Training for Visual Consulting Capability

If your clients haven't experienced visual consulting before, and you are getting results in the early phases, it is a good move to propose the following kinds of trainings to develop internal resources that can support initiatives and further change. These kinds of trainings are now well developed.

- ☐ **Basics of graphic recording** focuses on using flip charts, large paper, and tablets in virtual meetings. Many visual practitioners now offer this kind of help.
- ☐ **Principles of graphic facilitation** training focuses on learning basic display formats and managing the four flows of process.
- ☐ **Strategic visioning** training explores the use of large-scale templates
- ☐ **Leading change training,** develops literacy about change phases and challenges.
- ☐ **Critical conversations** training, helps with dialogic practices.

In addition to training programs, some of the most effective capacity building comes from working side-by-side with clients on change initiatives, letting them take the lead with you providing support.

You can also encourage them to get all the tools they need from suppliers like Grove Tools, Inc. and Neuland.

Summary

- ☐ **Pay attention to the inner dynamics**—supporting emergence, learning from new experiences, and taking enough time.
- ☐ **Support the process with outer structures**

1. **Communicate and visualize early wins**: Start initiatives early; use the agreed on vision to raise interest and even money, following the example of Cal Poly.
2. **Sustain a clear rhythm for the work**: Keep up a cadence of important meetings like the RE-AMP Annual Conference, or the multiyear commitment of DLR Group to doing five year strategic visions.
3. **Support new leaders and work groups**: Look for opportunities to enroll new people, like RE-AMPs work group that started their Global Warming Solutions work group.
4. **Build capacity**: Develop internal capability during the big change processes like National Semiconductor did or Headstart with coaching training. Take time to schedule and train internal resources and build new systems to support these skills, initiatives, and ongoing change.
5. **Facilitate learning processes:** Keep working as a visual consultant to supporting learning events. Introduce new concepts that catalyze learning.

5. Facilitate Learning Processes

As much as organizations say they want to learn, it is a constant struggle to get people to spend time standing back and reflecting. Holger, who we wrote about early in this chapter (SideStory 11.2), has managed by having the systems that support the innovations and learning be completely separate operations with different rules. Conducting these kinds of learning sessions is a great role for visual consultants, and a way to continue the work of change while clients are taking over ownership of initiatives and other actualizing work.

Introduce Concepts that Catalyze Reflection

One way to encourage learning is to introduce new content and concepts to help people wrestle with the challenges that emerge. At the California Roundtable on Water and Food Supply that we described in the first chapter of this book, Gisela introduced the value of standing back and articulating the methodology they used to come up with their connected benefits paradigm. Because this approach would be described in the Roundtable's final, highly visual report, the group spent quality time thinking about their process at a meta-level in order to agree on what was written. These insights helped a great deal in approaching their next challenge of working on groundwater.

At UC Merced Gisela introduced the idea of looking at the results from the summit through the lens of the iceberg model of change, which we will describe in the next chapter. This concept supported one of the more in-depth looks at some of the dynamics that underlie how the university was actually functioning.

12. Integrating Systemic Change

Take On New Processes & Behaviors

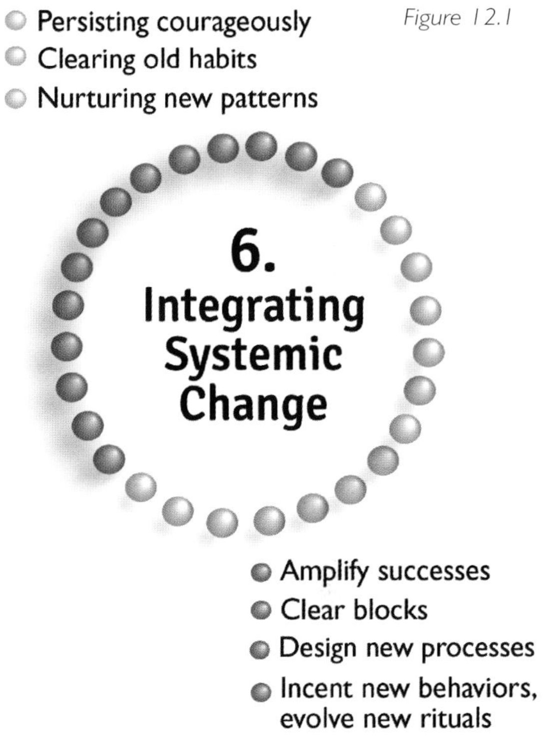

Figure 12.1

Committing to a new vision and visible actions gives momentum to change, but a longer-term challenge awaits. That is the job of integrating the new into the total organizational system so that it becomes a new baseline of normative behavior. This kind of work transcends the change initiatives, and requires taking a whole systems perspective on what has to shift to make change stick (Figure 12.1). Before we look at inner dynamics and outer structures, let's step back and think about the system as a whole.

The Iceberg Model

Have you ever attended a personal development workshop and learned about some new behavior that you felt would make a big difference in your life or work, and then returned to your regular life and experienced slipping right back into old patterns? That is because under our observable behaviors is an iceberg of factors that give rise to these behaviors. This iceberg model and its questions will help you look below the surface (Figure 12.2).

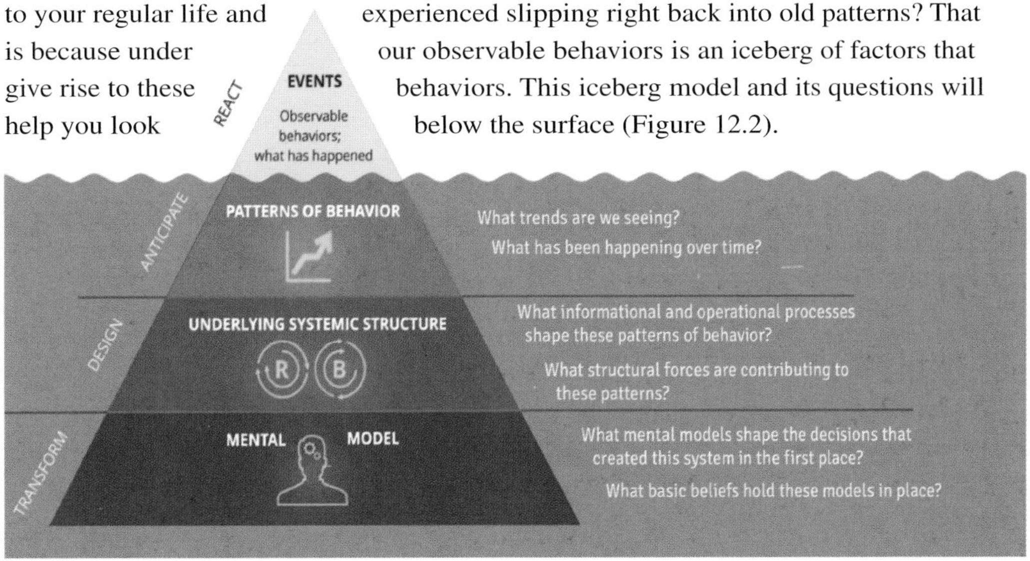

Figure 12.2

SideStory 12.1

Working with the Iceberg Model

There are many ways you can work with the iceberg model to raise awareness of how underlying systems dynamics shape behavior and culture.

1. **Analyze a problem that is blocking progress.** Simply post a big version of the model or draw it out yourself. Then brainstorm all aspects of the problem you can think about on sticky notes, and work with the group to sort them into the different levels.

2. **Organize inputs following stakeholder meetings.** When you have received input on initiative plans, roadmaps, visions, or other things, use the iceberg model to group items on the different levels.

3. **Reflect on a turning point event.** During change there will be times when big breakthroughs happen. Work with leadership to see what was under the surface of the turning point that led to its being possible.

Students of organizational development find the iceberg model useful because it invites you to look at what is not easily observable (SideStory 12.1). Above the surface are events and behaviors you can see. But these are the results of longer running patterns of activity below the surface of attention. And these patterns in turn are supported by underlying processes, like hiring and promotion policies, and structures reflected in physical environments, tools, and programs with built-in biases. Under all these are mental models and belief systems that guided the development of these systems in the first place, and gave rise to the social culture that surrounds them. For fundamental or transformational change to take place, shifts have to happen on all these levels. This is Change Challenge 6.

Why Is Keeping the Whole System in Mind Important?

A system is a collection of structures, tools, processes, and people that connect with each other in ways that result in a coherent, often self-reinforcing pattern of organizational functioning and behavior. Systems, once they are established, are amazingly resistant to change by tinkering or problem solving around single issues. The system might give a little at the point of focus, but then move to compensate in other areas. This is why the "program de jour" approach doesn't work very well. To work on a whole system you and the client have to develop a way to look at it and understand it as a living phenomenon, and operate on multiple levels. To do this a visual consultant faces two challenges.

- One is **continuously developing your own ability to keep the whole in mind while working on the parts**. Much of this book has been arguing that visualization is a key to this being possible. Working with robust mental models related to organization change underly this ability.
- A second challenge is **helping your client keep the whole in mind**.

Chapter 7 f provide a number of models for thinking about organizations as whole systems. We introduced them to help you scope out a consulting job and know what to inquire about. They continue to be helpful with later challenges. Most large organizations work with models like these as ways to understand internal functions and how they interrelate. Mapping interview data and other inputs on these kinds of models is a very effective way to help your clients and yourself develop systemic thinking capability. (If you have forgotten or skipped Chapter 7, go back and look at the models in Figures 7.8 through 7.11). When clear conceptual frameworks are used with interactive visual facilitation, everyone can collaboratively upgrade their mental models, think more systemically, and then commemorate insights visually. If clients have models of their own, build on them and evolve them. Let's look at what might being going on internally, when you are working on integrating systemic change.

Inner Dynamics of Integrating Systemic Change

1. **Persisting courageously**: Behind the scenes and under the surface people who have been at the forefront of leading change may well be getting exhausted. Setbacks can be discouraging. Even if this isn't the case, everyone will be struggling with the work it takes to keep change going. It may become obvious that certain big things need to happen. But it takes courage and persistence to tackle change systemically at all the levels we just addressed, and your clients may well be feeling challenged.
2. **Clearing old habits**: Change doesn't happen evenly in large systems. You may have positive new attitudes inspired by a new vision and direction and early wins in some areas, but other organizational norms aren't changing. There may also be backsliding behavior that people are reticent to admit to. Actually leaving old habits behind is not easy, and takes shifts in supportive structures and processes in addition to social acceptance and reinforcement of new habits. Inside, people may be struggling. Later we'll address some things you can do in regard to clearing blocks.

Keeping the Whole System in Mind While Working on the Parts

There are a number of ways you can use visualization to support your clients staying oriented to the whole system in which they are working.

- ☐ **Adopt a whole system framework** like the iceberg model (Figure 12.2) or the O'Reilly strategic alignment model (Figure 7.10) and keep it posted and visible.
- ☐ **Revisit & refine your stakeholder map** and keep it visible in meetings.
- ☐ **Update the change roadmap** and keep it visible and posted as a large mural in meetings.
- ☐ **Print large Vision Maps** and make them visible in meetings and key places like lobbies and gathering spots.
- ☐ **Develop measurable indicators** of progress and conduct periodic assessment and reviews. Map the findings visually.
- ☐ **Hold large stakeholder meetings** that allow a broad spectrum of people to share their perspectives on progress.
- ☐ **Conduct systemwide surveys** that cut across all the functions and provide a picture of the whole.

SideStory 12.3

Supporting Positive Deviance

Jerry Sternum and his wife successfully tackled postwar child malnutrition in Vietnam in the 1980's. Borrowing from his wife's sociology studies, Sternum wondered if the concept in that field, of all systems having deviant pockets that somehow manage to survive going against the dominant paradigm, would apply to child malnutrition. Their mental model theorized that when ideas come from within a system they will be more readily accepted and not rejected by the normal immune system of the organization.

They asked health nurses in two schools to weigh all the children and see who were not malnourished, but were still poor. They found a pocket of 5% or so. He then asked them to find out why not. They discovered the mothers were adding little crabs and spinach-like vegetables to their rice, and feeding them four times a day rather than two so they ate more! This was like discovering gold for the health nurses. Workshops that taught mothers how to do this were given over a year and spread the practice. The malnutrition problem was "solved" in 18 months at an extraordinarily low budget.

Sternum has passed away, but Tony Pascal has explained in *Positive Deviance* how Sternum's approach can be used in organizations as well as communities today.

3. **Nurturing new patterns**: New ways of working and new patterns of behavior are like little seedlings in a greenhouse. They need careful tending. Sometimes the impact isn't immediately visible. It is a challenge to have this nurturing, supportive behavior be a priority for your clients and the leaders of change because cultivating and tending over time doesn't always get rewarded, especially in systems that reward short-term gains and results.

   In addition, there are new processes and structures and new ways of thinking at a deeper level that take even more concentrated attention to change. The inner struggle that can emerge is between these kinds of repetitive, maintenance and "tending" tasks and new initiatives and projects that promise to attract more attention. When promotion dynamics emphasize standing out and taking credit, the job of nurturing can get subordinated. This is an important dynamics to keep in mind as change begins to spread systemwide (SideStory 12.2).

Outer Structures That Support Integrating System Change

There are four things that will make a difference at this point to move from visible successes to systemwide implementation of change.

1. **Amplify successes:** You can help your clients track and support things that are working in the right direction. Amplifying can occur operationally with new resources and tools. It can happen on the information level with communications about people experiencing successes. At the energetic level, new behaviors strengthen when people and teams that are succeeding are publicly celebrated, get direct reinforcement from leaders, and day-to-day positive reinforcement from managers. Amplifying also happens at the attentional level when leaders and managers make rewarding successes part of their jobs.

2. **Clear blocks:** Actively removing inhibiting, unnecessary, or outmoded processes

and structures is important at this stage. It works to help clients find the time and interest to discover what workers themselves think are the blocks and then respond. This is not only good practice but will also continue to strengthen the idea that each employee and their contributions are central to the success of the change, and thereby the success of the overall organization (SideStory 12.3).

Efforts to remove blocks need to be persistent and supported with strong underlying theory and example. Sometimes the block is a long-standing paradigm about how to organize work and communications (SideStory 12.4).

3. **Redesign processes**: At less paradigmatic levels, outdated processes need to be redesigned to support new directions. Organizations have hundreds of often nested processes that make them work. Core process, like hiring and promotion policies or production processes need to support your change. If processes for measuring success are focused on the wrong metrics, then trainings and visionary communications may not make much difference. On the flip side, if annual planning links explicitly to the new visions and direction, and budgets are analyzed for their fit with new directions, then change can accelerate. If your organization seeks more innovation and creativity, it may be that traditional planning needs to take on more agile, design-thinking approaches (see Figure 9.7).

4. **Incent new behaviors and evolve new rituals**: Studies of motivation from sources like Gallup suggest that the most powerful motivator for workers of any kind is support and recognition from their supervisors. This comes out as stronger than financial incentives, which are real, but not as motivating. In most jobs, people will invest in doing a good job, but often at 60–80% of their full capacity. They keep an extra 20% in reserve that really only gets tapped when deep wells of commitment and caring are tapped. If an organizational vision includes deeply inspiring intentions, as is often the case in "B" Corps like Patagonia that embody a social contribution orientation. (There are now more than 2,500 "B" corps.)

SideStory 12.4

Reinventing Organizations

A movement to change organizations into flatter, more human-centered systems is rising in Europe in response to widespread disillusionment in traditional hierarchical organizations, significantly supported by Frederick Laloux's best-selling, *Reinventing Organizations: A Guide to Creating Organizations Based on the Next Stage of Human Consciousness.* He argues that a collaborative paradigm is emerging and that looser, networked, competency-based structures with high trust can be evolved.

A remarkable number of people are responding to his thinking, and conferences are being held to push the ideas further.

Figure 12.3

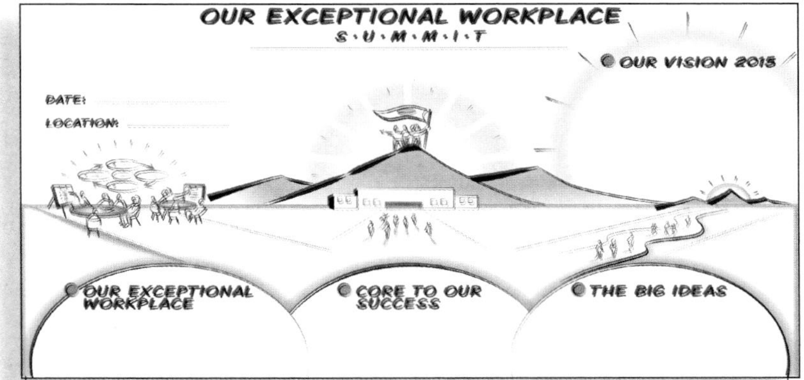

Appreciative Visualization

Diana Arsenian, former art director at The Grove Consultants International, is an experienced visual consultant. who has worked with David Cooperrider, founder of Appreciative Inquiry (AI), for more than 20 years facilitating the AI process and creating graphic templates like this one. David writes, "The source and center of all man's creative power. is his power of making images, or the power of imagination. This is what we do in our work with AI; we help organizations and individuals envision new images of what is possible in their future. One of the most powerful tools to support this work is graphic facilitation. Whether a small team meeting or a summit of 1,000, I have seen how it can be transformational. In this craft, Diana is . . . almost like a spiritual channel . . . It's an empathic art and skill that is experienced by the group as a gift."

In addition to consulting,do AI vision coaching within the growing network of practitioners.

1. Amplifying Success

A very successful dialogic approach to change is a method called Appreciative Inquiry or AI. David Cooperrider at Case Western University has helped evolve this approach over several decades now, arguing that traditional planning and problem solving is too focused on problems. If people pay attention instead to what works and making that stronger they would get further, he argues. The steady growth of this method has reinforced his assumption. Search online and you will find many resources supporting this approach. Visualization is a critical part of the method (see Figure 12.3).

The Power of Positive Feedback

Positive feedback for new ways of working from managers and supervisors is also critical. The consulting group called the Continuous Learning Group (CLG) has had tremendous success inside large organizations improving results inside their operating divisions with applied behavioral science. Their approach is informed by research suggesting that positive reinforcement is far and away the best motivator for changing behavior but needs to be applied systematically in support of behaviors that are needed to achieve new visions. They guide leaders through the following process in great depth.

1. **Getting clear on the new directions** for the divisions.
2. **Identifying new behaviors** needed to support that direction.

3. **Training all managers how to identify and provide positive reinforcement** for the new behavior.
4. **Train all managers to identify and avoid negative reinforcement**.

While this sounds fairly straightforward, the first two steps are challenging, and the training needs to be pervasive. But the results are so marked that other divisions in client organizations often begin requesting CLG's services.

2. Clear Blocks

People and their behaviors can be blocks to change. For instance, culture change can stall because of key executives who are loyal old managers, but unwilling to develop and model new behaviors (Figure 12.4). At one large multinational company, the CEO was a smart, professorial kind of person, who was well liked. He would engage managers and employees in educating them about his vision of an innovative, collaborative organization and what needed to be done to make this possible. But he wasn't fond of insisting on compliance or confronting people about bad results. His Chief Operating Officer, who was a tough manager, asked for and got financial results more by use of fear and bullying than anything else. While the culture change process was gaining traction, the COO's behavior was a double message that directly contradicted the vision. Many on the change team believed that progress stalled over this one issue.

At another large multinational, leaders wanted to support internal associates (their word for employees) being more transparent and collaborative. As a result they created open office plans for all associates, including the executives, with nearby closed-in conference rooms for small meetings. This new layout cleared blocks to sharing and interaction.

At UC Merced, the growing campus was bottle necked with a faculty and staff that were

Figure 12.4

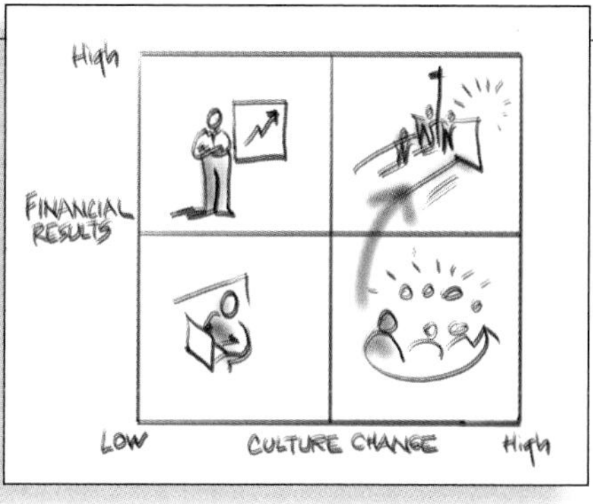

Strategic Compliance Model

This model pairs one axis of how strongly a leader supports a new culture change and another with how strongly a leader supports getting financial and other results.

Everyone agrees that leaders who are low on both should be developed or replaced. But organizational consultants argue if it is easier to support a leader who is strong on culture change to get results, than to support a results type of leader fully modeling and supporting culture change.

It takes courage to confront or remove a strong, results-oriented leader, even if their behavior sets people's teeth on edge. This points out the need for top management to stay involved and be willing to make important strategic decisions that support change. Personnel decisions can be one of the strongest symbolic moves a top executive can make to support change.

Figure 12.5

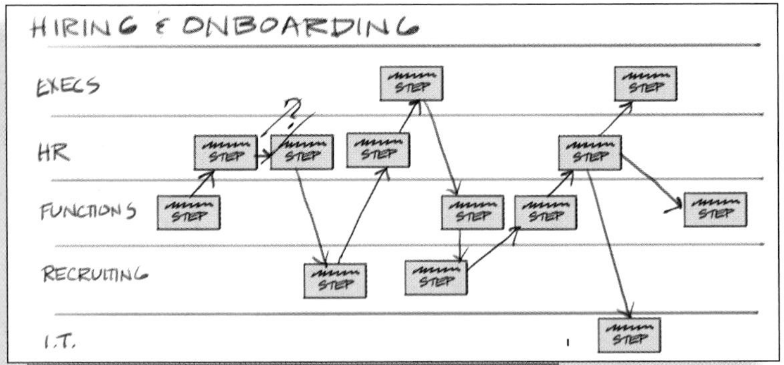

Work Flow Design

A common practice that you can add to your visual consulting tool kit is work flow design. The tools are simple. The art is being thorough with your questions and uncovering all the different functions and steps that are involved.

1. Identify a key process that needs changing.
2. Post a large sheet of paper. Create channels for the major functions involved in the process.
3. Use sticky notes to identify every current action and decision point in the process. Sequence these to represent the actual process.
4. Identify the steps that don't add any value or needed steps that are missing.
5. Illustrate the map to show the ideal state.

far flung with Internet connections unstable in many places. They decided to license a popular video conferencing program for system-wide use.

Marc Tognotti, a consultant working to support creation of a locally run nature preserve in Zambia found that one of the huge blocks to his working there was what he calls the "donor syndrome." As soon as Africans in the region where he was working heard he was connected with a donor, deep colonial acculturation took over and people wouldn't relate to him as a human being. He worked hard to remove some of these blocks through personal and direct sharing, and refusal to go along with what felt like a charade. He succeeded in facilitating a successful future search conference for 40 local people from 10 communities working alongside another 40 more institutional people to support the Mukungule Conservancy creating the preserve. Sometimes the cultural blocks to progress are the most challenging.

3. Design New Processes

Firms that specialize in re-engineering organizations to adopt new technologies often start with assessing all the processes. Any organization has dozens of processes and large ones have hundreds. Several dozen are probably considered core processes. The challenge is to carefully think through which combination of processes will be most important to work on to support whatever new direction you are moving (Figure 12.5).

As you move to design new processes and larger cross-organizational systems in an organization, you might benefit from using a framework like that illustrated in Chapter 9 (Figure 9.9 and SideStory 9.6). These organizational models illustrate the typical core processes in an organization. Of course you will need to create your own version reflecting the language used in the organization. Designing this kind of organizational improvement

Figure 12.6

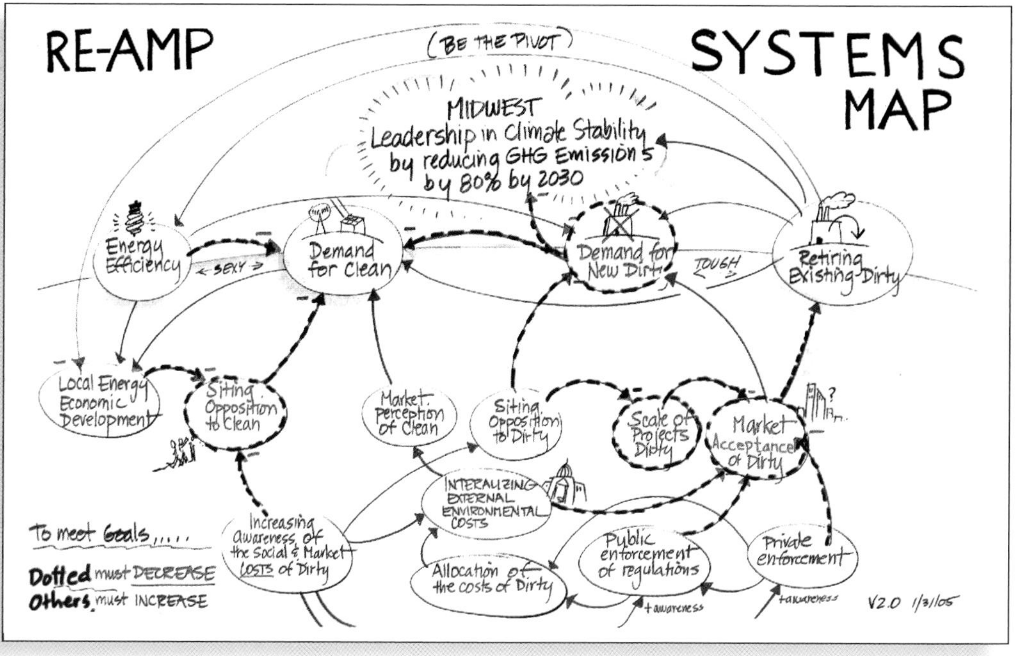

The System Surrounding Renewable Energy

This 15-factor diagram is a summary of a 175-factor map that allowed RE-AMP to keep their bigger picture in mind, created by Scott Spann, a consultant with expertise in systems analysis. Dotted line flows have a dampening effect and the solid-line flows increase system elements. This work brought them to realize that no renewable scenarios worked without having energy conservation active as part of the picture.

work at a structure level is an entire discipline in itself. For improving manufacturing and infrastructure process, you can research "lean manufacturing" and obtain a great deal of help. Some organizations use these methods beyond manufacturing to create more efficient processes. You can also look for total quality management and socio-technical system design for working on both social and technological efficiency together.

RE-AMP Reignites Energy Conservation

RE-AMP (Renewable Energy Alignment Mapping Network) softened a major block to developing new renewable energy conservation systems with a multistakeholder, policy formation approach.

As we described earlier, RE-AMP is working to clean up global warming pollutants in the upper Midwest. The original sponsor, Garfield Foundation, felt that if foundations and environmental NGOs worked together they might make more progress. They identified and committed to a bold vision and four working groups, based on a systems analysis phase of their process changes (Figure 12.6).

The working groups discovered that since the 1970s, almost no philanthropic grants had been given for energy conservation in the eight state region. It just wasn't being considered. This was partially a systemic problem. Energy conservation involves thousands of little changes in how building are built and insulated, how lighting is procured, how appliances are built, etc. And each state and municipality had layers and layers of different regulations and governing bodies. There was no one point that could be changed.

Out of this growing understanding emerged the idea that they might be able to persuade governors to start state-level task forces to encourage public support. They formed a new work group called Global Warming Solutions, as we described a bit in the last chapter. Over the next years RE-AMP influenced the creation of no fewer than five state initiatives on energy conservation, supported with RE-AMP research and policy ideas. And, seeing the process gap, foundations began funding conservation programs.

Figure 12.7

Integrating a New Vision into the Organization

John Schiavo, former CEO of Otis Spunkmeyer, is shown here orienting his I.T. function to the new vision for the company, as a prelude to having them do their annual functional planning. Each function in the company had John or another Executive team member do the same. To support this new leadership behavior of orienting annual planning to the new vision, a special session was held where the leadership team practiced telling the vision story with the big mural.

Otis Spunkmeyer Envisions Integrated Data

Otis Spunkmeyer linked their new vision with annual planning and a subsequent enterprise resource management (ERP) process. After a successful process of visualizing their company vision, John Schiavo, the CEO, suggested that all the functions use The Grove's Graphic Guides to support their work. To model a new annual planning process, David personally facilitated the first wave of meetings, leading functions through identifying their relevant contexts, doing a SPOT analysis of strengths, problems, opportunities, and threats, a vision, and the investment portfolio shown earlier in Figure 10.23.

In addition, their parent company decided to use Otis Spunkmeyer as a lead example of installing an ERP system. John asked the subject matter experts who were working with the technology consultants leading the project, to create their own vision for the ERP process (Figure 12.8) that would assure they could explain its benefit to all employees and

Figure 12.8

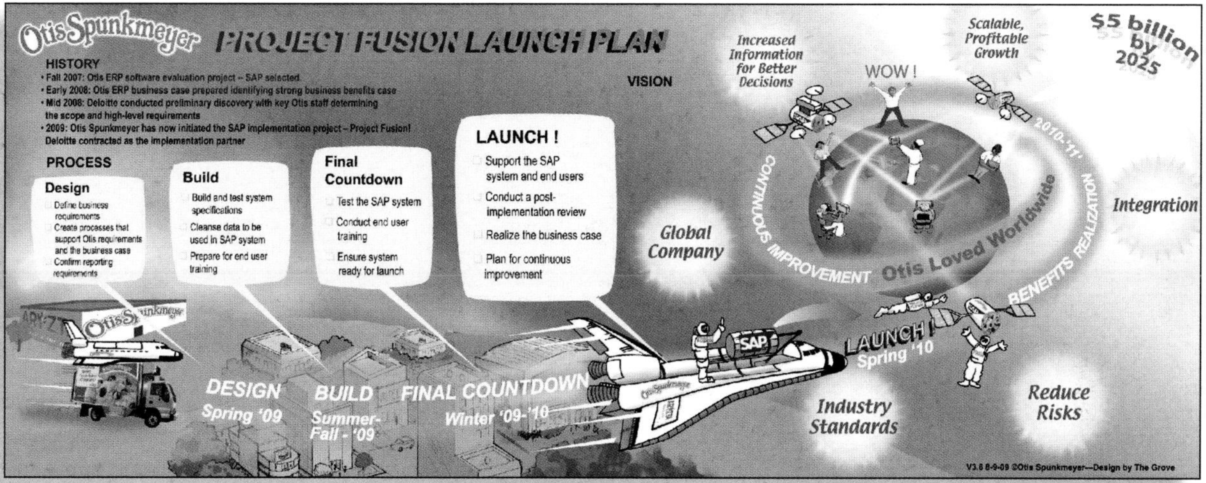

Otis Spunkmeyer's ERP Launch Map Reflects the Big Vision

To explain the benefit of Otis Spunkmeyer's big ERP process, called Project Fusion, the technology consultants and subject matter experts created this mural. It shows the goals and benefits of the project on an image to the right that mirrors the image of the larger company vision (Figure 12.7). Most helpfully, the mural-making process brought all parties to agreement on the actual launch schedule, shown in the talk balloons. The space ship image links to an earlier image of the company being "cleared for takeoff." In that case it was a DC-9 that Schiavo flew all around the country. The space vehicle evokes a more futuristic idea.

link it to the overall company vision (Figure 12.7).

UC Merced Adopts Decision Process for Creating Alignment

At UC Merced we introduced an iceberg model activity after the initial summit meetings to help the Change Alignment Team (CAT) think about next steps and outputs from the vision process. Out of this analysis came the insight that it was more important to achieve consensus on the criteria for prioritizing than to organize and prioritize all the projects five years ahead. If they could agree on these, they concluded, then the ongoing alignment could take place in their annual planning process. These criteria became a major feature of the final vision shown in Figure 10.17.

To anchor this new way of thinking, the new criteria emerging from the initial summits were then thoroughly discussed and tested in a second summit, which worked to develop specific goals and action plans linked to the vision elements. These criteria have now been adopted in their annual planning cycles.

4. Incent New Behaviors, Evolve New Rituals

We've already described some approaches to incenting new behaviors, with the CLG's approach to positive reinforcement, and Otis Spunkmeyer modeling visual planning through the organization. Here are some other things you can do:

1. **Make the new social norms visible**: i.e. motivate the herd (see SideStory 12.5).

SideStory 12.5

Motivate the Elephant

Chip and Dan Heath, in their popular book *Switch: How to Change Things When Change Is Hard,* detail out some of the strategies that work for behavior change with a compelling metaphor.

They organize the book around the image of a rider guiding an elephant. The rider represents our conscious mind. The elephant is all the unconscious, implicit, and subsurface feelings and dynamics—the bottom of the iceberg if you want to mix metaphors.

Elephants can learn to follow riders that give good direction, but clearly, if the elephant wants to do something different, there is little the rider can do to stop it.

So their rubric for change is

1. **Motivate the elephant.**
2. **Steer with good direction.**
3. **Clear the path.**

And when it comes to behavior, they emphasize motivating the herd. For elephants, like humans, are heavily influenced by their social context.

Some of the most successful vision maps over the years have had explicit behaviors indicated, preceeded by lots of discussion and agreement about what these should be as a way to get everyone clear on the new norms. Hearing about how people feel about the new visions and the attitudes and behaviors that will implement them in summits and other large gatherings is motivating. Visualizing new behaviors is the first step to getting them adopted.

2. **Encourage leadership modeling**: Leaders modeling new behaviors have a strong influence on cultures that are leader centered. It works both ways. Since modeling bad behavior can undermine change efforts, many organizations now use executive coaching, as in the Headstart case, to support leaders meeting this kind of challenge.

3. **Create environments that support new behavior**: Bill McDonough, a well-known architect leading in sustainability practices, designed a new manufacturing facility for Herman Miller that created spaces for employee breaks with access to nature and sunlight, as well as bringing sunlight and other features into the main working areas. Productivity increased dramatically. At Millikan Carpet, the CEO and other leaders hold annual "Sharing Rallies" that are like the Academy Awards for process improvement ideas, although it's not about winners and losers, but giving attention and recognition to all kinds of individuals and teams. Because the leadership is so enthusiastically involved, this culture produces thousands of ideas for improvement every year.

4. **Construct action triggers**: The Heaths (Figure 12.5), in other research cite that for staying motivated about keeping commitments, people who are asked to imagine specifically when and where they will do something have a vastly improved chance they will do it. This means being as specific as, "When I receive our annual planning calendar I will sit down that day and list my intentions for our unit in this planning cycle." The email will trigger the commitment. There are lots of implications here for how action agreements at the end of meetings are handled.

SideStory 12.6

5. **Use checklists:** Checklists seem simple but can be very important behavior changers. Hospital safety practitioners find that hospital infections drop dramatically when doctors and nurses follow checklists for things like infusions and surgical procedures. Pilots and other people who operate complex equipment use safety checklists.

Evolving New Rituals

Whatever changes you and your client are working on need to become embedded in the organizational culture. One of the ways cultures develop and strengthen is through ritual—patterns of behavior or symbolic acts that have special meaning. There are highly impactful and more formalized rituals, usually taking place less often, and there are ritual-like activities that are more frequent. In either case we can think of rituals having two dimensions. The outer dimension is what we can observe—a more public ceremonial aspect that people participate in. But there is also the inner dimension which is the felt experience of being in a ritual process. As we will explore in the next chapter, rituals provide opportunities to help catalyze changes or anchoring what needs to be stabilized.

Best practices, like starting meetings with a review of clear Outcomes, Agenda, Roles, and Rules, or the OARRs model we described early in this book (Figure 8.6) can become ritual-like when they are taken seriously and enough space and time are given for the various elements to come alive.

At our Leading Change Program at the Metropolitan Council in Minnesota, we start and end each three-day workshop with a simple ritual of sitting in a circle and sharing our current state of being as authentically as possible and what has our attention in work and life right now (SideStory 12.6). There are two ways we do this that have become ritualized.

Reflections as a Circle Practice

Participants in the Met Council's Leading Change Program end each day with a Takeaway Circle, reflecting on what has their attention and what was covered over the course of the day that resonated with them. It often starts with one person, and moves to their left around the circle until everyone in the group has had a chance to speak. Invariably, the takeaways are moving and surprising in their depth and variety.

This ritual-like activity brings good closure to the times together and informs the facilitator and the group about how the group is doing.

Summary

- ☐ **Use the Iceberg Model of Change** to grow systemic thinking
- ☐ **Pay attention to the inner dynamics**—persisting courageously, clearing old habits, and nurturing new patterns.
- ☐ **Support the process with outer structures**

1. **Amplify successes:** Support positive deviance, explore Appreciative Inquiry, use positive feedback.
2. **Clear blocks:** Work on strategic compliance with culture change, change environments, break through stuck behavior patterns.
3. **Redesign processes:** Learn visual work flow planning, identify core processes that support change, and learn from Lean practices. Appreciate a systems perspective like RE-AMP's can reveal new levers of change. Link new initiatives to the big vision, like Otis Spunkmeyer.
4. **Incent new behaviors;evolve new rituals:** Motivate the elephant, give clear directions, clear the path. Make new social norms visible, encourage leadership modeling, create supportive physical environments, create action triggers, and make checklists. Use meeting rituals like Takeaways and Stringing the Beads.

Figure 12.10

❑ **Stringing the Beads**: To begin meetings we often like to use a traditional practice called "Stringing the Beads," where each person and their voice represents a bead. When each have a turn to speak it strings everyone together into a metaphoric necklace (Figure 12.10). The process uses a talking piece.

In the words of Firehawk Hulin and Pele Rouge from the Center for Timeless Earth Wisdom, from whom we learned this practice, "the talking piece goes around the circle and becomes the energetic 'needle' carrying the thread of connection from person to person, 'stringing' the beads together into a complete necklace and an energetic whole. The talking piece and words are the thread of connection that create the larger fabric, the 'We,'much like a shuttle moves back and forth in a loom connecting/expanding/transforming the 'independent' strings into a woven fabric that contains the beauty of each thread and creates a larger beauty."

We ask people to begin stringing the beads with their name, and a brief statement about their current state of being—heart, mind, and body. We then usually ask a second question relevant to the work we will be doing. People end saying "I am complete." Invariably this practice brings everyone present, grounds them in a whole-person frame of mind, and begins the work from a place of being centered.

Takeaways: At the end of each day, or whenever a learning module is complete, we gather people in a circle and ask them to reflect a moment on what they are feeling and thinking about what they have done together, and what one or two things will they take away. It anchors people in the feeling of something having happened. In the language of the *Liminal Pathways Change Framework*, it gives voice to the "communitas," the group that is going through change together.

In the next chapter we will look at how more developed rituals play a part in both sustaining and transforming culture.

13. Sustaining Long Term
Evolving a New Culture

Figure 13.1

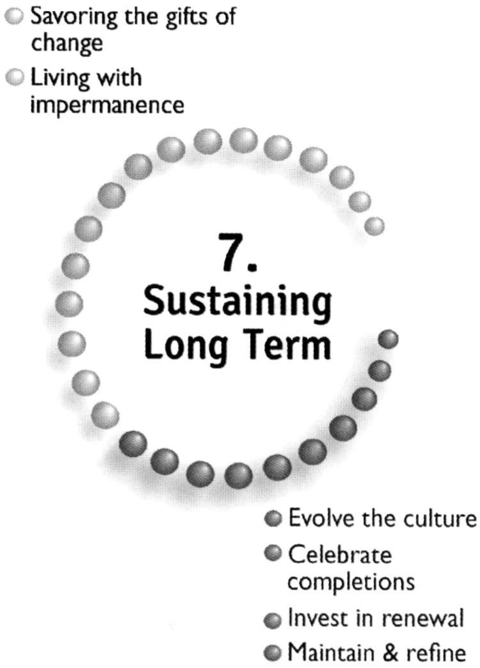

Creating, shaping, and evolving cultures is something that unfolds over long periods of time. In the last chapter we explored integrating the change in the more overt systems. But change ultimately has to be embodied in the culture if it hopes to sustain itself. The fact that change is always moving and happens at different frequencies (Figure 13.2) is part of the challenge, and the confusion. This is why cultural norms and practices exist. People need stability in the face of all the fluidity of life. After the intensity and disruption of a large change process, it is therefore helpful to stabilize new agreements in the culture itself. In fact, creating stable processes that support culture change is a key part of the art of process leadership. This chapter looks at ways you can help clients meet this challenge as visual consultants.

Figure 13.2

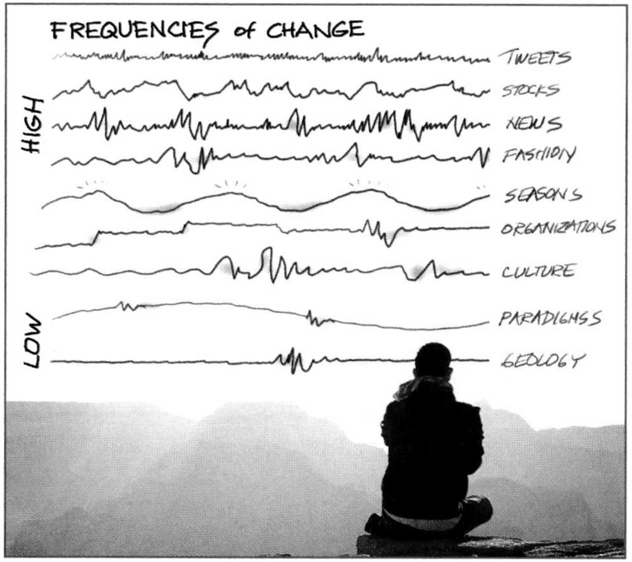

Confusing Activity with Change

Stocks and the news change at high frequency, but is this really change? Yes the word change is used for rapidly fluctuating phenomena, but the kind of change that can sustain long term is of lower frequency and a different order. Some more long-range thinkers like Stu Brand at the Long Now Foundation are very concerned our culture is losing its ability to track the long cycles of change, which they argue actually control and shape the shorter cycles. Part of working long term is not getting distracted by the buzz.

Figure 13.3

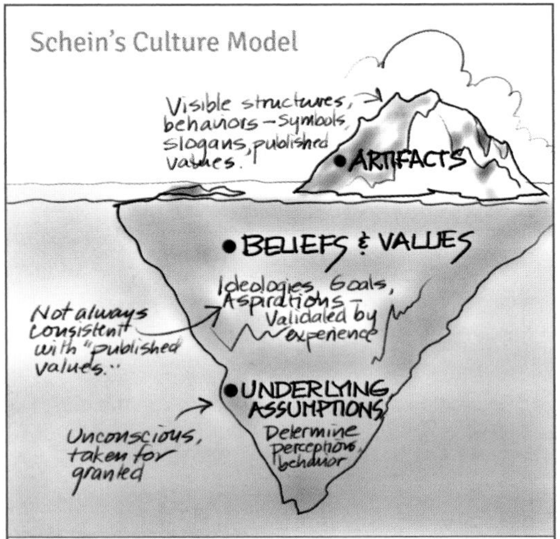

Culture Model

Ed Schein has shaped the way organization consultants think about culture. It maps onto the iceberg model we shared in Figure 12.2. He categorizes the key elements of culture as underlying assumptions, beliefs and values, and artifacts, which include behavior. Schein, along with many other organizational researchers, suggests that rituals point to these tacit and elusive aspects of organizational life as well as shape it.

From a visual consulting perspective, this second use of the iceberg model is a good example of how a basic metaphor can be used flexibly to clarify more refined distinctions.

Let's start by defining organizational culture. You can think of culture as all the ways that work actually gets done in an organization, including all the formal and informal aspects of it as well as the conscious and unconscious assumptions and motivations and what the organization aspires to be. Organizational researchers commonly define culture as having three key dimensions: cognitions, behaviors, and artifacts. Cognitions include the shared assumptions, values and beliefs, and emotional states. Behaviors include the norms and typical patterns of interaction. Artifacts include symbols as well as structures, technologies, or policies that are associated with a specific culture. Each dimension adds something that infuses the organization with a certain sense of personality and identity. (See Figure 13.3 for another perspective.) We like to say that identity is to the person as culture is to the organization.

Discerning Types of Change

We are moving toward practices that can help create the kind of culture and stability that will help you sustain long term (SideStory 13.1). But before delving into practices it will help to remind ourselves that different kinds of change have very different qualities in terms of what is meant by "long term."

- ❑ **Developmental change** is shaped by underlying patterns that are set in our biology and the dynamics of growing, living systems. Most people are familiar with development stages of human beings. It's understood that cycles from childhood, to adolescence, to young adult, to middle age, to mature, to senior, to elderly are each periods of 10–15 years, but what does it mean qualitatively? Traditional peoples' attention to marking the beginning and ending of developmental periods makes a huge difference in how quickly people integrate into the new phase and achieve enough stability to attend to the lessons and work of that stage. We will return to look at how rituals function in this regard later in this chapter.

Some organizational theorists analogize that organizations follow this same pattern, For sure organizations mature and grow old, but they don't necessarily have a biological imperative regarding aging. It's possible to renew organizations and have them last through generations. The model in Figure 13.4, based on Arthur M. Young's Theory of Process, suggests that organization can evolve to higher stages of freedom and contribution by mastering the earlier, more fundamental forms.

- **Volitional change**, such as the implementation of a new strategic vision, does not have a prescribed natural life, but depends on being refreshed and lived into in meaningful ways. This is where rituals for stabilization and creation of meaning are doubly important. Old habits have a way of coming back without conscious work.
- **Circumstantial change** often doesn't follow a pattern. Fires and earthquakes are unpredictable, except we know that they will happen. The changes resulting from global warming are similar. Many cycles of change are long enough to be outside our normal perception, except when specific "bifurcations"—a term used by biologists and geologists—occur, as when a large ice shelf in Antarctica calves off. Interestingly our new tools of visualization through video time compression and data visualization techniques are allowing humans to extend their perception into some of these phenomena and prepare for them.

If the deeply held assumptions underlying culture are shaped and held in place by internal narratives and images, that in turn are constructed by social interaction over time, then we can also appreciate that the various ways this circular process of reinforcing cultural processes can not only be disrupted and shifted but also stabilized. In the practices that follow we are more focused on this latter type of purposeful stabilization.

Inner Dynamics of Sustaining Long Term Change

When you and your clients reach this challenge of change, the inner dynamics can be

Deep Culture Visioning

Meryem Le Saget works with some of the largest companies in France to help them not only create new visions but embed them in the culture of the organization. She began her visual consulting work from a base of leadership and organizational development. while collaborating with Michael Doyle of Interaction Associates on "deep visioning." They had top management and a large cross section of stakeholders make personal, in-depth visits to customers in their homes, then used dialogue to make sense of their findings, create a long term vision, and integrate ideas throughout the company culture. A recent project she led involved training 250 internal managers to facilitate two-day visioning meetings that involved 22,000 associates in the company over several months. "I always work with visuals," Meryem says. "The engagement, creativity, and conversations give people a sense of accomplishment and deep connection to their culture." A huge part of her role is coaching senior management in how to inspire, lead, and support the change using collaborative processes.

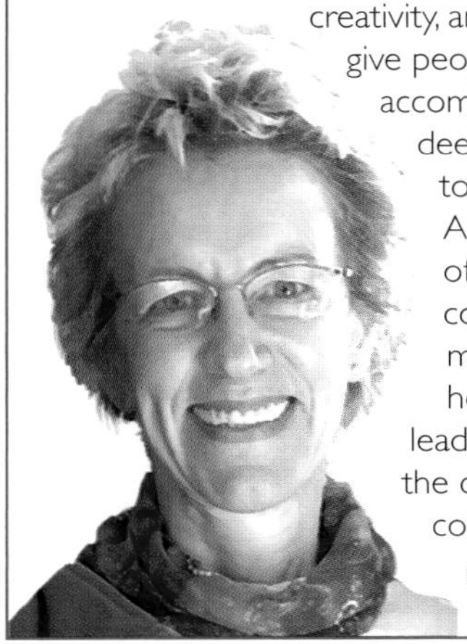

Figure 13.4

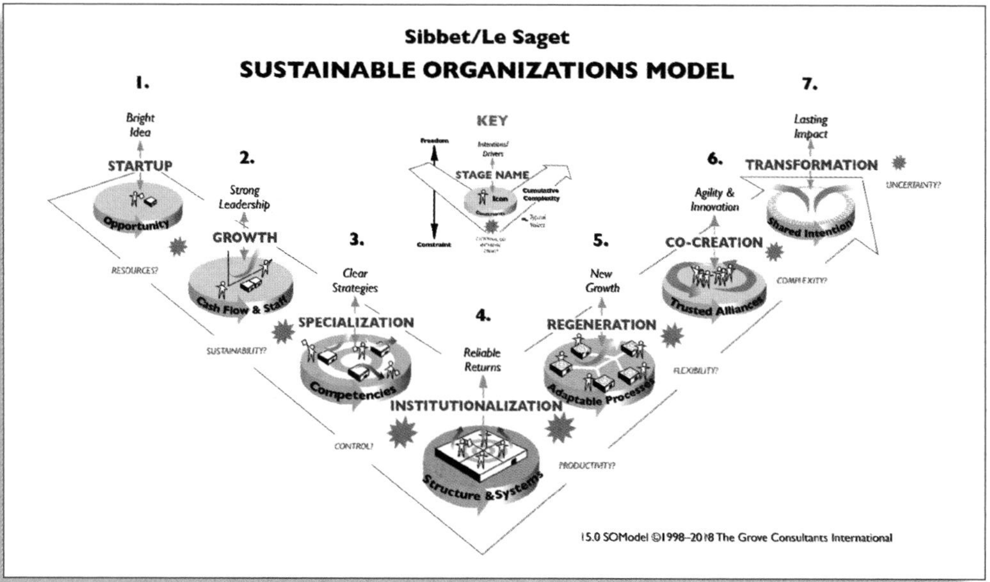

appreciated as moving in two directions. One is taking delight in the new opportunities that are emerging. The other is realizing that change is complex, multilayered and continuous, and that nothing is really permanent. We call these the inner dynamics:

1. **Savoring the gifts of change:** Transformational change can be exhilarating. A young person's developmental change from teenage to adult years is a turbulent transition, but after a while yields greatly widened choices. Persons recovering from disaster face huge challenges in the liminal phase, but often report a freedom from old patterns they had not anticipated. Volitional change, as when a company decides to integrate its enterprise-wide data, can be an enormous challenge initially and then later begin yielding insights and fluidity that was impossible before.

2. **Living with impermanence:** Something begins to shift in everyone's ability to deal with change when they take a longer view and realize that while nothing is permanent, certain patterns have a longer frequency and provide the stability that allows everyone to deal with the shorter-cycle challenges. Living with this feature of life means understanding the difference.

Archetypal Choices for Sustainable Organization

David and Meryem LeSaget (a colleague from France; see SideStory 13.1), have developed this framework for thinking about the different stages of organizational evolution. It is described in some detail in *Visual Leaders*, the third in the Wiley series on Visual Facilitation. It integrates Larry Griener's work on stages of organizational growth and crises, Arthur M. Young's Theory of Process, and David and Meryem's many years of consulting on organization change.

Rituals Can Cultivate, Harness, and Stabilize the Energy of Change

The consulting question is how to approach such complexity and move between different stages of growth or transformation. Let's return to the role of ritual. In Chapter 5, Basic Patterns of Change, we introduced the notion of rites of passages as a way of understanding how human systems change by emphasizing the phases of change and the inner process dynamics and outer process structures that support the change. But we did not write much about one of the most helpful things in culture change—the general role of ritual in organizational life and how the role of rites or rituals specifically support the movement through change processes, especially culture change. We identified crucibles as moments in time or special events that catalyze these forward movements, but didn't elaborate on how you work with them in practice. That is what we want to do now.

It helps to begin with some distinctions. Rituals can can be designed to help individuals and groups transition from one organizational role to another, maintain organization status, or build solidarity within the organization. Rituals can help create social meanings, emphasize values, and affirm or shape attitudes out of what otherwise would be ambiguous flux of experiences within organizations.

As we noted before, the terms rites, ceremony, and rituals are often used interchangeably. But they can also be understood as quite distinct. Rites and ceremonies are usually considered to be discrete and often public enactments that have a beginning, middle, and end. They are widely accepted social practices that are often repeated in full at certain intervals and special times. Victor Tuner refers to ceremony as the outward aspect, while ritual is the experience of the internal movements that happen within the individual. This inner and outer view is reflected in the *Seven Challenge of Change* framework.

Full Rituals and Ritual-Like Activities

Whether or not you consider these kinds of organizational processes to be ceremonies or rituals, they are forms of social action in which a group's values and identity is

Functions of Organizational Rituals

Following are the functions of rituals and ritual-like activities. Think about ones you have experienced in client organizations. Which of these functions are these activities fulfilling?

Ritual Functions

- ☐ Provide meaning
- ☐ Manage uncertainty and anxiety
- ☐ Catalyze new insight and vision
- ☐ Exemplify and reinforce old or new social order
- ☐ Communicate important values
- ☐ Enhance group solidarity
- ☐ Include and exclude
- ☐ Signal commitment
- ☐ End, establish new, and manage existing work structures
- ☐ Prescribe and reinforce significant events

Figure 13.5

How Rituals Prescribe Behavior

The takeaway practice we described in the previous chapter has ritual-like qualities. It marks the end of a meeting or phase of work. People become familiar with it and it becomes a routine, bringing to conscious awareness what has everyone's attention.

Doing "pop-up meetings" regularly reinforces, and you could say "prescribes," a cultural norm—that taking time for learning and reflection is important.

Taking a few minutes of silence before beginning an important meeting honors the inner aspects of our and the group's collective consciousness.

publicly demonstrated or enacted in a stylized manner. This may take place as part of a formal speech, a dinner for employees, or what we have come to call "special meetings" that are outside of the regular meeting structures. Coffee breaks and even virtual meetings can even be ritual-like.

Full organizational rituals are powerful and infrequent organizational events, while ritual-like activities are much more commonplace. Their repetitious enactments can still demand attention if they are not just mindless routines. They will tend to have greater impact than activities without any ritual elements (SideStory 13.2).

Why Are Rituals so Powerful for Shaping Culture?

In their literature survey on organizational ritual, *Organizational Rituals: Features, Functions and Mechanisms*, Aaron Smith and Bob Stewart identify three elements in meaningful rituals.

1. **Cognitive capture:** There is a connection between ritual performance and the transmission of content. When a ritual takes place in which the content that is shared matches the cognitive receptivity of the participants—such as their readiness to pay attention, to remember, to learn, or to make decisions—the ritual has more impact on the person.
2. **Affective anchoring and conditioning:** There is a strong connection between ritual performance and emotional impact. High-arousal rituals may instigate deeper meaning attributions and command greater transformative power. Rituals serve as an emotional anchor for social solidarity and belief. The practical consequence is that ritual performance leads to a "gut-feeling" about ideas and beliefs implicit to the ritual, even if it occurs on an unconscious level.
3. **Behavioral prescription:** There is a strong link between ritual performance and other,

subsequent activities (Figure 13.5). Ritualized action can reinforce new behavior and pull people out of routinized behavior. Routinized action is automatic, involves low attentional demands, and has limited emphasis on performance. In rituals with higher emotional engagement, the knowledge that is conveyed stands out, making reflection on it almost inevitable. While routine may be part of ritualized actions, it isn't the same as unconscious habit. Conscious practices and routines provide the learning pathways for new and stabilized behavior.

Outer Structures that Support Sustaining Long Term

We have identified four things that a visual consultant can learn about that will make a direct impact on an organizational or community culture being able to achieve some kind of new stability long term.

1. **Evolve the culture:** This set of practices focuses on specific ways of shaping the rituals and ritual-like activities that can reinforce and strengthen new cultural aspects that will support your new directions longer term. We will share how to design an organization ceremony that can introduce something new. We will also look at how to pay conscious attention to the stories, symbols, and practices that are being reinforced by leadership day-to-day.
2. **Celebrate completions:** Having clear endings for shorter processes frees up energy for other ones. There are wonderful rituals for ending special meetings or phases of projects that make it clear that the main work is completed and people can move their attention on to other things. Just as a farmer retires certain crops to free land for new ones, so the organization consultant learns to guide clients in the process of completing projects and processes and repurposing their resources.
3. **Invest in renewal:** Longer change cycles can lose vitality as they become taken for granted. People can settle into a phase of change and not give themselves time

The Paradox of Strong Cultures

Stories, symbols, language, rituals and relationships are the fabric of strong cultures. The paradox of attending to these in your consulting is that any given constellation of elements that form a culture can be both an enabler and a block to further change.

The paradox can be resolved a bit if you shift to a process mindset, and realize that the appropriateness of any given pattern has a lot to do with when it manifests in the longer cycle of change.

In the beginning stages of coming to a new way of working or behaving with one another and finding new, strong stories, metaphors and rituals help a great deal for the change to become embedded in peoples' everyday lives.

But the very same elements can be the tools used to block change by those who are benefiting from the status quo and refuse to adapt to new circumstances.

Visual consultants in particular need to be sensitive to where they are working in this regard. The sacred symbols of a deeply rooted culture are deeply rooted for reasons that need to be appreciated before they are challenged, especially when beginning to work with practices that can be confused with traditional religious or other doctrines. Context is paramount.

The Ambidextrous Organization

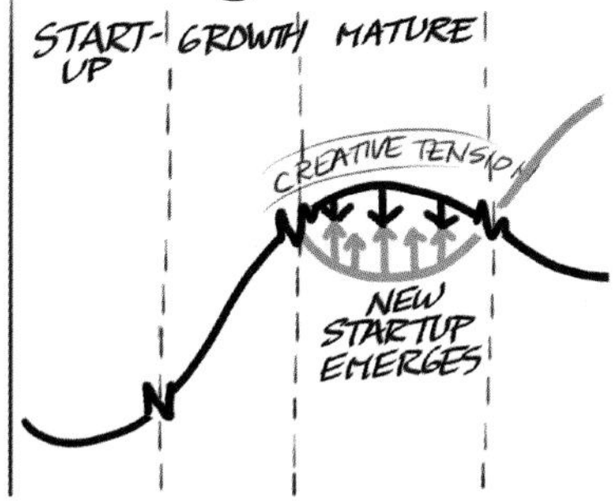

Products and businesses go through an "S" curve of change as they mature. Start-ups are creative, anything goes cultures. Growth organizations are focused and driven. Mature organizations focus on maintenance and refinement. It is the harvesting from the more mature elements that often feed the start-ups.

The challenge is to manage the overlap and creative tension. Charles O'Reilly at Stanford Business School has written extensively about this challenge in his *Winning Through Innovation: A Practical Guide to Leading Organizational Change and Renewal*. He argues for organizational ambidexterity, or the ability to manage both mature and innovative organizations. He contends it takes very different kinds of managers to lead start-up, growth,and mature cultures, and the bottleneck in current management is finding leaders who have the breadth of insight and flexibility to manage all three kinds.

and space to reconnect to the purpose of each phase and the renewal of motivation and energy it takes to integrate and stabilize the change. Learning and reflection activities are central to renewal. It takes time to gain a new perspective and bring in people with fresh ideas. These are all the kinds of things that make the phase of creating new directions so exciting. Well, they need to continue if change is to last. Being creative in developing reasons why your client should invest in renewal is part of the visual consulting contribution to this challenge.

4. **Maintain and refine**: The challenge of working long term is building maintenance and refinement into the very fabric of your culture. But not everything needs this kind of attention! Some processes in an organization or community are enablers of others, less critical processes. In the human body the cardiovascular system is fundamental. When it is weak or fails, all the other systems fail. In organizations, accounting functions are essential to making decisions and knowing how you are with cash flow and profitability. Hiring and promotion processes are central to culture shaping. Having discipline and stability around these enables the others.

   As a visual change consultant, part of your role is to help guide people in the early parts of a change process, as well as building in thinking and activities that prepare people for the latter stages (Sidestory 13.4). You may or may not be directly involved in the ideas we share next, but at a minimum you can bring them to your client's attention early so they have real choices when they reach the challenge of sustaining long term.

1. Evolve the Culture

Visual consultants can help cultures evolve in ways that support change by working outside the boundaries of traditional visual practice. Some of the elements that can be worked with can be appreciated through the lenses of the Four Flows framework.

1. **Presence and attention to higher purpose**: The quality of your presence in conversations and meetings is an intangible factor that makes a huge difference in the quality of what happens. In a culture moving to more trust and collaboration, your ability to be present with people in a way that respects their whole being can create an environment where others will step into that same field.

   Another aspect at the attentional level is how in touch you are with the higher purpose of the work you are doing, and how you help your clients connect with their own sense of purpose. When groups and leaders open up to the important reasons they are seeking change, a quickening of attention and spirit can flow through the entire process (Sidestory 13.5).

2. **Support for deep, energized engagements**: A meeting with no tables has a very different feeling than one where people are focusing on note taking and their computers. One of the reasons people who facilitate dialogue have people sit in a circle is to have everyone equally able to see the whole of every other person as they speak. Sitting in circle or at tables are choices that need to be made in context related to the goals of the meeting. However, if you are evolving a culture of mutual respect and trust then having some experiences that are deeply personal mixed in with other experiences is important. (See Gisela's cautionary story on the next page).

   You are also working with energy and experience of the group by supporting different kinds of informal socializing in meetings and gatherings. Meals, outdoor walks, reflective

Evolving Culture at the College of Business Administration

When the College of Business Administration (CBA) at Cal Poly Pomona began to consider what it would take to bring to life the operating principles they were developing, we suggested that the leadership team and the design team consider three dimensions of a developmental culture and a set of associated questions.

These distinctions come from *An Everyone Culture: Becoming A Deliberately Developmental Organization* by Robert Keagan and Lisa Lahey. They identify ways of creating organizations that are **BOTH effective as economic entities** and **dramatically support the development of individual and collective capabilities of their leaders, managers, and staff**. The dimensions they identify are:

Edge: Developmental Aspirations

Home: Developmental Communities

Groove: Developmental Practices

The questions we asked CBA to explore were:

Edge—What are CBA's overarching learning goals and what are the learning and development goals of the leaders, faculty, and staff and how would these be identified?

Home—What will you, as a collective, do to live into the culture you want? What will you do to support each other to practice your operating principles so that you are able to achieve your 2020 goals and 2025 vision?

Groove—What are your operating principles? What do they look like in action? How do they apply to each group and each person?

Deliberately developmental organizations are guided by aspirations expressed in operating principles and supported by communities of practice willing to try things out and to be vulnerable, inviting everyone to build a deliberately developmental culture, committed to individual learning goals that all reinforce each other.

SideStory 13.6

The Apple Leadership Expedition

In the early days of Apple Computer a special offsite called the Leadership Expedition was designed to help managers think like leaders more than managers. To make the point that this would be a different kind of experience, they entered the meeting room at Pajaro Dunes in the SF Bay Area to find huge mountains of furniture covered with white parachutes, symbolizing mountains.

Everyone was then asked to sit on the floor and experience a nine-projector slide show of a record-breaking climb up K2 in the Himalayas, the second-tallest mountain in the world. Jim Whittaker led the climb. It's an incredible, emotional story. As it finished Jim himself came from behind the screen and led a conversation about leadership, teamwork, and taking risk.

Then everyone was asked to take down the mountains of furniture and create their own base camp for the week-long session to follow. The agenda was graphically displayed on the wall as a series of climbs up the mountain.

The embodiment of the metaphor and using ritual-like elements in this start-up powerfully evoked the spirit of the week, which continued to embody surprise and challenge.

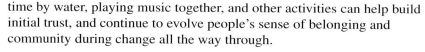

time by water, playing music together, and other activities can help build initial trust, and continue to evolve people's sense of belonging and community during change all the way through.

3. **Introduce new language and concepts**: New behavior and processes need anchoring in language. Sometimes this is a new story or metaphor. Sometimes it is a conceptual model that strikes a chord. The *Liminal Pathways Change Framework* is a good example. Simply having a way to normalize the ambiguity and potential confusion of the in-between times is a powerful support for change processes.

4. **Design new rituals and physical environments**. It is possible to design organizational ceremonies to mark special transitions in a change process (Chapter 5). It involves setting intention and planning beforehand, specific suggestions for how to step into the ceremony and the uses of symbolic acts during, and guidelines and suggestions for how to complete the ceremony and re-enter. Throughout, different people will play different roles, either leading aspects of it or holding space for the persons going through the process. If a group co-creates these kinds of activities they can have great emotional impact and meaning and catalyze needed energy for the initiative.

 Sometimes just changing physical spaces can anchor a desired change in behavior and process, or introduce new structures that reflect a new organization (see SideStory 13.6).

The Challenge of Getting Excited About New Methods

Establishing a new culture to support change is critical, but we would like to share a cautionary tale about imposing a process we love on people who aren't ready. This is a story from Gisela's years at Sonoma State University.

I first began teaching a core curriculum course in humanistic psychology to undergraduate students when I encountered an interesting culture problem. I had first experienced student-centered learning (SideStory 13.7) as an undergraduate and was eager to bring it forward now. I designed the course to bring those student-centered approaches to life. Rather than sitting in rows with the teacher in front, symbolizing a more teacher-centered approach, I asked students to sit in a circle emphasizing what they could learn from and with each other rather than just me as the professor.

Rather than offering extensive lectures, I would also do very short mini-presentations introducing topics and set up highly interactive, small and large-group explorations and invite dialogue about related topics that emphasized student interests.

In learning groups, they would take on areas of interest and share their learning with the others. This modeled learning as a process of discovery and that a topic could be approached more through the lenses of the other learners than those of the teacher.

What I did not do was lecture and give frequent multiple-choice tests. As a good designer of learning experiences, this format was not difficult for me. While I found that students initially were a bit baffled and disoriented about what they were supposed to do, after a few sessions our class times seemed really lively with explorations.

I was also satisfied with their projects and reports. However, the class evaluations baffled me. There were quite a few comments like "the class lacks structure," "the class is too organic," or "I did not know what was expected from me," and "the class is fun but I am not so sure what I learned." Wow. I was surprised. Then what occurred to me was that perhaps the very thoughtful structure I was introducing was so foreign to them, they did not recognize it as structure or something they would associate with being in college.

Afterwards I discussed these comments with one of my mentors, Arthur Warmoth,

SideStory 13.7

Student-Centered Learning Cultures

One of the significant contributions that Carl Rogers, one of the founders of humanistic psychology, made was the notion of student-centered learning. In this approach the student is at the center of the learning process, not the prescribed curriculum, the teacher, or the institution, which is often the case in mainstream academic institutions.

From the 1960's to 80's student-centered learning in its purest forms was a radical idea. In fact, it still is, although adult-learning theory recognizes that people are motivated to learn best when they are able to put their learning focus on topics relevant to their current situation and interest.

When bringing this approach to life, the student's learning interests drive the learning process and teachers function more as a resource, helping decide on the approach and offering guiding questions much like a good mentor or coach would do. In these situations, the typical hierarchy between the teacher and learner is more in the background. The learner rather than the teacher is in the driver's seat of the learning process.

Figure 13.6

from whom I learned quite a bit about student-centered learning. He suggested that the next time I teach the course I should slowly introduce this different approach, rather than all at once and see what happens.

Here are some of the things I did differently. I taught the first two classes standing in front lecturing, as most of the students would expect, but offered to stop lecturing as soon as they would let me know that they wanted to do something else, which they did in the third class. I also told them that they could turn their chairs into a circle so that we could better see each other while we were talking as a big group. Then at the beginning of class I let them choose if they wanted to sit in rows or in a circle. We went back and forth a number of times, ultimately settling on a half-circle format. This then gave us a chance to reflect on what we were doing and how this related to student-centered learning. And sure enough, those baffling comments pretty much disappeared from the evaluations.

Rather than assuming the students would adopt the norms without hesitation or confusion, I realized that a gradual introduction would bring them along and give them a chance to make them their own. We created our own classroom culture that was somewhere between the ideal and what was a comfortable stretch for them.

We hope this story helps you to appreciate the range of responses that can be evoked by imposing even a seemingly simple, new process but also the value of holding true to your intentions and improvising to get where you are going.

2. Celebrate Completions

In this book we've characterized change as a process that can be designed and guided. In real-life situations there are many simultaneous changes that begin to interact, with some starting and others bouncing back and forth between liminality and integration. A consultant can help clients by taking a look at what kind of things need ending or final completion so that attention, energy, and resources can be consciously focused on emerging processes.

Using Checkouts

In the Art of Hosting movement, which is expanding as people become more interested in high-engagement processes, meetings are often begun with a "check-in" and conclude with a "check-out" process. This is similar to the takeaways process described at the end of the previous chapter.

At the end of special ceremonies and workshop, a colleague of ours, Firehawk Hulin, loves to do a simple activity that beautifully marks the ending (Figure 13.6). He invites everyone to stand in a circle and then says. "I will say some words in the most neutral, unemotional way possible, and when I am done I want you to repeat them in the most celebratory, vibrant way possible." He then shuffles, looks at the ground, and says "This ceremony is now complete...and the next one has just begun." Then everyone shouts out the same words, with laughter and release all around.

Leave No Trace

On outdoor expeditions and special vision quest-type workshops a practice that marks the ending is to complete a ritual-like clean-up process, embodying the principle of "leave no trace." This practice is now adopted in many other situations (See SideStory 13.8). Brushing away footprints with fallen branches, picking up all litter, and returning everything that was moved to where it was before is all part of the ritual-like ending. It is good for the environment and clearly marks the completion.

Funeral for a Closing Plant

Back in the day when Hewlett-Packard was a standard setter for respecting employees, an

SideStory 13.8

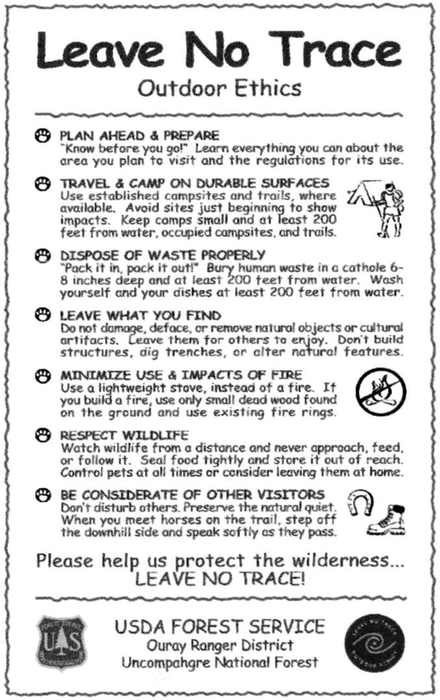

Leave No Trace

Outdoor Ethics

PLAN AHEAD & PREPARE
"Know before you go!" Learn everything you can about the area you plan to visit and the regulations for its use.

TRAVEL & CAMP ON DURABLE SURFACES
Use established campsites and trails, where available. Avoid sites just beginning to show impacts. Keep camps small and at least 200 feet from water, occupied campsites, and trails.

DISPOSE OF WASTE PROPERLY
"Pack it in, pack it out!" Bury human waste in a cathole 6-8 inches deep and at least 200 feet from water. Wash yourself and your dishes at least 200 feet from water.

LEAVE WHAT YOU FIND
Do not damage, deface, or remove natural objects or cultural artifacts. Leave them for others to enjoy. Don't build structures, dig trenches, or alter natural features.

MINIMIZE USE & IMPACTS OF FIRE
Use a lightweight stove, instead of a fire. If you build a fire, use only small dead wood found on the ground and use existing fire rings.

RESPECT WILDLIFE
Watch wildlife from a distance and never approach, feed, or follow it. Seal food tightly and store it out of reach. Control pets at all times or consider leaving them at home.

BE CONSIDERATE OF OTHER VISITORS
Don't disturb others. Preserve the natural quiet. When you meet horses on the trail, step off the downhill side and speak softly as they pass.

Please help us protect the wilderness...
LEAVE NO TRACE!

USDA FOREST SERVICE
Ouray Ranger District
Uncompahgre National Forest

Emerging Ecological Mindset

Increasingly people are aware that their impacts on the environment need attention. While "Leave No Trace" applies to campers, think about applying these kinds of principles to organizational interventions. Even this camping application includes consideration of social impacts. Ecological thinking is a good example of systemic awareness.

Figure 13.7

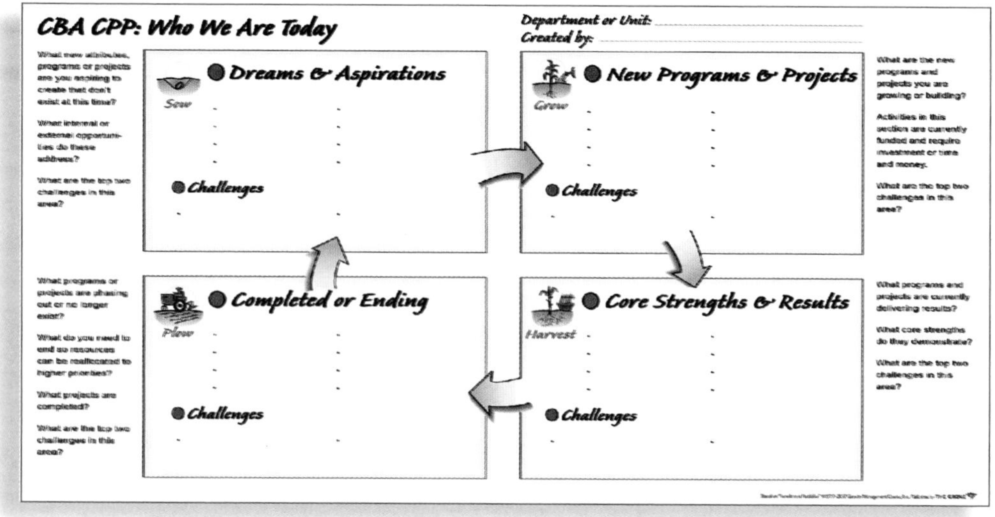

internal organizational consultant named Geoff Ainscow was tasked with helping bring an end to a plant in the Southwest that the company needed to close. The company took as much care as possible reassigning people, but it was still a huge change to close the plant. To mark this ending Geoff organized a New Orleans-style funeral. On the day of the event all the employees and their families gathered for a final goodbye gathering and meal. From the innards of the building a saxophone wailed out a traditional funeral dirge. Through the room a group of pall bearers wearing black garbage sacks carried a casket, and into it invited everyone to put favorite objects from their desks. When everyone had contributed, they moved outside to the gathering of families, and buried the casket. They then tore off the garbage sacks to reveal phoenix T-shirts and joined in a final celebration. The families of the HP employees were very moved that their company would go to this kind of trouble to acknowledge the contribution of the factory and its people.

Think Organically About Renewal

When Rob Eskridge originally developed this framework, as an alternative to a popular growth matrix that emphasized stars, problem children, cash cows, and dogs, he felt that thinking like a farmer was a much more sophisticated way to understand growth and renewal. It makes a difference which metaphor is underlying your base maps and visuals.

At Cal Poly Pomona, Gisela and Laurie adapted this template with headers that the College of Business Administration people could relate to more easily. Tuning templates to specific contexts is essential for getting full value from them.

3. Invest in Renewal

Renewal is name of the final stage in the *Drexler/Sibbet Team Performance Model*, another framework based on the Theory of Process (see *Visual Teams* from Wiley). On teams, real change mastery comes when people develop the ability to bring on new members, harvest learning, and celebrate endings—all part of renewal. People who have invested heavily in a change process need time to renew themselves for the longer term. In challenging circumstantial change, getting past immediate disasters is only the beginning of the challenge. Rebuilding the kind of social and physical infrastructures that are normally taken for granted is time and resource intensive. Organizations too need time and processes to allow for renewal. In developmental change, there are times in between the different stages when it helps to take care of ourselves and not push natural rhythms.

Work the Plow Section of Investment Portfolios

At the end of the chapter on Stepping into a New, Shared Vision we recommended grounding decisions in allocation of resources and included an example of The Grove's Investment Portfolio Graphic Guide (Figure 10.3). A practice that applies to the challenge of Sustaining Long Term is really working the "plow" section (Figure 13.7). If your clients don't have agricultural experience you might explain that plowing a field does not eliminate it completely, but is about freeing resources for a following cycle, perhaps with another crop, and is a part of renewal.

We are coming to appreciate that renewal is also about reconnecting to deeper purpose, vision, and inspiration, which are the real sources of energy and motivation in human beings. To have this kind of reconnection we need to step away from the day-to-day work and take reflective time to learn and refresh ourselves. SideStory 13.9 lists some of the kinds of things you as a visual consultant, can help plan and facilitate at this stage that can embody some of these qualities.

4. Maintain & Refine

The shadow side of growth and innovation is inattention to the things that created the new possibilities in the first place. These foundational elements are what you may have been working to establish in the Integrating Systemic Change, but they need to continue receiving attention. Too often leadership moves on (the average tenure of a CEO these days

SidesStory 13.9

Renewal Opportunities

Following are some tried-and-true activities that support organizational renewal. Which ones are you familiar with and which might you suggest to your clients?

- ☐ **Annual staff retreats** that include socializing and team building in addition to planning
- ☐ **Sharing rallies** where teams and individuals are honored for their contributions to the organization
- ☐ **Sabbaticals** available on a systematic basis for people with 6–20 year tenures
- ☐ **Retrospective learning events**, where the history of a special project or change process can be reviewed graphically, along with acknowledgment of contributions
- ☐ **Job rotation** for people who are burning out at a job they have been at too long
- ☐ **Group learning journeys and field trips** to other interesting organizations and relevant environments (A lot of relationship building and bonding occurs on these.)
- ☐ **Visioning refresh sessions,** where people get a chance to weave in new insights, learning,and experience and reconnect with the purpose of change

Summary

- ☐ **Understanding culture's role is critical to long term change.**
- ☐ **Pay attention to the inner dynamics**—savoring the gifts and living with impermanence.
- ☐ **Ritual plays an important part in anchoring culture.**
- ☐ **Support the process with outer structures**

  1. **Evolve the culture**: Connect with purpose, energized engagements, new language, new rituals, and environments. Bring in new processes—circle work, visual facilitation, and other innovations.
  2. **Celebrate completions**: Use takeaways and checkouts, ritual-like endings, and close analysis of what to plow under in your investments.
  3. **Invest in renewal**: Take time to reflect, connect with purpose, and hold special renewal activities.
  4. **Maintain and refine**: Understand how maintaining fundamental structure empowers all the others. Learn to balance innovation and maturity through becoming ambidextrous.

is 2.5 years) or long-term concerns are shelved to focus on short-term profits and advances. Nonprofits that work on big, long-term issues understand the slow and often ignored work it takes to keep working on change. Improving energy efficiency takes time. Restoring ecosystems and habitats takes time.

Balancing Maintenance with Innovation

Experienced organization consultants know that organizations are themselves, in reality, ecosystems composed of many different kinds of sub-organizations. Imagine the different choices for sustainable organizations (Figure 13.5) combining together in larger organizations. Developmental "S" curves can overlap (SideStory 13.4) with new start-ups in creative tension with more mature elements in the organization, upon whom they depend.

Within the complex web of interconnections that is the real world of private, public, and nonprofit sectors, think about the things that we all depend on that are not glamorous, but essential to all the rest. Think about our sewage systems, our roads and bridges. Think about the Internet and its vulnerabilities. Think about the relationship between our social capital, the number of relationships we sustain, and our educational and physical health. Unless we start bringing more attention to the foundational elements that make all the other changes possible, we will find ourselves overwhelmed with catch-up activity.

Maintenance and Refinement of Capability

For the visual consultant, this last challenge is the threshold you need to step over to become masterful. We'll end this book reflecting on this aspect, your personal practice. How do you set in motion the kinds of practices and habits of mind and awareness that allow you to be a lifelong contributor to change?

Part IV.

Expanding Your Resources

Continuing the Journey

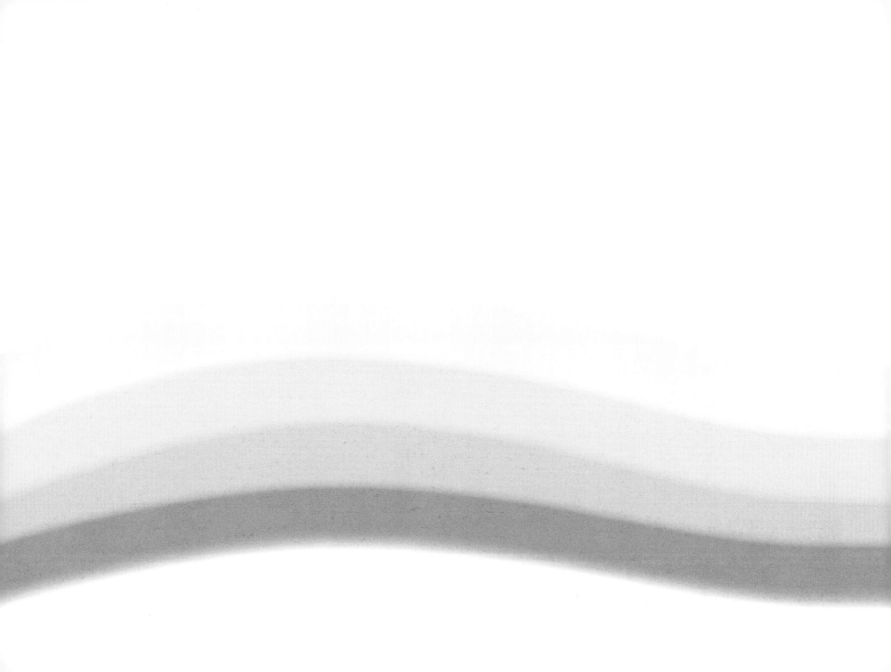

14. Toward Mastery
Purpose, Practice, & Passion

These timeless words of wisdom from 2,500 years ago still hold true about the work of leaders of change:

> *The wicked leader is he whom the people despise.*
>
> *The good leader is he whom the people revere.*
>
> *The great leader is he of whom the people say, "We did it ourselves."*
>
> *—Lao Tzu, Chinese philosopher*

Here we are at the last chapter of this book. We included it in the section along with the appendix and bibliography because these point you to resources for going deeper with this work. Walking the path to mastery means taking the exercises we suggest in the colored boxes and heading into working the four flows and challenges of change from wherever you start (Figure 14.1). It means practicing. The critical question is why? Why take on the challenges of change and the kind of process-leading that visual consulting can provide?

Working from Purpose and Intent

We are increasingly called to this work from our deep appreciation that during this current time period we may be at a potential tipping point. While the Internet has brought us together in ways never imagined, with access to imagery and information worldwide

Figure 14.1

Figure 14.2

Activating Collective Wisdom

Alan Briskin and **Amy Lenzo** pushed out into the digital realm creating a six-session video conference dialogue on collective wisdom exploring how the principles of collective wisdom find expression in our work and lives. Alan's research and writing on wisdom, combined with Amy's experience facilitating virtually, created a container for six rich exchanges. They collaborated with David to create a visual anchor for the work.

Their Collective Wisdom field book will be available through The GLEN in the future.

The gyrocompass metaphor and the images for the five principles emerged from several collaborative design sessions online, an expanding venue for visual consulting.

within hours and minutes, it is also bringing disinformation, images of violence and despair, and a constant appeal to trust the latest product rather than one's own resources. At the same time as our health and agricultural technologies are extending life, we are facing the decimation of indigenous peoples, global extinction of species, and mass migrations due to prolonged religious and military conflicts that by some estimates have left 1 in 10 people worldwide displaced from their homes. At the same time that the tools of education and literacy are ever more available, dictators and misogynist cultures repress the education of young girls and seek to control the media.

Now in many countries young people are turning away from traditional jobs and refusing employment at companies that don't respect the human qualities of their people. "We are crushing the pyramid," one colleague in Europe reported, "and learning to work in circle ways where collaboration and merit are respected." (See Figure 14.2.)

New Forms of Collaboration are Expanding Everywhere

The field of visual facilitation is currently growing at exponential rates. Why? we wonder. We suspect groups are responding to the human pace and sense of touch that live, visual practice provides, especially in organizations where the energy in meetings has been drained by dependency on slides and push communications.

For several weeks we have been participating in an online course called Meditate & Mediate, co-led by Thomas Hübl and William Ury. Thomas is a modern mystic originally from Austria. He teaches people how sensing inner dynamics and practicing mindfulness meditations can help heal and free people from trauma-induced reactivity and create space for feelings and new insights to emerge. William Ury, well known for co-authoring the mediator's go-to reference book, *Getting to Yes: Negotiating Agreements Without Giving In*, has been working on current conflicts in Korea.

Hübl and Ury are weaving a point of view that reconnects the lives and practices of individuals with the collective global community in which we all live. Their assumption is that we are actually profoundly interconnected and inter-resonant with each other. If this is so, then there is hope for tackling big problems, starting with encountering our own, personal struggles from being born into in a world of collective trauma and fragmentation. Can we become collaborative, social innovators in spite of this they wonder.

Hübl and Ury agree that the capabilities of self-awareness and mindfulness—walking in another shoes and being able to reflect on what is going on "from the balcony" (William Ury's metaphor) is not only possible but necessary. This means being able to love another and respect different perspectives, where the self is grounded, open, and responsive to our own and each others' emotional triggers in compassionate and constructive ways. You may not be a mediator, but if you are a consultant coming from respectful engagement with an intention to optimize mutual trust and collaboration, then your path will lead you to similar insights.

Both of us authors, in writing this book, have deepened our sense of the importance of this work in our times, with a sense of humility about what it takes to become masterful.

SideStory 14.1

Shokido

In Aikido one of the core practices is learning to first blend with your opponent, and then move. By reputation, Aikido is able to best the more aggressive martial arts, because it appreciates that all attackers are off balance and their energy can be used to move them and restore balance.

At one point we early practitioners of visual facilitation thought of it as conceptual Aikido. We take the imbalance in the group, receive it to the wall, and bring everything back to listening and balance again. Tomi Nagai Rothe, a Japanese American and long-time visual practitioner, named it Shokido, or whole-body calligraphy.

So process consultants, who use facilitation and dialogic methods, can deal with some of the most aggressive and challenging situations by practicing a kind of radical acceptance, blending through listening, and then moving to help restore connection, relationships, and balance.

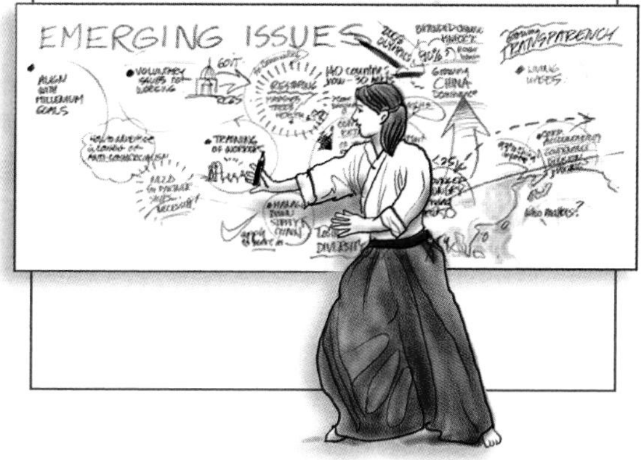

Figure 14.3

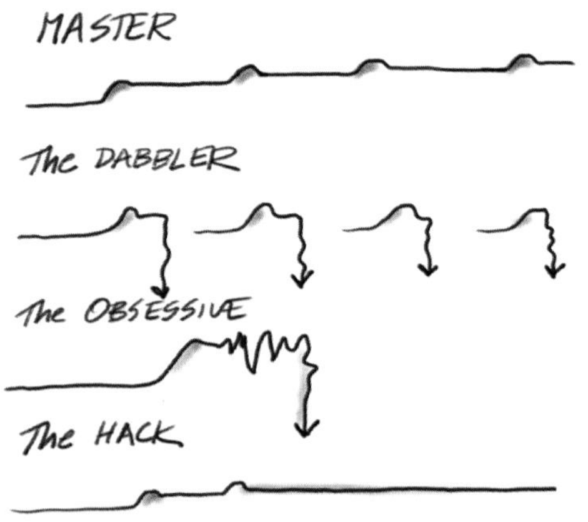

Visualizing Mastery

George Leonard, former editor of *Psychology Today* and Aikido master in his later years, uses graphics to define mastery in his wonderful book, *Mastery*. It's about small advances and long plateaus of refinement. He describes different ways to avoid mastery. The dabbler goes for the advances and ignores the plateaus. The obsessive tries to force through, again ignoring the plateau. The hacker (as in golf) gets a few improvements and then just hangs out with mediocrity.

Leonard's main point is that we have to learn to love the plateau, those long stretches where we don't see a big bump in progress, and then it happens.

Visual Consulting as a Path to Integrated Practice and Awareness

When visual consultants hang large sheets of white paper, then turn to the group to listen to people with understanding and respect, tracking patterns of feeling and thinking through visualization and conversation, and then sustain this kind of relationship over time in a change process, profound things happen. But it is demanding to do this. As practicing consultants we increasingly work collaboratively to hold the complexity, create emotional safety, and keep each other aware and honest. It is when we drop the certainty of our own point of view—being "the only" or "the right one"—and open up to real dialogue with people who are different, that collective wisdom emerges. Collaboration between a facilitator and designer, or consultant and visual facilitator, or dialogue leader and scribe keeps this kind of bridge-building and layered sense-making at the heart of the process.

Truly transformational change can happen when people come to trust that spirit and purpose can enter into a process at the most challenging, pivotal times. If we hold the space open long enough so that someone might speak their truth or share a new insight in a way that rings deeply true for everyone else, then in the heat of the crucible moments, breakthroughs free up energy that releases a new kind of coherence and positive action.

Combining Fields Is the Path to Mastery

It is in the combination of capabilities, with radical acceptance of current contexts and cultures, that a path can be sketched out toward a future of contribution and service in these fields.

Visual facilitation itself is a practice of radical acceptance—explicit and visible acceptance in fact. It is a commitment to reflect everyone's key meaning hour after hour, and finding patterns of insight and connection in a process of evolving clarity about what is so, what is needed, and what is being called for, without knowing where it will go ahead of time, but

Figure 14.4

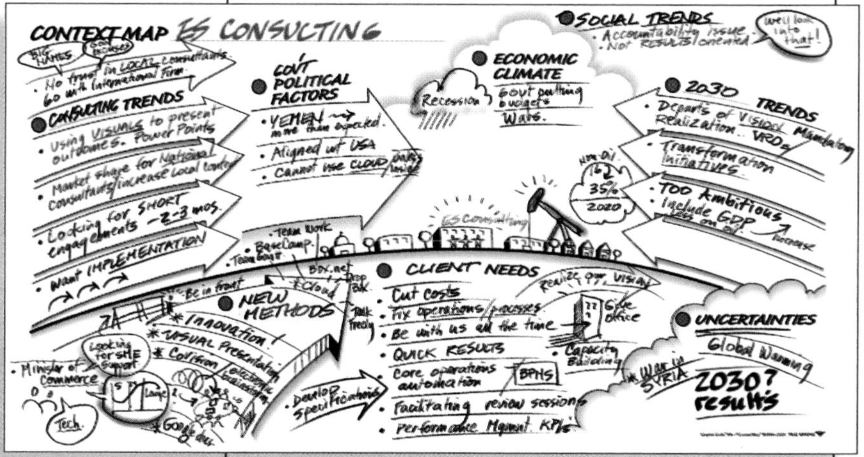

knowing that creating the conditions for receptivity provides soil for the seeds of the new when they appear.

Dialogic practice means both deconstructing and co-creating new narratives through conversation, inquiry, and deep listening, not only in regard to language, metaphor, and meaning, but also to the feelings and intention that give rise to them, while finding the generative images that fuel meaning and action.

Change work is having the persistence and trust that you can transform communications, organizations, and culture over time by coming to shared commitment about new visions and directions; evolving them creatively and intentionally; staying open to improvisation emerging surprises; building structures and processes to support them; and adding rounds of new people to add richness, embodiment, and ultimately sustainable responses to the big challenges.

Each of these fields is united in understanding that life and work is a process, and that process lives through each of us uniquely. By connecting with our own vitality and sense of purpose, the integration comes alive. Flowing between movement and stillness, change and stability is what it means to be alive. We inherently as humans need and know how to create and support both periods of stability as well as periods of transition, and in the midst of this we might experience quick jumps and bifurcation points that introduce radical changes. Today organizations and communities have lost many traditional moorings that traditional rites and rituals provided for guiding important change processes in a holistic, human way. We seldom allow ourselves the space and time to actually feel the experiences we are

Middle East Collaboration

Bassam Alkharashi is founder of ES Consulting in Riyadh, Saudi Arabia. He's building a network of strategy consultants. They conduct initial workshops to define client problems in visually facilitated ways, and collaborative design visions and roadmaps. Given the fluctuating business context they are in, ES delivers through focused workshops rather than long engagements, using visual templates to support their process, in what they call ES Consulting Co-Create. The image here is a context map created in a talk with David to think about their own ES strategy.

SideStory 14.2

Places to Start

Here are the capabilities that you could begin to work with. These are those that we consider fundamental.

DIALOGIC PRACTICE

- [ ] Working with intention
- [ ] Creating readiness
- [ ] Creating safe spaces
- [ ] Listening deeply
- [ ] Asking generative questions

VISUAL FACILITATION

- [ ] Framing
- [ ] Sketch talking
- [ ] Improvising
- [ ] Graphic process design
- [ ] Conceptual modeling
- [ ] Versioning

CHANGE WORK

- [ ] Working with stakeholders
- [ ] Understanding levels of intervention
- [ ] Designing process roadmaps
- [ ] Creating collaboration backbones
- [ ] Working with resistance
- [ ] Managing iterative process

USE OF SELF

- [ ] Knowing your own beliefs about change
- [ ] Tracking your own attention
- [ ] Context awareness
- [ ] Grounding yourself
- [ ] Knowing personal triggers
- [ ] Social contracting

going through. We wrote this book because we believe that having more practitioners who are willing to embrace working with both the inner and the outer dimensions of change simultaneously, will create a path forward that is quite different than working only on one-half or the other separately. We believe that by working collaboratively in our diverse and shifting contexts we can find a more complete approach. We hope that as more and more become engaged, these fields will continue to evolve and integrate (SideStory 14.2).

Designing & Leading Change

We chose to focus this book on the kind of consulting that supports change, arguing that any effort to consult and improve something requires change. Expert consultants are implicitly inviting consideration of their expertise in action. Free agent contractors working as a pair-of-hands are bringing about operational change. Process consultants address a wide range of challenges. In all of this, there are certain types of change that we especially hope the principles and practices in this book will address.

1. **Adaptability to circumstantial crisis**: We are convinced that the rate of impact of climate change on communities and organization, with its attendant weather, water, fires, and floods is going to profoundly escalate the need for processes and skilled people to help with these kinds of changes.

2. **Reestablishing developmental rites of passages:** Young people especially need containers for working out their responses to increasingly volatile and threatening times. What does it mean to be a young adult in a digital age, with rising violence and disinformation? Boomers need help learning how to be elders who can contribute and support the young. Parents working and raising kids need help understanding how to find renewal and support, so the traumas that drive their behavior don't just flow through to a new generation.

3. **Midwifing visions of a sustainable future:** Many believe a new vision of a more collaborative, equitable world is arising right alongside the expanding ambitions of strong-man leaders. For these volitional and culture changes to take root they need support and nourishment from capable, facilitative consultants. Some see organizations known for clear boundaries giving way to collaborative networks of cross-associating entities, knit together by new values and technology. Others see the emergence of new paradigms of consciousness that allow us to see the way creative tensions and paradox create greater wholes as we learn to embrace our differences.

Miracles in the Small Moments of Change

Our invitation is to step into change work invites a broad, inclusive perspective. But stepping into a more integrated way of working doesn't have to be big and grandiose to have impact (see SideStory 14.3). But it does start with working differently yourself. Both of us, in articulating the capabilities we think are required in visual facilitation, dialogic practice, change, and use of self, realize that all these can't be learned at once. We've picked out some fundamentals that are good places to start (see SideStory 14.2). In concluding, we also want to share a story of what it takes on a personal level to design and lead change.

Start with the Little Things—Recognizing Crucibles

This story is of finding a crucible moment with a client that we did not anticipate, and in accepting it, helping them free energy to move toward a brighter future.

Both of us were working with a department of over 200 employees. We had been brought in to do strategic visioning and to address several organizational effectiveness issues. In our initial scoping of the project it became clear that

SideStory 14.3

Mutual Regard in Africa

Marc Tognotti is working with tribal villages in Zambia to build the community-led Mukungule Community Nature Conservancy on a foundation of indigenous knowledge. He facilitated a successful Future Search Conference involving 40 local villagers from 10 villages and 40 institutional people, but the challenges of overcoming cultural stereotypes is huge.

"When I visit African tribal people on behalf of a U.S. donor, the communities often elevate me above themselves, sometimes even calling me 'father,' and themselves 'children in need.'

This attitude reflects an assumption common to all sides: that the developed world has all the wealth and expertise, while indigenous peoples have only their poverty. This assumption undermines indigenous pride and self-reliance, and prevents all parties from appreciating the unique gifts tribal people possess.

A now-popular adage enjoins: 'Don't give fish to those in need; teach them to fish.' I take that further. I now ask tribal communities, 'How can we together teach the world to fish?' It's an invitation to collaborate in achieving something greater than all of us. We can all rise into the magnanimous role of contributors, opening a space for everyone to bring their gifts in a spirit of mutual regard."

Photo Himba village in Namibia

SideStory 14.4

A Native Grieving Ritual

When someone in a native tribe in Canada dies, the tribe comes together to support the whole family to let go and to stay with the living rather than staying with their grief and loss.

A large rope is placed in the center of a circle. On one side of the rope is the family and on the other is the tribe. The family's task is to hold onto the rope with all their strength as they would hold onto the life of their beloved family member. This holding on is their expression of their love for the deceased and the grief that comes with accepting the loss and letting go.

Of course, the tribe with just a bit more strength pulls the family towards the other side of that grief.

this would entail several larger meetings between 40 to 70 people, as well as intensive work with the project leaders and a design team. The project leaders shared with us that their department had recently experienced a major loss, a traumatic death of someone who had been fired, and that the group needed to heal from this loss and what had transpired within the department since then. The impact of this situation, especially for those whom the person had worked closely with, was overwhelming, with increasing rounds of blame and finger-pointing. The organization's intention to focus on the future by generating a new vision seemed especially important at this time. However, it seemed difficult to refocus when the group was mired in a spiral of negative feelings and hurt. We were asked if we could help address the loss, blaming, and fragmentation so the group could move forward.

As part of initiating the visioning effort, we met with a design team of about 10 employees to begin designing an initial large-group visioning and organizational effectiveness session. We suggested that some kind of symbolic activity be included as a path for releasing the tension and mistrust. Our sense was that acknowledging the loss through a small, facilitated ritual would support the group to work with the issue in a low-risk way. At a minimum we would have created the space for people to acknowledge their sense of loss. If the group wanted to process this further, we would support them through stories and a well-facilitated process—in other words, in a crucible.

Surprisingly, when we shared our suggestions with the design team, the group fell into silence. The tension was palpable. Suddenly we had shifted out of a fairly animated meeting to total quiet. After a while, a few remarks were made. In essence, we were told by some individuals that this was not a topic that should be brought up in the large meeting and that the tension related to this was too intense.

At that moment both of us were at a choice point. We stopped working the process design chart. Should we trust our instincts, or should we delay until a later time, when it might come up organically but perhaps in unpredictable and more challenging ways?

Should we speak again to the importance of acknowledging the losses and taking the necessary steps that would support healing to occur? We hoped they might still support a process in the larger meeting.

Gisela had a sense something was about to move. She improvised, sharing a story about a grieving ritual used by a Native tribe in Canada (see SideStory 14.2). After she told the story, several people began to speak quietly about the loss of their co-worker and their pain. This was the reason they didn't want to go into it any further. We didn't move—just listened. Then one woman laid out in some detail just how upsetting this whole situation had been. She spoke their truth. It was clear that the opening we had in mind for the large-group meeting was occurring right there in the design team.

We let it flow. It turned out that the people in the design team who had been most reluctant about including a small ritual in the large group became our most helpful advocates for the larger project. We never included a symbolic act in the bigger meeting to acknowledge the passing of their co-worker. However the few times this issue came up, it was talked about with relative ease. Energy and aliveness had returned.

Both of us were amazed at how the energy could move in such a short period of time. And we were grateful that we were aware of the context. We experienced our intention—to work with the pain and suffering through the symbolic act of story telling—combining with our discipline of holding a safe space for whatever

SideStory 14.5

Evolving New Organization Cultures in Europe

Holger Scholz, co-founder of kommunikationslotsen in Germany, is one of a groundswell of visual consultants in Europe responding to the need for more human centric organizations. Twenty years ago he began visualizing on large boards in large group interventions. "We learned there is a lot we can do in initial conversations to bring across our consulting approach. We have visual thinking frameworks that explain our success factors. When you take the markers out, you have management attention from day one. We invite people to share their thinking and jump into the story themselves. We talk not about the story, but from the story. Our clients are the story."

This approach, combined with large-group intervention methods, Dynamic Facilitation, the Circle Way processes, and strategic conversations, has been well received in some of Germany's largest companies. Holger and his colleagues see a real revolution in approach happening, with a focus on working from higher purpose rather than profits alone. "All the talents are going with companies and community that are asking higher questions," Holger says. "Visualizing and sketching as a philosophical quest is the way we are going."

This visualization approach has worked so well they have created a separate company called bikablo® to teach these methods.

wanted to emerge to emerge, and a willingness to trust each other improvising in the moment.

Process Is Like Music and Dance

It's only fitting to end with a metaphor. If the *Seven Challenges of Change* is like a keyboard, then your process designs for change will be like compositions. How many times you face each of the challenges and how much repetition and back-casting you do will be driven by the situation you are in. But we believe you will find these seven to be the basic keys to working with change. And if a piano metaphor is too complex, then think of the basic pattern of change represented by the *Liminal Pathways Change Framework* as a flute, whose clear and ancient notes can lead the process across a threshold and on into the new.

Change involves humans, and humans have free will, emotions, unbelievably diverse thinking and cognitive patterns, and diverse environments and circumstances, all of which weave together in the complexity of change. Learning to work as a consultant is a lifetime work. The good news is, that if you learn to work in a collaborative, facilitative way, you don't have to have all the answers. You don't even need to know exactly what is going to happen. But you do need to have a repertoire of ideas you can suggest and try. We hope we provided you with that.

Global Learning & Exchange Network (The GLEN)

Our joint vision is to spend the next years supporting practitioner development in this field of visual consulting and change. We are going to continue to share principles and practices through The GLEN. You are welcome to enter into the inquiry and collaborative exploration we are supporting. We will be elaborating on these themes in our workshops and (very interactive) Exchanges. For us, ending this book is really a beginning. If you are walking this road too, visit us, and join us in designing and leading change.

Summary

- ☐ **Work with purpose and intent.**
- ☐ **Visual consulting is a path** to integrated awareness and contribution.
- ☐ **Combining fields of practice** is a key to mastery.
- ☐ **Design and lead change:** Tackle adaptability to climate, developing new rites of passage, and bringing forth new visions of our future.
- ☐ **Practice, practice, practice.**
- ☐ **Start with small things:** Recognize crucible moments; share stories of successful change.
- ☐ **Process is like music and dance:** Use the tools and frameworks in this book to create your own process "compositions."

THE GLEN
GLOBAL LEARNING
& EXCHANGE NETWORK

https://glen.grove.com

Appendix

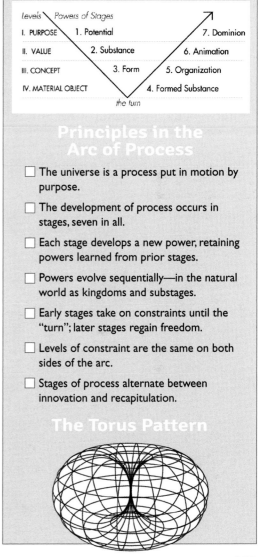

Arthur M. Young & the Theory of Process

Arthur M. Young received a degree in mathematics from Princeton in 1927 and studied relativity and quantum mechanics with Oswald Veblen. Young set out in the early 1930s to develop a unified theory of how universal systems relate to one another, caught up in the general efforts of the early twentieth century to describe a unified field theory integrating the major findings of science. In the process he spent a good number of years in the 1930s and 1940s grounding his thinking in the practical process of inventing and developing the world's first commercially licensed helicopter, the Bell 47.

He emerged from his work with Bell and parallel research believing that the unity of things cannot be explained by examining forms and structures and deterministic rules, but by appreciating the nature of process—the actions of the photon and fundamental particles upon which all else is based. He came to see that all process in the universe is playing out a creative tension between freedom and constraint, between the potential of the photons of light and the constraints of cause and effect at the molecular level. When matter discovers the combinatory rules at the molecular level, it can then turn back toward freedom through the evolved structures of plants, animals, and humans. This cycle is represented three-dimensionally by the torus and two-dimensionally in the arc of process.

The Theory of Process presents an integrated set of tools for understanding the evolution of life and consciousness in many fields of study. Students have applied the theory effectively in everything from the healing arts to international relations. Young evolved his theory of process by working deductively from basic principles and testing his ideas against both scientific fact and accepted theories over a period of 30 years. He was able to show that the process of nature is more fundamental than the structures it forms. He identified seven distinct phases of process that express themselves throughout seven kingdoms in nature (Figure A1). This is an abstraction of the ubiquitous torus pattern.

In practice, Young's ideas are clear and sensible, once you appreciate how to bring the role of purpose back into the scientific method. The fourfold aspects of nature and the seven-stage arc pattern, key elements in the theory, turn up not only in mathematics, quantum physics, chemistry, and biology but also in philosophy and religion. Because Young chose to express his philosophical ideas using geometry (as well as engineering formulas validated with philosophy and mythology), his work provides a basis for thinking visually about organizations, in this book's case, the basic pattern of change that challenges our expressions of purpose in practice. All the process models in the Wiley series are grounded in this theory. See **www.arthuryoung.com** for links to further resources or to obtain a canonical poster and summary of the theory by contacting David Sibbet www.davidsibbet.com.

Figure A1

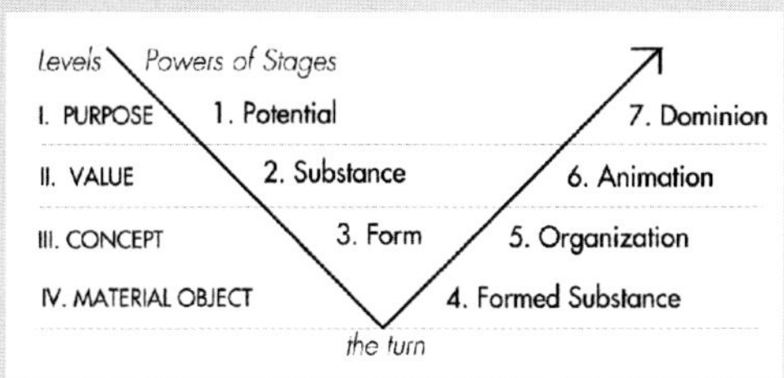

Principles in the Arc of Process

- ☐ The universe is a process put in motion by purpose.
- ☐ The development of process occurs in stages, seven in all.
- ☐ Each stage develops a new power, retaining powers learned from prior stages.
- ☐ Powers evolve sequentially—in the natural world as kingdoms and substages.
- ☐ Early stages take on constraints until the "turn"; later stages regain freedom.
- ☐ Levels of constraint are the same on both sides of the arc.
- ☐ Stages of process alternate between innovation and recapitulation.

The Torus Pattern

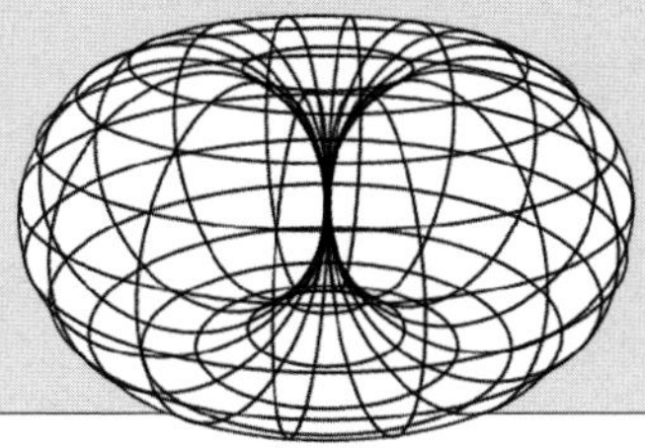

Links

Featured Visual Consultant Links

Bassam Alkarashi	esconsulting.com.sa
Diana Arsenian	soulcollage.com
Holger Balderhaar	https://next-u.de/team/holger-balderhaar
Bill Bancroft	conbrioconsulting.com
Alan Briskin	alanbriskin.com
Maaike Doyer	businessmodelsinc.com
Rob Eskridge	agendas.net
Mary Gelinas	gelinasjames.com
Reinhard Kuchenmüller	visuelle-protokolle.de
Amy Lenzo	wedialogue.com
Meryem Le Saget	lesaget.com
Kevin Souza	https://profiles.ucsf.edu/kevin.souza
Dan Roam	danroam.com
Holger Scholz	facilitation.kommunikationslotsen.de
Marc Tognotti	linkedin.com/in/marc-tognotti
Mathias Weitbrecht	visualfacilitators.com

The Grove Consultants International: The Grove is a full-service organization development and publishing firm in the Presidio of San Francisco, founded in 1977. See www.grove.com for information on services, workshops, and products.

Global Learning & Exchange Network (GLEN): This learning community is focused on evolving the methods and tools of collaboration. It is supported by The Grove and has members from around the world. See https://glen.grove.com to learn more.

Grove Tools, Inc: Is the product licensing and distribution arm of The Grove. Visit www.grovetools-inc to see the full line of products that are available to visually oriented consultants.

Bibliography

Axelrod, Robert. *The Evolution of Cooperation*. New York: Basic Books, 1984. Print.

Bateson, Gregory. *Mind and Nature: A Necessary Unity.* Cresskill: Hampton Press, 2002.

Bell, Catherine. *Ritual: Perspectives and Dimensions*. New York: Oxford University Press, 1997.

Bird, Kelvy. *Generative Scribing: A Social Art of the 21st Century*. Boston: PI Pres, 2018.

Bois, Samuel. *The Art of Awareness*. 3rd ed. Dubuque, IA: Wm. C. Brown Company, 1978.

Boulding, Kenneth. *The Image: Knowledge in Life & Society*. Minneapolis: University of Minnesota, 1956.

Bradford, David L. and Warner W Burke. *Reinventing Organization Development: New Approaches to Change in Organizations*. San Francisco. Pfeiffer; Chichester: Wiley, distributor, 2005.

Bridges, William. *The Way of Transition: Embracing Life's Most Difficult Moments*. Cambridge: Great Britain. Perseus Pub, 2001

Briskin, Alan. *The Power of Collective Wisdom and the Trap of Collective Folly.* Oakland, CA: Berrett-Koehler Publishers, Inc., 2009.

Brown, Tim. *Change by Design: How Design Thinking Transforms Organizations and Inspires Innovation.* New York: Harper Collins e-books, 2009.

Bunker, Barbara B., and Billie T. Alban. *Large Group Interventions: Engaging the Whole System for Rapid Change.* San Francisco: Jossey-Bass, 1997.

____. *The Handbook of Large Group Methods: Creating Systemic Change in Organizations and Communities*. San Francisco: Jossey-Bass, 2006.

California Roundtable on Water & Food Supply, *Applying the Connectivity Approach: Groundwater Management in California's Kings Basin*, Sebastopol, CA: Ag Innovations 2015.

____.*Applying the Connectivity Approach: Water and Food Supply Projects in California that Connect, Link, and Engage*. Sebastopol, CA: Ag Innovations, 2014.

______. *From Crises to Connectivity: Renewed Thinking About Managing California's Water and Food Supply*, Sebastopol, CA: Ag Innovations, 2014.

Capra, F. *The Web of Life: a New Scientific Understanding of Living Systems*. New York: Anchor Books, 1996.

Carson, Timothy L. *Liminal Reality and Transformational Power*. Lanham, NY: University Press, 1997.

Conklin, Jeff E. *Dialogue Mapping: Building Shared Understanding of Wicked Problems*. Chichester: Wiley, 2006.

Danskin, Karl and Lenny Lind. *Virtuous Meetings: Technology + Design for High Engagement in Large Groups*. San Francisco: Jossey-Bass, 2014.

Dressler, Larry. *Standing in the Fire: Leading High-Heat Meetings with Clarity, Calm, and Courage*. Oakland, CA: Berrett-Koehler Publishers, Inc., 2010.

Fisher, Rodger, and William L. Ury and Bruce Patton. *Getting to Yes: Negotiating Agreement Without Giving In*. New York: Penguin Books, 2011.

Gelinas, Mary V. *Talk Matters! Saving the World One Word at a Time. Solving Complex Issues Through Brain Science, Mindful Awareness & Effective Process*. Victoria: Friesen Press, 2016.

Gerard, Glenna, and Linda Ellinor. *Dialogue at Work: Skills for Leveraging Collective Understanding*. Williston, VT: Pegasus, 2001.

Gladwell, M. *The Tipping Point: How Little Things Can Make a Big Difference*. New York: Little, Brown and Company, 2000.

Gray, David and Sunni Brown and James Macanufo. *Gamestorming: A Playbook for Innovators, Rulebreakers, and Changemakers*. Sebastopol, CA: O'Reilly Media, 2010)

Gray, David. *Liminal Thinking: Create the Change You Want by Changing the Way You Think*. New York: Two Waves Books, 2016.

Hassan, Z. *The Social Labs Revolution: A New Approach to Solving Our Most Complex Challenges*. Oakland, CA: Berrett-Koehler Publishers, Inc., 2014.

Heath, Chip and Dan Heath. *Switch: How to Change Things When Change Is Hard.* New York: Currency, 2010.

Herzig, Maggie and Laura Chasin. *Fostering Dialogue Across Divides. The Nuts and Bolts Guide from the Public Conversations Project*. Watertown, MA: Public Conversation Project, 2006.

Holman, Peggy et al. *The Change Handbook: The Definitive Resource on Today's Best Methods for Engaging Whole Systems*. Oakland, CA: Berrett-Koehler Publishers, Inc., 2007.

Isaacs, David, and Juanita Brown. *The World Cafe: Shaping Our Futures Through Conversations That Matter.* Oakland, CA: Berrett-Koehler Publishers, Inc., 2005.

Isaacs, William. *Dialogue and Art of Thinking Together: A Pioneering Approach to Communicating in Business and in Life*. New York: Currency, 1999.

Jacobs, Roberts W. *Real Time Strategic Change: How to Involve an Entire Organization in Fast and Far-Reaching Change*. Oakland, CA: Berrett-Koehler Publishers, Inc., 1994.

Kahane, Adam. *Power and Love: A Theory and Practice of Social Change*. Oakland, CA: Berrett-Koehler Publishers, Inc., 2010.

Kania, John and Mark Kramer. "Collective Impact." *Stanford Social Innovation Review*, Vol. 9, #1, pp 35–41. Stanford, CA: Stanford University, 2011.

Keeney, Bradford. *Aesthetics of Change*. New York: Guilford Press, 1983.

____. *Kalahari Bushmen Healers*. Philadelphia: Ringing Rocks Press, 2000.

____. *The Bushman Shaman: Awakening the spirit through Ecstatic Dance*. Destiny Books, 2004.

Kegan, Robert and Lisa L. Lahey. *How the Way We Talk Can Change the Way We Work: Seven Languages for Transformation*. San Francisco: Jossey-Bass, 2001.

_____. Immunity to *Change: How to Overcome It and Unlock Potential in Yourself and Your Organization*. Boston, Mass: Harvard Business Press, 2009.

Kleiner, Art. *The Age of Heretics: A History of the Radical Thinkers Who Reinvented Corporate Management*. 2nd ed. San Francisco: Jossey-Bass, 2008.

Kotter, John P. *Leading Change*. Boston: John P. Kotter, 1996.

_____. and Holger Rathgeber. *Our Iceberg Is Melting: Changing and Succeeding under Any Conditions*. New York: St. Martin's Press, 2005.

Lakoff, George. and Mark Johnson. *Metaphors We Live By: A Leadership Fable*. Chicago: University of Chicago, 2003.

_____. *Philosophy in the Flesh: The Embodied Mind and Its Challenge to Western Thought*. New York: Basic Books, 1999.

Leonard, George. *Mastery: The Keys to Success and Long-Term Fulfillment*. Plume, 1992.

Marshak, Robert. and Gervase R Bushe. *The Dialogic Organization Development Approach to Transformation and Change*. San Francisco, Wiley, 2016.

McGoff, Chris. *The Primes: How Any Group Can Solve Any Problem.* Chichester: Wiley, 2012.

Merry, Uri. *Coping With Uncertainty: Insights from the New Sciences of Chaos, Self-Organization, and Complexity*. Westport, CT: Praeger, 1995.

Mezirow, Jack. *Learning as Transformation: Critical Perspectives on a Theory in Progress*. San Francisco: Jossey-Bass, 2000.

Mindell, Arnold. *Sitting in the Fire: Large Group Transformation Using Conflict and Diversity*. Portland, OR: Lao Tse Press, 1995.

____. *Working on Yourself Alone: Inner Dreambody Work*. Portland, OR: Lao Tse Press, 2002.

Mintzberg, Henry. *The Rise and Fall of Strategic Planning: Reconceiving Roles for Planning, Plans & Planners*. New York: N.Y., Free Press, 1994.

Moore, Robert L. *The Liminal and the Liminoid in Ritual Process and Analytical Practice*. Chicago: C. G. Jung Institute of Chicago, 1987.

Morgan, Gareth. *Images of Organization*. London: Sage Publications 1997.

_____. *Imagi-ni-zation: New Mindsets for Seeing, Organizing and Managing*. Oakland, CA: Berrett-Koehler Publishers, Inc., 1999.

Nanus, Burt. and Warren Bennis. *Leaders: The Strategies for Taking Charge*. New York: Harper & Row, 1985. This is a report on the shared characteristics of 90 acknowledged leaders. It's still a classic.

Neal, Craig, and Patricia Neal. *The Art of Convening: Authentic Engagement in Meetings, Gatherings and Conversations*. Oakland, CA: Berrett-Koehler Publishers, Inc., 2013.

Oshry, Berry. *Seeing Systems: Unlocking the Mysteries of Organizational Life*. Oakland, CA: Berrett-Koehler Publishers, Inc., 1995.

Osterwalder, Alexander and Yves Pigneur. *Business Model Generation: A Handbook for Visionaries, Game Changers, and Challengers,* Hoboken, NJ: Wiley, Inc., 2010.

Owen, Harrison. *Spirit: Transformation and Development in Organizations*. Potomac, MD: Abbott Publishing, 1987.

Pascale, Richard. *Managing on the Edge: How the Smartest Companies Use Conflict to Stay Ahead*. New York: Touchstone, 1991.

Plotkin, Bill. *Nature and the Human Soul: Cultivating Wholeness and Community in a Fragmented World*. Novato, CA: New World Library, 2008.

Roam, Dan. *Back of the Napkin: Solving Problems and Selling Ideas With Pictures*. London: Penguin Books, 2008.

_____. *Blah, Blah, Blah: What To Do When Words Don't Work*. London: Penguin Books, 2011.

_____. *Draw to Win: A Crash Course on How to Lead, Sell, and Innovate With Your Visual Mind.* New York: Portfolio/Penguin, 2014

Rogers, Carl. (1969) *Freedom to Learn*. Columbus, OH: Charles E. Merrill Publishing Co.,2010.

Scharmer, Otto C. *Theory U: Leading from the Future as it Emerges*. Oakland, CA: Berrett-Koehler, 2006.

Schein, Edger H. *Humble Consulting: How to Provide Real Help Faster*. Oakland, CA: Berrett-Koehler Publishers, Inc., 2016.

_____.*Organizational Culture and Leadership*. 4th ed. San Francisco; Jossey-Bass, 2010. Schein, Edger H. Process Consultation. Vol. 1, Its role in organization development, Addison-Wesley, 1988.

_____. *Process Consultation. Vol. 2, Lessons for Managers and Consultants*, Addison-Wesley, 1987.

Seashore, Charles and Seashore, Edith. *What Did You Say? The Art of Giving and Receiving Feed-back*. Columbia, MD: Bingham House Books, 1992.

Seashore, Edith. and Beverly Patwell. *Triple Impact Coaching: Use of Self in the Coaching Process*. Patwell Consulting, 2006.

Senge, Peter M. *The Fifth Discipline: The Art and Practice of the Learning Organization*. New York: Doubleday/Currency, 1990.

_____. *The Fifth Discipline Fieldbook: Strategies and Tools for Building a Learning Organization* Currency Book/Doubleday, 1994.

Sibbet, David. *Visual Leaders: New Tools for Visioning, Management & Organization Change*. Hoboken, NJ: Wiley, 2013.

_____. *Visual Meetings: How Graphics, Sticky Notes & Idea Mapping Can Transform Group Productivity*. Hoboken, NJ: Wiley, 2010. T

_____. *Visual Teams: Graphic Tools for Commitment, Innovation, & High Performance*. Hobo-ken, NJ: Wiley, 2011.

Solomon, Lisa K., Justin Lokitz and Patrick Van der Pijl. *Design A Better Business: New Tools, Skills, and Mindset for Strategy and Innovation*. New Jersey: Wiley, 2016.

Stewart, Bob and Aaron Smith. "Organizational Rituals: Features, Functions and Mechanisms". *International Journal of Management Reviews, Vol. 13*, pp 113–133. 2011.

Szakolczai, Arpad. *Reflexive Historical Sociology*. London: Routledge, 2000.

Turner, Victor. *The Ritual Process: Structure and Anti-Structure*. New York: Aldine De Gruyter, 2000.

_____. "Variations on a Theme of Liminality." In S. Moore & B. Myerhoff (Eds.), *Secular Ritual* (pp. 36-52). Assen/ Amsterdam, The Netherlands: Van Gorcum, 1977.

Tushman, Michael L., and Charles A. O'Reilly III. *Ambidextrous Organization: Resolving the Innovator's Dilemma*. Boston: Harvard Business School Press, 2009.

_____ . *Winning through Innovation: A Practical Guide to Leading Organizational Change and Renewal*. Boston: Harvard Business School Press, 1997.

Van Gennep, Arnold. The Rites of Passage. London: Routledge & Kegan Paul, (1906) 1960.

Weisbord, Marvin. "The Organization Development Contract", *OD Practitioner, Vol. 5*, # 2, pp. 1-4 Summer 1973.Reprinted in *Organization Development Classics: The Practice and Theory of Change*, 1987, pp. 107-118.

Weisbord, M. R. and Sandra Janoff. *Future Search: Finding Common Ground for Action in Organizations And Communities*. Oakland, CA: Berrett-Koehler Publishers, Inc., 1995.

_____ *Discovering Common Ground: How Future Search Conferences Bring People Together To Achieve Breakthrough Innovation, Empowerment, Shared Vision, And Collaborative Action*. Oakland, CA: Berrett-Koehler Publishers, Inc., 1993.

Weitbrecht, Mathias. *Co-Create! Das Visualisierungs-Buch*", Wiley Publishing, 2016.

Yankelovich, D. *The Magic of Dialogue: Transforming Conflict into Cooperation*. New York: Simon & Schuster, 1999.

Young, Arthur M. *Geometry of Meaning*. San Francisco: Delacourt Press, 1976.

_____ *Reflexive Universe*. San Francisco: Delacourt Press, 1976.

Zyphur, M. and G. Islam, "Rituals in Organizations: A Review and Expansion of Current Theory." *Group & Organization Management. Vol. 34*, #1, pp 114–139. Sage Publications, 2009.

Index

D

E

F

G

David Sibbet is founder and CEO of The Grove Consultants International, a full-service organization consulting firm in The Presidio national park's Thoreau Center for Sustainability in San Francisco. He is a master graphic facilitator, information designer, and considered a leader in the field of visual facilitation and process leadership. The Grove is hub to a global network of associates, partners, and other visual practitioners. He is co-directing the Grove's Global Learning & Exchange Network (GLEN) with Gisela, focused on evolving new approaches to collaboration and cross boundary work.

David consults on organization change worldwide across government, private, and nonprofit sectors. He is author of the best-selling Visual Facilitation series from Wiley, including *Visual Meetings, Visual Teams*, and *Visual Leaders*. David is also designer of the Grove's *Sustainable Organizations Model*, the Drexler/Sibbet *Team Performance System*, the Grove's Visual Planning Systems, and author of The *Grove's Facilitation Series*. He holds a masters degree in Journalism from Northwestern University, a BA in English from Occidental College, and a Coro Fellowship in Public Affairs. In 2013 he was awarded the Organizational Development Network's lifetime achievement award for creative contribution to the field of OD. For further information see **www.grove.com** and **www.davidsibbet.com**

Gisela and David are married and work together all over the world.

Gisela Wendling, PhD. is vice president of Global Learning at The Grove Consultants International. She provides organization development, change, and program design services to business, nonprofit organizations, and communities. Her expertise is based on 25 years of consulting and working within a wide range of organizations in the private and public sectors. Gisela has held leadership positions in the high-tech industry and education. She holds a doctorate from the School of Human and Organizational Systems at Fielding Graduate University. She is former director of the master's program in Organization Development at Sonoma State University, CA. For several years she facilitated the California Roundtable on Water and Food Supply, a statewide, multisector stakeholder initiative focused on applying whole systems approaches to developing sustainable water management solutions. At the Grove she leads Designing and Leading Change workshops and the Leading Change Program. She is co-director of the Grove's new Global Learning and Exchange Network (GLEN). She also teaches in the Professional Psychology PhD. program at Meridian University, CA.

Gisela brings a multicultural perspective (on change) to her work that includes field experiences in South America, Africa, and Australia, as well as herself being German-born and raised. Translating these deeply relevant perspectives into innovative approaches to organization and community development continues to inspire her and makes her work with her clients more insightful, culturally and globally sensitive, and ultimately more transformative. For further information see **https://glen.grove.com** and **www.giselawendling.com**.